CW01624065

A Practical Guide to Charity Law in Scotland

A Practical Guide to Charity Law in Scotland

James McNeill QC
Advocate with Axiom Advocates, accredited mediator, Judge of the Courts of Appeal of Jersey and Guernsey

Alastair Keatinge
Head of Charities and Social Enterprise, Lindsays Solicitors

Colin Liddell
WS, accredited specialist in charity law, J & H Mitchell

Simon A Mackintosh
WS, Chairman, Turcan Connell

Gavin McEwan
Head of Charities, Turcan Connell

Tom Murray
Partner, Gillespie Macandrew LLP

Stephen Phillips
Partner and Head of Third Sector Team, Burness Paull LLP

Malcolm H Rust
Partner and Head of Charities Group, Shepherd + Wedderburn LLP

Victoria JW Simpson
Head of the Charities Unit, Anderson Strathern LLP

Jandy Stevenson
formerly Partner and Head of Charities; Consultant to Charities Unit, Henderson Loggie

W. GREEN

THOMSON REUTERS

First Edition 2016

Published in 2016 by W. Green, 21 Alva Street, Edinburgh EH2 4PS part of Thomson Reuters (Professional) UK Limited (Registered in England & Wales, Company No.1679046. Registered Office and address for service: 2nd floor, 1 Mark Square, Leonard Street, London EC2A 4EG)

Typeset by Letterpart Limited, Caterham on the Hill, Surrey, CR3 5XL.

Printed and bound in Great Britain by CPI Group (UK) Ltd, Croydon, CR0 4YY.

No natural forests were destroyed to make this product; only farmed timber was used and replanted.

A CIP catalogue record of this book is available for the British Library.

http://www.wgreen.co.uk

ISBN: 978-0-414-03256-9

Thomson Reuters and the Thomson Reuters logo are trademarks of Thomson Reuters.

Crown copyright material is reproduced with the permission of the Controller of HMSO and the Queen's Printer for Scotland.

All rights reserved. No part of this publication may be reproduced, or transmitted in any form, or by any means, or stored in any retrieval system of any nature, without prior written permission, except for permitted fair dealing under the Copyright, Designs and Patents Act 1988, or in accordance with the terms of a licence issued by the Copyright Licensing Agency in respect of photocopying and/or reprographic reproduction. Application for permission for other use of copyright material, including permission to reproduce extracts in other published works should be made to the publishers. Full acknowledgement of the author, publisher and source must be given.

© 2016 Thomson Reuters (Professional) UK Limited

Foreword

Scotland's 24,000 charities enrich communities throughout the country. Their activity encompasses a vast range of endeavour and although some of our charities have been operating essentially unchanged for hundreds of years, the sector is also extremely dynamic, continually evolving and adjusting to changing social need and other external influences.

In April 2000, in the wake of devolution and the establishment of the Scottish Parliament, the McFadden Commission began its work setting out proposals for dedicated Scots charity law—this culminated in the passage of the Charities and Trustee Investment (Scotland) Act 2005 on which this compendium is in very large part a commentary. The Scottish Charity Regulator (OSCR), the independent regulator established under the Act, celebrated the 10th anniversary of the full assumption of its powers in April 2016, so this timely and important publication is able to draw on a substantial and growing body of operation and experience.

Being a charity trustee can be hugely rewarding but it is not an undertaking to be entered into lightly. Public trust and confidence relies on high standards of governance and propriety, so any source of guidance and support for trustees and their advisers is to be welcomed. Common sense and reasonableness will take trustees a long way, but having some readily available technical knowledge will be of enormous assistance.

The expert contributors to this comprehensive new guide are therefore to be commended for offering clear, practical advice on Scottish charity law. The guide deals with the establishment, running and dissolution of charities and, in a very accessible way, illustrated with a number of case studies and drawing on relevant case law, will be of interest not only to charity lawyers, but to all those involved in the setting up and operation of a charity of any size.

Mr McNeill and his team are to be congratulated for their initiative and for their industry. I am confident that this guide will prove an invaluable source of guidance for years to come, and will help ensure that Scotland's charities continue to operate with integrity and to deliver enormous public benefit.

David Robb
Chief Executive
Scottish Charity Regulator

TABLE OF CONTENTS

11. CROSS-BORDER ISSUES

12. VARIATION, REORGANISATION AND AMALGAMATION

TABLE OF CASES

TABLE OF STATUTES

TABLE OF SCOTTISH STATUTES

TABLE OF STATUTORY INSTRUMENTS

TABLE OF SCOTTISH STATUTORY INSTRUMENTS

CHAPTER 1

WHY CHARITIES MATTER

Tom Murray

INTRODUCTION

Since early medieval times the church has recognised the importance of institutions established for charitable purposes and in 1247 an exemption from papal taxation was provided to hospitals established for the treatment of leprosy patients. Following on from the Reformation in the 16th century came the decline of the monasteries and the breakdown of the pre-Reformation churches; and mediaeval society structure and many of the institutions which had been responsible for charity became defunct. Responsibility for the poor passed from the church to the state. **1–01**

The earliest Acts of the Scottish Parliament relating to the relief of the poor date from 1424 when beggars who were unable to earn their own living were given permission to beg. The basis of the system of poor relief in Scotland was established in 1579[1] and by 1597[2] the responsibility for carrying out poor relief was moved to the Kirk Sessions in each parish. **1–02**

Over the border in England each parish became liable for the support of its own aged and infirm poor in 1535[3] and the Poor Relief Act 1601[4] created a national poor law system for England and Wales. At the same time, the Charitable Uses Act of 1601[5] was fundamental in establishing charity law as we know it. Its preamble provided a list of charitable purposes (including relief of the poor and maintenance of "the sick and maimed soldiers and mariners, schools of learning, free schools and scholars of universities" as well as repairs of the likes of churches and ports and highways). It also placed charities under the supervision of the state. **1–03**

Charity law continued to evolve in both jurisdictions over the following centuries as new activities became recognised as charitable and some older charitable purposes (such as the marriages of poor maids recognised as a charitable purpose mentioned in the Statute of Elizabeth) ceased to be charitable. **1–04**

---

[1] Act for punischment of strang and idle beggars and reliefe of the pure and impotent (James VI c.24 No.12).

[2] Vagabonds Act (39 Eliz. 1).

[3] An Act for Punishment of Sturdy Vagabonds and Beggars (27 Henry VIII c.25).

[4] Poor Relief Act (43 Eliz I c.2).

[5] Charitable Gifts (43 Eliz I c.4).

1–05 The grounds for charitable exemption from income tax throughout the UK dates back to the "War Tax" Act of 1799 that introduced income tax as a temporary measure to pay for the Napoleonic War. In 1842 income tax was reintroduced and an exemption allowed for charitable purposes but confusion continued as no definition of "charity", "charitable purposes" or "charitable" was contained in the Act.

1–06 In 1891 Lord Macnaghten laid down four categories of charitable purposes being: (a) the relief of poverty; (b) the advancement of education; (c) the advancement of religion; and (d) any purposes of a charitable nature beneficial to the community not falling under any of the preceding heads[6] and it was subsequently settled that the concept of charitable purposes in Scotland was to be applied in accordance with the categorisation in English law for income tax purposes.[7]

1–07 Prior to 2005 there was no register of charities in Scotland and charitable status was effectively conferred by the Inland Revenue, applying UK tax law, to whom claims for exemption from taxes were made. The Court of Session as Court of Exchequer had jurisdiction to administer this branch of Scots law[8] and Scottish trust deeds continued to be construed in accordance with Scots law[9] but the charity test was essentially a UK test.

THE MODERN POSITION

1–08 The Charities and Trustee Investment (Scotland) Act 2005[10] (the 2005 Act) introduced a uniquely Scottish charity test (the charity test) and in order for an organisation to be entered on the Scottish Charity Register it must pass that test. A body entered on the register is entitled to call itself a "charity", "charitable body", "registered charity" or "a charity registered in Scotland".[11] Further, if a body is established under the law of Scotland, or is managed or controlled wholly or mainly in or from Scotland, it may also refer to itself as a "Scottish charity" or a "registered Scottish charity".[12]

1–09 Scottish charities that existed when the 2005 Act came into force were entered automatically on the Scottish Charity Register but if they subsequently fail the charity test they will be removed. Whilst the public are entitled to assume that a body on the Register passes the charity test the obligation to pass it is an ongoing one on those in management and control of that body.

---

6 *Commissioners for Special Purposes of the Income Tax v Pemsel* [1891] A.C. 531.
7 *Inland Revenue Commissioners v City of Glasgow Police Athletic Association*, 1953 S.C. (HL) 13.
8 *Inland Revenue Commissioners v City of Glasgow Police Athletic Association*, 1953 S.C. (HL) 13.
9 *Jackson's Trustees v Lord Advocate*, 1926 S.C. 579.
10 Charities and Trustee Investment (Scotland) Act 2005 (asp 10).
11 Charities and Trustee Investment (Scotland) Act 2005 s.13(1).
12 Charities and Trustee Investment (Scotland) Act 2005 s.13(2).

THE CHARITY TEST

A body meets the charity test if its purposes consist only of one or more of the charitable purposes, and it provides (or, in the case of a new applicant, provides or intends to provide) public benefit in Scotland or elsewhere.[13] 1–10

THE CHARITABLE PURPOSES

The 2005 Act introduces a definitive list of charitable purposes. This list was meant to encompass all the charitable purposes that had evolved since the categories of charitable purpose had been established in 1891[14] and it was not the intention of the Act to exclude any charitable purposes that were recognised immediately before its introduction on 1 April 2006 or to create any new charitable purposes. For example, prior to 2005 the promotion of the efficiency of the armed forces of the Crown was recognised as a charitable purpose in UK law[15] as was the promotion of efficiency of the police, fire and rescue services or ambulance services. The promotion of the efficiency of the armed forces of the Crown is not a stated charitable purpose in the 2005 Act but this activity would fall under the purposes of the saving of lives, as it is for the safety and protection of the country and also the advancement of citizenship. 1–11

Many charities have more than one charitable purpose and many charitable activities commonly carried out by charities encompass more than one purpose but a charity may be established only for charitable purposes and all its activities must further those purposes. 1–12

There has been little case law on the interpretation of charitable purposes at the time of writing and much of the following narrative is based on Office of the Scottish Charity Regulator's (OSCR) guidance.[16] 1–13

THE PREVENTION OR RELIEF OF POVERTY

"Poverty" is interpreted in accordance with changing economic and social standards. People suffering poverty include those unable to maintain a basic standard of living for themselves and their dependants. The definition of poverty falls short of destitution and it may be expressed as having to "go short" in the ordinary acceptance of that term.[17] Although it has been thought that "going short" ought to be relative to what in the past has been termed "station in life",[18] there may be some doubt as to how such a nuance would be viewed nowadays. For example, interim benevolent relief to provide food and necessities to an elderly person, with little income but living in a valuable house, and pending sale 1–14

---

[13] Charities and Trustee Investment (Scotland) Act 2005 s.7(1).
[14] *Commissioners for Special Purposes of the Income Tax v Pemsel* [1891] A.C. 531.
[15] *In Re Good* [1905] 2 Ch. 60; and *In Re Gray* [1925] Ch. 362.
[16] OSCR "Meeting the Charity Test: Guidance for applicants and existing charities" (August 2015).
[17] *Re Coulthurst* [1951] Ch. 661; and *Re de Carteret* [1933] Ch. 103.
[18] *Re Coulthurst* [1951] Ch. 661 at 666.

of the house, might be permissible. But funding a grander home in a style to which an individual had been accustomed might be more questionable.

1–15 The prevention of poverty includes preventing those who are poor from becoming poorer as well as preventing those who are at risk of being poor from becoming poor. Activity that enables individuals or groups to escape or avoid poverty such as training for work skills; the encouragement of fair trade activities; research into factors that contribute to poverty and campaigning on ways to prevent poverty may each provide benefit under this purpose.

1–16 Activities that seek to relieve poverty are those that address its consequences including direct help to individuals, families and communities. It must be possible to demonstrate that such activities are specifically targeted at people suffering, or at risk of, poverty.

THE ADVANCEMENT OF EDUCATION

1–17 This covers both formal education, such as that provided through schools and universities, and less formal education that may take place in the community. It covers education, training and research and the development of individual capabilities, skills and understanding. There is an expectation that the results of research should be published for a research charity to fall within this head.

1–18 The subject must be delivered in a structured way designed to educate, not just to inform and there must be educational merit from the activities carried out although the distinction between the mere provision of information and the provision of education is likely to vary according to the age and ability of the learner.

THE ADVANCEMENT OF RELIGION

1–19 Religion encompasses faith and worship of one or many gods or spiritual beliefs. The advancement of any philosophical beliefs that do not involve the belief in a god is analogous to this purpose.[19] Provision of public worship can provide benefit under this purpose, by enhancing spiritual wellbeing and a sense of spiritual and moral solidarity. Other activities such as religious instruction and dissemination of religious texts and materials may also provide benefit in the same way.

1–20 The benefits under this purpose must not be confined to a closed order that excludes the wider community[20] although the doctrines of a particular religion may mean that only people of a particular age or gender can attend or take part in certain ceremonies.

---

19 Charities and Trustee Investment (Scotland) Act 2005 s.7(3)(f).

20 *Gilmour v Coates* [1949] A.C. 426.

The advancement of religion also includes carrying out other charitable activities within the teachings of a particular faith[21] and when carrying out other activities to advance religion it may be possible to limit the class of beneficiaries if such limitation conforms to the doctrines of that religion. **1–21**

THE ADVANCEMENT OF HEALTH

"Health" encompasses both physical and mental health and its advancement includes both the prevention of disease as well as the relief of sickness and human suffering. This can be by conventional means or by complementary methods and alternative therapies. **1–22**

Where activity concentrates on a non-conventional form of treatment, independent evidence of impact may be required to assess benefit and, depending on how widely advanced the development of the treatment is, the standard of evidence may differ. **1–23**

Where activity surrounds finding new treatments it may be that there should be a realistic possibility that a cure may be found and the symptoms that the treatment seeks to address should be identifiable. **1–24**

THE SAVING OF LIVES

This includes a range of activity directed towards saving people whose lives are in danger and protecting life. Activities in pursuit of this purpose might include the provision of rescue services or training in first aid or other life saving techniques. **1–25**

THE ADVANCEMENT OF CITIZENSHIP OR COMMUNITY DEVELOPMENT

This purpose, including rural or urban regeneration and the promotion of civic responsibility, volunteering, the voluntary sector or the effectiveness or efficiency of charities, focuses on benefits to the community rather than the individual. Whilst this purpose can be used in relation to life skills, self confidence and citizenship by individuals the focus is on how such individuals will use such skills to benefit the community. **1–26**

Charities advancing citizenship seek to help people to be active citizens individually or through community organisations and networks. Such charities might help these organisations to work more closely with individuals to influence change in their communities. **1–27**

Charities set up to advance community development seek to help people and community groups to identify and articulate their needs, then take practical action to address those needs. **1–28**

---

[21] *St Margaret's Children and Family Care Society v Office of the Scottish Charity Regulator* (Case ref: APP 02/13).

1–29 Charities do not always need to target groups or areas that are categorised as deprived or disadvantaged. Community development activities can seek to address issues of inequality and social justice, bringing about changes that improve the quality of life for the whole community.

1–30 Communities vary in size and nature and can be defined by locality, interest or identity (for instance, ethnic origin or sexual orientation). While there is no minimum size, the openness and inclusiveness of communities to new members will be factors in deciding if organisations provide public benefit.

1–31 Giving grants or financial support to other community bodies may also advance community development but only where the grants would address an identifiable community need, or would result in identifiable benefits to the community as a whole. Whether this activity advances community development will depend on the type of organisations being supported, the reason for the financial support and what the intended outcome of the support is.

1–32 The advancement of citizenship or community development includes a number of different but connected areas. Among these, the 2005 Act includes[22]:

- the promotion of civic responsibility, volunteering, the voluntary sector or the effectiveness or efficiency of charities; and
- rural or urban regeneration.

THE PROMOTION OF CIVIC RESPONSIBILITY

1–33 Charities that advance citizenship may seek to develop and inspire civic responsibility. They may also seek to encourage voluntary and community activity. Advancing civic responsibility includes the development and teaching of civic values for the good of a community or society as a whole. For example, promoting democracy, equality and engagement with social and political processes.

THE PROMOTION OF VOLUNTEERING

1–34 Charities that fulfil this purpose encourage the concept of volunteering and the value and benefits that volunteering can bring, both for the volunteers and those who benefit from their activities. Simply engaging volunteers to carry out activities for a charity would not of itself qualify.

THE PROMOTION OF THE VOLUNTARY SECTOR

1–35 This refers to charities that provide services and assistance to voluntary organisations, whether charitable or not. Under this purpose, an organisation must promote the voluntary sector as a whole, or a sufficient section of it. Charities

[22] Charities and Trustee Investment (Scotland) Act 2005 s.7(3)(b).

falling within this purpose would include umbrella organisations for groups of charities serving beneficiaries with a common characteristic.

THE PROMOTION OF THE EFFECTIVENESS OR EFFICIENCY OF CHARITIES

This refers to activities that make sure that charities are well run or allow charitable resources to be used more effectively. For example, providing support and advisory services to voluntary organisations to improve their management, administration and operations. **1–36**

RURAL OR URBAN REGENERATION

Regeneration is the process of reversing the economic, physical and social decline of places where market forces alone are not enough. **1–37**

Charities set up for regeneration must have an overall goal of improving the social, economic and/or physical quality of life of the whole community in areas where the need for improvement can be clearly demonstrated (for example, by indicators of social or economic deprivation). **1–38**

Charities registered under this purpose are often led by the community and identify the issues and opportunities in their area. They make the decisions and are responsible for delivering the economic, social and environmental change. **1–39**

To be charitable, a regeneration organisation will normally need to demonstrate that an area is in need of regeneration, and that its activities will cover a broad spectrum of regeneration work. **1–40**

THE ADVANCEMENT OF THE ARTS, HERITAGE, CULTURE OR SCIENCE

The advancement of the arts covers art at a national or professional level as well as at a local or amateur level. Benefit may be provided by the provision of arts facilities and encouraging high standards in the arts: for instance, by bodies encouraging the playing or appreciation of a particular type of music, arts festivals or bodies aiming to improve facilities for the arts, such as theatres or concert venues. **1–41**

Heritage can be seen as part of a country's local or national history and traditions as well as its historic land, buildings and built environment. Where a body aims to provide benefit by preserving a building or site, independent evidence may be required to prove that heritage benefit would result from the activity and public access must be available. **1–42**

Culture can refer to a range of activities which are distinctive of a society or group within a society: for example, food, fashion, dancing, children's play or games. There is frequently an overlap with the other categories within this purpose, and the other purposes: for example, sports, beliefs, education and recreation. "Culture" shares with "heritage" activities that are part of local or national history or tradition. Activities such as cross-cultural exchanges, **1–43** multicultural events and activities designed to promote tolerance and understanding of other cultures are charitable activities under this purpose.

1–44 The advancement of science includes scientific research and charities connected with learned societies and institutions. Research and development carried out for commercial gain is unlikely to be charitable and there is an expectation that the research will be published.

THE ADVANCEMENT OF PUBLIC PARTICIPATION IN SPORT

1–45 Then 2005 Act specifies that sport must involve physical skill and exertion. This reflects the fact that the advancement of public participation in sport is included as a charitable purpose mainly because of the health benefits that it can provide.

1–46 If there is any doubt about whether any activity constitutes a sport, factors to be taken into account will include whether the activity has been recognised as a sport by a national body; whether it is regulated by a set of rules and customs; whether there is a governing body for the sport and how it is organised and whether the activity increases the health and fitness of the participants.

1–47 Whilst provision for elite or professional athletes is acceptable as part of a charity's activities the charity must demonstrate that its activities are open to all. This would generally mean that a wide range of participants (in terms of skill or ability level, physical condition, age, etc.) will be catered for.

THE PROVISION OF RECREATIONAL FACILITIES

1–48 When a charity is not providing facilities or activities to the public as a whole but only to a limited section of the public, that section must be defined in terms of need as set out in the 2005 Act. If this is the case then the charity must be able to demonstrate that the benefit is being provided to that section of the public that suffers from particular disadvantage because of that need. Examples could include a club providing recreational or sporting facilities for people with learning difficulties or an activity club for senior citizens.

1–49 The purpose encompasses the organisation of recreational activities, with the object improving the conditions of life for the persons from whom the facilities or activities are primarily intended, but only in relation to recreational facilities or activities that are primarily intended for persons who have need of them by reason of their age, ill-health, disability, financial hardship or other disadvantage or available to members of the public at large or to male or female members of the public at large. Care needs to be taken to ensure that a body relying on this purpose does not breach the Equality Act 2010.

THE ADVANCEMENT OF HUMAN RIGHTS, CONFLICT RESOLUTION OR RECONCILIATION

This covers relieving the victims of human rights abuse, raising awareness of human rights, advocacy and securing the enforcement of human rights law. Human rights are a broad and constantly evolving concept widely recognised in a number of international treaties and enshrined in national law and it is to these that one should look when considering whether a particular right is a human right. 1–50

This also includes the resolution of international conflicts and relieving the suffering, poverty and distress arising through conflict on a national or international scale by identifying the causes of the conflict and seeking to resolve such a conflict. The promotion of restorative justice and mediation or reconciliation between persons, organisations, authorities or groups may also fall within this purpose. 1–51

THE PROMOTION OF RELIGIOUS OR RACIAL HARMONY

These are purposes that actively aim to promote harmony and the lessening of conflict between people from different races, religions or belief systems. There must be a real risk of disharmony that the purposes aim to prevent amongst the group it is intended to work with. Activities under this purpose might include schemes intended to bring together immigrants and existing residents in a particular area, or the provision of structures for interfaith dialogue. 1–52

THE PROMOTION OF EQUALITY AND DIVERSITY

This includes the elimination of discrimination and promotion of diversity in society. Benefit might, for example, be provided under this purpose by advocacy or campaigning by or on behalf of, disabled people for better access to public facilities. The elimination of discrimination must be a main focus of the charity and not just a secondary outcome. 1–53

THE ADVANCEMENT OF ENVIRONMENTAL PROTECTION OR IMPROVEMENT

The advancement of environmental protection or improvement includes preservation and conservation of the natural environment and the promotion of sustainable development. It also includes the conservation of a particular animal, bird, or of wildlife in general, or the conservation of a specific plant species or habitat or area of land or water, including areas of natural beauty and scientific interest. In such cases, the assessment of public benefit may require independent evidence of the environmental benefit likely to derive from the body's activities. 1–54

Sustainable development activities must be designed to balance the different, often competing, needs of the community with an awareness of environmental, social and economic limitations so as not to compromise the ability of future generations to enjoy the protected environment. Sustainable development is 1–55 development that meets the needs of the present without compromising the ability of future generations to meet their own needs.

THE RELIEF OF THOSE IN NEED BY REASON OF AGE, ILL-HEALTH, DISABILITY, FINANCIAL HARDSHIP OR OTHER DISADVANTAGE

1–56 This purpose, which encompasses relief, given by provision of acommodation or care, involves helping people who suffer a particular disadvantage compared to other people in general and activities in furtherance of this purpose are only open to them and not to the public at large.

1–57 This purpose will be relevant to organisations concerned with the care or upbringing of children or young people (for example, children's homes) or organisations concerned with the relief of effects of old age or disability (for example, by providing specialist advice or equipment, or drop-in centres). It will also be relevant to housing associations[23] and registered social landlords and to bodies aiming to relieve the effects of ill-health.

1–58 The assistance given under this purpose must be linked to the needs associated with the disadvantage in question.

THE ADVANCEMENT OF ANIMAL WELFARE

1–59 The advancement of animal welfare includes any purpose directed towards the prevention or suppression of cruelty to animals or the prevention or relief of suffering by animals.

1–60 This purpose does not include the conservation of a particular animal or wildlife in general. This would be covered by "the advancement of environmental protection and improvement".

ANY OTHER ANALOGOUS PURPOSE

1–61 By including as a charitable purpose any other purpose that may reasonably be regarded as analogous to any of the listed charitable purposes, the 2005 Act provides the necessary flexibility to allow charitable purposes to evolve as society changes.

1–62 The 2005 Act specifically states that the advancement of any philosophical belief, whether or not involving belief in a god, is analogous to the advancement of religion but otherwise as of the coming into force of the Act all the then Scottish charitable purposes were covered by the charitable purposes outlined above.

1–63 A purpose might be recognised as analogous to one or more of the existing purposes in the Act and therefore as a charitable purpose when:

[23] Under the Housing (Scotland) Act 2010 (asp 17).

(a) it combines aspects of established charitable purposes into a distinctive and coherent whole reflecting current social contexts and necessities;
(b) it includes or resembles certain aspects of the existing purposes but also includes novel or differing aspects; and
(c) it becomes appropriate in a changed social or practical context to consider as a freestanding purpose something previously considered as an activity in furtherance of an existing charitable purpose.

SPECIFIC EXCEPTIONS

A body that would otherwise meet the charity test does not meet the charity test if: (a) its constitution allows it to distribute or otherwise apply any of its property on being wound up (or at any other time) for a purpose that is not a charitable purpose; (b) its constitution expressly permits the Scottish Ministers or a Minister of the Crown to direct or otherwise control its activities; or (c) it is, or one of its purposes is to advance, a political party. **1–64**

The Scottish Ministers may by order disapply either or both of parts (a) and (b) but not part (c) in relation to any body or type of body specified in the order.[24] **1–65**

PROHIBITION ON DISTRIBUTION OR USE OF PROPERTY FOR NON-CHARITABLE PURPOSES

The 2005 Act states that a body will not pass the charity test if its constitution allows it to distribute or otherwise apply any of its property for a non-charitable purpose, whether on being wound up or at any other time.[25] Further as a result of this rule a charity may not share any surplus that it may make with a non-charitable body. **1–66**

This does not mean that on winding-up the property can only be transferred to a charity registered in Scotland: the requirement is that it may only be used for charitable purposes which are charitable under the 2005 Act. However, when transferring funds to be used by non-Scottish charities care must be taken to ensure that the property is only used in a way that is charitable both in Scots Law and UK tax law. **1–67**

As noted in para.1–65 above, the Scottish Ministers may by order disapply this rule. **1–68**

A CHARITY MUST NOT BE SUBJECT TO MINISTERIAL CONTROL

A Scottish charity must be independent from the control of Scottish Ministers or a Minister of the Crown.[26] If an organisation's constitution contains an explicit power of direction by a Minister or a Minister's consent or approval is required **1–69**

[24] Charities and Trustee Investment (Scotland) Act 2005 s.7(5).
[25] Charities and Trustee Investment (Scotland) Act 2005 s.7(4)(a).
[26] Charities and Trustee Investment (Scotland) Act 2005 s.7(4)(b).

for any actions it will fail the charity test. A charity may have a constitution that allows Ministers of the Crown to appoint the charity trustees provided that once appointed the trustees act independently. What needs to be considered is whether the Minister has any power over and above such powers as are ordinarily vested in members of a company.

1–70 This prohibition only applies to Scottish Ministers or Ministers of the Crown. It does not mention or include powers of direction or control by local authorities or any other type of third party.

1–71 Any powers of control resulting from grant conditions, service level agreements or legislation do not amount to ministerial control provided that such powers do not form a part of the constitution.

1–72 Again as noted in para.1–65 above, the Scottish Ministers may by order disapply this rule.

A CHARITY CANNOT BE FOR PARTY POLITICAL PURPOSES

1–73 Even if it appears to have charitable purposes and provide public benefit, a body cannot be a charity if the organisation is, or if one of its purposes is to advance, a political party.[27] However, a charity whose direct and principal purpose is not political may apply political means to campaign or lobby to change the law or the policy of political bodies where this is in furtherance of their non-political charitable purposes.[28]

IDENTIFYING THE PURPOSES OF A CHARITY

1–74 Ideally the constitution should state, expressly and clearly, the purposes for which the charity is established; and the purposes of a charity applying to be on the Register for the first time should always be clear in their governing document. Where such purposes are not expressly and clearly stated, they may fall to be ascertained by interpreting the document establishing the charity or from evidence of what the charity has done.[29] This is done, not for the purpose of construing its constitution, but for the purpose of assisting in assessing whether the implementation of the purposes would achieve a charitable end result including providing a public benefit.

1–75 The principles that apply to the interpretation of a document relating to a charity are those that apply generally to the interpretation of documents. Thus, the document is to be given the meaning that it would convey to a reasonable person having all the background knowledge that would reasonably be available to the audience to whom the document is addressed.[30]

---

[27] Charities and Trustee Investment (Scotland) Act 2005 s.7(4)(c).

[28] *McGovern v Attorney General* [1982] Ch. 321 at 343.

[29] See, for example, *Re Resch* [1969] 1 A.C. 514.

[30] *Attorney General of Belize v Belize Telecom Ltd* [2009] 1 W.L.R. 1988.

Where a charity is established by a document with clearly stated purposes, the motives and intentions of the founders are irrelevant to the interpretation of the document and what the charity has done since it was established will not normally be admissible as an aid to ascertaining its interpretation.[31] 1–76

PUBLIC BENEFIT

How much benefit and when?

Generally speaking, to meet the public benefit test charities must in some way actively provide public benefit, and not simply intend to provide it. This means that there must be activity on the part of a charity in the pursuit of its stated purposes. The 2005 Act does not set a minimum amount of benefit that needs to be provided before there can be said to be public benefit nor is it part of the charity test assessment to make a judgement on the effectiveness or efficiency of the charity in providing benefit. 1–77

Benefit does not need to be linked to financial output or even current activity but such inactivity may only last for a determinable, reasonable time and the eventual benefit should be definable. 1–78

It is possible to establish a charity in expectation of a future event. For example, a charity could be established to provide for the relief of flood victims in a place where floods are likely. Such a charity would hold funds but not carry out any activity until the flood occurred. However, for such a charity to pass the charity test there must be a reasonable likelihood of flooding occurring. 1–79

Another example of types of charities that do not immediately carry out activities to provide public benefit are anticipatory charities. These are charities set up with minimal trust property only, the intention being that they will receive property (usually a legacy or bequest on the death of the truster) at a later date. The trust deed should provide for the trust to undertake particular activities in pursuit of its charitable purposes from that point on. 1–80

It is also possible for a charity to become dormant yet still meet the charity test where there is a possibility that it may receive funds in the future that can then be applied for its original charitable purpose. For example, a charity may remain in existence after its activities, assets and liabilities have been transferred to another charity, its purpose being to "catch" any legacies left to the original charity and then to transfer these to the new charity. 1–81

A sufficient section of the public

When applying the rule that, to be charitable, a purpose must be for the benefit of the public generally or of a sufficient section of the public, it is necessary to identify the class of individuals whom the purpose primarily benefits. Where the purpose primarily benefits the public in general, the rule is satisfied. If the 1–82

---

[31] *James Miller and Partners Ltd v Whitworth Street Estates (Manchester) Ltd* [1970] A.C. 583.

definition of the section of the public is too limited then the restriction will be regarded as unduly restrictive and the public benefit test will not be met.[32]

1–83 Accordingly, where the benefit is restricted to a class of persons the question is whether that class can be regarded as a sufficient section of the public. The inhabitants of a defined geographical area will normally constitute a sufficient section of the public, unless perhaps the area is, without adequate justification, very small. Persons with a shared characteristic such as a defined disability may constitute a sufficient section of the public even if that disability is rare. A section of the public may be defined by their trade or profession.

1–84 Where the potential beneficiaries of a purpose are not a sufficient section of the public, the wider indirect benefit that the public may receive from the advancement of the purpose will not make it charitable. For example, a trust established by a father for the education of his son is not a charity. The public element is not supplied by the fact that from that son's education all may benefit.[33]

1–85 Except in the case of the relief of poverty it has generally been accepted that no matter how numerous the group of persons may be, if the link between them is their relationship to a particular person they cannot be a section of the public for charitable purposes.[34] Such a condition would be unduly restrictive. For example, a fund collected for the purpose of the relief of distress among air raid victims whose potential beneficiaries were linked by employment to one employer was held not to be charitable. In that example one ground for the decision was that the potential beneficiaries, being in common employment and not limited to the poor, were not a section of the public.[35]

1–86 An exception to the rule that those linked by common employment are not a sufficient section of the public can be made where the employer has a monopoly, for example, the armed and civil services. In such cases the employees are considered to be linked by a common trade or profession and therefore can form a sufficient section of the public.

1–87 Private individuals, or a fluctuating body of private individuals—as opposed to a community or important class—cannot constitute a sufficient section of the public[36] even in relation to the relief of poverty.

1–88 The question of whether the prospective beneficiaries are sufficient to be regarded as a section of the public also depends on the charitable purpose being furthered and differs as between the charitable purposes set out in the 2005 Act.[37] The group that qualifies as a section of the public and the charitable purpose in question are interdependent and sufficiency varies on a case by case basis. For example, there could be a valid trust for the promotion of religion benefiting a

---

32 Charities and Trustee Investment (Scotland) Act 2005 s.8.

33 *Oppenheim v Tobacco Securities Trust Co Ltd* [1951] A.C. 297 at 306 (Lord Simonds).

34 *Oppenheim v Tobacco Securities Trust Co Ltd* [1951] A.C. 297 at 306.

35 *Re Hobourn Aero Components Ltd's Air Raid Distress Fund* [1946] Ch. 194 at 206, 207–209 (Lord Greene MR).

36 *Verge v Somerville* [1924] A.C. 496 at 499.

37 *Gilmour v Coats* [1949] A.C. 426 at 449 (Lord Simonds).

very small class but it does not follow that a recreation ground for the exclusive use of the same class would be a valid charity.[38]

The purpose in which the section of the public may be the smallest is the relief of poverty. It has been stated that the relief even of one person's poverty is a benefit to the whole community; but this does not permit a charity merely to be for the benefit of one named individual.[39] Further, in relation to this charitable purpose only, the potential beneficiaries may be linked by descent from one individual or by employment by one employer or by membership of an unincorporated association.[40] **1–89**

What must be considered in each case is whether any criteria for and limitations on who may benefit are justifiable and reasonable. What is justifiable and reasonable will depend on the nature of the body's charitable purpose and the nature of any limits, including any payments for services or fees and how these limits are operated. **1–90**

Charities charging fees for their services

Where charities provide benefit to a section of the public only and charge fees for those services the question that needs to be considered is whether such fees are unduly restrictive. **1–91**

The fact that a charity provides benefits that will be charged for and will be provided mainly to people who can afford and choose to pay the charges does not of itself mean that the charity does not provide public benefit. There is no objection in principle to the charging of fees for services provided by charities. It has never been held that purposes, otherwise charitable, cease to be charitable if beneficiaries are required to make payments for what they receive.[41] **1–92**

The overall approach is to assess whether a fee constitutes an unduly restrictive condition by focusing on access to the benefit a charity provides. The courts will consider whether and to what extent in the context of the cost of providing the benefits, access may be restricted; how the charity itself responds to mitigate the impact of the financial restriction on access, and any other external factors which mitigate this. **1–93**

Whatever the scale of fees a charity should be able to demonstrate that its fee structure and arrangements to facilitate access are well publicised. Transparency is important. **1–94**

In the case of small or insignificant fees less evidence is generally required to assess whether they constitute an undue restriction although, where benefit depends on a small fee regularly paid over a long period, the cumulative result of such fees may be considered unduly restrictive. The greater any fee, the more **1–95**

---

38 *IRC v Baddeley* [1955] A.C. 572 at 615 (Lord Somervell of Harrow).

39 In *Re Compton* [1945] Ch. 123.

40 *Attorney General v Charity Commission (The Poverty Reference)* [2012] W.T.L.R. 977.

41 *Scottish Burial Reform and Cremation Society Ltd v Glasgow Corporation* [1968] A.C. 138, per Lord Reid at 147.

evidence may be needed, and the more important any measures on the part of the charity or others to mitigate the impact of the fee becomes.

1–96 Where a charity charges for only some of its services the scale of those fees will be balanced against the full scope of the benefits provided by that charity.

1–97 The cost of providing the benefit that is being charged for is also relevant to assessing whether any fee or charge is unduly restrictive. Some benefits are expensive to provide and charities must be able to cover the cost of providing them. Keeping fees charged to individual beneficiaries low by covering the cost in part from other sources such as donations can, in some circumstances, be an appropriate means of ensuring that fees are not unduly restrictive.

1–98 Where a fee is charged that may affect the access to a benefit, there should be some kind of facilitated access or other mitigation in place such as means tested benefits payments, discounts, bursaries and fee waivers for people with a wide range of incomes, including low incomes. Forms of facilitated access that are clearly linked to the financial situation of potential beneficiaries are likely to have the greatest impact in addressing undue restriction in this context.

1–99 There is no requirement for the profile of beneficiaries of any charity to reflect the profile of the population as a whole, or the profile of the local population. Facilitated access arrangements, such as support to pay any fees, that come from a body that is not a charity or is not connected with the charity can and do in practice facilitate access to the benefit a charity provides. What matters is that the source of support is reliable, and how much impact the arrangements have on opening up access. Where the charity itself funds the support arrangements this will be recognised as a positive contribution to its provision of public benefit.

No particular purpose is presumed to be for the public benefit

1–100 The law relating to public benefit is evolving on a case-by-case basis and no particular purpose is, for the purposes of establishing whether the charity test has been met, to be presumed to be for the public benefit.[42] Case law does not provide a comprehensive statement of the public benefit requirement but provides, rather, a series of examples of when the public benefit requirement is or is not satisfied. There is no application of some overarching, coherent, principle by which the courts have been guided.[43] In determining whether a body provides or intends to provide public benefit, regard must be had to a number of criteria.

1–101 Public benefit should be capable of being identified and defined and the nature of benefit may be either tangible or intangible.

1–102 A tangible benefit may be material or measurable. For example, if a charity relieves a person's sickness or financial hardship, the person's health or financial circumstances can be measurably improved. On the other hand, intangible benefits may be more difficult to measure, but should still be identifiable. These

[42] Charities and Trustee Investment (Scotland) Act 2005 s.8(1).
[43] *Attorney General v Charity Commission (The Poverty Reference)* [2012] W.T.L.R. 977 at [34].

can include, for example, many of the benefits of education or religion, or promoting appreciation of historic buildings. Both tangible and intangible benefits will be taken into account.

Indirect as well as direct benefits will be taken into account in assessing whether a body provides benefit to the public. A direct benefit is one that is directly related to the activities carried out in pursuit of the charitable purpose and benefits the intended group of beneficiaries. For example, there is a direct benefit to the people who receive medical care if they are sick; to the people whose conditions of life have been improved by taking part in recreational activities; or to the people whose skills have been developed by taking part in a training programme. **1–103**

Indirect benefit exists when the benefit can be said to extend beyond the immediate beneficiary group, in many cases to the public generally. In most cases a charity will provide both direct and indirect benefits as a result of its activities, but to different degrees depending on individual circumstances. It is possible for charities to provide indirect benefit only. Charities for the advancement of animal welfare do not directly benefit any individual but indirectly the whole of society benefits from the charities activities. **1–104**

The legal concept of charity, including the concept of public benefit in charity law, is not static. Changing social perceptions have, in the past, resulted in changes in what is seen as for the benefit of society and, accordingly, of what is properly to be accorded charitable status.[44] There must be a link between the charity's purposes, its activities in furtherance of those purposes and the benefits that arise from those activities. If the link is not clear, the benefits will not be relevant in assessing public benefit. **1–105**

The court should take into account the general consensus of fair-minded and unprejudiced opinion when deciding whether there is a public benefit but public opinion cannot by itself determine what is and is not charitable. The question whether a gift is or may be operative for the public benefit is a question to be answered by the court by forming an opinion upon the evidence before it.[45] Further a donor's subjective belief that the purpose for which they make a gift is for the public benefit is not relevant. **1–106**

The benefit must be identifiable and, in principle, must be capable of being proved by evidence[46]: the court can have regard to the consequences of pursuing a charitable purpose in order to determine whether it is for the public benefit. The requirement for evidence is in practice tempered in a number of respects. The court will regard some benefits as being too obvious to require formal proof.[47] **1–107**

---

[44] *R (Independent Schools Council) v Charity Commission* [2012] Ch. 214 at [14] (Upper Chamber, Warren J).

[45] *Re Hummeltenberg* [1923] 1 Ch. 237 (Russell J).

[46] *Scottish Burial Reform and Cremation Society Ltd v Glasgow Corporation* [1968] A.C. 138 at 146 (Lord Reid).

[47] *Re Shaw's Will Trusts* [1952] Ch. 163 at 169 (Vaisey J).

The court will also take account of statute law as indicating what Parliament regards as being for the public benefit,[48] and will take judicial notice of some obvious facts.[49]

1–108 If the court regards the public benefit of a purpose as incapable of proof one way or another, the court will not recognise it as a charitable purpose.[50]

PRIVATE BENEFIT

1–109 Although a charity must be set up to provide a public benefit, in many cases it will also confer benefits on individuals. For example, a school established as a charity will benefit its scholars[51] and such private benefit will be regarded as incidental. Likewise the social benefits of membership of a synagogue have been regarded as incidental to charitable religious purposes.[52] Any benefit conferred on someone as an individual as opposed to as a member of the class of beneficiaries is a private benefit.

1–110 A charitable purpose may confer benefits on persons who are not in charitable need, if to do so is incidental to advancing a charitable purpose. For example, the provision of a home of rest for nurses was held to be charitable, as it was conducive to the efficiency of a hospital, and so for the advancement of health.[53] Overall, a judgement must be made on the balance between the private benefit and the public benefit resulting from the activities of a body. The fact that some private benefit exists does not in itself mean the charity test is not met. The private benefit needs to be seen in the context of the benefit the body provides as a whole.

1–111 Where benefit to individuals is not in furtherance of the body's purposes, any private benefit should be necessary and/or incidental to the pursuit of the charity's purposes. There should be a link between the benefit to the individual that is not of itself charitable and the charity's purposes. Necessary means that the public benefit the charity provides would be difficult to provide without incurring the degree and kind of private benefit involved. For example, it may be necessary for a charity to employ staff to fulfil its activities and it would be necessary to pay reasonable remuneration. It is also possible for a Scottish charity to make an ex gratia payment to another individual or organisation that does not share the charity's purposes provided such a payment is in the best interest of the charity. Incidental means that the private benefit arises as a secondary consequence of activity producing benefit to the public and is not an end in itself.

---

[48] See, for example, *Scottish Burial Reform and Cremation Society Ltd v Glasgow Corporation* [1968] A.C. 138 at 146,

[49] *R (Independent Schools Council) v Charity Commission* [2012] Ch. 214 at [70].

[50] *McGovern v Attorney General* [1982] Ch. 321 at 334 (Slade J).

[51] *London Hospital Medical College v IRC* [1976] 1 W.L.R. 613, 620 (Brightman J).

[52] *Neville Estates v Madden* [1962] Ch 832 at 851–852 (Cross J).

[53] *Re White's Will Trusts* [1951] 1 All E.R. 528.

Provided that less than half of their number are remunerated a charity may pay some of its trustees provided that such payments is in the best interest of the charity and the arrangements under which it is made are recorded in writing.[54] **1–112**

MEMBERSHIP ORGANISATIONS

It is, in principle, acceptable for charities to adopt membership structures that include membership benefits, but where charities do so and the members are given special benefits by the charity, such benefits must be reasonable and necessary and/or incidental to the purpose of the charity. Benefits that are inconsequential or of little measureable value will not usually cause a problem. **1–113**

It may be that the members of an organisation are at the same time the main beneficiaries of the body (for example, guides, scouts or similar groups). In these cases there must be a clear link between the charitable purpose for which the organisation was established and the benefit conferred on the members. The purpose must be altruistic and membership must be open to a sufficient section of the public. Special care is needed where membership is made up of both potential beneficiaries and other supporters of the charity's aims.[55] **1–114**

Membership bodies are constitutionally varied, so in some instances it may be that members (who are beneficiaries) are also charity trustees. While membership charities will be able to draw their charity trustees from their membership and these charity trustees will be able to continue to receive the same benefits as any other member, they will have to pay particular attention to the charity trustees' duty to act in the interests of the charity and avoid conflicts of interest.[56] Care also needs to be taken to avoid falling foul of the rules on trustee remuneration.[57] **1–115**

However, if the main beneficiaries of a body are its members, and all these members are also to be charity trustees (and there are no other potential members or beneficiaries), then the body exists for self-interest or private benefit only and cannot provide public benefit. **1–116**

DISBENEFIT

Disbenefit, whilst perhaps a new word, is not a new concept. Disbenefit is the opposite of benefit. It is therefore more than the mere absence of benefit. Disbenefit is equivalent to detriment or harm. **1–117**

When deciding whether a purpose is beneficial to the public, the court has always weighed any benefit that will result to the public from the pursuit of the purpose against any detriment. **1–118**

In considering whether there is disbenefit to the public, the same general principles will apply as when deciding whether there is benefit to the public. As **1–119**

---

54 See paras 4–140—4–133.

55 See paras 5–77—5–89.

56 See paras 5–77—5–89.

57 See paras 4–140—4–133.

with benefit, disbenefit can vary in nature, scale and the immediacy or visibility of the impact or result. Again, as with benefit, it should be possible to identify and describe the disbenefit caused. To be taken into account, the disbenefit should affect the public at large or a relevant section of the public.

1–120 Great weight will be given to a purpose that would, ordinarily, be charitable before the alleged disadvantages can be given much weight, but the benefits need to be clearly demonstrated. Thus, it has been held by the House of Lords that the question of whether the promotion of a change in the law to abolish vivisection was a charitable purpose was not concluded by the assertion of the moral benefits that would flow from the cessation of vivisection, but required a comparison of those benefits with the practical benefits that were proved to flow from the practice of vivisection.[58]

1–121 Many of the everyday actions of organisations (and individuals) may cause a degree of disbenefit to others, either directly or indirectly. This fact should not unnecessarily stifle the operations of charities. Where any disbenefit caused stems from reasonable and necessary actions in connection with the charity's purpose and is the inevitable and generally accepted result of such reasonable actions in the society in which they take place, then such disbenefit may be largely disregarded.

1–122 Disbenefit also arises where the activities of a charity are unlawful. A major area where this can affect charities relates to discrimination under equality legislation.

DISCRIMINATION BY CHARITIES

1–123 Equality legislation provides that it is illegal to discriminate against anyone with a protected characteristic.[59] The protected characteristics are:

- age;
- disability;
- gender reassignment;
- marriage and civil partnership;
- pregnancy and maternity;
- race;
- religion or belief;
- sex; or
- sexual orientation.

1–124 Charities are liable to find themselves discriminating in that respect when they carry out a number of activities:

- providing services;
- making grants and non-monetary support;
- limitations on beneficiaries; and

---

58 *National Anti-Vivisection Society v Inland Revenue Commissioners* [1948] A.C. 31.
59 Equality Act 2010 (c.15) ss.4 and 13.

- employment practices.

THE CHARITY EXEMPTION

The benefit conferred by many charities is restricted by reference to a group of people who share a particular protected characteristic, for example, charities for the elderly or for children discriminate on grounds of age. Charities for people with a particular infirmity discriminate on grounds of disability. Clearly it was not the intention of legislators to legislate against these worthy charities and so the Equality Act contains an exemption for charities.[60] **1–125**

The 2005 Act allows a charity to restrict its benefits to people with a shared protected characteristic provided that certain tests are met. **1–126**

First, the restriction must be allowed by the constitution that sets out the charity's purposes.[61] The charity purposes must specifically restrict their services or benefits to a particular class of beneficiaries by a shared protected characteristic. For example, a charity set up to alleviate the sufferers of a particular disability must state in its constitution that this is this suffering that it set out to alleviate. Conversely a charity set up with purposes to alleviate disabilities generally cannot just focus on one disability as it would be discriminating against everyone with any other disability. **1–127**

The exception to this rule is for religious and belief charities that do not need a governing document restriction to be able to discriminate on grounds of religion or sexual orientation. **1–128**

Secondly, the discrimination must be justified either because it helps to tackle disadvantages that particularly affect someone with a protected characteristic[62]; or because such discrimination is a fair, balanced and reasonable ("proportionate") way of achieving a legitimate aim.[63] **1–129**

The proposed restriction of benefit to a particular group of people with particular needs should be based on the needs or disadvantages experienced by that particular group. For example, charities may look after the particular needs of people at different ages when they are particularly vulnerable (children or the aged). However, a charity cannot restrict benefit to part of a group sharing a protected characteristic where that part does not suffer any additional or different disadvantage. Thus, a charity established to feed only homeless men would be discriminatory unless it could be shown that they were at a greater disadvantage than homeless women. **1–130**

If a charity is unable to demonstrate that the proposed discrimination can be based on the needs or disadvantages experienced by that particular group then it should consider whether the discrimination is for some other reason a fair, balanced and reasonable ("proportionate") way of achieving a legitimate aim. **1–131**

60 Equality Act 2010 s.193.
61 Equality Act 2010 s.193(1)(a).
62 Equality Act 2010 s.193(2)(b).
63 Equality Act 2010 s.193(2)(a).

This test depends on the particular circumstances both of the charity and the environment in which it operates. A particularly convincing and weighty reasons is needed to justify the proposed discrimination.[64] The negative attitudes of third parties and the private prejudices of charitable donors of themselves cannot be an adequate justification for discrimination.[65]

1–132 There is an exception for charities whose purpose is the advancement of religion.[66] They can discriminate on the grounds of a person's religion or belief or their sexual orientation. They can impose limits in respect of membership; participation in the organisation's activities; the services they provide and the use of their premises. If the charity seeks to discriminate on the grounds of religion or belief it can only do so either because promoting those beliefs is the organisation's purpose or to avoid causing offence to followers of the religion or belief on which the organisation is founded. A charity whose purpose is the advancement of religion that seeks to discriminate on the grounds of sexual orientation can only do so in order to comply with the organisation's doctrine or to avoid conflict with the religious or belief based convictions of many followers of the organisation. Even if these tests are met, religious charities cannot discriminate because of sexual orientation if they are providing a service on behalf of a public authority.

---

[64] *Catholic Care (Diocese of Leeds) v Charity Commission for England and Wales* [2013] 1 W.L.R. 2105; [2012] CA/2010/0007 UKUT.

[65] *St Margaret's Children and Family Care Society v Office of the Scottish Charity Regulator* (Case ref: APP 02/13).

[66] Equality Act 2010 Sch.23.

CHAPTER 2

OFFICE OF THE SCOTTISH CHARITY REGULATOR

James McNeill

THE REGULATOR

Supervision of charities in Scotland is under the control of an office named the Office of the Scottish Charity Regulator.[1] The holder of the office is a corporate body, the Scottish Charity Regulator,[2] commonly called OSCR.[3] OSCR comprises a number of members, appointed by the Scottish Ministers, together with a chief executive and staff appointed by OSCR.[4] It is independent of the Scottish Government.[5] OSCR publishes annual reports on the exercise of its functions.[6] It maintains a website.[7] **2–01**

The formation, operation and dissolution of charities in Scotland are overseen by OSCR. Its principal general functions are: (a) determining whether bodies are charities and granting charitable status; (b) keeping a public register of charities; (c) encouraging, facilitating and monitoring compliance by charities with regulatory requirements; (d) identifying and investigating apparent misconduct in the administration of charities and taking any necessary remedial or protective action; and (e) giving information[8] or advice,[9] and making proposals, to the Scottish Ministers.[10] It is also the principal authority for the approval of reorganisation schemes for charities,[11] of restricted funds[12] and for conversions.[13] **2–02**

The function of encouraging, facilitating and monitoring regulatory compliance by charities is of particular importance.[14] With over 23,500 registered charities in Scotland the maintenance of good compliance is clearly an essential building block both for the regulator and for medium sized charities. Another important **2–03**

---

[1] Charities and Trustee Investment (Scotland) Act 2005 (asp 10) s.1(1).
[2] Charities and Trustee Investment (Scotland) Act 2005 s.1(2).
[3] Charities and Trustee Investment (Scotland) Act 2005 s.1(3).
[4] Charities and Trustee Investment (Scotland) Act 2005 Sch.1.
[5] And see the Charities and Trustee Investment (Scotland) Act 2005 (Consequential Provisions and Modifications) Order 2006 (SI 2006/242) para.2.
[6] Charities and Trustee Investment (Scotland) Act 2005 s.2.
[7] *http://www.oscr.org.uk/* [Accessed 18 May 2016].
[8] An instance in respect of a decision to grant charitable status in a complex matter was the Raeburn Place Foundation Note of May 2014.
[9] A practical example being the advice on safe methods of giving support to Syria dated July 2014.
[10] Charities and Trustee Investment (Scotland) Act 2005 s.1.
[11] Charities and Trustee Investment (Scotland) Act 2005 ss.39 and 40.
[12] Charities and Trustee Investment (Scotland) Act 2005 ss.43A–43D.
[13] Charities and Trustee Investment (Scotland) Act 2005 s.56.
[14] Charities and Trustee Investment (Scotland) Act 2005 s.1(5)(c).

aim is the encouragement of transparency within charities because of the significant part that integrity and accountability have to play in public confidence.[15]

THE REGULATED

2–04 Entry on the register kept by OSCR is the keystone to the entitlement of a body to represent itself as a charity in Scotland. As a general rule, only a body entered in that register may refer to itself in Scotland as a "charity", a "charitable body", a "registered charity" or a "charity registered in Scotland".[16] If the body is established under Scots law, or is in the main managed or controlled in or from Scotland, it may also refer to itself as a "Scottish charity" or a "registered Scottish charity".[17] An exception permits a charitable body to refer to itself in Scotland as a "charity" where it is established under the law of another territory, entitled there to refer to itself as a "charity" or suchlike and is in the main managed or controlled outside of Scotland. This exemption from Scottish registration does not apply if the body occupies land or premises within Scotland or if it carries out activities from office, shop or similar premises within Scotland.[18] It follows that a body referring to itself in Scotland as a "charity" or a "charitable body" might be subject to the supervisory powers of OSCR. If the exceptions do not apply, a body wishing to refer to itself in Scotland as a "charity" or a "charitable body" must seek registration with OSCR.[19]

2–05 Representation is taken by OSCR to mean any public reference to the organisation being a charity, made by the organisation itself or made by a person acting on behalf of the organisation. The representation might be any written or verbal communication with any person external to the organisation itself. An example of a relevant representation might be a funding application or a request for rates relief in which the organisation makes reference to being a charity; but a letter sent only to the organisation's own members would not be treated as a public representation.[20]

2–06 Penalties may be imposed for failure to comply with a direction from OSCR[21] to stop representation as a charity in Scotland.[22]

---

[15] See OSCR "Annual Report and Accounts 2013–2014", pp 4–5.
[16] Charities and Trustee Investment (Scotland) Act 2005 s.13(1).
[17] Charities and Trustee Investment (Scotland) Act 2005 s.13(2).
[18] Charities and Trustee Investment (Scotland) Act 2005 s.14.
[19] Charities and Trustee Investment (Scotland) Act 2005 s.4.
[20] See OSCR, "Seeking charitable status in Scotland" (Guidance for England and Wales charities) para.4.2.
[21] Charities and Trustee Investment (Scotland) Act 2005 s.32(5).
[22] Charities and Trustee Investment (Scotland) Act 2005 s.31(5).

THE REGISTER

Application for entry in the Register requires presentation not only of details of the applicant and of the charitable purposes but also of a copy of a constitution together with information as to who will be the charity trustees, how the charity will provide a public benefit, whether there will be any private benefit and whether there will be any restrictions on receiving benefit.[23] The application is determined by OSCR.[24] In relation to public benefit OSCR will look for objective independent evidence of claims.[25] The register is publicly accessible,[26] effectively nowadays through the OSCR website. The information publicly available[27] comprises the principal details of the charity such as the full name and charity number, the principal office,[28] as also the website address together with the identity of any parent body. The charitable purposes are specified, as are operational details such as whether the charity is active, its geographical spread of operation, any restriction as to beneficiaries and how it carries out its activities. Financial information is given together with a general breakdown both of income and of expenditure. Directions given by OSCR as to the charity's constitution or operations will be identified. OSCR has power to require provision of relevant documentary and other information in relation to the entry.[29] **2–07**

There is no requirement on OSCR to maintain a register of trustees of a charity, but OSCR views the publication of charitable accounts on the register as a key priority.[30] In effect, this would lead to something close to the maintenance of a register of charity trustees as (except in cases of potential safety or security concerns[31]) the identity of the trustees should appear on the annual accounts and report on activities.[32] In any event, that document as well as the constitution are to be made available to the public by the charity, subject to meeting any request for reimbursement of the cost of supply.[33] **2–08**

Where a charity (other than a Scottish charitable incorporated organisation) applies to be removed from the Register, OSCR must do so within 28 days.[34] When a body is removed from the register, its assets continue to be dedicated to its constitutional purposes and OSCR may seek a court order to protect assets.[35] **2–09**

---

[23] Charities and Trustee Investment (Scotland) Act 2005 s.4.
[24] Charities and Trustee Investment (Scotland) Act 2005 s.5.
[25] See, for example, the OSCR, "Inquiry Report regarding a body known as Campbell's Ozone Therapy Trust", *http://www.oscr.org.uk/media/1776/2015-01-12-inquiry-report-campbells-ozone-therapy-trust-v2.pdf* [Accessed 18 May 2016].
[26] Charities and Trustee Investment (Scotland) Act 2005 s.21.
[27] Charities and Trustee Investment (Scotland) Act 2005 s.3.
[28] Charities and Trustee Investment (Scotland) Act 2005 s.3(3).
[29] Charities and Trustee Investment (Scotland) Act 2005 s.22(1).
[30] See OSCR, "Annual Report and Accounts 2014–2015", p.11.
[31] Charities and Trustee Investment (Scotland) Act 2005 s.3(4).
[32] Charities and Trustee Investment (Scotland) Act 2005 s.44; and see the Charities Accounts (Scotland) Regulations 2006 (SSI 2006/218) Sch.2, para.4.
[33] Charities and Trustee Investment (Scotland) Act 2005 s.23.
[34] Charities and Trustee Investment (Scotland) Act 2005 s.18.
[35] Charities and Trustee Investment (Scotland) Act 2005 s.19.

USE OF INFORMATION

2–10 OSCR is under a duty to secure cooperation with other relevant regulatory bodies.[36] OSCR is also empowered to disclose information to other bodies whether in Scotland, in the remainder of the UK or further afield.[37] HMRC is empowered to disclose to OSCR any information concerning bodies of whom they have knowledge through exercise of their functions.[38]

2–11 On occasion a body might be subject to the jurisdiction both of OSCR and of another overseeing body. An example exists with the Scottish Public Services Ombudsman. In such circumstances it is likely that the jurisdiction of OSCR will extend to consideration of charitable trustee misconduct, mismanagement and the protection of charitable assets.[39]

DECISIONS

2–12 Many decisions taken by OSCR[40] must be notified to relevant persons, with reasons.[41] Those decisions, on application by someone notified within 21 days, can be made the subject of a review by OSCR.[42] OSCR may confirm, vary, reverse or revoke the decision and must give notice of the review determination, with reasons.[43] There is a right to appeal against such decisions, within 28 days, to the Scottish Charity Appeals Panel.[44] On appeal the Panel may confirm a decision, quash with directions or remit with reasons.[45] Decisions of the Panel may be appealed to the Court of Session.[46] On a remit OSCR must reconsider its decision and give notice of its new decision, with reasons.[47]

REGULATING CHANGES

2–13 The consent of OSCR is required where a charity wishes to amend its charitable purposes, to enter into an amalgamation or to commence a winding up.[48] For these steps, 42 days' notice must be given to OSCR. Amendment of charitable purposes requires actual consent from OSCR,[49] but in the other matters, unless

---

36 Charities and Trustee Investment (Scotland) Act 2005 s.20.

37 Charities and Trustee Investment (Scotland) Act 2005 s.24; and see the Memorandum of Understanding between OSCR and FCA December 2013.

38 See the Charities and Trustee Investment (Scotland) Act 2005 (Consequential Provisions and Modifications) Order 2006 (SI 2006/242) para.3.

39 See the Memorandum of Understanding between OSCR and SPSO 28 May 2007 (reviewed 2009).

40 Charities and Trustee Investment (Scotland) Act 2005 s.71.

41 Charities and Trustee Investment (Scotland) Act 2005 s.72.

42 Charities and Trustee Investment (Scotland) Act 2005 s.74; and see OSCR's "Review Procedures" (June 2014).

43 Charities and Trustee Investment (Scotland) Act 2005 s.74.

44 Charities and Trustee Investment (Scotland) Act 2005 s.75; and see paras 2–68–2–71 below.

45 Charities and Trustee Investment (Scotland) Act 2005 s.76.

46 Charities and Trustee Investment (Scotland) Act 2005 s.78.

47 Charities and Trustee Investment (Scotland) Act 2005 s.77.

48 Charities and Trustee Investment (Scotland) Act 2005 s.16.

49 Charities and Trustee Investment (Scotland) Act 2005 s.16(5).

OSCR has refused consent or issues a direction imposing a six month moratorium, failure by OSCR to respond to the notice will result in deemed consent.[50] OSCR may make appropriate enquiries after issuing a direction that action by the charity is not to be taken for a six month period.[51]

Some changes must be notified to OSCR, but do not require its consent. These include: (i) change to the principal office, to other details set out in the register entry, or to the constitution (other than in respect of purposes); and (ii) administration and winding up orders or receivership appointments.[52] Notification of changes must be given within three months of the event or action.[53] Notification of orders and appointments must be given within one month.[54] **2–14**

SUPERVISION

Supervision can include encouraging, facilitating and monitoring compliance by charities with regulatory requirements, as well as identifying and investigating apparent misconduct in the administration of charities and taking any necessary remedial or protective action. Through this OSCR tries: (i) to increase public confidence in charities through effective regulation; (ii) to have increased transparency and public accountability of charities; (iii) to encourage increased compliance by charity trustees with the 2005 Act; and (iv) to establish and maintain OSCR as a trusted, effective and innovative regulator whilst at the same time seeking to minimise the burden of regulation.[55] **2–15**

Active and proactive supervision lie at the heart of the 2005 Act. It was the discovery of irregularities (albeit not amounting to fraud) in the running of a number of charities in Scotland, in a sector without systematic supervision, which was a material compulsitor for the legislation creating the Regulator. The statutory provisions governing OSCR's supervisory powers are therefore of such importance that it is appropriate to quote the principal inquisitorial provision in full[56]: **2–16**

> "**Section 28 Inquiries about charities, etc.**
> (1) OSCR may at any time make inquiries, either generally or for particular purposes, with regard to—
> (a) a charity,
> (b) a body controlled by a charity (or by two or more charities, when taken together),
> (c) a body which is not entered in the Register which appears to OSCR to represent itself as a charity (or which would, but for section 14, so appear),
> (d) a person not falling within paragraph (a) to (c) who appears to OSCR to act, or to represent itself as acting, for or on behalf of—
> (i) a charity, or
> (ii) a body falling within paragraph (b) or (c),

[50] Charities and Trustee Investment (Scotland) Act 2005 s.16(6).
[51] Charities and Trustee Investment (Scotland) Act 2005 s.16(8).
[52] Charities and Trustee Investment (Scotland) Act 2005 s.17(1).
[53] Charities and Trustee Investment (Scotland) Act 2005 s.17(3).
[54] Charities and Trustee Investment (Scotland) Act 2005 s.17(4).
[55] OSCR, "Inquiry Policy Guidance" (August 2014), p.4.
[56] Charities and Trustee Investment (Scotland) Act 2005 s.28.

(e) a person who appears to OSCR to represent a body which is not entered in the Register as a charity,
(f) any particular type of charity, of body falling within paragraph (b) or (c), or of person falling within paragraph (d) or (e).

(2) OSCR may make inquiries under subsection (1) of its own accord or on the representation of any person.

(3) OSCR may direct any charity, body or person with regard to which it is making inquiries under subsection (1) not to undertake activities specified in the direction for such period of not more than 6 months as is specified in the direction.

(4) A direction under subsection (3) given to a person falling within paragraph (d) or (e) of subsection (1) may be given only in relation to activities which that person undertakes for or on behalf of the charity or body to which the inquiries relate.

(5) A direction under subsection (3)—
(a) may be revoked at any time,
(b) may be varied, but not so as to have effect for a period of more than 6 months from the date on which it is given.

(6) A person who, without reasonable excuse, refuses or fails to comply with a direction under subsection (3) is guilty of an offence.

(7) A person guilty of an offence under subsection (6) is liable on summary conviction to a fine not exceeding level 4 on the standard scale or imprisonment for a period not exceeding 3 months, or to both."

2–17 These provisions therefore empower:

- inquiries either of a particular or of a general nature;
- inquiries about charitable bodies and about other bodies and individuals;
- inquiries whether or not prompted by the representation of a third party;
- the making of directions as part of the inquiry process[57]; and
- the imposition of a fine or imprisonment in the event of failure to comply with directions.

2–18 OSCR may therefore institute an inquiry arising from:

- a complaint from a member of the public;
- concerns raised by parties connected to a charity (for example, trustees, members, employees or volunteers);
- a referral from another organisation including other regulators;
- matters referred from an auditor or independent examiner; and
- the internal identification by OSCR of the need for a referral (for example, when issues of interest emerge from annual returns or from media reports[58]).

THE INQUIRY PROCEDURE: GENERAL

2–19 OSCR itself decides whether or not to proceed with an inquiry; and when an inquiry takes place OSCR must act in the public interest and not on behalf of a complainant, other body or interest group. If the inquiry is based on a complaint,

---

57 See, for example, the OSCR interim directions in respect of the Cameron Fund: *http://www.oscr.org.uk/media/1872/2015-04-23-cameron-fund-section-33-report-updated.pdf* [Accessed 18 May 2016].

58 See, for example, the OSCR report into "The Kiltwalk": *http://www.oscr.org.uk/media/1868/2015-04-17-inquiry-report-the-kiltwalk.pdf* [Accessed 18 May 2016].

OSCR should have considered the information provided, have identified that the issue falls within its regulatory remit and have determined the most proportionate response.

OSCR receives about 20–30 indications of concern a month; in 2013–2014 it produced six inquiry reports, and three in 2014–2015.[59] It is not bound to take forward a matter complained of. OSCR ought also to confirm that any information presented with a complaint—and, indeed, throughout an inquiry—is correct and credible. It is an offence under the 2005 Act—punishable with fine or imprisonment or both—for a person knowingly or recklessly to provide OSCR with any information or explanation that is false or misleading in a material respect, or to destroy or conceal any document that is required for the conduct of any OSCR inquiry.[60] **2–20**

In determining to take action following on from external or internal information it is likely that OSCR will have identified concerns such as: **2–21**

> "a. risk of significant damage to the charity, its assets or beneficiaries;
> b. apparent breach of trustee duties;
> c. apparent serious or sustained misconduct by those in management and control of the charity;
> d. indications that the charity does not meet the charity and public benefit tests; and
> e. indications that there is improper misrepresentation as to being a charity in Scotland.[61]"

Each of these concerns carries with it a noteworthy external element. It is clear, however, that OSCR does not have discretion to overrule a decision of charity trustees that has been validly taken. Accordingly, where a complaint is made regarding internal matters that do not suggest misconduct it is unlikely that OSCR would intervene. Examples are: (i) problems or disagreements with which it is the duty of trustees to deal, such as employment or contractual disputes; (ii) criminal activity such as embezzlement; (iii) disputes relating to service delivery, which should be dealt with through the charity's own complaints procedures; (iii) disputes between charity trustees; (iv) disputes between trustees and members of a charity, such as decisions about policies pursued or actions taken so long as they are within the law and the charity's governing document. OSCR is also unlikely to intervene where another regulator also has a supervisory role and is likely to be more suited to the issue that has arisen.[62] **2–22**

When a complaint has been made but OSCR decides either that there is no proper evidence or that intervention is not appropriate, as a general rule it will not contact the charity unless it appears that it would be in the best interests of the charity to make charity trustees aware of the issues or concerns raised.[63] OSCR will advise the complainant of its determination, with reasons, within six to eight **2–23**

[59] OSCR, "Annual Report and Accounts 2013–2014", p.7; "Annual Report 2014–2015", p.7.
[60] Charities and Trustee Investment (Scotland) Act 2005 s.26.
[61] OSCR, "Inquiry Policy Guidance" (August 2014), p.2.
[62] OSCR, "Inquiry Policy Guidance" (August 2014), p.2.
[63] OSCR, "Inquiry Policy Guidance" (August 2014), p.3.

weeks of the initial complaint having been received but will neither enter into more detailed discussions nor issue findings on each and every allegation made.[64]

2–24 If OSCR establishes that there are grounds upon which to conduct an investigation, it might either contact the charity immediately or think it appropriate to conduct background inquiries first as part of its assessment. It might also refrain from contact at the initial stages where the issues suggest that contact with the charity trustees might impair the investigation or place assets at risk.[65]

2–25 On initial contact, the charity will be made aware of the general grounds of the complaint or of the cause for concern, but the name of a complainant will be withheld except with their permission or by court order.[66]

2–26 Throughout an inquiry or investigation OSCR aims to keep to a minimum any disruption to the work of the charity, staff, volunteers and trustees. However, it has power to ask for information from any trustee, person connected with the charity or appropriate public bodies. That power, again, is supported by statutory punishment in the event of failure to comply.

2–27 The power given to OSCR for the purpose of its inquiries under s.28 is, by notice, to require any person to provide it with any document or type of document, or copy or extract from any document, together with any information or explanation which OSCR considers necessary for the purposes of those inquiries. The notice must specify: (i) the documents, type of documents, information or explanation to be produced; (ii) the date by which the recipient must do so; and (iii) the existence of the statutory penalty for failure to comply.[67] The penalty is a fine, imprisonment for a period up to three months, or both.[68] The reasonable cost of complying with the notice may be paid.[69]

2–28 However, these powers do not authorise OSCR to require disclosure of anything that would be protected from recovery in a court process on grounds of confidentiality.[70] Further, OSCR must not disclose any document or information provided except for the purposes of the inquiries in question.[71]

THE INQUIRY PROCEDURE: DIRECTIONS, SUSPENSIONS AND OFFENCES

2–29 If OSCR reaches the view that a charity no longer meets the charity test, it is usual that the charity will be given a direction to take such steps specified by OSCR, in a time frame specified by OSCR, as OSCR considers necessary for the purposes of meeting the charity test: under notice that, otherwise, the charity will

---

64 OSCR, "Inquiry Policy Guidance" (August 2014), p.3.
65 OSCR, "Inquiry Policy Guidance" (August 2014), p.4.
66 OSCR, "Inquiry Policy Guidance" (August 2014), p.3.
67 Charities and Trustee Investment (Scotland) Act 2005 s.29.
68 Charities and Trustee Investment (Scotland) Act 2005 s.29(6).
69 Charities and Trustee Investment (Scotland) Act 2005 s.29(3) .
70 Charities and Trustee Investment (Scotland) Act 2005 s.29(3).
71 Charities and Trustee Investment (Scotland) Act 2005 s.29(4) .

be removed from the Register.[72] Orders may be varied or revoked.[73] On a failure to comply with a direction, the charity will be removed.[74] Specified steps may include applying to OSCR for approval under s.39 of a reorganisation scheme.[75]

Separately, the inquiry might suggest that there has been misconduct in the administration of the charity, or of a body controlling it; or OSCR might identify that it is necessary or desirable either to act to protect the charity's property or to secure proper application of the property for the charitable purposes. In these instances OSCR has detailed and far reaching powers of suspension and direction.[76] **2–30**

Suspension of an individual may be ordered. This can occur if a person is part of the management or control of the charity and: (a) appears to have been responsible for or privy to misconduct; (b) appears to have contributed to, or facilitated it; or (c) appears to be unable or unfit to perform their functions within the charity or body.[77] But there is an exception for those who appear to have been acting honestly and reasonably and ought to be excused.[78] **2–31**

Suspensions and directions may have effect for up to six months.[79] The notification procedure is set out in the 2005 Act.[80] A person who, without reasonable excuse contravenes a suspension or refuses or fails to comply with a direction will be guilty of an offence and liable on summary conviction to a fine or imprisonment for a period not exceeding six months, or to both.[81] **2–32**

In instances of misconduct, restrictions on transactions can be imposed. OSCR has power to issue a direction restricting the transactions which can be entered into otherwise than with its consent, or the nature or amount of payments to be made.[82] There is also a power to give a direction not to dispose of, or part with, property to such financial institutions or other parties as OSCR may direct.[83] OSCR has no power to recover funds that have already been paid improperly by a charity. **2–33**

Instances of improper representation may result in: (a) a body being directed to stop representing itself as a charity; (b) a person being directed to stop representing a body as a charity; (c) a charity being directed to stop representing itself as being established under the law of Scotland or as being managed or controlled wholly or mainly in or from Scotland; and (d) a person being directed **2–34**

---

72 Charities and Trustee Investment (Scotland) Act 2005 s.30.
73 Charities and Trustee Investment (Scotland) Act 2005 s.30(2A).
74 Charities and Trustee Investment (Scotland) Act 2005 s.30(3).
75 Charities and Trustee Investment (Scotland) Act 2005 s.30(2).
76 Charities and Trustee Investment (Scotland) Act 2005 s.31.
77 Charities and Trustee Investment (Scotland) Act 2005 s.31(4): see, for example, the steps taken in regard to the Alfred Stewart Trust: *http://www.oscr.org.uk/media/1925/2015-07-23-updated-s33-report-re-ast.pdf* [Accessed 18 May 2016].
78 Charities and Trustee Investment (Scotland) Act 2005 s.31(10).
79 Charities and Trustee Investment (Scotland) Act 2005 s.32(1).
80 Charities and Trustee Investment (Scotland) Act 2005 s.32.
81 Charities and Trustee Investment (Scotland) Act 2005 s.32(5).
82 Charities and Trustee Investment (Scotland) Act 2005 s.31(6).
83 Charities and Trustee Investment (Scotland) Act 2005 s.31(7).

to stop representing the charity as being so established, managed or controlled.[84] Again there is a power to give a direction not to dispose of, or part with, property to such financial institutions or other parties as OSCR may direct.[85]

2–35 Where there seems to be misconduct by a person appearing to act, or to represent themselves as acting, for or on behalf of a charity,[86] OSCR may direct the person to cease acting on behalf of the charity or body, and to pay to the charity any sums collected for the charity.[87] It may also make directions regarding financial institutions or others holding property representing sums collected for the charity.[88]

2–36 In carrying out its regulatory functions OSCR must have regard to the principles of best regulatory practice. These include ensuring that any use of its powers is proportionate, accountable consistent, transparent and targeted only where action is necessary. It will also consider the risk of misconduct that charity trustees pose to other charities of which they are also trustees and may consider proactive monitoring of those charities.[89]

2–37 Such suspensions and directions may have effect for up to six months, may be revoked and varied.[90] Contravention of a suspension and refusal or failure to comply with a direction constitute offences liable to a fine or imprisonment for a period not exceeding six months, or to both.[91]

THE INQUIRY PROCEDURE: REPORTS

2–38 OSCR prepares and publishes reports on inquiries. It must prepare a formal report on an inquiry under s.28 if the result is a direction or removal under s.30, a suspension under s.31, or a direction under s.31.[92] It must prepare a formal report if requested to do so by the person in respect of whom the inquiries were made.[93] OSCR is also empowered to prepare a report on any other s.28 inquiry[94] and may prepare a single report relating to more than one inquiry.[95]

2–39 A report will identify the person in respect of whom inquiries were made.[96] However, unless OSCR considers it necessary to do so, a report made under s.33

---

[84] Charities and Trustee Investment (Scotland) Act 2005 s.31(5): see, for example, the direction in the OSCR, "Inquiry Report regarding a body known as Campbell's Ozone Therapy Trust": *http://www.oscr.org.uk/media/1288/campbellsozonetherapytrust.pdf* [Accessed 18 May 2016].

[85] Charities and Trustee Investment (Scotland) Act 2005 s.31(2) and (7): see, for example, the steps taken in regard to the Alfred Stewart Trust: *http://www.oscr.org.uk/media/1925/2015-07-23-updated-s33-report-re-ast.pdf* [Accessed 19 May 2016].

[86] Charities and Trustee Investment (Scotland) Act 2005 s.28(1)(d).

[87] Charities and Trustee Investment (Scotland) Act 2005 s.31(8).

[88] Charities and Trustee Investment (Scotland) Act 2005 s.31(9).

[89] See, generally, the OSCR, "Arms Length External Organisations" (January 2015): *http://www.oscr.org.uk/media/1778/2015-01-09-oscr-aleo-report.pdf* [Accessed 19 May 2016].

[90] Charities and Trustee Investment (Scotland) Act 2005 s.32(1).

[91] Charities and Trustee Investment (Scotland) Act 2005 s.31(5).

[92] Charities and Trustee Investment (Scotland) Act 2005 s.33(1)(a).

[93] Charities and Trustee Investment (Scotland) Act 2005 s.33(1)(b).

[94] Charities and Trustee Investment (Scotland) Act 2005 s.33(2).

[95] Charities and Trustee Investment (Scotland) Act 2005 s.33(3).

[96] Charities and Trustee Investment (Scotland) Act 2005 s.33(4).

must not mention the name of any other person, or contain particulars likely to identify any person, if they can be omitted without impairing the effectiveness of the report.[97]

A copy of the report must be sent to the person in respect of whom the inquiries were made.[98] Most importantly, OSCR must publish these reports or such other statement of the result of inquiries as it thinks fit and in such manner as it thinks fit.[99] 2–40

There is also public notification. Formal direction and suspension notices issued to a charity as a consequence of an inquiry or investigation will be displayed on the charity's entry on the Scottish Charity Register with appropriate links given to reports.[100] Where statutory powers are exercised with consent of the court, these will not only be in the public domain, but will also be reflected on the charity's Register entry. 2–41

Press statements or reports about individual inquiries or the exercise of intervention powers may be issued by OSCR, whether or not there has been an application to the court, albeit taking into account the rights of organisations and individuals concerned. It is also to be borne in mind that OSCR will respond to any requests for information in accordance with its obligations under the Freedom of Information (Scotland) Act 2002. 2–42

POWERS OF THE COURT

In cases that it considers particularly serious, OSCR has power to apply to the Court of Session for orders relating to the charity and individuals concerned. In some cases the orders of the court are similar to those that OSCR may issue, but bring the added impetus that failure to comply will carry the greater penalty of contempt of court. In other matters, the powers available to the court permit greater intervention. 2–43

In cases of misconduct, or of expediency for the protection of charitable assets, the court, on the application of OSCR, may interdict the charity or body from such action as the court thinks fit, on either a temporary or permanent basis.[101] In an extreme case it may appoint a judicial factor to manage the affairs of the charity or body, again on a temporary or permanent basis. [102] 2–44

The appointment of a judicial factor is a course of last resort due to the costs that will be incurred; but the sanction is an important spur to compliance. Less costly but equally important powers of intervention are those to have a trustee appointed 2–45

[97] Charities and Trustee Investment (Scotland) Act 2005 s.33(4).
[98] Charities and Trustee Investment (Scotland) Act 2005 s.33(5)(a).
[99] Charities and Trustee Investment (Scotland) Act 2005 s.33(5)(b).
[100] OSCR, "Inquiry Policy Guidance" (August 2014), p.5.
[101] Charities and Trustee Investment (Scotland) Act 2005 s.34(1), (5)(a).
[102] Charities and Trustee Investment (Scotland) Act 2005 s.34(1), (5)(c): see, for example, the steps taken in regard to the Alfred Stewart Trust: *http://www.oscr.org.uk/media/1925/2015-07-23-updated-s33-report-re-ast.pdf* [Accessed 19 May 2016].

where the charity or body is a trust,[103] and to have an order for suspension or removal of any person concerned in the management or control of the charity or body.[104]

2–46 Other powers reflect those given to OSCR, such as ordering that property is not to be disposed of without court consent,[105] or restricting the transactions that may be entered into without the court's consent.[106] The powers can be exercised even where the person is no longer concerned in the management or control of the charity or body, or the body is no longer a charity.[107]

2–47 In instances where a body that is not a charity is or has been representing itself as a charity, the court may exercise those same powers as well as having power to interdict the body from representing itself as a charity or from such other action as the court thinks fit.[108]

2–48 When individuals have been representing that a body that is not a charity is a charity, similar powers of financial restriction may be imposed as well as orders of interdict from making representations.[109]

2–49 Further, in instances where a person appears to act or to represent themselves as acting for a charity or other relevant body and there is apparent misconduct in any activity which the person undertakes for or on behalf of the charity or body, the court may pronounce an interdict of the individual, order the person to pay to the charity sums that they have collected, and order relevant financial institutions or others not to part with relevant property without the consent of the court.[110]

REMOVAL FROM THE REGISTER

2–50 At the outset the Register comprised each body then entitled by statute[111] to describe itself as a "Scottish charity".[112] New charities have been admitted by application.[113]

2–51 Charities that do not submit required documents to OSCR on time, may be considered to be in default of registration requirements and placed on the defaulting charities list. Those failing to provide OSCR with required forms after six months of a submission deadline may be considered for removal from the Register.[114] OSCR then carries out potentially wide-ranging[115] enquiries to

---

[103] Charities and Trustee Investment (Scotland) Act 2005 s.34(1), (5)(d).
[104] Charities and Trustee Investment (Scotland) Act 2005 s.34(1), (5)(e).
[105] Charities and Trustee Investment (Scotland) Act 2005 s.34(1), (5)(f).
[106] Charities and Trustee Investment (Scotland) Act 2005 s.34(1), (5)(g).
[107] Charities and Trustee Investment (Scotland) Act 2005 s.34(5)(ea).
[108] Charities and Trustee Investment (Scotland) Act 2005 s.34(2), (5)(b)–(5)(g).
[109] Charities and Trustee Investment (Scotland) Act 2005 s.34(3), (5)(f)–(5)(h).
[110] Charities and Trustee Investment (Scotland) Act 2005 s.34(8), (9).
[111] Law Reform (Miscellaneous Provisions)(Scotland) Act 1990 (c.40) s.1(7).
[112] Charities and Trustee Investment (Scotland) Act 2005 s.99(1).
[113] Charities and Trustee Investment (Scotland) Act 2005 s.4.
[114] See the OSCR, "Monitoring Policy" (August 2013), p.2; and Charities and Trustee Investment (Scotland) Act 2005 s.30.
[115] See the OSCR, "Monitoring Policy" (August 2013).

establish whether these charities can be found, or whether they have apparently ceased to exist or operate. A charity that has ceased to exist or operate does not provide public benefit and, therefore, does not meet the charity test and will be taken off the Register.[116]

If a charity disagrees with OSCR's decision to remove it from the Register, there is a right[117] to request a review of the decision. To do so the charity must make a formal communication[118] within 21 days of the charity being listed for removal. OSCR should respond within 21 days. **2–52**

The position in respect of dormant charities may be more flexible. But a charity that has stopped all activities, holds no property and is not expecting either a particular donation or a particular event in which it might participate is unlikely to be providing a public benefit.[119] The fact that someone at some future point may wish to revive the charity is unlikely to be sufficient reason to avoid removal.[120] **2–53**

WORKING WITH CHARITIES

As part of its work in facilitating, supporting and monitoring regulatory compliance, OSCR operates a proactive monitoring programme based on a review of the annual return and accounts, together with a supplementary monitoring return for charities with a gross income in excess of £25,000.[121] OSCR's current annual return includes increasingly detailed queries for charities with an annual income in excess of £25,000 on subjects such as reviews of the constitution, the number of trustees, whether any trustees receive any payment or benefit, whether there are any particularly significant sources of funding and what internal control procedures exist.[122] **2–54**

If charity trustees fail to submit returns, accounts or other required documents on time, OSCR will consider them to be in default of their registration and the charity will be placed on the defaulting charities list. The Charity Register entry for the entity will be highlighted in red to inform the public that returns and accounts are overdue. If trustees fail to provide OSCR with the required forms within 12 months of the submission deadline, OSCR may consider removing the charity from the register. **2–55**

Any supplementary monitoring returns are assessed by reference to areas of risk that OSCR has identified. When one of OSCR's priority action risks is triggered, the charity will be notified with requests for further information. **2–56**

---

116 Charities and Trustee Investment (Scotland) Act 2005 s.30(1)(b).

117 Charities and Trustee Investment (Scotland) Act 2005 s.74; and see the OSCR, "Review Procedures" (June 2014).

118 Charities and Trustee Investment (Scotland) Act 2005 s.100(4).

119 See the OSCR, "Apparently Inactive Charities" (October 2009), p.5.

120 See the OSCR, "Apparently Inactive Charities" (October 2009), p.5.

121 See the OSCR, "Monitoring Policy" (August 2013).

122 See *http://www.oscr.org.uk/media/2161/2016-03-15-new-paper-ar-form_web-version.pdf* [Accessed 19 May 2016].

2–57 OSCR also conducts tailored monitoring for individual charities where certain criteria are met.

2–58 There are limited powers available to OSCR to delegate to certain other public regulatory authorities some of its powers in relation to identified charities.[123]

2–59 Timeframes for compliance are issued and monitored. Following the giving of advice OSCR will seek trustee assurances or commitment to take action, with the statutory inquiry procedure being used only as a last resort.

2–60 New charities may be the subject of special monitoring. If, at the stage of the application for registration, there is limited information as to how the charity will conduct its affairs or deliver public benefit OSCR may perceive a degree of risk. In these cases a specific monitoring programme may be instituted, and the charity told of the additional information and timescales required to enable OSCR to assess compliance.

SPECIFIC MONITORING

2–61 OSCR also undertakes specific monitoring operations. An example is the use of assets of charities removed from the Register.[124]

2–62 Under s.19 a body removed from the Register continues to be under a duty to apply its property in accordance with its purposes; and there is also a continuing duty to keep proper accounting records and to prepare and submit accounts to OSCR. The consequences of removals, therefore, are part of OSCR's monitoring processes.

2–63 At the point of removal, information on assets is sought from the charity, unless the assets are negligible, or a charity ceases to exist due to a merger or some other union with another charity. For example, requirements for continued reporting under s.19 will be given and a request made for confirmation of charitable assets held at the date of removal. Checks for validity are made by comparison with recent accounts and any other information available regarding the former charity.

2–64 OSCR has published guidance on s.19 monitoring in order to assist charities in making an informed decision regarding removal from the Register and enable them to understand fully the implications of removal before any such action is undertaken.[125]

[123] Charities and Trustee Investment (Scotland) Act 2005 s.38.

[124] See OSCR, "Monitoring of charitable assets following removal from the Scottish Charity Register—a guide to OSCR Monitoring under Section 19" (August 2010).

[125] See OSCR, "Monitoring of charitable assets following removal from the Scottish Charity Register—a guide to OSCR Monitoring under Section 19" (August 2010).

Consultation

In 2013 OSCR established an external Charities Reference Group with a view to introducing an increasingly proactive and risk-based approach to regulation. Minutes were published on the website.[126] The group provided views on matters such as the development of a risk framework to prioritise regulatory risk, possible changes to the annual return form, whether charity accounts should be published on the Register and whether there should be a Register of Charity Trustees. In 2014 OSCR consulted more widely on proposals for a new targeted regulation framework. **2–65**

Complaints about OSCR

For complaints as to OSCR's handling of matters, there is published guidance.[127] **2–66**

However, OSCR also holds an unacceptable actions policy to protect both staff and functions. Some demands may be viewed as unacceptable and unreasonable if they start to impact substantially on its work by taking up an excessive amount of staff time to the disadvantage of other functions.[128] Examples of actions viewed in this way are the demanding of responses within an unreasonable timescale, the insisting on seeing or speaking to a particular member of staff, the continual making of phone calls, or continually sending letters stating the same thing, repeatedly. Unacceptable behaviour in making complaints can include changing the substance of the concern, or the frequent raising of unrelated concerns. **2–67**

Scottish Charity Appeals Panel

An appeals panel system exists to consider appeals from decisions of OSCR.[129] The Panel is independent both from the Scottish Government and from OSCR. **2–68**

It is for the person whose request or earlier appeal caused OSCR to confirm or reconfirm its decision to make an appeal.[130] The appeal must be made within 28 days of the appellant being given notice of the confirmation or reconfirmation.[131] The notice is to be addressed to the Secretary[132] and it follows that the panel secretariat must receive a notice of appeal within that time. The process before the Panel can be expected to be relatively swift.[133] Hearings are in public unless **2–69**

---

126 See the OSCR, "Charities Reference Group" (2013).

127 See the OSCR, "The Model Complaints Handling Procedure (Model CHP) for OSCR" (January 2014).

128 See the OSCR. "Unacceptable Actions Policy" (2013).

129 Charities and Trustee Investment (Scotland) Act 2005 s.75 and Sch.2; Panel website: *http://www.scap.gov.uk/appeal/index.html* [Accessed 19 May 2016].

130 Charities and Trustee Investment (Scotland) Act 2005 s.76(3).

131 Charities and Trustee Investment (Scotland) Act 2005 s.76(4).

132 See the Scottish Charity Appeals Panel Rules 2006 (SSI 2006/571) r.3(2).

133 Scottish Charity Appeals Panel Rules 2006 rr.4, 8 and 15 (and see the appeal guidance given in the website of the Scottish Charity Appeals.

there are exceptional circumstances.[134] On an appeal, the Panel may confirm a decision, quash a decision and direct OSCR to take such other action, if any, as the Panel thinks fit by such time as may be specified in the direction, or remit a decision back to OSCR for reconsideration, together with the Panel's reasons for doing so, for reconsideration.[135] Decisions are given with 21 days,[136] are registered[137] and published.[138] Orders for expenses may be made.[139]

2–70 Within 14 days of a decision being remitted to it OSCR must reconsider the decision, confirm, vary, reverse or revoke it, and give notice of its decision and reasons to the person who appealed to the Panel.[140]

2–71 Any decision of the Panel may be appealed to the Court of Session by the person who appealed to the Panel, or by OSCR, to the Court of Session. The Court of Session may confirm the decision appealed to it, or quash the decision and direct OSCR to take such action, if any, as the court thinks fit by such time as may be specified in the direction.[141]

---

[134] Scottish Charity Appeals Panel Rules 2006 r.13.
[135] Charities and Trustee Investment (Scotland) Act 2005 s.76(5).
[136] Scottish Charity Appeals Panel Rules 2006 r.18(3).
[137] Scottish Charity Appeals Panel Rules 2006 r.20(3)(e).
[138] Scottish Charity Appeals Panel Rules 2006 r.19.
[139] Scottish Charity Appeals Panel Rules 2006 r.21.
[140] Charities and Trustee Investment (Scotland) Act 2005 s.77.
[141] Charities and Trustee Investment (Scotland) Act 2005 s.78.

CHAPTER 3

SETTING UP A CHARITY

Stephen Phillips

PRELIMINARY

Before taking forward the detailed steps associated with setting up a charity, it is important that those involved are satisfied that charitable status is in fact appropriate. Reference should be made to the material set out in Ch.1, but by way of summary, the key issues are generally as follows: **3–01**

- Are the aims which the organisation is to pursue recognised as charitable purposes under the Charities and Trustee Investment (Scotland) Act 2005[1] (the 2005 Act)?
- Are there any aspects of the organisation's activities that are likely to make it difficult or impossible to satisfy the public benefit test?
- Is there sufficient information available on the proposed activities of the organisation to satisfy the kinds of factual questions that the Office of the Scottish Charity Regulator (OSCR) is likely to raise in determining whether or not the public benefit test is satisfied?
- Are those concerned in the setting up of the charity prepared to accommodate the principle that a majority of the board members must not be remunerated by the charity?
- Is the burden of additional legal obligations and restrictions associated with charitable status outweighed by the financial and other benefits of charitable status?

In considering the first three of these issues, the focus should be on the aims that represent the main drivers in relation to the organisation's activities. In order to qualify for charitable status, an organisation's aims must be *exclusively* charitable; it is, however, fairly common[2] for activities that are not regarded as being in direct furtherance of a charitable purpose to be carried on by a subsidiary company or companies, thus allowing the parent organisation to qualify for charitable status. **3–02**

Looking at the fourth issue, the restrictions under the 2005 Act relating to remuneration of board members[3] may be particularly relevant in the context of **3–03**

[1] Charities and Trustee Investment (Scotland) Act 2005 (asp 10).

[2] See para.3–64 below.

[3] See paras 4–120—4–133.

setting up a social enterprise,[4] where there may be a desire on the part of those setting up the social enterprise to draw sufficient remuneration to enable them to support themselves through working for the new organisation. In that situation, they would require to be outnumbered on the board by people who are *not* drawing remuneration from the organisation, in order for the organisation to qualify for charitable status—and the implications of that, from the point of view of losing control over the future direction of the organisation, would require to be carefully considered. The community interest company (CIC) model provides an alternative to charitable status for a social enterprise; the CIC legislation does not impose any restrictions on remuneration of directors, beyond the broad principle that the level of remuneration must not be inconsistent with satisfying the community interest test.[5]

3–04 Finally, the other legal restrictions associated with charitable status also need to be carefully considered. Broadly speaking, a charity can only expend its funds either:

- in direct furtherance of its charitable purposes (with the impact, in terms of furtherance of those objectives, being commensurate with the sum expended); or
- as a sound investment, with a reasonable financial return for the charity and without the charity taking on undue risk.

3–05 If an organisation wishes to use its funds in ways that would not be regarded as being in direct furtherance of a charitable purpose, the above restrictions may be a significant source of concern. It is important to recognise that certain objectives can readily be seen as being for the benefit of the local community, without necessarily being regarded as directly furthering a purpose that is *charitable*. One example might be a body set up to promote economic development, making loans to small businesses to allow them to expand and thus contribute to a more dynamic local economy. That sort of initiative would generally be regarded by members of the public as being for the public benefit, but it is likely that OSCR would not regard this as a proper expenditure of charitable funds (in the absence of special circumstances), on the grounds that it did not advance a charitable purpose[6]; in addition, there could be serious tax consequences if HMRC Charities were to take a similar view.

3–06 The regulatory framework associated with being a charity is also sometimes put forward as a significant disadvantage of charitable status. At a practical level,

---

[4] See para.3–56 below.

[5] Companies (Audit, Investigations etc.) Act 2004 s.35; and Community Interest Company Regulations 2005 (SI 2005/1788) Pt 2.

[6] In the context of a charity established to advance urban or rural regeneration, for example, a case could be made that it did advance that charitable purpose providing the public benefit test (see paras 1–77 to 1–108) was satisfied.

however, the requirements are not particularly onerous; leaving aside matters that will arise only very rarely (e.g. winding-up of a charity), the main elements are as follows[7]:

- the need to file annual accounts and a (fairly simple) return with OSCR on an annual basis;
- the requirement to obtain OSCR's consent prior to changing the name of the organisation, or amending its charitable purposes;
- the obligation to notify OSCR after making any change to the organisation's constitution; and
- the obligation to report the occurrence of a "notifiable event" to OSCR.[8]

Beyond that, it is important that those involved give some consideration to the legal duties that will attach to board members if the organisation is to be a charity (see paras 4–60 to 4–78). At the end of the day, however, the charity trustee duties set out in the 2005 Act[9] are not greatly different from those which the law would almost certainly apply to anyone serving on the board of a voluntary sector organisation,[10] whether it was a charity or not. **3–07**

Generally it should be noted that—with the exception of the Scottish Charitable Incorporated Organisation (SCIO) model (see para.3–12)—it is possible to form the legal entity first, and then pursue charitable status at a later date. That approach may be appropriate where the legal entity is required earlier than the normal OSCR turnaround time for applications (see para.3–75) would permit. It may also be appropriate where those setting up the charity are still in the process of developing their ideas regarding the activities that the organisation will be carrying on; such that difficulties could be anticipated in addressing the questions that OSCR might raise in the course of the application process (see paras 3–72 to 3–74 below).[11] A further possibility is that those involved in setting up the organisation may not yet be certain whether charitable status would offer significant benefits in the short term, and hence they decide to postpone an application for charitable status until such time as it becomes evident that charitable status would be advantageous. **3–08**

In the absence of special circumstances, however, the best approach is to keep the governing document (whether trust deed, constitution, articles of association or rules) in draft form when submitting the application for charitable status—as that **3–09**

[7] OSCR has indicated that it intends at some future date to introduce a requirement to notify OSCR of changes in the charity trustees.

[8] See, generally: *http://www.oscr.org.uk/media/2155/2016-03-15_guidance-for-notifiable-events_web-version.pdf* [Accessed 19 May 2016].

[9] See para.4–60.

[10] The charity trustee duties are also quite similar to those which apply under the Companies Act 2006 to directors of a company (whether the company is a charity or not).

[11] One example of that kind of situation would be where those establishing a community organisation had identified a wide range of projects that the community felt could usefully be progressed, but there was no clarity as to how those projects would be funded, or the nature or extent of that organisation's role in delivering them; in circumstances of that kind, OSCR may ask those applying for charitable status to withdraw their application, on the understanding that they could reapply once the proposals had been developed further.

means that adjustments can very readily be made in response to points raised by OSCR on the detailed wording in the course of the application process. If, for example, a company has already been incorporated prior to the application being submitted to OSCR, any adjustments to the articles to meet comments from OSCR would require to be effected in accordance with the formal requirements for a general meeting (or written resolution) under the company's articles of association, and there would also be a need to comply with Companies House filing formalities.

3–10 The material that follows provides practical guidance on the key issues to be addressed in the context of setting up a charity, as from the point at which a group comes to the view that charitable status is appropriate. It is arranged in the following order:

- types of legal entity;
- governance models;
- key issues in tailoring the constitution;
- particular types of charity;
- more complex models; and
- application for charitable status.

TYPES OF LEGAL ENTITY

3–11 The types of legal entity that can be adopted in the context of an organisation that is seeking charitable status are as follows:

- unincorporated association;
- company limited by guarantee;
- SCIO;
- trust;
- company limited by shares;
- community benefit society (BenCom); and
- body incorporated by Royal Charter or Act of Parliament.

3–12 Careful consideration should be given to the advantages and disadvantages of each of these types of legal entity in deciding what is appropriate in a given case. The key features of each can be summarised as follows:

- Unincorporated association—This is not a separate legal entity.[12] With only a few exceptions (e.g. tax legislation), an unincorporated association is not regarded by the law as having any existence in its own right. That creates difficulties where an unincorporated association is to hold property, enter into contracts, become a tenant under a lease or employ people. The solution that is generally adopted is to have, say, three main office bearers

[12] A useful summary of the law relating to unincorporated associations is contained in the Scottish Law Commission's Report (No.217) of November 2009 at *http://www.scotlawcom.gov.uk/law-reform-projects/completed-projects/unincorporated-associations/* [Accessed 19 May 2016].

as parties to contracts, leases and so on—but this is far from ideal, as (particularly in the case of ownership, or leases of land or buildings) there may then be a need to provide evidence of the linkage between the office bearers who signed the original document and those holding office at a future date (e.g. at the time when the property is being sold or the lease is being transferred). A further consideration is that there is a significant risk that the members of the management committee could be personally liable if there were outstanding debts or liabilities which the unincorporated association was unable to meet. For these reasons, the use of the unincorporated association legal form as a vehicle for new charities is falling out of favour, with the SCIO being a much more attractive option for all but the very smallest charities.

- The company limited by guarantee (or "guarantee company") is widely recognised as a tried and tested model, and the existence of a wide body of companies legislation and case law is seen by many as providing a robust regulatory framework. A guarantee company—in common with the BenCom model and the SCIO model—provides a separate legal entity that can enter into contracts, hold property, etc. in its own name; and it provides the benefit of limited liability for the members of the organisation. The question of whether the more detailed statutory framework for guarantee companies—as compared with the statutory provisions relating to SCIOs—provides significant additional safeguards is the subject of some debate. Certainly, it could be argued that a high proportion of the body of law applying to companies in general is irrelevant to guarantee companies; and the likelihood of formal intervention (other than in relation to a few specific areas such as delays in filing annual accounts) is extremely low in practice. For many of those involved in the governance of charities, the existence of such a wide body of legal requirements, over and above what is stated in the constitution, is seen as intimidating; and there may in certain contexts be difficulties in attracting board members for that reason.
- The SCIO legal form is increasingly being regarded as the preferred legal form for most new charities.[13] The SCIO—in common with the guarantee company with charitable status and the BenCom model—has a separate legal identity (and can thus enter into contracts, hold property, etc. in its own name) and provides limited liability for its members. The members of a SCIO have no liability to contribute to the debts and liabilities of the SCIO if it is wound up.[14] The SCIO was developed through a process that involved a systematic review of the legislation governing existing legal forms (including company law), identifying those features that were considered to be of greatest relevance in supporting good governance in a charity setting—so it is reasonable to assume that it will (in most cases) provide the best fit for a new charity, as compared with other legal forms. The registrar for SCIOs is OSCR—eliminating the requirement to deal with two authorities that applies to a guarantee company (OSCR and Companies

[13] The OSCR "Annual Review 2014–2015" indicates that 44 per cent of new charity applications involve a new SCIO.

[14] Charities and Trustee Investment (Scotland) Act 2005 s.49(4).

House) or BenCom with charitable status (OSCR and the Financial Conduct Authority (FCA)). The requirements as regards notifications to OSCR are less onerous than for companies (e.g. there is currently[15] no requirement to notify changes in board members, other than through the annual return); but OSCR is a much more active regulator (as regards investigations and interventions) than Companies House or the FCA, thus providing a greater level of public assurance.

- A trust—in the legal sense (i.e. operating under a trust deed or declaration of trust)—is not a corporate body; the assets are vested in the individuals (or corporate body) who serve as trustees, and their successors in office. There are greater risks of trustees incurring personal liability than for those serving on the board of a company, SCIO or BenCom.[16] A further point is that where the trust is to hold land or buildings (either through ownership or under a lease), there will generally be a need to evidence the linkage between the trustees in office at the time when the interest in the property was acquired and those holding office at the time when a disposal or other transaction is to be effected. Similar technical issues can come into play in the context of the holding of shares and other investments, though that is often addressed through the use of nominee companies or stockbrokers' nominees. The question of how significant the risk of personal liability may be for trustees is linked to some extent with the nature of what the trust does—the likelihood of a problem of that kind arising in practice is much lower for a trust that simply holds a large fund from which it gives financial support to other charities, than for a trust that is actively involved in delivery of care services, for example. It should be noted that many charities use the word "trust" in their name, without adopting the legal form of a trust, and many generic terms used to describe types of organisation can also be misleading in this respect, e.g. the vast majority of development trusts are in fact guarantee companies. The comments in this section relate only to a situation where the trustees are operating under a trust deed or declaration of trust.
- Company limited by shares—the essence of a company limited by shares is that the shareholders have not just powers of control (in common with members of a guarantee company) but also have a property right, in the form of the shares they hold—providing them with an entitlement to dividends and an asset that (at least in principle) could rise in value in line with the growth of the company. The principle of distribution of dividends is inconsistent with what would generally be considered appropriate in the context of a charity, and would fall foul of the "public benefit" test (see paras 1–77 to 1–108). A company limited by shares with charitable status might, however, be appropriate where the shareholder or shareholders

[15] It should be noted, however, that it is anticipated that OSCR will, at some future date, introduce a requirement—for all charities, irrespective of legal form—to notify OSCR of changes in charity trustees.

[16] See paras 4–80 to 4–90.

consist solely of bodies which themselves have charitable status.[17] One application of that model would be in the context of a consortium structure (see below, under the heading of "more complex models").

- The BenCom legal form[18] is regulated by legislation[19] that is widely regarded as lagging significantly behind companies legislation (although a gradual process of reform and updating is being taken forward). Also, the registrar for BenComs is the FCA, rather than Companies House; and the processes and timescales associated with formal procedures effected through the FCA are significantly less efficient than those associated with equivalent procedures effected through Companies House. The BenCom legal form provides the benefit of limited liability for its members and it shares many of the characteristics of a guarantee company. Where the desired features for a new charity's constitution closely match one of the sets of model rules accepted by the FCA, the set-up process for a BenCom can be relatively straightforward. If, however, that is not the case, the set-up process for a BenCom will be significantly more involved than it would be for a guarantee company or SCIO; and also there could be a fairly substantial fee payable to the FCA. Accordingly, unless there are very specific reasons why a BenCom is favoured,[20] a guarantee company or SCIO would be chosen in preference.
- A body incorporated by Royal Charter or Act of Parliament represents, at least in principle, a possible option for a new charity. As a matter of practice, however, it is extremely rare for new charities to be formed using either of these routes. The processes and procedures associated with forming a new charity by Royal Charter or Act of Parliament are outwith the scope of this publication.

Choosing between a company limited by guarantee and SCIO

While it is appropriate to give consideration to the long list of possible options as outlined above, for the vast majority of new charities the choice will lie between the guarantee company and the SCIO. **3–13**

The existence of a compact and readily accessible legislative framework for the SCIO ought in practice to support good governance, particularly when allied to an active regulator in the form of OSCR. In addition, SCIO board members have to comply with the duties attaching under charities legislation to charity trustees[21] **3–14**

[17] An alternative—in a situation where the member bodies were not looking to receive dividends or benefit from an increase in the capital value of their interest in the joint body—would be a guarantee company or SCIO.

[18] There are two types of registered society available under the Co-operative and Community Benefit Societies Act 2014: (1) a co-operative; and (2) a community benefit society ("BenCom"). A cooperative will generally not satisfy the "public benefit" test (see para.1–116), given that it exists for the benefit of its own members.

[19] Co-operative and Community Benefit Societies Act 2014.

[20] The most common factor in practice being the possibility of making use of the special exemptions from financial services regulations available for public issues of shares by a BenCom, which are not available to a company.

[21] See para.4–60.

(a single set of easily-understood legal duties) whereas board members of a guarantee company or BenCom have to comply both with the legal duties attaching to their legal form and with charity trustees' duties.

3–15 It should be noted that a SCIO cannot grant a floating charge—a type of security that extends to moveable property (e.g. equipment, furniture, intellectual property) and catches whatever assets a body has, at the point when the security is called up. A SCIO can, however, grant standard securities over land or buildings and any other form of fixed security. In general, fixed securities tend to be of greater value to lenders and grant funders, and it is unlikely that the inability to grant a floating charge will represent a significant factor in the decision on whether or not to adopt the SCIO legal form.

3–16 A SCIO is currently a less familiar legal form than the guarantee company, and that is something which should be taken into account if the charity will be carrying on a major part of its activities outwith the UK or if it will be contracting regularly with non-UK bodies; in those circumstances, a guarantee company may be a more appropriate legal model.

3–17 For completeness, mention should be made of certain other factors that are sometimes thought to be significant in the context of a choice between the SCIO and the guarantee company.

3–18 In particular, concerns are sometimes expressed with regard to the implications of a SCIO losing charitable status, i.e. being removed from the Scottish Charity Register. So far as the technical position is concerned, unlike a guarantee company or BenCom (which would cease to have charitable status, but continue to exist as a legal entity), a SCIO ceases to exist if it is removed from the Scottish Charity Register. It is argued by some that this raises significant risks for lenders, landlords and others having dealings with a SCIO. It is important to note, however, that a SCIO would lose its charitable status only if OSCR actively took the requisite steps towards removal from the Scottish charity register,[22] and the likelihood of OSCR removing charitable status from a SCIO without exhaustive enquiries, and without using its extensive powers to protect the interests of creditors and others, is extremely remote. If there were particular areas of concern, it is much more likely that OSCR would engage with the SCIO to explore ways in which these could be addressed (e.g. by transferring particular activities to a non-charitable entity), and it would be a key consideration for OSCR, as much as for those involved in the SCIO, to ensure that no steps were taken which might undermine public confidence in the SCIO model.

---

[22] In the case of a SCIO, the general power of OSCR to remove a body from the register of charities if it no longer meets the charity test (s.30 of the 2005 Act) does not apply. Instead, reg.8 of the Scottish Charitable Incorporated Organisations (Removal from Register and Dissolution) Regulations 2011 (SSI 2011/237) states that where there is a failure to meet the charity test, OSCR may direct the SCIO to apply to be removed from the register of charities and be dissolved; the review and appeals processes provided for in the 2005 Act apply, in relation to any direction of that nature. If the SCIO declines to comply with the direction, OSCR must apply to the Court of Session for an appropriate order. The Court of Session may hear witnesses, and has power to deal with the matter as the court sees fit.

It is also important to recognise that, notwithstanding that this is less evident from the wording of the legislation, a guarantee company would be in a comparable position to a SCIO—at a practical level—if it were to lose charitable status. Again, OSCR would not remove a guarantee company from the register without exhausting every other means to resolve the issues of concern; but if matters did reach a point where OSCR felt that that was the only option, it would be highly unrealistic to assume that OSCR would simply remove charitable status and leave the guarantee company to continue as before. OSCR has wide-ranging powers under the 2005 Act to protect the assets of a former charity[23]—and therefore the likelihood is that OSCR would either impose strict requirements on the company regarding the future use of its assets or would apply to the Court of Session for an order divesting the guarantee company entirely of its assets, such that these were placed in the hands of another charity. **3–19**

A further point which is sometimes made is that a SCIO is only able to merge or amalgamate with another SCIO. That is not in fact accurate as a statement of the legal position. The 2005 Act includes a set of provisions that allow a SCIO-to-SCIO merger or amalgamation to be effected through a special process that avoids the need for the formal assignation (transfer) of leases, contracts and so on. It would, however, be perfectly possible for a SCIO to use the alternative routes for merger of one charity with another that are routinely adopted for companies limited by guarantee and other types of legal entity in the charity sector. A SCIO, therefore, has the same flexibility as regards merger/amalgamations as any other legal form—but with the added advantage of a simpler route where the charity with which it is merging or amalgamating is itself a SCIO. **3–20**

GOVERNANCE MODELS

Assuming the decision is taken to proceed with the setting-up of a charity, one of the key issues to be addressed at an early stage is the general nature of the governance model that should be adopted. **3–21**

In broad terms, governance models can be split into two categories: **3–22**

- a two-tier model; and
- a single-tier model.

The differences between the two relate to the way in which decision-making is structured within the constitution. **3–23**

[23] Section 19(1) of the 2005 Act states that where a body is removed from the Scottish Charity Register it continues to be under a duty to apply the property previously acquired by it (and income accruing on that property—as well as assets purchased with that income) in accordance with the charitable purposes that were entered against it in the Scottish Charity Register immediately before it was removed. Also, s.19(4) of the 2005 Act gives OSCR the power to apply to the Court of Session for a scheme for transfer to a charity of any property and income that falls within the duty under s.19(1).

Two-tier model

3–24 A two-tier model involves two levels of decision-making:

- The members—who take decisions in relation to alterations to the constitution itself (including any change to the organisation's name or to its charitable purposes); they also have power to pass a resolution for the winding-up of the organisation; and they have powers in relation to the appointment and reappointment of all or some of the board members.
- The board—who exercise overall control and supervision in relation to the activities of the organisation; they are responsible for maintaining the accounting records and for complying with the requirements relating to annual accounts; and they have the duties attaching, under the 2005 Act, to charity trustees (see para.4–60).

3–25 The two-tier model is by far the more prevalent of the two within the charity sector as a whole—although that can be obscured by the fact that many charities whose constitutions are based on the principle of a wider membership extending beyond those serving on the board make very little effort to encourage new members; also, members' meetings (e.g. annual general meetings) tend to have poor attendance. Nevertheless, the principle of reserving certain decisions to a wider membership is considered by many in the charity sector to be critically important, for a number of reasons:

- It creates a framework under which the smaller group of people (the board) with responsibility for overseeing the operations of the organisation have to operate; and on the basis that that framework cannot be altered by the board themselves but only by bringing in a wider group of stakeholders (the membership).
- On a similar note, the fact that the wider membership requires to endorse any proposal to wind-up the organisation ensures that fundamental decisions of that kind are taken by a wider group of stakeholders, and not just the board.
- When combined with the usual provisions for periodic retiral and re-election of board members (and with provisions allowing any new candidate to put themselves forward for election at the annual general meeting), this helps to reduce the risk of a small self-perpetuating group of people remaining in office as board members.
- The fact that the membership is able to raise questions of the board at the annual general meeting introduces an important element of accountability; this provides a degree of protection against misconduct by board members and also helps to ensure that the board remains attuned to the aspirations of the stakeholders (assuming they are appropriately represented in the membership (see para.3–30 below)).

Single-tier model

Turning to the single-tier model, this—as the name would suggest—involves only a single level of decision-making. The most obvious example of a single-tier governance structure is the traditional charitable trust—with a board of trustees operating under a trust deed or declaration of trust.[24] 3–26

In a few cases the trust deed may require the trustees to obtain the consent of the individual or individuals or body who set up the trust in relation to, e.g. an alteration to the terms of the trust deed; and the trust deed may occasionally include power for the individual(s) or body/bodies who set up the trust to appoint new trustees. Also, the power of the trustees to alter the trust deed may well be limited in other ways by the constitution. Subject to those points, though, the only formal decision-making processes under the trust deed or declaration of trust rest with the trustees alone. Occasionally, a trust deed may provide that the trustees must hold an annual meeting involving the local community (or other stakeholders); but those attending that meeting (other than the trustees themselves) have no voting rights—and so an annual general meeting in that context is only an opportunity for the trustees to gain informal feedback from the stakeholders. 3–27

In determining whether a single-tier model or two-tier model is more appropriate, a useful test is to consider whether or not those involved in the project anticipate having annual general meetings; if they do—and if this is also allied with the concept of people being elected or re-elected onto the board—then a two-tier model should be adopted. For some types of charity the idea of a body of people/organisations (over and above the board) making certain decisions via an annual general meeting (or other members' meeting) may not be particularly appropriate or relevant; some examples would be: 3–28

- certain grant-giving charities (especially those administering a fund donated or bequeathed by one or more individual donors);
- some charities involved in research; and
- certain arts organisations where audience feedback is seen as more significant.

The fact that the group may be unsure as to who, as a matter of practice, will be interested in joining the organisation as a member is not conclusive; it is very common for a membership base to be built up only quite slowly during the initial years of a new organisation. The group do, however, need to be reasonably confident that there will be at least some individuals or bodies—outwith the board themselves—who will be willing to become members in the future.

---

[24] It is also possible to tailor articles of association for a guarantee company, or a constitution for a SCIO or unincorporated association, in such a way as to achieve a similar single-tier governance structure at a practical level. In the case of a company or SCIO, however, there would still be a need for the individuals involved to take certain decisions in their capacity as members (rather than as directors or charity trustees) in order to comply with the legislation.

Variants of the two-tier model

3–29 If the decision is taken to pursue a two-tier model, that in turn should lead on to consideration of three variants of that model:

- a membership-led model;
- a partnership model; and
- a blended model.

3–30 Taking each of these in turn:

- The membership-led model: This is by far the most common in the charity sector. The principle is that there should be a wide membership, to provide a balanced spread of input from the key stakeholders. The constitution of the charity ought ideally to set out the specific qualifications for membership that are considered to be appropriate; and having regard to the significant powers over the charity (e.g. alterations to the constitution, a winding-up resolution) which the members are able to exercise. In a community-based organisation, for example, the qualification for membership is likely to be stated in terms of being a resident of the local community. A charity that was focused on a particular medical condition might include within its constitution a provision stating that only someone with that medical condition (or caring for someone with that condition) could apply for membership. In certain contexts—and councils of voluntary service (CVS) are an obvious example—membership would be open to organisations, rather than individuals; and the membership qualification would then be likely to relate to their being third sector organisations operating within a defined area.
- The partnership model: This would be appropriate in a situation where there are a fairly limited number of key partner bodies taking forward a joint initiative (see, for example, under "more complex models" at para.3–63 below). The constitution of the charity would name each of the partner bodies as prospective members—and, on the basis that those bodies would participate in any decisions relating to alterations to the constitution, etc.; each would also be given power to appoint one or more individuals to the board of the charity; and to remove its appointee(s) at any time.
- Blended model: This would involve a combination of the membership-led model and partnership model. Certain key partner bodies would be named in the constitution as members and would have reserved seats on the board; the remainder of the membership would be more fluid, consisting of those individuals or organisations who fulfilled the membership qualifications, and on the basis that they would in turn elect a specified number of people to the board.

3–31 Under all three models outlined above, it would be possible (and indeed quite common) to include provisions whereby the board elected or appointed by the members could in turn appoint additional board members (up to a specified limit), selected on the basis either of the special skills and experience that they could bring to the board or on the basis that they had been nominated by bodies with which the organisation had close contact in the course of its activities.

KEY ISSUES IN TAILORING THE CONSTITUTION

Those involved in the setting up of a charity will need to reach a view in relation to the governance model and type of legal entity (see paras 3–11—3–31 above) before the process of tailoring a constitution for the charity can be taken forward. For simplicity, the word "constitution" is used below, but the form that this takes will vary depending on the type of legal entity, as follows: 3–32

- Unincorporated association—constitution.
- Company limited by guarantee—articles of association.
- SCIO—constitution.
- Trust—trust deed or declaration of trust.
- BenCom—rules.
- Company limited by shares—articles of association.

Name

Those involved will, of course, have to think of a suitable name for the charity. In the case of a guarantee company or BenCom, the name can—but need not—include the word "limited". In the case of a SCIO, the name of the organisation can end with the words "Scottish Charitable Incorporated Organisation" or "SCIO"; but again, that is not necessary in terms of the legislation. If the word "limited" is not used at the end of a company name, the fact that the organisation is a company has to be stated on the organisation's notepaper. A similar principle applies where "Scottish Charitable Incorporation Organisation" or "SCIO" is not used in the name of a SCIO. 3–33

OSCR can refuse to register a charity name[25] if it considers that the name is: 3–34

- the same as, or too like, the name of another charity;
- likely to mislead the public as to the true nature of the purposes of the organisation (or of the activities which it intends to carry on);
- likely to give the impression that the body is connected to the Scottish Government, the UK Government or any other local authority (or indeed any other person) when it is not in fact connected; or
- offensive.

In addition, there are risks associated with the common law principles associated with "passing-off". This is the ability of an existing body with a name similar to that adopted by a new organisation to challenge the use of that name by the new organisation on the grounds that the public would be misled, through the 3–35

[25] Charities and Trustee Investment (Scotland) Act 2005 s.10.

similarity in the names, into thinking that there was some connection between the two bodies. It would not be necessary in that context for the existing body to be able to prove that there had been a deliberate intention on the part of the new charity to mislead people. From a practical point of view, it might be advisable to check for similar names in any directory or database listing local or national charities (including the register of Scottish charities kept by OSCR and any listing maintained by the local council for voluntary service or third sector interface); an internet search would obviously be the quickest way of researching this. If the name is of a kind where a private sector business might potentially be using a similar name, then some investigation through online business listings, etc. would also be advisable. A check for similar company names at Companies House would also be helpful, even where some other legal form is to be adopted by the new charity.

3–36 At a practical level, the extent of the investigations that are carried out to check whether there is an existing body with a similar name will depend on the perception of the likelihood of a challenge. If the name that has been chosen for the new charity is very unusual or the new charity will be operating only within a small geographical area, the question of conflict with an existing body in relation to the name may be less significant.

3–37 It should also be noted that the Companies and Business Names Regulations[26] may be relevant in this context.

3–38 A further dimension is that company names are regulated by specific provisions within the Companies Act 2006; and Companies House has developed guidance with regard to the approach that it takes in practice in relation to a number of "sensitive words" in the context of company names.[27]

Purposes

3–39 Irrespective of the type of legal form, the constitution will require to set out clearly the main purposes which the charity is to pursue. It is important that these are carefully drafted so as to reflect the aims which it is intended that the charity will be pursuing in practice.

3–40 The choice of terminology will be limited to some extent by the need to stay within the confines of what are defined under the 2005 Act as charitable purposes. To take one example, while concepts such as "social exclusion" are now widely accepted in a political context and have a reasonably well-defined meaning within the voluntary sector, OSCR would be likely to take the view that activities under that heading could potentially extend beyond the charity field; and it would therefore be preferable to adopt purposes that referred to "prevention and/or relief of poverty" and/or other recognised charitable purposes.

---

[26] The Company, Limited Liability Partnership and Business Names (Sensitive Words and Expressions) Regulations 2014 (SI 2014/3140) and the Company and Business Names (Miscellaneous Provisions) Regulations 2009 (SI 2009/2404).

[27] Companies House: Incorporation and Names (GP1, March 2016).

As a general principle, the purposes clause has two main aspects. It guides future boards in relation to the range of activities that the charity should pursue; and it identifies for those dealing with the organisation what the organisation was set up to do. This could include people considering whether or not to join as members; and, importantly, bodies that are considering whether or not to provide funding to the organisation. In certain contexts, the inclusion of particular terminology within the purposes clause can improve the prospects of obtaining grant funding and/or other forms of support; and that may represent part of the consultation with outside organisations/agencies that is often carried out as part of the wider processes associated with setting up a new charity. **3–41**

Some guidance in relation to the sort of wording that would be appropriate for a purposes clause can be obtained through reviewing the purposes (sometimes referred to as "objects") clauses of other bodies operating in a similar field. Having said that, the following points should be borne in mind: **3–42**

- Every charity is different, and so it is very important that the wording that is used in the constitution does accurately reflect the aims and activities that the organisation will be pursuing in practice; it would be highly inadvisable to adopt a particular form of words as a "passport" to charitable status or particular sources of grant funding if in fact those aims are unlikely to be pursued.
- Many purposes clauses contain very old-fashioned language and/or redundant material, and it is worth considering whether, even if the general message is the same, an element of "translation" into modern language would be useful.

A further consideration that may occasionally come into play in the context of a charity being established with a large initial donation, is whether the purposes are wide enough to use the funds being generated; if there is a large donation, the courts may give a wide interpretation to the wording in the purposes clause, on the basis that it would be reasonable to assume that the charity was intended to have a range of activity that enabled it to make full use of that donation.[28] **3–43**

Reference should also be made to the meeting the charity test guidance[29] issued by OSCR. **3–44**

Membership

As noted above (see para.3–24), under a two-tier structure it is the members—rather than the board—who have ultimate control in relation to fundamental aspects of the structure, including the constitution itself. It is very important, therefore, that careful consideration is given to the question of who ought to be eligible for membership. **3–45**

---

[28] *The Trustees of the RS Macdonald Charitable Trust*, 2009 S.C. 6.

[29] OSCR, "Meeting the Charity Test Guidance": *http://www.oscr.org.uk/media/1977/v50_meeting-the-charity-test-guidance_final.pdf* [Accessed 19 May 2016].

3–46 The key issues under that heading would normally include the following:

- What should be the membership qualification(s)?
- Should bodies, as distinct from individuals, be entitled to be members? And if so, should there be special voting provisions to balance the voting rights of bodies as against individuals?
- Should the board have power to veto any application for membership? And if so, should that be limited by setting out certain specific grounds for refusing admission?
- Should someone who no longer fulfils the qualifications automatically cease to be a member?

Board

3–47 The composition of the board is a key issue—and that applies in relation to both single-tier and two-tier models (see paras 3–24 to 3–31 above). The board's role is to set overall strategy and control and supervise the activities of the charity. It will meet on a regular basis (monthly, bi-monthly or quarterly) to receive reports from members of staff, discuss important issues which have arisen, plan for the future and, importantly, monitor the financial position of the charity. Careful thought, therefore, should be given to the composition of the board.

3–48 The key issues under this heading would include the following:

- What should be the maximum number of board members?
- Should all board members be subject to periodic retiral or reappointment procedures?
- Should all board members retire from office each year, or should this be limited to, say, one third of board members (in the interests of continuity)?
- Should there be a maximum period in office for board members?
- Are there any outside bodies which should be named as having power to appoint or nominate people to serve on the board?

3–49 Once the more significant issues—as outlined above—have been agreed, attention can then focus on more detailed points for the constitution:

- the use of different categories of membership, in order to achieve a balance of voting power across different stakeholder groups;
- the inclusion or otherwise of provision for an annual membership subscription (and perhaps allowing for differing levels of subscription for various categories of membership or in line with, e.g. size of member organisations) or an annual reregistration process;
- the inclusion or otherwise[30] of provisions allowing for proxy voting at members' meetings;
- the quorum for members' meetings;

---

[30] It should be noted that in the case of a company there is a requirement under the Companies Act 2006 s.324 to allow proxy voting by members.

- whether the chairperson of a members' meeting should have a casting vote[31];
- the inclusion or otherwise of provisions intended to provide a balance among different stakeholder groups at board level and/or to reflect principles of diversity in the composition of the board;
- the process for appointment/election of the chair and other office bearers;
- the term of office for the chair and other office bearers;
- the quorum for board meetings;
- the inclusion or otherwise of provisions allowing a board member to participate in board meetings by way of video conference facilities, etc.;
- the ability or otherwise for a board member to appoint a substitute to attend board meetings in their place;
- the inclusion or otherwise of provisions referring to specific subcommittees and advisory groups;
- the detailed provisions which are to apply in relation to conflict-of-interest; and
- the inclusion or otherwise of provisions allowing the board to expel a board member on the grounds of failure to attend board meetings for an extended period and/or breach of a code of conduct.

The above checklist is given by way of general guidance only. The issues identified above will not be relevant in every case; and it should also be borne in mind that additional points for the constitution may well require to be considered, depending on the nature of the organisation and its stakeholders. **3–50**

PARTICULAR TYPES OF CHARITY

Within the charity sector as a whole, there is a wide range of types of charity, many of which have their own umbrella body and with a strong sense of their own distinctive identity within the sector. It should be noted, however, that although certain legal forms may be more prevalent within certain of these groupings, the "label" attaching to these various types of charity does not generally have any legal force. As noted above, the use of the word "trust" does not indicate that charities within that grouping use the legal form of a trust, e.g. the membership of Development Trusts Association Scotland extends (at the time of publication) to around 250 development trusts, of whom it is estimated that around 98 per cent have adopted the guarantee company legal form. **3–51**

Accordingly, the question of whether or not a charity can be classified as a development trust, a social enterprise, an environment trust, a building preservation trust, a voluntary health organisation, etc. is not a matter of legal classification, but rather a classification that may be helpful in the context of **3–52**

---

[31] Under the Companies Act 2006, it is not possible for the chairperson of a members' meeting to have a casting vote unless they are a member of the company and the additional vote is cast in their capacity as a member; that rule does not apply, however, where the articles of association allowed for a chairperson to have a casting vote before the relevant provisions of the Companies Act 2006 came into force. In order to avoid technical complications, therefore, it is usual for new articles of association to state that the chairperson of a members' meeting will not have a casting vote.

accessing funding and other support. From the point of view of the legal issues to be addressed in setting up a new charity, there are certain characteristics associated with a few types of charity which may raise special considerations from a charity law point of view, and these are addressed below.

Development trusts

3–53 The generally-accepted definition of development trusts is[32]:

> "Community organisations which:
> - are owned and managed by the local community;
> - aim to achieve the sustainable regeneration of a community or address a range of economic, social, environmental and cultural issues within a community;
> - are independent but seek to work in partnership with other private, public and third sector organisations;
> - aim to reduce dependency on grant support by generating income through enterprise and the ownership of assets;
> - and in which all trading surpluses are principally reinvested in the organisation or the community."

3–54 One of the key characteristics of a development trust is that it takes a strategic and wide-ranging approach to furthering community development and promoting urban/rural regeneration within the local community in which it is based. That in turn means that, in furthering those strategic objectives, it can engage in a number of different ways:

- It can develop a strategic plan for the community, and monitor the work of others (including public sector agencies) in implementing particular elements of that overall plan.
- It may set up subsidiary companies and/or other entities (often non-charitable) to take forward particular projects.
- It can deliver services directly.

3–55 Accordingly, a key requirement, in pursuing an application for charitable status in the context of a development trust, is to identify clearly what projects and initiatives the development trust will be delivering directly, those that will be delivered through a wholly owned subsidiary (or other offshoot body, e.g. a joint venture), and those that will be carried through by other organisations.

Social enterprises

3–56 As regards social enterprises, Social Enterprise Scotland[33] (the leading umbrella organisation for Scottish social enterprises) has set out what it describes as five essential elements of a social enterprise. These are as follows:

---

[32] Adopted by Development Trusts Association Scotland: see *http://www.dtascot.org.uk/content/what-is-a-development-trust* [Accessed 19 May 2016].

[33] *http://www.socialenterprisescotland.org.uk* [Accessed 19 May 2016].

(1) A social enterprise is a trading business—selling goods and services—but whose primary objective is to achieve social and/or environmental benefit. Social enterprises are different from those charities and voluntary organisations that do not aspire to financial independence through trading.
(2) Regardless of its legal form, the constitution of a social enterprise will include the requirement that profits are reinvested in the business or in the beneficiary community—and not distributed to private owners, shareholders or investors.
(3) The constitution will always require that, on dissolution, the assets of the social enterprise are reinvested in another organisation with similar aims and objectives. Taken together, criteria 2 and 3 are referred to as the "asset lock"—the defining characteristic of a social enterprise—that distinguishes it from the private sector.
(4) Social enterprises are constituted and managed in an accountable and transparent way—particularly with regard to the community they serve.
(5) Social enterprises are distinct from the public sector and cannot be the subsidiary of a public body.

A key challenge from a charity law point of view, in the context of many social enterprises is the "enterprise" dimension to the organisation's activities. There can often be a similarity—as regards the interface with the general public—between the activities of a social enterprise and the activities of a private sector trading company. The key issue therefore (leaving aside the possibilities associated with a non-trading subsidiary or subsidiaries) is to focus on the nature of the trading activity itself—that is to say, in order to be compatible with charity law and charity law principles, the trading activity must either directly further a charitable purpose or the work in connection with the trade must be mainly carried out by beneficiaries of the charity (using the terminology contained in the tax legislation). **3–57**

Social firms

A "social firm" is defined by Social Firms Scotland[34] (the umbrella body for Scottish social firms) as **3–58**

> "a distinct type of social enterprise; social firms are market-led enterprises, working in a wide range of sectors with a specific social mission to create employment for people most disadvantaged in the labour market".

This is stated to include people who have a disability or a history of mental health problems, as well as others who face major barriers to employment, for example, because they have a criminal record or a drug or alcohol dependency. Social firms use enterprise to achieve their social mission and are thus different from more traditional models of employment provision or support for disabled people, such as sheltered workshops. The definition of a social firm would, for Social Firms **3–59**

[34] *http://socialfirms.org.uk/* [Accessed 19 May 2016].

Scotland, involve an expectation that an emerging social firm would be trading and working towards achieving targets of:

- generating over 50 per cent of its income through sales of goods and/or services; and
- ensuring that at least 25 per cent of the people it employs are at a particular disadvantage in the labour market.

3–60 Again, the essence of a social firm is that it should carry on trading activities—but on the basis that the trading activities provide a working environment for people who would be unable to access jobs in the mainstream labour market. As with certain social enterprises, that may raise concerns in the context of an application for charitable status. In particular, OSCR will be concerned to establish that:

- the true focus of the organisation's aims and activities is indeed supporting people who would be unable to access employment in the wider jobs market; and
- there is no suggestion of exploitation, in relation to those who will be carrying out the work.

More complex models

3–61 The charity sector is very diverse—and from time to time there will be a need to develop more complex models in the context of setting up a charity. Some examples are set out below.

3–62 In the case of an individual charitable body, there may be a requirement to attract membership from across a wide geographical area (e.g. Scotland-wide) or to encourage local groups to take an active part in fundraising or delivery of services and support. That may point to the development of a constitution that explicitly acknowledges local branches within the overall governance framework. A key consideration, however, is to ensure that the overarching role of the board is clear, so that there is no dubiety around the question of who would be deemed to be "charity trustees" for the purposes of the 2005 Act. In addition, if local branches are to be given a degree of delegated authority in relation to fundraising and/or expenditure, the constitution should make explicit reference to the power of the board to define the appropriate financial thresholds and other parameters.

3–63 A further feature of the charity environment is the growing use of consortium models. These can be adopted as a mechanism to facilitate the sharing of back office resource, applications for grant funding in the context of larger-scale projects, or larger-scale contracts for the delivery of public services. If a jointly-controlled corporate body is to be used as a consortium vehicle, the nature of that vehicle will need to be carefully considered. In certain contexts, the consortium vehicle could itself be a charity—and that could simplify the flows of funds to and from the participating charities and minimise the impact of taxation.

A feature of the increasing emphasis on charities creating their own sources of self-generated income is the growth in the use of non-charitable companies as the vehicle for trading activities. A non-charitable subsidiary is not, however, required in every case where a charity is carrying on activities which would be regarded as trading for tax purposes. Reference should be made to the material in Ch.10. Where a non-charitable subsidiary forms part of the overall legal structure, care should be taken in relation to the relationship between the charity and the wholly-owned subsidiary; in particular: 3–64

- So far as the general principles are concerned, the charity should not make payments to a non-charitable subsidiary company otherwise than:
  - as a sound investment (with a commercial rate of return and appropriate security);
  - in exchange for services supplied by the subsidiary to the parent charity (and with the sum payable being in line with the value of the services received by the parent charity);
  - by way of reimbursing employment costs, in respect of work done by the subsidiary's staff for the benefit of the charity; or
  - by way of funding all or part of the cost of activities carried on by the subsidiary which directly advance the parent charity's charitable purposes (and, again, with the payment being in line with the extent of the impacts achieved, in terms of furtherance of those charitable purposes).
- Any use of the parent charity's staff or other resources should be the subject of a charge by the parent charity, and on the basis of full cost recovery.
- The charity should not incur liability in relation to matters that relate to the operations of the trading subsidiary, e.g. the charity should not have the role of grant applicant (and thus be liable for compliance with grant conditions) where the grant is for the benefit of the non-charitable subsidiary.

Leaving aside tax considerations (see Ch.10), the use of a trading subsidiary can serve as a very useful mechanism to protect the assets of the charity against the risks associated with a given trading activity. Assuming the usual arrangement is adopted where the charity holds fully paid-up shares in the subsidiary and (in line with the charity law principles outlined above) does not issue any guarantee in relation to the subsidiary's debts or take on any other obligations relating to the subsidiary's operations, the principle of limited liability means that the charity will have no liability even if the subsidiary goes into liquidation with substantial debts. For that reason, a subsidiary company will sometimes be used to protect the main assets of the charity in the context of a new strand of operations which is regarded as carrying significant risks—even where those operations fall within the charitable field. 3–65

The use of a subsidiary can offer other advantages: 3–66

- the ability to put in place a more compact board, possibly with a greater proportion of people with relevant commercial expertise (as compared with the board of the charity)—giving a sharper commercial focus to the trading operations; and
- the ability to offer to a commercial lender (or a grant funder) a legal entity that is concerned only with the particular activities that they wish to fund—enabling the lender or grant funder to assess the financial prospects and risks with more confidence, and also potentially creating a more attractive security package in support of the funding.

APPLICATION FOR CHARITABLE STATUS

3–67 Applying for charitable status involves the following:

- a completed application form,[35] signed by one of the proposed charity trustees (on behalf of all of the proposed charity trustees);
- completed charity trustee declaration forms—signed by each of the proposed initial charity trustees—confirming that they are aware of their responsibilities as charity trustees, are not disqualified from acting as charity trustees, and are prepared to serve as charity trustees;
- in the case of a person disqualified from acting as a charity trustee, an application for waiver[36];
- a copy of the constitution (or, as the case may be, draft constitution—see para.3–09 above);
- in the case of an organisation which is already in operation—a copy of the most recent annual accounts; and
- documents in support of the application for charitable status—such as a business plan, application for grant funding and/or proposal document.

3–68 Some of the information required in the application form is quite straightforward—the proposed legal name of the charity, any other name by which the organisation will be known, the principal contact details, the website address (if any), the proposed legal form, and the accounting reference date (if known). In addition, the form asks for information with regard to any connected bodies (e.g. a parent charity).

3–69 The remainder of the application form is intended to provide OSCR with information to guide its assessment of whether or not the organisation meets the charity test (see para.1–10 and following). The form, as currently structured, asks first for a statement of the charitable purposes as stated in the constitution (or, as the case may be, draft constitution). It then goes on to ask for information on how the organisation intends to achieve its charitable purposes and provide public benefit. That involves an outline of the main activities and information regarding

[35] Available from the OSCR website.

[36] Charities and Trustee Investment (Scotland) Act 2005 s.69.

delivery of activities and benefit provided to the public; as well as some material that demonstrates the linkage between these activities and the charitable purposes.

A further section within the application form is directed towards identifying any issues of potential concern to OSCR around private benefit (see paras 1–109 to 1–116)—in particular, information is required in relation to any payments to individuals (including charity trustees and connected persons) and membership benefits. The fact that the proposals may envisage remuneration being payable to one of the charity trustees or that particular benefits would be available only to members of the organisation, would not, however, be fatal to the application; rather, the inclusion of these questions within the form is intended to highlight to OSCR whether any features of that kind are envisaged. At a practical level, if information is disclosed in this section which would suggest that there could be a degree of private benefit, OSCR will, as a matter of course, request additional information to assess the extent of the private benefit and satisfy itself that these arrangements are reasonable in the circumstances. **3–70**

A further set of questions is focused on access to benefit—tying in with the requirement under the 2005 Act that there must not be unduly restrictive conditions on accessing benefit.[37] In particular, the questions focus on who can benefit from the charity's activities to ensure that the class of beneficiaries is not unduly restricted (see paras 1–82 to 1–90 above). The request for information on fees, charges, concessions, membership fees, physical or practical restrictions and equalities aspects are also based on the issue of whether there are unduly restrictive conditions. Again, the fact that fees may be charged for accessing services is not necessarily a serious problem; but it does mean that OSCR will require full information on the proposed charging structure, so that it can come to a decision on whether or not the level of charges is such that a significant proportion of the general public will be unable to afford the services of the organisation. In a similar vein, the form also captures an outline of the key features of the proposed charity regarding the nature of its activities—in particular, whether financial assistance is given to individuals or organisations or the charity carries out activities itself; the beneficiary groups (children or young people, older people, people with disabilities, etc.); and geographical spread (a specific community, a local authority area, etc.). **3–71**

After the full package of documentation (including the application form itself) has been submitted to OSCR, an acknowledgement will be received from OSCR—identifying the case officer who has been assigned to the application. The process is then likely to involve a series of questions raised by the case officer regarding the activities of the proposed charity—focusing particularly on the linkage between the charitable purposes and the activities that will be carried on at a practical level; as well as exploring any particular points of concern arising from the question of public versus private benefit. **3–72**

OSCR may also raise queries or suggestions regarding provisions within the constitution (or, as the case may be, draft constitution). In the context of an **3–73**

[37] Charities and Trustee Investment (Scotland) Act 2005 s.8(2)(b).

application for formation of a SCIO, OSCR will be seeking to ensure that the constitution covers all of the various matters that require, under the 2005 Act and the SCIO Regulations,[38] to be covered within the constitution of a SCIO. In relation to other types of legal entity, the focus will be primarily on the purposes clause, the provisions prohibiting distribution of profits and application of surplus assets on a winding-up; as well as any provisions regarding remuneration for charity trustees. In addition, if OSCR has any reservations with regard to the proposed name of the charity (see para.3–34) these would also be raised at this stage.

3–74 The level of detail that OSCR requires as regards the proposed activities of the organisation varies from case to case. It should be noted that although the 2005 Act requires that all the purposes of the organisation be charitable purposes as set out in the 2005 Act and must deliver, or be intended to deliver, public benefit, OSCR—as a matter of practice—will not allow a charitable purpose to remain in the purposes clause of a proposed charity's constitution unless OSCR is satisfied that there are reasonably concrete proposals describing how the proposed charity will further that particular charitable purpose at a practical level.

3–75 OSCR's target in relation to issuing a decision on a routine application for charitable status is three months. In practice, the timescale varies considerably—and much will depend on the nature of the aims and activities of the charity—with more challenging applications (particularly where there could be significant concerns around private benefit) potentially taking longer than the three-month target period. The process is generally conducted through email—but in the context of applications that raise issues of special difficulty and/or if the correspondence becomes protracted, a face-to-face meeting may be beneficial in resolving the remaining concerns.

3–76 As and when OSCR has satisfied itself that the organisation (or proposed organisation) satisfies the charity test, it will issue a letter to that effect—accepting the application in principle. Where the legal entity has not yet been formed (see para.3–09), those involved should then proceed with the incorporation process with Companies House (or the FCA in the case of a BenCom) or with the signing of the trust deed or declaration of trust. Once the company or BenCom has been incorporated—or, as the case may be, the trust deed or declaration of trust has been signed—the application process can then be completed by forwarding a certified copy of the trust deed or declaration of trust or, as the case may be, a copy of the certificate of incorporation and the final form of the articles of association or rules—to OSCR; and OSCR will then issue the formal charity recognition letter (referred to by OSCR as the "status award letter") and enter the name of the organisation on the register of Scottish charities. The details of the new charity will then be visible on the OSCR website.

3–77 In the case of a SCIO, the decision by OSCR that the proposed organisation satisfies the charity test will involve both the grant of charitable status and at the

[38] The Scottish Charitable Incorporated Organisation Regulations (SSI 2011/44).

same time completion of the incorporation process. The SCIO will come into existence with effect from the time when OSCR enters it on the Scottish Charity Register.

Recognition of an organisation as a Scottish charity does not in itself give the organisation access to tax exemptions and other provisions of the tax legislation applicable to charities. In order to achieve that position, a separate application form[39] requires to be completed and submitted (online only) to HMRC Charities. So far as the statutory provisions are concerned, HMRC Charities will apply the charity law of England and Wales, rather than Scottish charity law, in determining whether or not a body should be recognised as a charity for the purposes of the tax legislation. In theory, therefore, it would be open to HMRC Charities to decline to accept a body as a charity for tax purposes, notwithstanding that it had been entered on the Scottish Charity Register. As a matter of practice, however, it is extremely unlikely that any such situation would arise. HMRC Charities and OSCR are both committed to seeking to achieve consistency so far as possible, and are aware of the difficulties that would emerge if there were significant divergences in approach. **3–78**

If OSCR declines to accept an organisation as a charity, it is open to the proposed charity trustees to seek a review of that decision or to make a formal appeal against the decision.[40] In practice, however, reviews and appeals are quite rare.[41] **3–79**

---

[39] Available online at *https://www.gov.uk/charity-recognition-hmrc* [Accessed 19 May 2016].

[40] See para.2–12.

[41] Out of the applications for charitable status received by OSCR during the period from 1 January 2014–30 June 2016, 15 were the subject of a request for review of the decision under s.74 of the 2005 Act. During the period to 30 June 2016, there were no appeals to the Scottish Charity Appeal Panel arising out of refusal of an application for charitable status.

CHAPTER 4

CHARITY TRUSTEES

Malcolm H Rust

WHAT IS A "CHARITY TRUSTEE"?

Charity trustees, generally speaking, are the people who make up the governing body of the charity and have general control and management of it. They are responsible for making sure that their charity is administered effectively and can account for its activities and outcomes. The expression "charity trustee" is used to describe those subject to the duties laid down[1] in the Charities and Trustee Investment (Scotland) Act 2005 (the 2005 Act). The context in which they operate may direct that they assume another title. For example, in a trust they will be trustees, but they may also be directors (in a charitable company), management committee members (in an unincorporated association), board members or committee members (in a Scottish Charitable Incorporated Organisation (SCIO)).[2] **4–01**

THE CONCEPT OF THE TRUST IN SCOTS LAW

Those considering accepting an invitation to join a charity as a charity trustee, as well as those advising a charity, need to understand the concept of the trust in Scots law. Any analysis of charity trusteeship needs to be firmly rooted in an understanding of the separation of rights and duties as a charity trustee from those as an individual, and of the standard of care that must be adopted at all times as a charity trustee. **4–02**

Although the trustee is the "owner" of the trust property once a trust has been created, the property is not theirs to deal with just as they like. It is quite separate from private property. A fundamental characteristic of a Scottish trust is that a right to the trust property vests in the trustee but that the beneficiaries also have a right that they can enforce against the trustees to ensure that the trust purposes are carried out.[3] For a charity, the beneficiaries are those members of the public most likely to have an interest in the affairs of the charity, but in theory the ambit of beneficiaries is as wide as the public at large. **4–03**

---

1 Charities and Trustee Investment (Scotland) Act 2005 s.66.

2 OSCR, "Guidance and Good Practice for Charity Trustees" (June 2016), p.5 "Who are the charity trustees?"

3 *Inland Revenue v Clark's Trustees*, 1939 S.C. 11.

4–04 A trustee will always have their own private property. If a person becomes insolvent all of that private property is vulnerable to claims by creditors.

4–05 When a person becomes a trustee they acquire a separate set of property (owned jointly with any other trustees): the trust property. These two sets of property are distinct as a matter of law and should be kept distinct in practice.[4] It is similar to a director who manages the affairs of a company—the company's assets and the director's assets are quite separate in law.

4–06 In this way trust property is never vulnerable to the claims of the trustee's personal creditors. Even if there is nothing in the private property for personal creditors to claim, they still cannot claim from the trust property—it is entirely separate. The reverse is not necessarily the case—a charity's creditors may make a claim against a charity trustee's personal property in circumstances where the charity does not provide limited liability. This understanding of the two separate sets of property is fundamental to appreciating the very real separation of interests and duties of trustees and the imposition of standards of care specific to the role of a charity trustee.

APPOINTMENT AND RESIGNATION OF CHARITY TRUSTEES

4–07 The composition of a charity's governing body is key to its effectiveness. Choosing appropriate individuals can be a difficult and sensitive area both at the start and during operation because people often become too close to a charity to take an objective view. It can lead to charities lacking effective and challenging leadership and in the most extreme cases can give rise to complaints of mismanagement. A charity's governing body needs a certain mix of skills and experience to manage the charity's affairs effectively. It is essential that trustees (and those setting up charities) identify the skills needed by the charity. The range of skills should include financial or accountancy, legal or regulatory, and operational, tailored to the charity's core purposes. The most effective charities have a broad spectrum of backgrounds represented by their trustees.

4–08 The size of the governing body is equally important. Charities with too many trustees serving can struggle to maintain focus and decision-making can be compromised. Outdated constitutions sometimes direct a certain number and composition of charity trustee appointments, leading to enforced and ineffective participation often across a diverse and fragmented membership. Smaller governing bodies can be as problematic, lacking challenge and leading to strategic focus being directed by a few or one. For a smaller group of charity trustees, a charity is exposed to the real risk of the charity's governance failing through a key member dying or leaving.

4–09 Some charities engage with other groups and organisations and have such stakeholders represented on their governing body. The principle of democratic accountability in the charity sector is a dominant one and often conflicts arise

---

[4] KGC Reid, "*Patrimony Not Equity: the trust in Scotland*" (2000) 8 E.R.P.L. 427, 432–33.

between the desire of the membership of a charity to support a particular candidate, and the need to balance and engage the correct skills on the charity's governing body.

It is important to have these issues in mind both when setting up a charity and/or during its operational life. Once operational, succession planning on all aspects relating to charity trustee composition is therefore vital. **4–10**

METHODS OF APPOINTMENT

Once a charity is operational, there is no obligation to inform the Office of the Scottish Charity Regulator (OSCR) of the appointment of a new trustee, nor to seek OSCR's consent, although as at the date of publication this is something that is under review by OSCR and may well change. Evidence as to who sits on a charity's governing body at any time is not held on OSCR's website. A search over any charity using OSCR's search engine will highlight that OSCR does not keep a register of Scottish charity trustees, as this is not part of OSCR's statutory functions nor something that OSCR is resourced to do. This may be something that in time is added to the Register akin to the practice under Companies House and it must be regarded as the next obvious step in the development of OSCR's supervisory role and wholly within the spirit of transparency and accountability to the general public. The Charities Commission in England and Wales operates an advanced search system that allows full disclosure of the individual names of the trustees of any charity monitored by it. It also operates a powerful cross-referencing option to allow sight over which other charities a specific individual may be involved with as a charity trustee. Until a similar option is available under OSCR's system, for those members of the public seeking such information on Scottish registered charities reference should be made to the charity's report and accounts that require to carry such details, although care should be taken here as such information in the report may only be up-to-date to the preceding year end. **4–11**

If the appointment means a change of contact details for the charity[5] notice must be given to OSCR within three months.[6] The particular means of appointment depends on the legal structure of the charity and the specific terms of its constitution. Here are the typical approaches taken with different types of constitution, although reference should be made in every case to the constitution as appointment provisions do vary: **4–12**

Trust: It is necessary to look first at the trust deed.[7] The trust deed may specify a mechanism and provide for either or both a minimum and a maximum number of trustees. Some deeds may be silent on the matter, but all trustees have statutory power to appoint new trustees[8] unless the trust deed itself includes a contrary intention. There is an overriding jurisdiction of the Court of Session to appoint **4–13**

[5] Charities and Trustee Investment (Scotland) Act 2005 s.17.

[6] Charities and Trustee Investment (Scotland) Act 2005 s.17(3).

[7] The word often used for "appoint" in trust deeds is "assume".

[8] Trusts (Scotland) Act 1921 s.3(b).

trustees in cases where trustees cannot be appointed under any trust deed or the sole trustee lacks capacity by reason of physical or mental disability or is continuously absent from the UK for at least six months.[9]

4–14 Where a trust deed gives trustees power to appoint new trustees, the power might also require some other consent. This might be from the truster (the individual who "declared" or established the trust at the outset)[10] or some other person. If the charity trustee is itself a trustee company, the individual directors of that company[11] will not on the face of it be evident. A look to establish the trustee company's directors through a search on Companies House records may therefore be necessary.

4–15 The minute of a meeting appointing a new trustee is sufficient evidence of the appointment; however, use of a formal deed of assumption,[12] usually followed by registration in the Books of Council and Session to ensure that the original is never lost, is needed to effect a valid transfer of assets where the trust property includes land. The trust deed sometimes allows for an outside body to appoint or remove a trustee by written notice, and trustees may also be appointed automatically by virtue of the office or post they hold.[13]

4–16 **Company limited by guarantee:** Where the charity is a company, the company's articles of association should specify the method of appointment. Ordinarily, a director may be appointed at a general meeting of the company by either a special (rare) or ordinary resolution. Frequently the articles provide for an election process that avoids the need for an ordinary resolution. The board of a charitable company will usually be able to co-opt a director from the membership, subject to that person standing down at the next annual general meeting (AGM), enabling the members to decide whether the same person should serve another term. Another possibility is an outside body or bodies being given the power under the articles to appoint or remove a director by notice to the company. Where the charity is a company, the "charity trustee" is also a director and there are additional statutory rules that apply.[14] As with all charity trustees[15] there is a minimum age of 16 for directors,[16] and the company must maintain a register of directors.[17] Directors' details (excluding residential address) can be viewed at Companies House. New directors are notified to Companies House by using Form AP01, which is completed and signed before being sent to Companies House. It is nevertheless important that evidence of the appointment (minutes of

[9] Trusts (Scotland) Act 1921 s.22.

[10] Unusual in charitable trusts.

[11] With a trustee company as charity trustee it is only the company that has the charity trustee duties imposed by the Charities and Trustee Investment (Scotland) Act 2005 in relation to the charitable trust, and the directors of the trustee company will only have charity trustee duties in relation to the company if it is itself a charity.

[12] Trusts (Scotland) Act 1921 s.21 and Sch.B.

[13] Usually referred to as trustees "ex officio".

[14] Companies Act 2006 as amended from time to time.

[15] Age of Legal Capacity (Scotland) Act 1991 s.9(f).

[16] Companies Act 2006 s.157.

[17] Companies Act 2006 s.162.

the general meeting or board meeting or notice of appointment and also letters of resignation) are kept as well, as the notification process may on occasion fail to correctly reflect the true position.

SCIO: In the case of a SCIO, the details of how a charity trustee is appointed must be laid down in the SCIO's constitution, in accordance with s.50(2)(b) of the 2005 Act which states that: 4–17

> "A SCIO's constitution must make provision for the appointment of 3 or more persons ("charity trustees") who are to be charged with the general control of the SCIO's administration, and about any conditions of eligibility for becoming a charity trustee."

Normal good practice would suggest that for both single-tier and two-tier SCIOs, for instance, there should be included a prohibition against appointing any employee of the organisation as a charity trustee. Similar provisions often appear in articles of association of charitable companies as well as registered societies and unincorporated associations with charitable status. OSCR has stated that it would be

> " ... prepared to accept a key employee (e.g. project director or equivalent) serving on the board providing this could be justified as being of significant benefit to the charity from the point of view of improving its management and administration".[18]

It may be important to bear in mind that some funding bodies will not entertain applications from a body which has an employee, however valued, on the board of trustees. As a general rule, the members of the SCIO will vote on the appointment of new charity trustees although the charity trustees themselves have power to appoint new charity trustees as well. Alternatively the board of an outside body may be able to appoint, depending on the terms of the SCIO's constitution.

Unincorporated association: In an unincorporated association registered as a charity the management committee members are the charity trustees. An unincorporated association registered as a charity should have a written constitution. It may govern how the management committee members are appointed, and there may be provisions specifying notice to members. Typically, an unincorporated association will evidence the appointment or resignation of its management committee members within minutes of meetings held. It is important to check the constitutional provisions surrounding the calling of, and voting at such meetings, to ensure compliance, particularly given the likely involvement of membership groups in the decision-making around the office holders. Unless some other means is specified, a vote of the members may be adequate to appoint a new management committee member however the constitution may supplement this by allowing the management committee to appoint, and again an outside body or bodies may also be given power to appoint. An unincorporated association may also hold land or buildings either directly 4–18

---

[18] Scottish Council for Voluntary Organisations, "Drafting your constitution—Voluntary Association: A Clause by Clause Commentary" (2011), p.4.

through its office bearers or indirectly through a nominee arrangement and there may be separate provisions for their appointment.

4–19 **Registered society:** Housing associations tend to use the registered society legal form and reference to it should be made for the appointment/removal provisions of its board members.

Resignation

4–20 In a traditional charitable trust there is a statutory power to resign.[19] Resignations sometimes include a form of discharge to the resigning charity trustee of all their actions as trustee, excluding gross negligence or fraud. Care should be taken in each case to critically assess whether granting a discharge is actually in the charity's best interests.

4–21 For the other charitable vehicles, the constitutions in each should be checked for specific provisions as there may be stipulated periods of notice applying to resignations or to a specified form in which such a notice needs to be given. In the case of a charitable company, Companies House will expect Form TM01 (to record the resignation of a director) is used in the same way as Form AP01.[20]

4–22 Charity trustees may cease to act in other circumstances beyond their control. Owing to the collective responsibility of all charity trustees, any who cease to act may obtain a discharge of subsequent actions, if it can be shown that they played no part in such actions and that their ceasing to act was outwith their control, e.g. due to incapacity. This is, however, a matter of facts and circumstances and in each case it is best practice to be clear at the earliest stage that a charity trustee no longer acts as such and is therefore no longer responsible for the actions of the rest of the group. A charity trustee might not be re-elected at the end of an AGM and will then vacate automatically. Evidence of this through minutes of the meeting is sufficient to record the fact. Equally, if a trustee fails to attend meetings, or is sequestrated or convicted of an offence, any of these may give rise to automatic removal as a trustee. Minutes again best identify the circumstances and notice should be given to the trustee of the removal.

Appointment of temporary trustees

4–23 If a charity has an insufficient number of charity trustees to be able to appoint a charity trustee under its constitution, OSCR has power either upon the request of the majority of the charity trustees, or if there are only two charity trustees by either of them, to appoint a person temporarily as an acting charity trustee of the charity.[21]

[19] Trusts (Scotland) Act 1921 s.19(1) and Sch A.
[20] See para.4–16.
[21] Charities and Trustee Investment (Scotland) Act 2005 s.70A(2)(b).

OSCR may appoint more than one trustee but only as many as are needed for the charity itself to be able to appoint charity trustees under its constitution.[22] 4–24

A person appointed as an acting charity trustee is appointed for a period of 12 months (or shorter if OSCR sees fit) starting with the date of appointment and they have the same functions as a charity trustee appointed under the charity's constitution.[23] 4–25

If, at the end of the 12 month period, the charity is still not able to appoint a charity trustee under its constitution, the period of appointment may be extended by up to three months.[24] 4–26

Ex officio trustees

It is relatively common for charity constitutions to be subject to the involvement of other organisations. These organisations may have power to appoint one or more charity trustees, or the constitution of the charity might provide that the holder of an office in the other organisation is to be a charity trustee: these are known as trustees ex officio. This can add significant skills and impetus to governance. In this case the individual acts personally, but holds office through the will of the other body. Ex officio trustees have power to assume other ex officio trustees into the trust.[25] 4–27

Difficulties can arise with these appointments: 4–28

- Does the office holder have the ordinary power of any trustee to resign,[26] and where that would leave the charity without one of its trustees?
- How do you remove a trustee or try to remove an office?[27]
- How easy is it to remove an ex officio trustee by notification to OSCR?[28]

As a generality, no person, including someone proposed as an ex officio trustee, can be compelled to accept the role of a trustee,[29] and there may be an impasse either if it is a condition of accepting the principal office that the person also accepts the position of trustee of the charity or that it is a condition of being a trustee of the charity that the individual proposed affirms their support of a specified ethos of the charity. Practical problems can also arise where someone is not aware they have become an ex officio trustee and challenges the apparent appointment. 4–29

---

[22] Charities and Trustee Investment (Scotland) Act 2005 s.70A(3).

[23] Charities and Trustee Investment (Scotland) Act 2005 s.70A(4)(a) and 70A(b).

[24] Charities and Trustee Investment (Scotland) Act 2005 s.70A(5)(a) and 70A(b).

[25] *Winning, Petitioners*, 1999 S.C. 51.

[26] Trusts (Scotland) Act 1921 s.3(a).

[27] Scottish Law Commission Discussion Paper on Supplementary and Miscellaneous Issues relating to Trust Law (Discussion Paper 148) Ch.8, paras 8.8–8.10.

[28] Charities and Trustee Investment (Scotland) Act 2005 s.17.

[29] *Vestry of St Silas Church v Trustees of St Silas Church*, 1945 S.C. 110, per Lord Justice-Clerk (Cooper) at 121).

The problem of the shadow trustee

4–30 Charities should be in the control of properly appointed charity trustees. Those charity trustees may be at risk if they allow control to be exercised by an outsider, and that outsider may find themselves being subjected to the same regulation as if they were a properly appointed charity trustee.

4–31 The 2005 Act defines "charity trustees" as those who are in "the general control and management of the administration of a charity".[30] The OSCR "Guidance and Good Practice for Charity Trustees", explains that situations can arise where people can exercise influence and control even though they have not been formally appointed as charity trustees. We might refer to these people as "shadow trustees".[31] There is no statutory basis for the term "shadow trustee" and it draws on the corporate definition of a "shadow director" namely "a person in accordance with whose directions or instructions the directors of the company are accustomed to act".[32] The concept of "shadow trustee" therefore is very wide and many faceted.

4–32 The importance of the concept of "shadow trustee" lies in the situation where control is lost to, or shared with, an outside hand, exerting unaccountable influence over a charity's governing body that otherwise should be in control, to the potential damage of the assets or reputation of the charity.

4–33 A person attending, whether or not participating, at trustee or board meetings exposes themselves to liability as if they were a charity trustee, if the influence they bring is sufficiently significant. A "shadow trustee" can be a dead hand, but also can be a willing helper, unconsciously attracting for themselves responsibilities, liabilities and duties well beyond their own understanding of their role. This can happen because of poor oversight on the part of the charity's governing body and unclear operating parameters. For example, charity trustees need to ensure that appropriate levels of participation from invited guests at meetings are maintained at all times, adopting sections of meetings for invited guests and maintaining "closed sessions" for the charity trustees alone to deliberate and decide matters discussed previously with the guests.

4–34 Consider the situation where a general manager or chief executive is taking too active a part in board meetings, participating in or actively encouraging decision-making just as much as the real directors. Equally, it may be a funder dictating to a board what they should be doing.

4–35 Another example may arise where the charity is linked in some way to another body. That body makes a suggestion to the charity's governing body to make a decision in a certain way. Depending on how the governing body treats the suggestion, a failure to debate the issue might lead to the outsider being treated as a shadow trustee. The charity trustees may feel they have operated autonomously, but in practice they have followed rather than led because they did not challenge. There are a number of useful examples given of cases where control is lost or

[30] Charities and Trustee Investment (Scotland) Act 2005 s.106.

[31] OSCR, "Guidance and Good Practice for Charity Trustees" (June 2016), p.5.

[32] Companies Act 2006 s.251(1).

diluted to an unacceptable level in OSCR's publication "Who's in Charge: Control and Independence of Scottish Charities".

CASE STUDIES

Shetland Charitable Trust (SCT)[33]: OSCR highlighted the action taken against SCT given the significant influence of the Shetland Islands Council on the board (24 trustees of whom 22 were councillors). The issue of conflict of interest arose here and the lessons arising highlight the importance of managing board composition to ensure the independence of decision making and also how a charity may be viewed by the public. **4–36**

Lloyds TSB Foundation for Scotland[34]: here the independence of the board of a charity to make its own decisions in the face of directions from a funder was highlighted. Ensuring that a board operates independently and questions what is in the best interests of the charity at all times is key. **4–37**

This is not to say that trustees cannot delegate. Delegation and the power to delegate, including investment management functions,[35] nevertheless require that charity trustees retain responsibility for a charity's affairs. Day-to-day operational and administrative functions aside, charity trustees should, however, remain in overall charge. Ineffective reporting lines from a charity's governing body to its subcommittees and back again, a failure to oversee and monitor, and at the most extreme end, a complete abdication of responsibility over a particular project, all strike at the heart of the charity trustee duties.[36] **4–38**

The structure or relationships a charity has will often highlight ahead of time problem areas where the "shadow trustee" may emerge. Common themes to watch out for include: **4–39**

- where there is some exertion of central government control. Central government links need to be carefully watched as charitable status will be at risk where a constitution expressly allows the Scottish Ministers or a Minister of the Crown to direct or control a charity's activities[37];
- where a charity is linked to another body:
  - if there is identical or similar board composition to the other body;
  - if the charity has been established by the other body; or
  - if finances are secured from the other body.
- where the charity has complex governance arrangements that might reduce accountability, confuse reporting lines or create a lack of clarity around the hierarchy of decision-making.

---

33 OSCR, "Who's in Charge: Control and Independence of Scottish Charities" (2011) p.14.

34 OSCR, "Who's in Charge: Control and Independence of Scottish Charities" (2011) p.18.

35 Charities and Trustee Investment (Scotland) Act 2005 s.94, inserting Trusts (Scotland) Act 1921 s.4C.

36 Charities and Trustee Investment (Scotland) Act 2005 s.66(1).

37 Charities and Trustee Investment (Scotland) Act 2005 s.7(4)(b).

For any charity, it is a challenge to maintain focus on the management functions at every level. Clear operating protocols and reporting requirements best address the need to keep control at the top.

4–40 From 6 April 2016 companies (including charitable companies) must keep a register of individuals or legal entities who have control over them (people with significant control (PSCs)), with a requirement to update Companies House from 30 June 2016. As such, new companies created on or after 30 June 2016 will need to include a statement of their PSCs (or legal entities—"relevant legal entities" or RLEs) when they apply for incorporation, and existing companies will need to include this information when they complete their "confirmation statement" at Companies House. This comes on the back of a drive to increase transparency promoted by the Government, drilling in to who exactly is in control of the UK's companies.

4–41 Charitable companies limited by guarantee (and the few rare ones that are limited by shares) together with wholly owned trading subsidiary companies of charities, all fall under the spotlight of the new regime. It seems that the rules do not sit happily in a charitable context as a lot stems from seeking to understand who the beneficial owner of a company is, and of course, for charities that concept of "beneficial ownership" really does not make much sense, as charities are not as such "owned" by anyone, but simply exist to further their stated purposes.

4–42 An example of where the rules would bite would be a charitable trust (not itself being a corporate entity), with a wholly owned trading subsidiary. There the PSCs would be all the trustees of the charitable trust, so every time there was a change of trustee, the PSC details would need to be changed. It must be questioned as to whether this new obligation, when applied in a charitable context, will have any practical benefit and as such it can only really be regarded as yet another reporting requirement that charities need to factor in.

4–43 Further information and discussion on the provisions can be found in the Department for Business Innovation & Skills publication entitled "Register of People with Significant Control—Guidance for Companies, Societates Europaeae and Limited Liability Partnerships", Version 4, dated 11 April 2016.

(DIS)QUALIFICATION OF TRUSTEES

4–44 Focusing solely on disqualification may overlook the sometimes more difficult question of qualification, in the sense of acting as a charity trustee, and this section looks at the principles underlying who qualifies, and who does not.

4–45 The following are disqualified from acting as charity trustees:

- someone with a conviction for dishonesty or for an offence under the 2005 Act[38];
- an undischarged bankrupt[39];

[38] Charities and Trustee Investment (Scotland) Act 2005 s.69(2)(a)(i)–(ii).
[39] Charities and Trustee Investment (Scotland) Act 2005 s.69(2)(b).

- someone who has been removed under either Scottish or English law or the courts from being a charity trustee.[40] The reference here to the Law Reform (Miscellaneous Provisions) (Scotland) Act 1990, s.7 does not only apply to trustees but covers managers as well, so disqualification as a manager under s.8 will disqualify the same person as trustee under s.69 of the 2005 Act; and
- a person disqualified from being a company director (Company Director Disqualification Act 1986 or the equivalent order in Northern Ireland)[41] (examples of misconduct include fraud, trading to the detriment of the Crown/creditors, failure to keep adequate company accounts).

It is a criminal offence under the 2005 Act for anyone to act as charity trustee while disqualified.[42] **4–46**

Any person convicted of an offence is liable to up to two years in prison or a fine, or both.[43] **4–47**

OSCR has power to waive the disqualification[44] either generally or in relation to a particular charity or type of charity. Charities often seek declarations from prospective charity trustees that they are not disqualified from acting as a charity trustee, and this is considered to be good practice. In addition, HMRC's "fit and proper person" test[45] must now be adhered to in order to comply with the requirement of the Finance Act 2010 that a charitable organisation must satisfy the "management condition". Declarations require to be signed and submitted to HMRC confirming the charity trustee is a "fit and proper" person. Charities need to consider a prospective charity trustee's ability to fulfil the test as well as their qualifications to act on the charity's governing body. In the course of assessing suitability, disclosure checks for charity trustees may be required particularly for those charities operating with vulnerable adults or children. **4–48**

OSCR guidance[46] states that it is the responsibility of individual charity trustees to ensure that they are not personally disqualified from being a charity trustee. Whilst there is no obligation to do so, it is suggested that it would be in the interests of the charity for charity trustees to collectively ensure the qualification of each charity trustee. An example of good practice would be for prospective charity trustees to sign a form before their appointment to confirm that they are not disqualified from acting as a charity trustee. **4–49**

As a general principle anyone can accept trusteeship unless lacking in legal capacity.[47] The constitution may stipulate conditions that apply, minimum/maximum number of trustees, lengths of tenure and rotational provisions, but at **4–50**

---

[40] Charities and Trustee Investment (Scotland) Act 2005 s.69(2)(c) and (d).

[41] Charities and Trustee Investment (Scotland) Act 2005 s.69(2)(e).

[42] Charities and Trustee Investment (Scotland) Act 2005 s.70.

[43] Charities and Trustee Investment (Scotland) Act 2005 s.70(1)(a) and (b).

[44] Charities and Trustee Investment (Scotland) Act 2005 s.69(4).

[45] HMRC, *Guidance on the Fit and Proper Persons test* (3 May 2016).

[46] OSCR, "Guidance and Good Practice for Charity Trustees" (June 2016), p.5.

[47] John McLaren, *The Law of Scotland in Relation to Wills and Succession*, 3rd edn (Edinburgh: Bell and Bradfute, 1894), Vol.II, para.1618.

the most basic level, provided someone has legal capacity, they can act. As to whether they demonstrate the right skills and have the right experience to act is another matter, and one which is covered under appointment. While the 2005 Act does not prescribe a minimum age for charity trustees to act, s.1 and s.9 of the Age of Legal Capacity (Scotland) Act 1991 provides that no person under the age of 16 can act as a trustee. Equally, s.157(1) of the Companies Act 2006 requires a company director to be aged 16 or over.

4–51 In certain cases a charity trustee may be conflicted in a decision-making process. It is one of the fundamental duties of a charity trustee that in circumstances of potential conflict, they put the charity's interests before that of a body appointing them.[48] Where they cannot do so they must disclose the conflict, refrain from participating in relevant decisions and should declare themselves removed.[49] An example is where an organisation responsible for the appointment of one of the charity trustees makes application for a grant to the charity on which the individual sits as charity trustee. In such a case the charity trustee will, almost inevitably, be prevented by their duty to the organisation from putting the charity's interests first. They must refrain from participating in any decisions in connection with that application.

TIME RESTRICTIONS ON APPOINTMENT

4–52 Charity constitutions often place limits on a charity trustee's tenure, typically linked with provisions allowing re-election. Such provisions are intended to ensure that governing bodies do not stagnate and that unduly dominant personalities can be managed out of a charity. It can be transformational to a charity's fortunes to change a board's composition, enabling fresh eyes to assess strategic direction and structures and perhaps make changes to redundant practices or deficient policies. Where rotational provisions do not exist, the charity's governing body should hold the mirror up to itself and often make difficult decisions about tenure and composition. Often that discipline is lacking without the provisions being in place.

4–53 The older constitutions are unlikely to contain tenure provisions and in the context of a reorganisation or amendment to a charity's constitution, such administrative controls are well worth considering in terms of adding to the effective governance of the charity. The role of the chairperson in persuading trustees, who have been acting for many years, to demit office, is often very important. The requirements of good governance to regularly attend meetings and ensure proper attention to the charity's affairs can enable a chairperson to persuade trustees who have been in office as such for some time, to step aside in favour of new blood.

4–54 In setting up a new charity it is good practice to provide that terms of office are staggered to ensure that the charity trustees do not all demit office at the same

[48] Charities and Trustee Investment (Scotland) Act 2005 s.66(1)(c)(i) and 66(1)(c)(ii); and see para.4–113.

[49] See para.4–114.

time. There are model constitutions for both a single-tier SCIO and a two tier SCIO, respectively which provide for the entire body of charity trustees retiring from office—good practice would suggest it is better staggering retirements and appointments. Regarding single-tier SCIOs, cl.26 states "[a]t each AGM, all of the charity trustees must retire from office—but may then be re-elected under clause 27". For a two tier SCIO, cl.60 provides equivalent wording. Supplementary guidance for two tier SCIOs provides an additional clause to be added after cl.60. This provides for a maximum period in office for charity trustees:

> "A person who has served on the board for a period of [*specify*] years shall automatically vacate office on expiry of that [*specify*] year period and shall then not be eligible for re-election until a further year has elapsed."[50]

Similar provisions are very common in articles of association for companies as well as rules of registered societies and constitutions of unincorporated associations.

REMOVAL OF TRUSTEES

All charity trustees must take steps not only to ensure any breach of duty is corrected and not repeated by the errant charity trustee,[51] but also that if any charity trustee is in serious or persistent breach of either of these duties, they are removed as a charity trustee. **4–55**

To enable fulfilment of this requirement, the charity's constitution should set out the procedure for dealing with a charity trustee who has consistently failed to act appropriately in the interests of the charity and, if appropriate, that the constitution affords a procedure to remove them. **4–56**

In many trust deeds there is no such procedure and in such cases a costly court application may appear the only route available to have a charity trustee removed.[52] The alternative is to reorganise and have a specific power inserted in the constitution to allow for removal, through an application to OSCR under the Reorganisation provisions contained in the 2005 Act.[53] **4–57**

Some constitutions make provision allowing for the removal of a trustee without need to resort to the courts. Where they do, but do not make full provision for the mechanism by which this can be achieved, best practice should be that the decision to remove should be made by a significant majority—if not all—of the remaining trustees, that the proposed decision should be intimated to the errant trustee and that they should be given the opportunity to discuss the issue with the others. A person is, after all, a trustee until removed and ought to be given notice **4–58**

---

50 *http://www.scvo.org.uk/setting-up-a-charity/write-your-constitution/scottish-charitable-incorporated-organisation/* [Accessing 20 May 2016].

51 Charities and Trustee Investment (Scotland) Act 2005 s.66(5)(a).

52 Trusts (Scotland) Act 1921 s.23.

53 Charities and Trustee Investment (Scotland) Act 2005 s.42(2)(d) and see Ch.12.

of trustee meetings.[54] The constitutions of SCIOs invariably provide for removal by resolution but with prior notice to the trustee whose removal is proposed, with an opportunity for that trustee to address the meeting prior to the resolution being put, and in cases of material misconduct or persistent breach with a requirement for two-thirds of the whole trustees then in office.

4–59 Other membership organisations such as companies limited by guarantee and unincorporated associations, may confer rights on their members to vote on the appointment or removal of charity trustees; and, for companies, the removal of a charity trustee director would fall under the Companies Acts with the resolution being notified to Companies House under Form TM01.

GENERAL DUTIES

4–60 Any charity trustee induction is not complete without a close analysis and discussion of a charity trustee's duties and the first stop here is to reflect upon the general duties as expressed within s.66 of the 2005 Act. It is as well to set them out in full:

CHARITIES AND TRUSTEE INVESTMENT (SCOTLAND) ACT 2005 S.66

4–61 **"66 Charity trustees: general duties**

(1) A charity trustee must, in exercising functions in that capacity, act in the interests of the charity and must, in particular—
- (a) seek, in good faith, to ensure that the charity acts in a manner which is consistent with its purposes,
- (b) act with the care and diligence that it is reasonable to expect of a person who is managing the affairs of another person, and
- (c) in circumstances capable of giving rise to a conflict of interest between the charity and any person responsible for the appointment of the charity trustee—
  - (i) put the interests of the charity before those of the other person, or
  - (ii) where any other duty prevents the charity trustee from doing so, disclose the conflicting interest to the charity and refrain from participating in any deliberation or decision of the other charity trustees with respect to the matter in question.

(2) The charity trustees of a charity must ensure that the charity complies with any direction, requirement, notice or duty imposed on it by virtue of this Act.

(3) Subsections (1) and (2) are without prejudice to any other duty imposed by enactment or otherwise on a charity trustee in relation to the exercise of functions in that capacity.

(4) Any breach of the duty under subsection (1) or (2) is to be treated as being misconduct in the administration of the charity.

(5) All charity trustees must take such steps as are reasonably practicable for the purposes of ensuring—
- (a) that any breach of a duty under subsection (1) or (2) is corrected by the trustee concerned and not repeated, and
- (b) that any trustee who has been in serious or persistent breach of either or both of those duties is removed as a trustee."

4–62 The principal feature of s.66 is to lay down the basic ground rules by which every charity trustee should conduct themselves (a code of conduct) and as such it is one of the most important sections of the 2005 Act. In essence, it says no more

[54] *Gibb v Stanners*, 1975 S.L.T. (Notes) 30.

than one would expect to see demonstrated in any well-managed charity and as such its requirements should not surprise nor worry a prospective charity trustee or a charity trustee sitting on an effectively operating charity. For those not so placed, it can lead to some worryingly close analysis of failings. It is misconduct to breach any duty imposed[55] by the section, and it is made the collective responsibility of all charity trustees to take such steps as are reasonably practicable to ensure that the breach is corrected by the charity trustee concerned and not repeated and that any charity trustee in serious or persistent breach is removed from office.[56]

In OSCR's "Guidance and Good Practice for Charity Trustees"[57] areas of good practice are highlighted that inform our understanding of what OSCR is seeking behind the statutory provisions. For example, acting in the best interests of the charity is underpinned by ensuring there is an up to date register of interests maintained and that a charity has conflicts of interest and remuneration policies.[58] **4–63**

OSCR expresses s.66(1) in its current "Guidance and Good Practice for Charity Trustees" as four key duties: **4–64**

To act in the interests of the charity Essentially this means putting the charity before oneself or other organisations, e.g. that the charity trustee is connected with. It covers conflicts of interest and avoiding those and how to distance the charity trustee from the conflict. The guidance helpfully identifies three possible scenarios where conflicts most commonly arise.[59] **4–65**

The guidance seeks to draw out lessons from each situation and points to the importance of maintaining an up to date register of interests for all charity trustees, of charity trustees declaring conflicts when they arise and absenting themselves from any discussion or decision relating to the conflict, of developing a conflicts policy/code of conduct for managing conflicts and of ensuring in cases of persistent breach there is power to remove a charity trustee under the constitution.[60]

For charitable trusts the power to remove charity trustees under the general law is limited to an application under the Trusts (Scotland) Act 1921.[61] Otherwise the court has a common law power to remove a charity trustee.[62] It is very difficult to remove a charity trustee from office without the power to do so included within the constitution. There are also the costs of a court action. Hence OSCR's suggestion that constitutions are reviewed to see that a power to remove is available, leaving aside issues of intimation.[63] As an alternative to court action, a **4–66**

---

[55] Charities and Trustee Investment (Scotland) Act 2005 s.66(4).

[56] Charities and Trustee Investment (Scotland) Act 2005 s.66(5)(a).

[57] *http://www.oscr.org.uk/media/2272/2016-06-10-charity-trustee-duties-guidance-final-for-publication.pdf* [Accessed 20 May 2016].

[58] OSCR, "Guidance and Good Practice for Charity Trustees" (June 2016), p.10.

[59] OSCR, "Guidance and Good Practice for Charity Trustees" (June 2016), pp.22 and 23.

[60] Charities and Trustee Investment (Scotland) Act 2005 s.66(5)(b) and see para.5–27.

[61] Trusts (Scotland) Act 1921 s.23.

[62] *MacGilchrist's Trustees v MacGilchrist*, 1930 S.C. 635, per Lord President Clyde at 638.

[63] *Gibb v Stanners*, 1975 S.L.T. (Notes) 30.

reorganisation scheme under the 2005 Act to add in a power to remove a trustee may be a cheaper alternative if there is no such power to remove.

In a charitable company a director may be removed by resolution.[64]

4–67 Within the 2005 Act there are powers reserved to OSCR and the Court of Session to suspend or remove a person concerned in the management or control of the charity in cases of misconduct.[65]

4–68 **To operate in a manner consistent with the charity's purposes** Charity trustees should carry out their duties in accordance with the specific terms of their charity's constitution. The constitution will set out the aims of the charity and the powers it has to act.

4–69 **To act with care and diligence** The care that is expected a charity trustee takes in discharging their duties is that which they would apply in managing the affairs of another person. It is therefore a higher standard of care than would be applied to a charity trustee's own affairs and that expected of trustees under the general law.[66]

4–70 The professional charity trustee (e.g. lawyer/accountant/investment adviser) has no higher standard of care imposed upon them acting as charity trustees, although that might arise under separate statutory provisions, for example, those applying to directors of charitable companies.[67] Often a professional charity trustee's own firm may be providing services to the charity—e.g. legal/accountancy. The firm owes duties and responsibilities to the charity to undertake the tasks it has been set competently and professionally. The professional charity trustee, acting in their capacity as adviser, will bring upon themselves additional standards of care acting in that capacity, separate from their role acting as a charity trustee.

OSCR provide in their Guidance examples of good practice and this is required reading in this area. In particular, it gives examples of what OSCR is looking to see from charity trustees acting with care and diligence.

4–71 The guidance points to certain key actions to demonstrate effective compliance with this duty. No area is beyond the scope of a charity trustee's view in so far as it relates to the charity's activities and charity trustees need to run themselves and their charity with constant rigour and a healthy degree of self-analysis and self-criticism. In practical cases, where charity trustees have fallen down, it is most commonly seen in the areas of governance and control such as developing policies and maintaining protocols around meetings—one might say the "boring" housekeeping tasks. Usually the slipping of the basics around regular meetings can be indicative of a much more deep rooted set of problems in the operations of the charity.

4–72 **To comply with the 2005 Act and other legislation** Subsections (1) and (2) of s.66 do not displace any other duties imposed on charity trustees (and by

---

[64] Companies Act 2006 s.168.

[65] Charities and Trustee Investment (Scotland) Act 2005 ss.31(1)(a) and 34(1)(a).

[66] *Raes v Meek* (1889) 16 R. (H.L.) 31, per Lord Herschell at 33.

[67] Companies Act 2006 Pt 10 Ch.2.

extension on the charity) by other legislation[68] (and by extension, other regulators) and reference is made in the OSCR Guidance to examples of other legislation that might be included here. This is obviously not an exhaustive list and to it could be added, by way of example, equality and discrimination law, bribery law, and specific operational laws and regulations pertinent to the sector in which a charity is working, such as the protection of vulnerable groups. Charity governing bodies must be mindful of their duties to other regulators, aside from OSCR, and address specific requirements demanded from those regulators in carrying out their purposes. Other regulators include:

(1) Care Inspectorate.
(2) Health and Safety Executive and Healthcare Improvement Scotland.
(3) Information Commissioner's Office.
(4) Companies House.
(5) Equality and Human Rights Commission.
(6) Financial Conduct Authority.
(7) HMRC.

Underlying the reference in subs.(3) of s.66 to other duties on charity trustees imposed by enactment or otherwise, there is a clear focus on cooperation and the sharing of information between OSCR and various other regulators and groups established to police such laws. A list of the memoranda of understanding between OSCR and other organisations is available on OSCR's website.[69] **4–73**

SPECIFIC DUTIES UNDER THE 2005 ACT

As well as the general duties imposed on charity trustees under s.66, the 2005 Act also contains more specific duties which focus more on operational activities. **4–74**

Financial duties

A charity must keep adequate financial records and each year must prepare a statement of account, including a report on its activities.[70] This can be contrasted with the position under the CA 2006 where the duty is imposed on directors personally.[71] The statement of account needs to be independently examined or audited[72] and after examination or audit a copy needs to be sent to OSCR in accordance with regulations.[73] Accounting records need to be kept by a charity for six years after the end of the financial year in which they are made.[74] Section 46 is a whistleblowing section for auditors or others completing accounts to inform OSCR of any matter that may have a material impact on OSCR's work. **4–75**

---

68 Charities and Trustee Investment (Scotland) Act 2005 s.66(3).
69 *http://www.oscr.org.uk* [Accessed 20 May 2016].
70 Charities and Trustee Investment (Scotland) Act 2005 s.44(1)(a) and 44(1)(b).
71 Companies Act 2006 Pt 15 Ch.2.
72 Charities and Trustee Investment (Scotland) Act 2005 s.44(1)(c).
73 Charities and Trustee Investment (Scotland) Act 2005 s.44(1)(d).
74 Charities and Trustee Investment (Scotland) Act 2005 s.44(2).

Duties owed to the general public

4–76 In the spirit of transparency and accountability to the general public, charity trustees owe certain duties to offer and supply information. Scottish Ministers may make regulations compelling charities to state certain information on documents issued or signed on their behalf.[75] The regulations are now contained within the Charities References in Documents (Scotland) Regulations 2007 (as amended). OSCR have provided a very helpful guide to this area that sets out the types of documents that must contain certain details about a charity, for example its name, charity number and the fact that it is a charity.[76]

4–77 If the request is reasonable, a charity must provide a copy of its constitution and its latest accounts to any person so requesting them and that person may also request the form in which the information is provided, again if such request is reasonable.[77] Charities may charge a fee for complying with such a request provided the fee does not exceed the cost (e.g. photocopying and postage) of actually supplying the documents requested.[78] As to what constitutes an unreasonable request, it is hard to see many circumstances short of harassment, e.g. repeated requests from the same party, coming close to an unreasonable request, and the reasonableness test needs therefore to be viewed against the facts and circumstances of the case. Unreasonable timeframes and unreasonable demands in relation to formats for the information to be supplied, might also be rejected, but care needs to be taken to avoid complaints being made to OSCR for failing to supply the information requested.

Duties to report

4–78 (i) At the heart of the 2005 Act is the Scottish Charity Register, the maintenance of which is one of OSCR's key roles. Those charities that are listed on the Register need to supply OSCR with certain information to ensure the Register is kept up to date. The information that is contained in the Register is prescribed by the 2005 Act[79] and if there are any changes to the information held by OSCR on any charity, it is a statutory duty imposed on charities (and by extension, charity trustees) to notify OSCR.[80] This emphasises the need to provide a clear and accurate picture of each charity operating in the sector, which must be accessible to public inspection.[81]

(ii) Prospective charity trustees, at the stage of applying for charitable status, are required to sign a declaration stating that they are aware of the charity's aims and purposes, and their duties and responsibilities as charity trustees, and that they are not disqualified from acting as charity trustees. Specific

[75] Charities and Trustee Investment (Scotland) Act 2005 s.15(1).
[76] OSCR, "References to Charitable Status—A Guide to the Charities References in Documents (Scotland) Regulations 2007 (as amended)" (2008).
[77] Charities and Trustee Investment (Scotland) Act 2005 s.23(1)(a) and 23(1)(b).
[78] Charities and Trustee Investment (Scotland) Act 2005 s.23(2).
[79] Charities and Trustee Investment (Scotland) Act 2005 s.3.
[80] Charities and Trustee Investment (Scotland) Act 2005 s.17.
[81] Charities and Trustee Investment (Scotland) Act 2005 s.21.

reference is made in the declaration to ss.69 and 70 of the 2005 Act that cover disqualification. There is no such requirement for charity trustees joining after charitable status has been granted.

(iii) Charity trustees are also under an obligation to complete an annual return, and if their gross income is £25,000 or more, a supplementary monitoring return is also required. The supplementary monitoring return seeks additional information on a charity's accounts, its fundraising activities, any remuneration agreements in place with individual charity trustees and any dealings with connected trading companies. The annual return and the supplementary monitoring return must be filed within nine months of a charity's financial year end. OSCR has consulted on changes to the annual return and other aspects of its monitoring role and has rolled out a series of revised processes aimed at streamlining its monitoring of charities to better enable it to direct its attention to areas where public confidence in the sector may be at risk.[82] **4–79**

(iv) There are reporting requirements under either the notifications or consents procedures contained with the 2005 Act.

(v) In addition to the above, OSCR has introduced guidance on the reporting of notifiable events.[83]

PERSONAL LIABILITY

Whichever legal structure governs the charity trustees, none can completely absolve the charity trustees from potential personal liability either to beneficiaries or to third parties. **4–80**

Charity trustees of traditional charitable trusts should act only in accordance with the powers conferred upon them under the charitable trust deed or the general law; if they act outside these powers a breach of trust will have occurred and if as a consequence a loss results to the charitable trust, then the charity trustees may be held personally liable. **4–81**

Further, the 2005 Act imposes a duty on a charity trustee to act with the care and diligence that is reasonable to expect of a person who is managing the affairs of another person.[84] **4–82**

In a charity, the beneficiaries are members of the general public and so claims can arise from a grouping that is on the face of it wider than that which can be ascertained. This can be seen as part of a charity's general obligations to the public to be accountable. It is fair to say that such claims are rare and tend to arise from particular groups with an interest in the operations of a charity. **4–83**

Third party claims tend to arise from those with whom a charity has entered into contracts. Charity trustees, with the exception of those in SCIOs and guarantee companies, may incur personal liability for such contracts.[85] Normally it is not an **4–84**

---

[82] OSCR, "Targeted Regulation of Scottish Charities" (March 2015).

[83] OSCR, "Reporting Notifiable Events" (March 2016), p.7.

[84] Charities and Trustee Investment (Scotland) Act 2005 s.66(1)(b).

[85] But see para.5–123.

issue as the charity will have sufficient funds to meet its obligations under a contract, but in cases where a charity becomes insolvent, issues of personal liability of the charity trustees may come in to focus. Potential liability for the charity's debts, particularly with charitable trusts and unincorporated associations, links in with general guidance supplied by OSCR that a charity trustee must ensure a charity is run "properly, responsibly and lawfully" and that it is solvent.[86] OSCR's emphasis here is on charity trustees taking their role seriously in the interests of the charity. In contracting with third parties charity trustees should assess the risks of entering into each contract in advance and regularly review the ability of the charity to meet its obligations whether these be to its beneficiaries, contractors or employees. Scrutiny of monthly management accounts and income/expenditure forecasts assists with this, but ultimately it is up to each charity's governing body to assess the most appropriate level and frequency of scrutiny to adopt to its own particular operations. More complex/larger charities will demand a greater level of reporting and scrutiny than smaller charities.

4–85 Charity trustees are entitled to be indemnified from the charity's assets if they enter into contracts properly, responsibly and lawfully, however contracts, entered into beyond the scope of the powers conferred upon the charity trustees may give rise to potential personal liability should a loss thereby occur.

4–86 The personal liability of one charity trustee's actions may become the personal liability of all of the charity trustees as a group if the actions were agreed in advance or subsequently approved. Joint and several liability applies and as such charity governing bodies need to be particularly clear on the delegated authority they allow to one of their number to enter in to contracts, and to review the exercise of that authority on a regular basis. Liability for the acts or omissions of a charity's employee acting in the course of their employment also requires to be considered.

4–87 OSCR underlines its view on a charity governing body's collective responsibilities in its guidance—the general collective duty of care is emphasised[87] as well as the importance within governing bodies of policing their own and ensuring compliance with the 2005 Act. Persistent breaches are to be addressed by removing the charity trustee in question that leads to the need to address in each constitution whether there is power to remove a charity trustee who is in serious or persistent breach.

4–88 The 2005 Act enables OSCR to take action against charity trustees who are in breach of their duties, although the sanctions available to OSCR, such as removal and disqualification, do not include a claim for pecuniary damages. To date no cases have been taken under the 2005 Act pursuing pecuniary damages against a charity trustee.

4–89 Immunity clauses have grown up in traditional charitable trust deeds. They seek to limit the charity trustees' liabilities and over time have become quite complex and legalistic in their terms, but what can and do they actually protect? There is

---

86 OSCR, "Guidance and Good Practice for Charity Trustees" (June 2016), p.11.

87 OSCR, "Guidance and Good Practice for Charity Trustees" (June 2016), p.10.

much debate around that. It should be understood by any new charity trustee that an immunity clause is not a complete exemption from liability. Gross negligence and fraud[88] will always be excluded and as such will continue to give rise to personal liability but otherwise such immunity clauses afford a degree of protection. Generally the courts take a strict view here on interpretation and so if the clause is in any way ambiguous, the charity trustee will not be given the benefit of the doubt. OSCR has not commented on the effectiveness of these clauses and the 2005 Act makes no mention of them. However, at its most fundamental level the existence of such a clause must not be regarded by any charity trustee as a complete solution to the issue of personal liability and is certainly no substitute to adopting a rigorous approach to governance at all levels.

Whilst statute affords some protection in the context of a charitable trust, as each charity trustee is deemed liable for "his own acts and intromissions and shall not be liable for the acts and intromission of co-trustees"[89] adoption or approval can make the acts of one, the acts of all. A clear understanding therefore of the true extent of personal liability, shorn of protections, is a fundamental requirement in any induction process for new charity trustees. **4–90**

Corporate structures afford considerable protection in terms of limitation of liability, but the general duties of charity trustees as expressed in the 2005 Act nevertheless still apply to charity directors, as they do to any other charity trustee. In the case of a charitable company limited by guarantee, not only do the directors need to comply with the rules and duties imposed upon them by the 2005 Act, but they also have the duties imposed upon them by the Companies Acts to consider and adhere to, and in particular the CA 2006 Pt 10 Ch.2. Breach of those duties brings with it the same sanctions potentially, with the added burden of civil action against such a breach contained within CA 2006.[90] **4–91**

INDEMNITY INSURANCE

In response to the issue of personal liability, indemnity insurance has been seen by some as a partial answer. Here the position in England and Wales has for some time stood apart from the position in Scotland, with the Charity Commission permitting charities to purchase such insurance for their charity trustees to afford protection against claims for breach of trust and liability to third parties; provided the constitution includes a power to reimburse reasonable expenses, the premiums can be funded from the charity's assets. As a general principle under Scots law, it is accepted that charity trustees may pay for such insurance out of the charity's assets, provided that there is a suitable power contained within the charitable trust deed and that the insurance does not cover liabilities arising from a breach of trust that was committed knowingly or recklessly.[91] **4–92**

---

[88] *Knox v Mackinnon* (1888) 15 R. (HL) 83; *Raes v Meek* (1889) 16 R. (HL) 31; *Lutea Trustees Ltd v Orbis Trustees Guernsey Ltd*, 1997 S.C. 255.

[89] Trusts (Scotland) Act 1921 s.3(d).

[90] Companies Act 2006 s.178.

[91] *Dollar Academy Trust, Governors of v Lord Advocate*, 1995 S.L.T. 596.

4–93 In Scotland, OSCR's original position considered the purchase of such insurance as amounting to a benefit and as such falling under the rules applying to remuneration. Statute now specifically permits the arrangement of indemnity insurance.[92] This is a welcome relaxation.

4–94 Charities may purchase indemnity insurance on the terms permitted by the 2005 Act unless their constitutions expressly prohibit it.[93] A general prohibition in the constitution on charity trustees receiving a personal benefit does not constitute a prohibition.[94]

4–95 To fall within permitted limits set down by the legislation, a charity trustee indemnity policy must not indemnify charity trustees for any liability to pay:

- a fine imposed in criminal proceedings or a sum due to a regulatory authority as a penalty for non-compliance with a regulatory requirement[95];
- the costs of representation in criminal proceedings if the charity trustee is convicted of an offence arising from fraud, dishonesty or wilful or reckless misconduct[96]; or
- a liability to the charity that arises out of conduct that the charity trustee knew or must reasonably be assumed to have known, was not in the interests of the charity or where the charity trustee did not care whether it was in the charity's interests.[97]

SCIO CHARITY TRUSTEES

4–96 The SCIO provides an alternative to the traditional charitable trust structure, the company limited by guarantee, the unincorporated association and the registered society.

4–97 There are two structures available for the SCIO. Under the two tier structure, a SCIO's charity trustees are appointed by, and on many matters must answer to, the members of the organisation. The single-tier structure most closely resembles that of the traditional trust, with charity trustees appointing new charity trustees and being answerable primarily to themselves, rather than to any wider membership.

SCIO trustee liability

4–98 The SCIO, as a corporate body, is a separate legal entity that, on the whole, has the same status as a natural person. This means that it has the same rights, protections, privileges, responsibilities and liabilities as an individual would have

92 Charities and Trustee Investment (Scotland) Act 2005 s.68A.
93 Charities and Trustee Investment (Scotland) Act 2005 s.68A(4)(a).
94 Charities and Trustee Investment (Scotland) Act 2005 s.68A(4)(b).
95 Charities and Trustee Investment (Scotland) Act 2005 s.68A(2)(a)(i) and 68A(2)(a)(ii).
96 Charities and Trustee Investment (Scotland) Act 2005 s.68A(2)(b).
97 Charities and Trustee Investment (Scotland) Act 2005 s.68A(2)(c).

under the law and may enter into the same types of transactions as a natural person can, including entering into contracts, employing staff, incurring debts, owning property, suing and being sued.

As the transactions of the SCIO are undertaken by it directly, rather than by its charity trustees on its behalf, the SCIO charity trustees are in the main protected from incurring personal liability. **4–99**

As with any other type of corporate body, this protection is however not absolute and, in some circumstances, SCIO charity trustees may be held personally liable for the actions of the SCIO. These may occur where the SCIO charity trustees have been reckless, negligent, have acted illegally or have acted outwith their powers in the management and control of the SCIO. The issue of personal liability of SCIO charity trustees is at the date of publication so far untested by the courts. It could be that in the context of health and safety regulations or cases of corporate manslaughter, SCIO charity trustees may be held personally liable. **4–100**

The extent to which the limited liability of a SCIO offers any real benefit in the protection to a charity trustee compared to, say, a charitable trust structure depends upon the terms of the individual constitution. **4–101**

The separate legal personality of a SCIO also means that it is the SCIO itself that is responsible for any debts, obligations and liabilities incurred in furthering the purposes of the charity. Even where a SCIO has insufficient assets to meet its liabilities, the charity trustees themselves will not be held personally liable. **4–102**

SCIO trustee powers

A SCIO is governed by its constitution. While there is no standard format for the constitution to take, key aspects of governance must be covered within its provisions. Specifically, the constitution must state the purposes of the SCIO.[98] This is no different from any of the other charitable structures that can be adopted. A difference from other charitable structures is the existence of regulations specifying the features that need to appear in the constitution of a SCIO. **4–103**

SCIO charity trustees must use and apply the property of the SCIO in furtherance of its purposes and in accordance with its constitution.[99] Again this is identical to the position under any of the other charitable structures. **4–104**

SCIO v traditional charitable trust

It is worth considering the main differences between a SCIO and a charitable trust: a SCIO is a separate legal entity from its charity trustees whereas a charitable trust is not legally separate, the trustees there acting directly and potentially incurring personal liability. **4–105**

---

[98] Charities and Trustee Investment (Scotland) Act 2005 s.50(1).
[99] Charities and Trustee Investment (Scotland) Act 2005 s.50(4).

4–106 However, trustees of a traditional charitable trust may be protected from the impact of personal liability by being entitled to have recourse to the trust assets assuming they have acted honestly and reasonably.[100]

4–107 Similarly, the powers and duties of charity trustees of a charity constituted by a traditional charitable trust are governed principally by their trust deed. The trust deed of a traditional charitable trust directs how the trust will operate and anything that is at variance with the provisions of the trust deed could amount to a breach of trust on the part of the charity trustee.[101]

4–108 Whilst some traditional charitable trust deeds may be liberal in the powers that they confer upon their charity trustees in the administration of the trust, other trust deeds may be particularly restrictive. As such, while SCIO charity trustees have unlimited powers to further the purposes of the SCIO, traditional charitable trustees may find that the terms of their trust deed significantly limit the extent to which they can administer the trust fund.

4–109 The extent to which the powers of a SCIO charity trustee may be compared with the powers of a traditional charitable trustee therefore depend entirely upon the precise wording of the governing document. In each case there is no substitution for a close analysis of the constitution of any charity to establish the precise extent of the powers and protections afforded to its charity trustees.

4–110 One potentially problematic area relating to SCIOs concerns the interaction and relationship between the members and the charity trustees, where the composition of each differs. Section 66(1)(a) of the 2005 Act lays out the principal duty of the members of the SCIO (which is one of the duties that also falls on the charity trustees), being to "seek, in good faith, to ensure that the charity acts in a manner which is consistent with its purposes". Where agreement between the members and the charity trustees can be reached as to what those purposes are and what action is required to ensure consistency with those purposes, such a duty remains unproblematic. Issues may arise, however, where differences in opinion emerge between the two groups as to what is meant by "consistent with [its] purposes". In such circumstances, the 2005 Act provides no guidance as to how such differences should be reconciled. Again, the terms of the SCIO constitution must be considered; however, where this remains silent, there is the very real possibility that the opinions of a minority group (the SCIO's charity trustees) are simply treated as being inconsistent with the purposes of the charity.[102] As a matter of effective governance, the potential for conflict is quite apparent here, with a divided view as between members and charity trustees. That, however, is the nature of the SCIO, in that the members have significant control and have an annual opportunity to vote off trustees.

---

[100] *Andrews v Ewart's Trustees* (1886) 13 R. (HL) 69.

[101] *Goodsir v Carruthers* (1858) 20 D. 1141 at 1145.

[102] Stuart Cross, "A new legal form for charities: the Scottish Charitable Incorporated Organisation", 2007 S.L.T. , 39, 281–284.

SCIO trustee general duties

Section 66 of the 2005 Act outlines the general duties that are applicable to charity trustees. These duties apply equally to trustees under traditional charitable trust structures as they do to charity trustees operating under a SCIO structure. **4–111**

INFORMING OSCR OF CHANGES

In terms of s.16 of the 2005 Act, charities must seek prior consent from OSCR before undertaking certain actions. Changes to the composition of a charity's body of charity trustees does not fall within this.[103] **4–112**

CHANGES TO THE STRUCTURE OR CONSTITUTION OF A CHARITY

A charity can only make changes to its constitution or governing document if the constitution or governing document gives it the power to do so and, in making the changes, the terms of the constitution or governing body are followed. **4–113**

Some changes that a charity may wish to make can only be made with the consent of OSCR and on 42 days notice[104]:

- changing the name of the charity;
- amending the charitable purposes—42 days' notice must be given to OSCR;
- amalgamation with another body;
- winding up or dissolving the charity; and
- applying to the court in relation to amending its purpose, amalgamating or winding up.

How to manage conflicts of interest

Every trustee must put aside their personal interests when dealing with the trust affairs, but sensitive issues arise for some charities who have individuals appointed as charity trustees to their governing bodies under agreement with other organisations. This is often observed with charitable or non-charitable groups operating in similar fields, with particular expertise or insights to bring to the charity in question, or operations that are perhaps similar or relevant to the charity's own purposes. Key stakeholders such as local authorities, may often have the right to appoint an individual or individuals to charity trustee positions on charity governing bodies. Such broad engagement with other organisations is a healthy feature of the charity sector, where collaboration can drive efficiencies as well as promote a wider delivery of services to the target recipients. Clearly such structures can also give rise to potential and actual conflicts of interest and irrespective of which group, body or organisation the individual participant on the **4–114**

[103] There is likely to be a requirement in the future to notify OSCR on an on-going basis of changes in a charity's trustees.

[104] Charities and Trustee Investment (Scotland) Act 2005 ss.11 and 16.

charity's governing body may arise from, it is incumbent upon each individual to act in the best interests of the charity for whom they are a trustee and importantly exercise their own personal judgement in carrying out their role as a charity trustee.

4–115 How does this work where an individual is a trustee of two charities that have connected interests? Where a charity trustee is faced with a conflict of interest between the charity and the person who appointed him, the charity trustee must put the interests of the charity before those of the appointer[105] or if prevented from so doing because of another duty, must disclose the conflicting interest and take no further part in relation to the deliberations or decision of the charity's governing body on the matter.[106]

4–116 For such charity trustees, it is particularly important that they appreciate the extent of their duties here, and that they understand the notion of conflict of interest clearly and unequivocally. Failure to properly manage this area constitutes a breach under the 2005 Act and as such amounts to misconduct under the 2005 Act.[107] This is as relevant for the charity trustees who are not so conflicted as it is for the charity trustee who is, and the obligations therefore fall on all charity trustees to take steps to correct the breach[108] and to remove a charity trustee in serious or persistent breach.[109]

FUNDRAISING

4–117 The 2005 Act provides charities and, therefore, charity trustees, with greater control over those who fundraise for them—this applies not just to charities but to all benevolent organisations.[110] Section 81 requires a formal agreement between the charity or other benevolent body and any professional fundraiser or commercial organisation that is involved in raising funds for then.

4–118 The agreement must state the level of remuneration and expenses to be paid to the fundraiser, and satisfy a number of requirements that will be set out in the forthcoming fundraising regulations. If these requirements are not met the agreement is only enforceable against the charity or other benevolent body by an order of the sheriff.

4–119 Section 82 allows charities or other benevolent organisations, under certain circumstances, to obtain an interdict banning fundraising on their behalf, e.g. if an organisation objects to the method of fundraising, if the person involved is not a fit and proper person to fundraise or if the organisation does not want to be associated with the venture.

---

[105] Charities and Trustee Investment (Scotland) Act 2005 s.66(1)(c)(i).
[106] Charities and Trustee Investment (Scotland) Act 2005 s.66(1)(c)(ii).
[107] Charities and Trustee Investment (Scotland) Act 2005 s.66(4).
[108] Charities and Trustee Investment (Scotland) Act 2005 s.66(5)(a).
[109] Charities and Trustee Investment (Scotland) Act 2005 s.66(5)(b).
[110] See Ch.7.

The 2005 Act also allows Scottish Ministers to make regulations controlling both the collection of money from the public and those carrying out such collections.[111]

REMUNERATION AND BENEFITS

Some charity constitutions permit trustees to receive remuneration or benefits such as accommodation, but the primary rule is that a trustee must avoid receiving any personal benefit from their position as trustee as that might create conflict between their personal interests and the interests of the trust. **4–120**

Trustee "charging clauses" are nowadays fairly commonplace, usually drafted on the basis that a trustee can be paid for work done on a professional basis. In the absence of such a clause a charity trustee requiring to be paid for services would have no option but to resign. This does not cover out of pocket expenses for which a charity trustee is entitled to be reimbursed. **4–121**

For trusts other than charitable trusts, the Scottish Law Commission (SLC) is of the view that this rule should be changed so that, unless there were a contrary intention expressed in the trust deed, trustees should be allowed to appoint one of their own number as agent and to allow that person reasonable remuneration for the services provided.[112] The SLC *Report on Trust Law* recommends that this should apply to public trusts,[113] and that it should not be necessary, in fixing the remuneration for the trustees, to consider any other benefit that the remunerated trustee may receive from the trust.[114] **4–122**

Under the present statutory provisions, charity trustees "may not" be remunerated unless certain conditions are met.[115] OSCR makes the comment in its "Guidance and Good Practice for Charity Trustees" sets out when charity trustees (and those who are connected to them) can receive payments from the charity for services they have supplied.[116] **4–123**

It is necessary to understand the scope of what constitutes "remuneration". It covers any payment or benefit in kind: **4–124**

- for being a charity trustee;
- under a contract of employment; and
- for other services to or on behalf of the charity.

Trustee indemnity insurance is not regarded as a benefit for these purposes.[117] **4–125**

---

[111] Charities and Trustee Investment (Scotland) Act 2005 s.83.

[112] Scottish Law Commission, *Report on Trust Law* (Scot. Law. Comm. No.239), p.144, para.12.73, cl.54(1).

[113] Scottish Law Commission, *Report on Trust Law* (Scot. Law. Comm. No.239), p.144, para.12.73, cl.54(2).

[114] Scottish Law Commission, *Report on Trust Law* (Scot. Law. Comm. No.239), p.144, para.12.73, cl.54(3).

[115] Charities and Trustee Investment (Scotland) Act 2005 s.67(1).

[116] OSCR, "Guidance and Good Practice for Charity Trustees" (June 2016), p.33.

[117] See paras 4–92, 4–93.

4–126 The provision against remuneration applies not only to charity trustees, but also to "a person with whom the trustee is connected".[118] "Connected" here is defined in terms of s.68(2) as:

- any person who is married to the charity trustee, who is in a civil partnership, or any person with whom the charity trustee is living as husband and wife or if in an equivalent same sex relationship[119];
- any child, parent, grandchild, grandparent, brother or sister of the charity trustee (and any spouse of any such person)[120];
- any institution that is controlled (directly or through a nominee) by the charity trustee, any person connected to the charity trustee as defined above or two or more persons falling within subparas (i)–(ii)[121];
- a body corporate in which the charity trustee or anyone connected with the charity trustee has a substantial interest[122] ("substantial interest" and "control of an institution" are defined in s.105[123]); and
- a Scottish partnership in which one or more of the partners is the charity trustee or someone connected with the charity trustee under para (a) or (b).[124]

4–127 For the purposes of this section a person who is another person's stepchild or brought up or treated by another person as if the person were a child of the other person, is treated as that other person's child.[125]

4–128 The connections are therefore very wide and in practice it is for every charity governing body to assess carefully the potential and actual links that exist when looking at remunerating one or more of its charity trustees and/or family members, companies, etc. connected with any of them.

4–129 The conditions for remuneration are set out in s.67(3) and state that the maximum amount of remuneration:

- is set out in a written agreement[126]; and
- is reasonable in the circumstances.[127]

4–130 It must also be shown that:

---

[118] Charities and Trustee Investment (Scotland) Act 2005 s.67(2)(b).
[119] Charities and Trustee Investment (Scotland) Act 2005 s.68(2)(a)(i)–68(2)(a)(iii).
[120] Charities and Trustee Investment (Scotland) Act 2005 s.68(2)(b).
[121] Charities and Trustee Investment (Scotland) Act 2005 s.68(2)(c)(i)–68(2)(c)(iii).
[122] Charities and Trustee Investment (Scotland) Act 2005 s.68(2)(d).
[123] A person who is able to secure that the affairs of an institution are conducted in accordance with the person's wishes is to be treated as being in control of the institution and a person who is interested in shares comprised in the equity share capital of a body corporate of a nominal value of more than one-fifth of that share capital or is entitled to exercise more than one-fifth of the voting power at any general meeting of a body corporate is treated as having a substantial interest in the body corporate. Charities and Trustee Investment (Scotland) Act 2005 s.105(2)(a) and 105(2)(b).
[124] Charities and Trustee Investment (Scotland) Act 2005 s.68(2)(e)(i) and 68(2)(e)(ii).
[125] Charities and Trustee Investment (Scotland) Act 2005 s.68(3)(a) and 68(3)(b).
[126] Charities and Trustee Investment (Scotland) Act 2005 s.67(3)(a)(i).
[127] Charities and Trustee Investment (Scotland) Act 2005 s.67(3)(a)(ii).

- it is in the interests of the charity for the services to be provided by the service provider for that amount.[128] "Service provider" includes the charity trustee or someone who provides the services with whom the charity trustee is connected[129];
- after the agreement is entered in to less than one-half of the charity trustees or those connected to the charity trustee receive remuneration[130]; and
- the charity's constitution does not expressly prohibit the remuneration.[131]

It is for each charity to assess what is "reasonable remuneration" and to do so with an adequate knowledge of the market, basing any such decision on a detailed comparison of similar functions and roles. The level of enquiry required here will depend on the precise scope and level of remunerated services being engaged. It is essential, however, that charity governing bodies are able to demonstrate this market testing analysis has been undertaken with a degree of rigour and that they document their decisions based on that. 4–131

It should be noted that two exemptions exist, although the circumstances where they apply are limited and the exemptions do not absolve the charity trustees from acting in the best interests of the charity to ensure that the remuneration is not excessive. The exemptions are: 4–132

- that the charity's constitution contains a provision authorising the remuneration, which provision was in force on 15 November 2004 (being the date the Charities and Trustee Investment (Scotland) Bill came before the Scottish Parliament)[132];
- that the remuneration is authorised by an order of the Court of Session.[133]

The sanction for receiving remuneration in breach of s.67 is that the charity may recover the remuneration and if so directed by OSCR, recovery proceedings must be taken.[134] 4–133

BREACH

If there has been found to be misconduct in the administration of a charity, OSCR has powers under s.31 to take action. In their publication and statements, OSCR highlights the regulatory imperatives of acting proportionately and fairly, offering support where charity trustees have encountered difficulties in fulfilling their requirements, yet taking robust action when required. The nature of any action depends very much on the seriousness of the misconduct, and here every case will turn on its own particular facts and circumstances. 4–134

The powers OSCR has at its disposal are wide-ranging. They cover: 4–135

[128] Charities and Trustee Investment (Scotland) Act 2005 s.67(3)(b).
[129] Charities and Trustee Investment (Scotland) Act 2005 s.67(2)(a) and 67(2)(b).
[130] Charities and Trustee Investment (Scotland) Act 2005 s.67(3)(c).
[131] Charities and Trustee Investment (Scotland) Act 2005 s.67(3)(d).
[132] Charities and Trustee Investment (Scotland) Act 2005 s.67(5)(a).
[133] Charities and Trustee Investment (Scotland) Act 2005 s.67(5)(b).
[134] Charities and Trustee Investment (Scotland) Act 2005 s.67(7).

- suspension of any person concerned in the management or control of the charity who has been responsible for or privy to the misconduct,[135] who has contributed to, or facilitated, the misconduct[136] or who is unable or unfit to perform that person's functions in relation to the property of the charity. On the face of it, this is a very wide power to suspend, however subs.(10) states that this "does not apply if OSCR considers that the person has acted honestly and reasonably in relation to the misconduct concerned and ought fairly to be excused". This ties in with OSCR's stated proportionate approach to regulation;
- directing that the body representing itself as a charity, the person representing the body as a charity, the charity representing itself as being established as a Scottish charity, or the person representing the charity as a Scottish charity, to cease doing so[137];
- directing the restriction of transactions undertaken, or the amount of payments made, in the administration of the charity without consent from OSCR[138]; and
- directing a third party holding property on behalf of a charity, not to part with the property without OSCR's consent.[139]

4–136 Breach of the statutory duty is not one of the grounds for removal of a charity trustee under s.23 of the Trusts (Scotland) Act 1921.

4–137 Going to court to remove a charity trustee will involve the charity in expense and it has to be questioned whether the requirement to take such steps as are reasonably practicable to remove a charity trustee who has been in breach of their statutory duties, goes as far as requiring the charity trustees to pursue a court action for their removal. It may be possible to apply to OSCR under the reorganisation procedure[140] for the addition of a power of removal that may be more cost effective than pursuing a court action.

TRANSPARENCY

4–138 Transparency and confidence in the charity sector go hand in hand, and this underpins the importance of the maintenance of up to date information on every charity, and is supported by the provisions of the 2005 Act.

4–139 OSCR can therefore require, by notice, charity trustees to provide information on any documents or other information that OSCR requires in connection with a charity's entry in the Charity Register.[141]

4–140 Reference is made here to a charity trustee's duties owed to the general public under Pt 13—this all adds to the transparency and confidence in the charitable

---

135 Charities and Trustee Investment (Scotland) Act 2005 s.31(4)(a).
136 Charities and Trustee Investment (Scotland) Act 2005 s.31(4)(b).
137 Charities and Trustee Investment (Scotland) Act 2005 s.31(5)(a), 31(5)(b), 31(5)(c) and 31(5)(d).
138 Charities and Trustee Investment (Scotland) Act 2005 s.31(6).
139 Charities and Trustee Investment (Scotland) Act 2005 s.31(7).
140 See Ch.12.
141 Charities and Trustee Investment (Scotland) Act 2005 s.22(1).

sector. Particularly relevant here is s.23 and the right of a member of the public to request information on a charity (constitution and accounts). This is dealt with in more detail above.

The relevant legislation that underpins the issue of transparency is as follows: **4–141**

- Section 21 of 2005 Act—Information about charities:
  - The Register should be made available to the public by OSCR at all reasonable times at its principal office, at all other places as it thinks fit and otherwise as it thinks fit.[142]
  - OSCR may determine the form and manner in which the Register is made available.[143]
  - OSCR may charge a fee (no more than the cost of supply), for providing the information.[144]
- Section 22—Power of OSCR to obtain information from charities:
  - OSCR may by notice require any charity to provide to it:
    - any document, or copy or extract from any document[145];
    - documents of any type, or copies or extracts of such documents[146];
    - other information or explanation[147] that OSCR requires in relation to the charity's entry in the Register.
  - The notice must specify documents, type of documents, and date which the charity must supply and by when it must do so (the date must be at least 14 days after the date on which the notice is given).[148]
  - A charity may be entitled to refuse to give information if it would fall under grounds of confidentiality in proceedings in the Court of Session.[149]
- Section 23—Entitlement to information about charities:
  - A person is entitled to be given a copy of a charity's constitution or latest statement of account, if it is a reasonable request.[150]
  - A charity may charge such fee as it thinks fit—but such a fee must not exceed the cost of supplying the document requested.[151]
- Section 24—Disclosure of information by and to OSCR:
  - OSCR may disclose any information to any public body or office-holder for any purpose connected with the exercise of OSCR's functions or for the purpose of enabling or assisting the public body or office holder to exercise any functions.[152]

---

[142] Charities and Trustee Investment (Scotland) Act 2005 s.21(1).
[143] Charities and Trustee Investment (Scotland) Act 2005 s.21(2).
[144] Charities and Trustee Investment (Scotland) Act 2005 s.21(4).
[145] Charities and Trustee Investment (Scotland) Act 2005 s.22(1)(a).
[146] Charities and Trustee Investment (Scotland) Act 2005 s.22(1)(b).
[147] Charities and Trustee Investment (Scotland) Act 2005 s.22(1)(c).
[148] Charities and Trustee Investment (Scotland) Act 2005 s.22(2)(a) and 22(2)(b).
[149] Charities and Trustee Investment (Scotland) Act 2005 s.22(3).
[150] Charities and Trustee Investment (Scotland) Act 2005 s.23(1).
[151] Charities and Trustee Investment (Scotland) Act 2005 s.23(2).
[152] Charities and Trustee Investment (Scotland) Act 2005 s.24(1)(a) and 24(1)(b).

- any office holder in the Scottish administration, the Scottish Parliamentary Corporate Body, any local authority, any constable and any other Scottish public authority with mixed functions or no reserved functions, may disclose any information to OSCR for the purpose of enabling or assisting OSCR to exercise these functions.[153]
- The power to disclose information (unless otherwise provided for by s.25) is subject to any obligation as to secrecy or other restriction on disclosure of information.[154]

- Section 25—Removal of restrictions on disclosure of certain information:
  - No obligation as to secrecy or other restriction on disclosure of information, however imposed, prevents:
    - OSCR from disclosing any information to a designated body for any purpose connected with the exercise of OSCR's functions or the purpose of enabling or assisting that body to exercise any functions[155];
    - a designated body from disclosing any information to OSCR for the purpose of enabling or assisting OSCR to exercise any functions[156];
    - a charity trustee from disclosing any information about that charity to OSCR for the purpose of enabling and assisting OSCR to exercise any functions[157];
    - any person from disclosing any information to OSCR about any matter in respect of which the person is required or authorised by s.46 to make a report to OSCR[158]; or
    - a relevant financial institution from disclosing any information to OSCR for the purpose of enabling or assisting OSCR to exercise any functions under s.47.[159]
- Section 26—False or misleading information, etc.
  - It is an offence for a person to provide any information or explanation to OSCR or any other person if:
    - the person providing the information or explanation knows it to be, or is reckless as to whether it is, false or misleading in a material respect and the information provided is in purported compliance with a requirement by or under this 2005 Act[160];
    - or in other circumstances in which the person providing it knows or could reasonably be expected to know, that it would be used by OSCR, or provided to OSCR for use, in connection with the exercise of its functions.[161]

[153] Charities and Trustee Investment (Scotland) Act 2005 s.24(2) and 24(3).
[154] Charities and Trustee Investment (Scotland) Act 2005 s.24(4).
[155] Charities and Trustee Investment (Scotland) Act 2005 s.25(1)(a)(i) and 25(1)(a)(ii).
[156] Charities and Trustee Investment (Scotland) Act 2005 s.25(1)(b).
[157] Charities and Trustee Investment (Scotland) Act 2005 s.25(1)(c).
[158] Charities and Trustee Investment (Scotland) Act 2005 s.25(1)(d).
[159] Charities and Trustee Investment (Scotland) Act 2005 s.25(1)(e).
[160] Charities and Trustee Investment (Scotland) Act 2005 s.26(1)(a) and 26(1)(b)(i).
[161] Charities and Trustee Investment (Scotland) Act 2005 s.26(1)(b)(ii).

— It is an offence for a person deliberately to alter, suppress, conceal or destroy any document which the person is, or which that person knows it, required by or under this Act to provide to OSCR.[162]
— A person guilty under this offence is liable on summary conviction to a fine or imprisonment for a period not exceeding six months or to both.[163]

CHARITABLE TRUSTS—THE FUTURE

With the SLC's *Reports on Trust Law*[164] and on *Unincorporated Associations*[165] now published, there are a number of areas of interest for charity trustees to consider. Whilst the proposals seek to consolidate all current trust legislation, the 2005 Act remains. Even though on the face of it the landscape for charities may appear potentially unaltered by the recommendations contained within the report, it would be quite wrong for charity trustees to ignore the recommendations, and where such will have potential application to the operations of their charities. **4–142**

Particular aspects of the *Report on Trust Law* where charity trustees will have an interest are as follows: **4–143**

- more effective powers to allow charity trustees to deal with the removal of ex officio trustees and their office to be replaced by nominated trustees;
- reform of provisions around appointment, resignation, removal and discharge of trustees; and
- a new general power of administration to allow the delegation of administrative functions with possible savings for smaller charities by pooling resources.

---

162 Charities and Trustee Investment (Scotland) Act 2005 s.26(2).
163 Charities and Trustee Investment (Scotland) Act 2005 s.26(3).
164 Scottish Law Commission, *Report on Trust Law* (2014) (Scot. Law Comm. No.239).
165 Scottish Law Commission, *Report on Unincorporated Associations* (2009) (Scot. Law Comm. No.217).

CHAPTER 5

GOVERNANCE AND ADMINISTRATION

Alastair Keatinge

WHAT IS GOVERNANCE?

This chapter is about the day to day running of a charity. All charity trustees, especially chairs and secretaries, must have a thorough knowledge of the ways in which a charity ought to be run. This is often referred to as good governance. There is no statutory definition of governance, but the Good Governance Code suggests the processes that sustain the effectiveness, and good administration of the charity.[1] **5–01**

The principles of governance underpin the fact that charity trustees must accept ultimate responsibility for everything the charity does, or does not do. In short, in line with their statutory duties,[2] trustees must act always in the best interests of the charity. This chapter seeks to reflect the current state of good governance at the time of writing. **5–02**

The Good Governance Code suggests six principles of good practice for trustees[3]: **5–03**

(i) knowing your constitution and your charity's vision (understanding your role);
(ii) good operational and financial plans (ensuring delivery);
(iii) appropriate skills, experience and diversity within the trustees (working effectively);
(iv) checks on management, on financial controls and on risks (exercising control);
(v) be independent, and always act with probity (behaving with integrity); and
(vi) good communication with management, staff, stakeholders, supporters and beneficiaries (being open and accountable).

A well run charity will work out its own annual cycle of business and events that have to be arranged and managed at specific times. This is the start of good governance. In this chapter we will look at: **5–04**

- understanding the charity trustee's role: paras 5–05 to 5–23;

---

[1] See Good Governance, "A Code for the Voluntary and Community Sector" (the "Good Governance Code"): *http://www.governancecode.org* [Accessed 23 May 2016].
[2] See paras 4–60 to 4–65.
[3] See the "Good Governance Code".

- operational working: paras 5–24 to 5–33;
- meetings: paras 5–34 to 5–62;
- modern management: paras 5–63 to 5–76;
- integrity: paras 5–77 to 5–91;
- understanding the role of members: paras 5–92 to 5–112; and
- administration: paras 5–113 to 5–145.

UNDERSTANDING THE CHARITY TRUSTEE'S ROLE

Powers of administration

5–05 Charity trustees need to be aware of the powers which they have in order to operate their charity. The powers for the administration of charities come from three sources:

- express powers conferred by a constitution;
- powers that can be implied into a constitution; and
- powers conferred by law, primarily by statute.

A distinction must be made between "powers" and "purposes" (or objects). Powers are only exercisable in order to advance the charitable purposes of a charity.

5–06 The powers of charity trustees are often set out in some detail in the constitution. Trustees and those dealing with them may need to be aware that the existence of detailed provisions may mean that a particular action they are considering may not be open to the trustees as being a legitimate exercise of their powers.

5–07 Particularly where charities are transacting with third parties, both the charity trustees and the third parties engaging with the charity will want to be quite clear that the charity has the powers required to transact in the way that the parties have in mind.

5–08 The specific powers available to a particular charity will depend on its legal structure: guarantee company, Scottish Charitable Incorporated Organisation (SCIO), trust, unincorporated association, registered society or some other form of entity, such as Royal Charter.

Express powers for guarantee companies

5–09 For a modern charitable company (a "guarantee company"), its purposes and powers are set out in its articles of association.[4] Older charitable companies have their powers set out in their memorandum of sssociation (unless they have subsequently adopted articles in the new form).

---

[4] Companies Act 2006 (Commencement No.8, Transitional Provisions and Savings) Order 2008 (SI 2008/2860)—applies to companies incorporated after 1 October 2009.

Adding or modifying powers can usually be done by virtue of a members' special resolution to amend the articles of association. 5–10

The validity of any act done by a company cannot be called into question by reason of anything in the company's constitution.[5] The constitution comprises the company's articles of association and resolutions[6] (and the memorandum of association for older companies—see para.5–09). The power of the directors to bind the company is also deemed to be free from limitation under the constitution.[7] For guarantee companies, however, the third party seeking to rely on this must either not know that the company is a charity, or give value and at the same time be unaware that the company had no power to do the act or that procedures were not observed.[8] 5–11

Even so, it is the duty of the directors to comply with the provisions of the constitution in relation to the exercise of powers and they can be liable to the company for failing to comply with that duty. In addition, any member of a company may take action to restrain the directors or trustees from undertaking activities that are outwith the company's powers. 5–12

Express powers for Scottish Charitable Incorporated Organisations

A SCIO has the power to do anything that is "calculated to further its purposes or is conducive or incidental to doing so".[9] This power is subject to any restriction in the SCIO's constitution. For the purposes of managing the affairs of a SCIO, its charity trustees may exercise all the SCIO's powers.[10] 5–13

A person dealing with a SCIO in good faith and for value is not required to enquire whether: (1) anything in the SCIO's constitution prevents it acting in the way it is; or (2) any limit on the powers of the charity trustees under its constitution prevents them from binding the SCIO or authorising others to do so.[11] 5–14

If there is no express power where one is thought to be required, it will usually be possible to add one or to modify any restriction on an existing power. This requires a members' resolution (the required majority being not less than two-thirds of the members who vote) (see paras 5–24 and 5–38) to amend the constitution. Sometimes issues do arise, particularly with banks, if there are no specific powers, such as a power to borrow. 5–15

5 Companies Act 2006 s.39.
6 Companies Act 2006 s.17.
7 Companies Act 2006 s.40.
8 Companies Act 1989 s.112 (Companies Act 2006 s.42 does not apply to Scotland).
9 Charities and Trustee Investment (Scotland) Act 2005 s.50(5).
10 Charities and Trustee Investment (Scotland) Act 2005 s.50(6).
11 Charities and Trustee Investment (Scotland) Act 2005 s.62(1).

Express powers for trusts and unincorporated associations

5–16 The express powers of a charity that is constituted as a trust or as an unincorporated association ought to be set out in its trust deed or other constitution. On occasion they may be found elsewhere, for example, in title deeds. Such powers may be expressed in a very individual manner and the precise wording may need to be construed in the context of the document as a whole. There is no provision protecting third parties similar to the statutory rule that applies in relation to companies and SCIOs.[12]

5–17 For trusts in which there is no express power to carry out the proposed action, the trustees may have a sufficiently wide power of amendment to enable them to add a new power or modify an existing power. How the power must be exercised will depend on the particular provisions of the trust deed. Unincorporated associations are likely to be in the same position.

5–18 If it appears that the trustees or the members of the unincorporated association do not have adequate powers to amend, it may be possible to make an application to OSCR to approve a reorganisation scheme.[13]

Implied powers for all charities

5–19 If there are no express powers to authorise an action that a charity proposes to take, and there is no adequate power of amendment, it may be possible to imply a power into its constitution. This will depend on how the charity is constituted, what its constitution says and the approach taken by its trustees and any third party with whom the charity engages. With implied powers the position can never be determined with absolute certainty without a decision of the courts. However, where a transaction is to proceed upon the basis that a power can be implied, it is only in rare instances that the parties should feel forced to apply to the courts for a determination. A formal instruction to an appropriately experienced counsel or specialist solicitor, agreed between solicitors for the parties, has always been considered satisfactory clarification. A good guide may be to ask whether the proposed action is consistent with the charity's purposes and vision.

Investment powers

5–20 Charitable trustees (like all other trustees) have power to make any kind of investment of the trust property, unless the constitution says otherwise.[14] This includes investment in heritable property (that is, land and buildings). They also have power to acquire heritable property for any other reason.[15]

---

[12] See the Scottish Law Commission, *Report on Trust Law* (2014) (Scot. Law Comm. No.239), Ch.13.

[13] Charities and Trustee Investment (Scotland) Act 2005 s.39: see para.12–45 onwards.

[14] See the Trusts (Scotland) Act 1921 Act s.4, as amended by Charities and Trustee Investment (Scotland) Act 2005 s.93.

[15] Charities and Trustee Investment (Scotland) Act 2005 s.93(2)(b).

All charities also have power to participate in common investment schemes and common deposit schemes[16] unless the constitution specifically excludes this. **5–21**

Restrictions on powers

Any restriction on the exercise of express powers set out in a charity's constitution must be observed. These could include, for example, obtaining any third party consent to the sale of an asset, borrowing only up to a specified limit or buying only particular types of investment. **5–22**

Advice

In exercising their powers trustees must consider whether they first need to take advice on the issue they are considering. Certain statutory powers impose an express obligation to take advice or at least consider taking it, e.g. making investments.[17] If charity trustees decide not to follow proper advice that has been obtained from a suitably qualified person, they should minute on what basis the advice has been rejected.[18] **5–23**

OPERATIONAL WORKING

Acting together

Unless the constitution states otherwise, decisions of trustees will be by majority vote. It is always necessary to keep in mind whether the constitution stipulates that in some circumstances a special majority decision (e.g. two thirds or three quarters) is required. **5–24**

Collective responsibility

Charity trustees as a body are collectively responsible for all the activities of the charity. This means that all charity trustees are equally accountable. They have a collective general duty of care for the charity and the charitable assets. Charity trustees are expected to act together to realise the values and purposes of the charity and to comply with legislative and regulatory requirements. **5–25**

It is the charity trustees (as opposed to the charity's employees or agents) who have an absolute duty for meeting the statutory commitments of the charity under the Charities and Trustee Investment (Scotland) Act 2005 (2005 Act)[19] and any other duty imposed by statute or otherwise on charity trustees, e.g. under employment law or health and safety legislation.[20] **5–26**

---

16 Charities and Trustee Investment (Scotland) Act 2005 s.96 and para.9–17 onwards.

17 Charities and Trustee Investment (Scotland) Act 2005 s.94.

18 See paras 9–25, 9–26.

19 Charities and Trustee Investment (Scotland) Act 2005 s.66(2).

20 Charities and Trustee Investment (Scotland) Act 2005 s.66(3).

5–27 If a charity trustee fails in their statutory duties,[21] it is the obligation of the other charity trustees to take reasonable steps to ensure that the misconduct is rectified and not repeated. They also need to ensure that anyone guilty of serious or persistent misconduct or breaches of their duties no longer remains a charity trustee.[22] For a charity where the constitution does not provide a power to remove a trustee, the constitution should be amended, if possible, to include one and avoid the need to engage the assistance of OSCR. Where the constitution does not permit such an amendment an application for a reorganisation scheme may be required.

Trustees not to act without reference to colleagues

5–28 The chair, secretary and treasurer of a charity are referred to as "office-bearers", particularly in unincorporated associations, but they do not have any general implied authority to bind the charity. Often, however, these individuals will be given particular delegated authority, either in the constitution or by the body of trustees.

Standing orders and policies

5–29 The constitution of the charity is the primary source for stipulations as to how the charity is to operate: for example, by specifying the minimum number of meetings of trustees to take place each year. Some constitutions allow the trustees to agree secondary instruments of authority and these may be called standing orders, rules, regulations, governing instruments or byelaws. Once adopted these will be just as binding as provisions in the constitution, subject to any power to review or amend them.

5–30 Even where the constitution does not make specific provision to do so, trustees should agree and adopt appropriate governance policies. These might be divided into board policies, policies required by law or regulation and policies under which a chief executive is to operate. Examples are trustee recruitment, anti-bribery and anti-fraud, complaints, confidentiality (often within a broader code of conduct for trustees), conflicts of interest, data protection, delegated decision making, financial controls, health and safety, human resourses (recruitment procedures, equal opportunities, etc.), reserves and risk management and policies relating to confidentiality, attendance at meetings (and consequences of non-attendance), use of email, audit and management of risks. It is good practice for all constitutional documents, policies, regulations and protocols to be kept together as a single document.

---

[21] See para.4–60 and 4–74.

[22] Charities and Trustee Investment (Scotland) Act 2005 s.66(5)—see also Scottish Law Commission, *Report on Trust Law* (Scot. Law Comm. No.239), para.12.96. and see para.4–115.

The trustee induction pack

A charity trustee cannot be expected to understand the nature or extent of their role and responsibilities without some form of trustees induction pack. All charity trustees are under a duty to ensure that they familiarise themselves with the charity's constitution, purposes, assets and current work. Office bearers who stand in the way of the provision of this information will be at risk of some form of censure. At *minimum* a new charity trustee should be given the following items both in hard copy and, where available, electronically: 5–31

- a copy of the charity's constitution and any other governing instruments;
- the terms of reference for the charity trustees generally, including in particular the period of initial appointment;
- copies of minutes for the preceding 12 months;
- a copy of the charity's latest report and accounts (including an explanation of how the charity operates to achieve its charitable purposes) together with any recent budget control or management accounts;
- copies of all trustee policies including, for example, policies on investments, expenses and conflicts of interest;
- committee structure and remits, conflicts of interest requirements, details of staff structure and reporting, all scheduled meeting dates (board and committees);
- the schedule of trustees' work for the year ahead[23];
- details of the usual place and anticipated dates of trustee meetings and of the information that will be made available for meetings and when it will be made available; and
- a summary of the charity's internal financial controls.

In addition there should be an informal meeting with the chair. Increasingly, this is where the chair will also offer the allocation of an existing trustee to act as mentor to the new trustee for a limited induction period. It also enables the chair to explain about any annual assessment of trustees that the charity may expect. No matter how large or small the body of trustees, it is essential that a new trustee feels at ease and valued. An informal occasion when the new trustee has an opportunity to ask questions about the operation of the charity is an important start to trusteeship. This can also be an opportunity to discuss the likelihood of conflicts of interest arising[24] and the training needs of the trustees, both individually and as a group. 5–32

Schedule of year's work

Trustees often have many other commitments and it is important to schedule and forward plan meetings of the trustees and of any subcommittees. It is also good practice to schedule the ordinary business to be transacted throughout the year 5–33

[23] See para.5–33.
[24] See paras 5–77—5–85.

(approval of accounts, report to OSCR, receiving the reports of subcommittees) so that business is taken at appropriate times. This scheduling by means of a "year plan" or "forward look" should be approved annually by the trustees in advance of the year ahead. It can also helpful to schedule an annual away-day or strategy day (where funds permit) so that there is time and space to discuss the direction in which the charity is moving or the possible implications of important decisions.

MEETINGS

Charities other than guarantee companies

Meetings of trustees

5–34 Good governance requires well run and effective meetings and guidance exists as to how to achieve an effective meeting of trustees.[25]

5–35 There should be a sufficient number of (and appropriately spaced) meetings to ensure that the required business is dealt with effectively. The number of meetings will vary according to the size of the charity and the amount of decision-making needed. Urgent business can be transacted without a meeting.[26] Consultation by way of telephone, email, Skype, video-conferencing and other internet based methods of communication can be used, where the constitution permits, to obtain decisions of the trustees where required.[27]

Notice for trustees' meetings

5–36 In the case of a charity that is not a company, there are no legal rules that govern the periods of notice required for trustees' meetings. The notice period is governed solely by the provisions, if any, in the charity's constitution. If none is specified, between 10 and 14 days notice is a good guide. The secretary should circulate not only the proposed agenda but also the up to date budget statement and any reports. Draft minutes of the preceding meeting should also be included. Any confidential matter covered at the preceding meeting—and probably minuted in a separate paper—should not be sent. In many cases this work will be done electronically unless the constitution requires notice to be in writing.

---

[25] Charity Commission, *Guidance: Charities and meetings* (CC No.48, 2012).

[26] See para.5–63. See also Scottish Law Commission, *Report on Trust Law* (Scot. Law Comm. No.239), para.5.3.

[27] See paras 5–63—5–66 below and the Scottish Law Commission, *Report on Trust Law* (Scot Law Comm. No.239), para.5.3.

Quorum at trustees' meetings

A charity's constitution will usually specify the quorum that applies at a meeting. In other cases, the quorum may be set out in rules or regulations in relation to the conduct of meetings. Proxies are not relevant to trustees' meetings unless the charity's constitution or rules and regulations in relation to meetings expressly provide that they should be. It is not sufficient for establishing a quorum that a trustee indicates in advance their agreement with proposed courses of action. Some constitutions or adopted rules may allow a quorum to be established if a trustee participates throughout a meeting by conference call or other electronic aid.[28] **5–37**

Voting at trustees' meetings

Voting at trustees' meetings will be in accordance with the charity's constitution but, if the constitution is silent, a simple majority can pass resolutions. A simple majority exists where more members vote for a particular resolution than against it. A charity's constitution may also provide that a higher or special majority is required in relation to a particular resolution: for example, a resolution to amend the constitution or dissolve a charity will often require a two-thirds majority vote in order to pass it. **5–38**

The majority in question is a majority of the charity's trustees present at the relevant meeting unless otherwise specified in relation to certain resolutions: examples might be decisions on winding up or dissolution. Charity constitutions often provide that the chair has a second or casting vote in the event that the votes of trustees are equal. If one or more trustees cannot vote because of an adverse interest, a majority or quorum is established by reference to those trustees who are not conflicted. Some trust constitutions do make provision for participation by trustees even although they have a particular, potentially conflicting, interest. The handling of this requires great care and good practice does not approve of such participation.[29] **5–39**

Minutes

Whether there is an express legal requirement on a charity to take and retain minutes of its trustees' meetings will depend upon the terms of its constitution, but the obligation to maintain good records is a part of the trustees' duty to safeguard its assets. For this reason, all charities should maintain comprehensive and accurate records of the business transacted at their trustees' meetings. This does not require a verbatim account, but a minute of topics covered at a meeting, reports received, decisions taken and allocation of any further work required. Matters properly to be treated as confidential should not be recorded in the main minute but the fact of the item of business having been discussed should be recorded in the minute and a full note set out in a paper apart, to be kept in a **5–40**

[28] See paras 5–63 to 5–66 below.

[29] See para.5–83 below.

separate file from the minute book. On confidential matters, which regularly might relate to employment issues, it is of the utmost importance that the issue discussed, any discussion appropriate to narrate, and the decision, should be recorded with clarity. Minutes should be set out on consecutively numbered sheets. Minutes should be approved at the ensuing meeting of trustees and signed by the chair and secretary, and any approved amendments marked on the minutes and noted in the minutes of the subsequent meeting. A confidential "paper apart" from a preceding meeting should be read out at the subsequent meeting, approved and signed.

5–41 Copies of approved minutes and of confidential "papers apart" must be retained in a form that continues to allow access throughout the lifetime of the charity. They are the only proof of the business transacted at any meeting, and who attended a meeting. Traditionally, it was thought that they should be kept securely in lever arch files. The electronic age and a desire to restrict the use of paper has seen some changes of view.[30] For those confident of electronic systems and with appropriate backing up there seems no reason why electronic storage alone should not be used. This would probably require scanning of the signed minutes.

Meetings of members

5–42 A charity with members will generally hold meetings of its members from time to time. The position will be determined by a charity's constitution, which will usually require meetings to be held (usually including an annual general meeting (AGM)) and, if so, will spell out in some detail the way in which they are convened, the business that should be transacted at them and the voting and quorum requirements.

Notice for members' meetings

5–43 In the case of a charity which is not a company or a SCIO, there are no legal rules that govern the periods of notice that are required for members' meetings. The notice period is governed solely by the provisions, if any, in the charity's constitution. If none is specified, between 10 and 14 days is a good guide. The charity's constitution will often identify who is able to call a meeting. If it does not, the charity's trustees will be able to do so, but the constitution may also provide for this to be done by a specified minimum number of members. It is good practice to circulate not only the proposed agenda but also the up to date budget statement, management accounts and any reports. Draft minutes of the preceding meeting should also be included.

[30] See also Scottish Law Commission, *Report on Trust Law* (Scot. Law Comm. No.239), para.11.25.

Quorum at members' meetings

A charity's constitution will usually specify the quorum that applies at a meeting. In other cases, the quorum may be set out in rules or regulations in relation to the conduct of meetings. If there are corporate members, an authorised representative of a corporate member will represent the corporate member "in person".[31] Otherwise, proxy holders will not count as representing the granter "in person" unless the charity's constitution or rules and regulations in relation to meetings expressly provide that they may do so. **5–44**

Voting at members' meetings

Voting at members' meetings will be in accordance with the charity's constitution but, if the constitution is silent, a simple majority can pass resolutions. A simple majority exists where more members vote for a particular resolution than against it. A charity's constitution may also provide that a higher or special majority is required in relation to a particular resolution: for example, a resolution to amend the constitution or dissolve a charity will often (always in a SCIO) require a two-thirds majority vote in order to pass it. **5–45**

The majority in question is a majority of the charity's members present at the relevant meeting unless otherwise specified in relation to certain resolutions: examples might be decisions on winding up or dissolution. Charity constitutions may provide that the chair has a second or casting vote in the event that the votes of members are equal. **5–46**

If the charity's constitution is silent on the manner of voting, voting will be on a show of hands. A vote may also be taken using a poll; that is votes cast in writing, which may be important to ensure precision in counting especially if there are any weighted voting rights. There is a common law right for any member to demand a poll on a particular resolution, although this can generally be limited or excluded by express provisions in the charity's constitution. Polls will generally be conducted in such manner as the chair directs.[32] They require voting slips and the appointment of scrutineers. If the demand is made before the meeting, these can be arranged in advance; but if the demand is made during the meeting the poll will have to be arranged for a meeting at later date (usually within 30 days). **5–47**

Minutes

Charities should maintain accurate records of the business transacted at their members' meetings. This does not require a verbatim account, but a minute of topics covered at a meeting, reports received, decisions taken and allocation of any further work required. It is unlikely that members' meetings will cover confidential matters such as employment issues, but any matters properly to be treated as confidential should not be recorded in the main minute but the fact of **5–48**

---

[31] Companies Act 2006 s.324.

[32] See, for example, the Stair Memorial Encyclopaedia, *Companies* Vol.4, p.329, para.399.

the item of business having been discussed should be recorded in the minute and a full note set out in a paper apart, to be kept in a separate file from the minute book. Minutes should be set out on consecutively numbered sheets. Minutes should be approved at the ensuing meeting of members and signed by the chair and secretary, and any approved amendments marked on the minutes and noted in the minutes of the subsequent meeting. Any confidential "paper apart" from a preceding meeting should be read out at the subsequent meeting, approved and signed. Copies of approved minutes and of confidential "papers apart" should be kept securely. As with trustee minutes,[33] for those confident of electronic systems and with appropriate backing up there seems no reason why electronic storage alone should not be used rather than the traditional method of storage in lever arch files. This would probably require scanning of the signed minutes.

Guarantee companies

Company meetings

5–49 The Companies Act 2006 abolished the requirement for private companies to hold an AGM. Many charitable companies still hold an AGM each year, and must do so if required by their constitution. The main purpose of the AGM is to lay the company's accounts before the members, re-appoint the company's auditors or independent financial examiners (and fix their remuneration) and deal with any retirement by rotation of the trustees. Some constitutions enable the accounts to be approved by the trustees and be exhibited to the members. Alternatively, some constitutions require the members to formally approve the accounts.

5–50 Any meeting of the members of a charitable company other than an AGM is, under the Companies Act 2006, simply a "general meeting" or "GM". However, many charities will still refer to this as an "extraordinary general meeting" or "EGM". There is no requirement that a GM should ever be held, but both the directors and members have the power to call one.[34]

Notice

5–51 The procedures for convening meetings of members are set out in the Companies Act 2006.[35] Broadly:

- The charitable company's trustees have the power to convene a GM whenever they think it appropriate in the interests of the charity. Most charitable companies' constitutions will give trustees an express power to convene a GM in any event.
- The trustees of a charitable company must also convene a GM on a "members requisition". This is a demand by those members representing

33 See para.5–41.
34 Companies Act 2006 ss.302 and 303.
35 Companies Act 2006 ss.307–313.

not less than one-twentieth of the total voting rights of all of the members, as at the date of the requisition, who are able to vote at general meetings.

- Notice of any meeting must be sent to anyone who is entitled, under the terms of the company's constitution, to receive notice. In general, this will be all of the members of the charitable company. The charitable company's auditors or independent financial examiners are also entitled to receive notice of any meeting.
- A charitable company's constitution will usually specify that notice of a meeting must be given to its members in writing. This includes giving notice electronically, either to an email address or via a website. If this is to be done via the website, members must be notified of the presence of the notice, that it concerns a company meeting and specifying the place, date and time of the meeting.[36]
- The charitable company's constitution will also usually specify when notice is deemed to be given. Notices should be sent to the address recorded for a particular member in the register of members. This includes an electronic address.
- The notice must confirm the date, time and place of the meeting and state its purpose sufficiently clearly. The key point is that the notice must contain sufficient information about the matters that will be considered to enable members to decide whether or not to attend the meetings. The wording of any special resolution must be included in full.
- The period of notice required is specified by s.307 of the Companies Act 2006 as 14 days' notice in writing. The period of notice required excludes both the day on which the notice is received by the member and the day on which the meeting is held.
- Where the statute provides that special notice is to be given for particular resolutions, such as a resolution to remove a director or an auditor by ordinary resolution, the period of special notice is not less than 28 days before the meeting at which the relevant resolution is to be proposed.

Voting

Voting will be in accordance with the charity's constitution. The majority required in respect of various categories of resolution will be determined by company law, unless the constitution requires a greater majority. **5–52**

Resolutions passed by a simple majority are usually referred to as "ordinary resolutions" in the context of charitable companies. References to "resolutions" in the Companies Acts should be interpreted as references to "ordinary resolutions". A "special resolution" of the members means a resolution passed by a majority of not less than 75 per cent of those members present and eligible to vote in person or by proxy.[37] Some constitutions require that abstentions be disregarded in reaching the 75 per cent majority (as otherwise the statutory **5–53**

[36] Companies Act 2006 s.309.

[37] Companies Act 2006 s.283.

provision will prevail, i.e. those abstaining/not voting are counted as a vote against the resolution). This will include, for example, a resolution to alter a charitable company's constitution.

5–54 A charitable company's constitution will determine how members' votes are cast and counted. In general, voting will be by way of a show of hands. However, there is both a common law and a statutory right for members to demand that voting should be by way of a poll: that is, votes cast in writing. This right cannot be excluded by the terms of the charitable company's constitution. The statutory right enables five or more members, or a member or members holding not less than one tenth of the total voting rights of all members,[38] to demand a poll.

5–55 The purpose of a vote by poll is to ensure that votes cast are recorded in writing, which may be important to ensure precision in counting, especially if there are any weighted voting rights.

5–56 A charitable company incorporated under the Companies Act 1985 or earlier may have a provision in its constitution specifying that the chairman of the members' meeting should exercise a casting or second vote in the event of deadlock. In the absence of a provision of this kind, the chairman has no second or casting vote in addition to any other vote he or she may have. Companies incorporated after 1 October 2007 cannot pass a resolution using a chairman's casting vote.[39]

Written resolutions

5–57 Decision-making by a private company can be carried out by way of a "written resolution" procedure where a written resolution can be passed when the "required majority" of members have signed it.[40] The required majority is the number of members who would be required to vote for a particular ordinary or special resolution at a meeting. The ability to pass written resolutions of this kind is subject to a number of detailed requirements in relation to the circulation of written resolutions to all members.[41] In brief:

(a) the usual majority rules apply, but in respect of "eligible votes";
(b) it cannot be used for removing a director or auditor;
(c) the circulation of and the signifying of agreement to a "written resolution" includes electronic form but the company must circulate the resolution with a statement informing members how to signify agreement and the date by which the resolution must be passed;
(d) a member's agreement cannot, once signified, be revoked; and
(e) a written resolution will still need to be sent to the auditors or independent financial examiners.

---

38 Companies Act 2006 s.321.
39 The result of the terms of the Companies Act 2006 ss.281 and 282.
40 Companies Act 2006 s.281.
41 Companies Act 2006 ss.288–300.

Quorum and proxies

The constitution will usually specify the quorum that applies at a meeting but, if no quorum is specified, the quorum is two "qualifying persons" personally present.[42] (A "qualifying person" includes: (a) an individual member; (b) a corporate representative; or (c) a proxy holder.) In the case of a single-member charitable company, the quorum is reduced to one person. **5–58**

The quorum required by a charitable company's constitution may vary depending upon the resolution that is proposed. Typically, the quorum will be the "lower of" or "greater of" a fixed number or proportion of members, so that they can keep pace with a changing number of members. The number of members necessary for the quorum must be present at the meeting "in person". If there are corporate members, an authorised representative of a corporate member will represent the corporate member "in person".[43] **5–59**

A member of a company is entitled to appoint another person as their proxy to attend, speak, demand a poll and vote at a meeting of the company. **5–60**

Other attendees

A charitable company's auditors or independent financial examiners have a right to attend general meetings. Who else can or should attend will generally depend upon the terms of the charity's constitution. **5–61**

Every charitable company is required to keep minutes of all of the proceedings of its general meetings. Any minute that is signed by the chairman of the meeting, or by the chairman of the next succeeding meeting, is evidence of the proceedings.[44] **5–62**

MODERN MANAGEMENT

Electronic aids—electronic attendance

Many charities wish to take advantage of electronic communication to enable participation in board and other meetings. However, the generally accepted rule is that a meeting can be validly held only where the participants can both see and hear each other. It follows that, unless a charity's constitution expressly prohibits it, trustees can hold meetings by electronic means including by way of video conferencing, webcam or Skype. **5–63**

As a telephone conference does not allow trustees to see each other, it may not constitute a "meeting" unless the charity's constitution expressly provides for meetings to be held on this basis. If there is no specific power to conduct trustees' meetings by telephone conference call, some trustees may still be able to phone into a physical meeting of trustees provided that, discounting the trustees who are on the telephone, they can form a valid quorum for the meeting. **5–64**

---

[42] Companies Act 2006 s.318.

[43] Companies Act 2006 s.323.

[44] Companies Act 2006 s.356(4).

5–65 Accepted modern practice is that decisions can be made by trustees without a meeting being held. The most obvious means is by way of email, instituted by the secretary in consultation with the chair. All trustees must (so far as reasonably practicable) be given adequate prior notice of the matters to be decided and an opportunity to put forward their views.[45] The secretary should keep the email streams with the minutes so that the views expressed and decision reached are evidenced.

5–66 Trustees may wish to set their own appropriate regulations or protocols with regard to when and which electronic aids may be used to achieve attendance at board meetings, particularly where trustees reside in distant geographical locations from each other.

Delegation

5–67 The charity trustees are the persons having the general control and management of the administration of the charity.[46] Accordingly, delegation to others does not absolve a trustee of responsibility.

5–68 Without an appropriate power of delegation that is exercised properly by the charity trustees, decisions taken and acts carried out by people to whom the trustees' power have purportedly been delegated will have no legal effect. The consequence of that will vary from case to case but the scope for potential liability of a breach of trust by the charity trustees is clear, with some potential personal liability also for the people to whom powers were purportedly delegated.

5–69 The powers of delegation available to charity trustees will depend upon the constitution of the charity. Day-to-day operational and administrative functions of trusts have always been subject to some form of delegation. The employment of a factor on large landed estates is a clear example. There is no reason why trustees of charities may not delegate such functions.[47]

5–70 Larger charities with more complex operational requirements are likely to use delegation as an important aspect of their governance arrangements. By creating committees of the board with non-trustees as members, the board may be able to harness the skills and experience of a wider range of people who do not have the time, or perhaps may not be willing, to become trustees themselves or could only do so at the risk of increasing the number of members on the board until it becomes unworkable. Power to delegate to a committee of the board will usually be set out as an express provision in the charity's constitution.

5–71 The scope of any delegated authority should be clear and in writing and reviewed regularly. Individuals and committees with delegated authority should report back to the trustees and be held to account by the trustee body. Charity trustees will want to be clear about the style and frequency of reporting which will be provided by the investment managers and whether that will meet the charity's

---

[45] Scottish Law Commission, *Report on Trust Law* (Scot Law Comm. No.239) paras 5.1–5.5.

[46] Charities and Trustee Investment (Scotland) Act 2005 s.106.

[47] Note the provisions of s.4C(1) of the Trusts (Scotland) Act 1921, inserted by s.94 of Charities and Trustee Investment (Scotland) Act 2005 specifically in relation to investment management.

needs. They will often also want to ensure that their investment manager is accessible and is willing to attend occasional meetings of the trustees, and that is also a point to raise at the appointment stage. Trustees should not attempt to delegate:

(a) any function relating to the distribution of assets;
(b) any decision as to whether payments should be from income or capital;
(c) any power to appoint trustees to the trust; and
(d) any statutory power to delegate.[48]

Guarantee companies

The constitution of a guarantee company will generally contain an express provision to the effect that the business of the charity will be managed by the trustees who may exercise all of its powers. The articles will usually include an express power to delegate any of the trustees' powers to any committee consisting of one or more persons, at least one of whom must be a trustee. **5–72**

Another power of delegation available to trustees of a guarantee company is the ability to appoint "alternate directors". There is no provision within the companies legislation dealing with alternate directors in a private company and a provision providing for "alternate directors" must be contained in the articles of association. The statutory provisions relating to possible alternate directors in public companies provide a guide.[49] **5–73**

An alternate director is any person appointed by a charity trustee to act in their place. The relevant provisions will normally provide for the alternate to act in the place of the trustee who has appointed them where the trustee is absent, set out the basis on which the alternate is appointed and the scope of their powers. The alternate will usually require to be approved by the other directors and should cease to be an alternate director if the person ceases to be a trustee. **5–74**

The power to appoint an alternate director should be employed sparingly. It might be thought to disrupt continuity and to introduce a decision-maker who is not well acquainted with the workings of the charity. But it can be useful in practice where a trustee is likely to be absent for a period of time perhaps through working abroad or through illness. They may therefore wish to appoint someone (preferably someone agreed to with the chair or the other trustees) to act in their place for a limited time and to preserve their interest; and the other trustees might see this approach as indeed preserving continuity. The power will not usually be used to delegate particular trustee powers or functions. Alternate directors are an exception to the usual rule that those appointing delegates will remain responsible for the delegate's acts and decisions. A charitable company's constitution may expressly provide that an alternate director is solely responsible for their own acts and defaults to the exclusion of any liability for the trustee who has appointed them. **5–75**

---

[48] See the Scottish Law Commission, *Report on Trust Law* (Scot. Law Comm. No.239), paras 8.1–8.8.

[49] Companies (Model Articles) Regulations 2008 (SI 2008/3229) Sch.3 arts 25–27.

Unincorporated charities

5–76 Many unincorporated charities will have an express power in their constitution authorising the delegation of trustees' powers and functions to other people. Where there is an express power, its provisions must be properly observed, particularly in relation to any conditions that apply (for example, that those to whom powers are delegated must themselves be trustees or that any act or decision taken by those to whom powers are delegated must be ratified by the trustees in order to become effective). A power of delegation contained in the constitution of an unincorporated charity will often be expressed as a power to employ and appoint agents.

INTEGRITY

Managing conflicts

5–77 Overlooking potential conflicts of interest for an individual trustee risks damaging the integrity and reputation of the charity in the eyes of beneficiaries, stakeholders and the public. For many charities the means of allaying this prospect is by keeping a register of trustees' individual outside interests. Even so, every charity should have in place a protocol for dealing with potential conflicts. A standard formulation in the constitution of a SCIO might suggest that a charity trustee must not vote at a meeting on any resolution relating to something in which they have a personal interest or duty that conflicts (or may conflict) with the interests of the charity and must withdraw from the meeting while an item of that nature is being dealt with.

5–78 Every charity trustee owes their principal duty to the charity whose affairs they are dealing with at the relevant time.[50] It follows that the charity trustee has a duty to avoid any conflict between their duties to the relevant charity and their own personal interests. Charity trustees also have a duty to avoid any conflicts between their duties to the charity and the duties they may owe, or feel that they owe, to some other person or entity notwithstanding that their personal interests are not involved.

5–79 A frequent, innocent, instance is where a trustee holds their trusteeship by virtue of another office that they hold. Where a charity trustee has been appointed by an outside person or body, if there are circumstances capable of giving rise to a conflict of interest between a charity and any person responsible for the appointment of the charity trustee, the charity trustee must:

(i) put the interests of the charity before those of the other person; or

---

[50] Charities and Trustee Investment (Scotland) Act 2005 s.66.

(ii) where any other duty prevents the charity trustee from doing so, disclose the conflicting interest to the charity and refrain from participating in any deliberation or decision of the charity trustees with respect to the matter in question.[51]

At the other end of the scale, a trustee who while acting as trustee furthers their own interests, such as by buying assets of the charity or doing business with the charity or carrying on a business in competition with the charity, acts in breach of fiduciary duty. These transactions can be undone by the courts and any profits recovered from the trustee. It does not matter if the transaction was fair or the trustee acted reasonably.[52] However well meant, it can cause damage to the charity. If a trustee believes or knows that another trustee is conflicted, the trustee has a duty to raise the conflict either at the trustee meeting or with the chair. 5–80

If the constitution does not make provision for dealing with conflicts of interest, there should be a protocol to cover them. In addition, charities should seek to identify which possible conflicts are likely to be significant or a constant issue for them: as with the example above where a trustee is appointed by a stakeholder member to whom they owe duties as a trustee or employee. 5–81

It is good practice to arrange that all trustees are asked to declare any conflicts in relation to the business of the meeting at the start of each trustee meeting. It may be important to explore whether what has been declared as a conflict is in fact so. Principal examples are[53]: 5–82

- a charity trustee could get direct financial benefit from a decision the charity has to make;
- a charity trustee is discussing a contract or business arrangement with an organisation their family have links to;
- a charity trustee is also an employee of a company that the charity is doing business with; and
- an employee, or potential employee, of the charity is a person connected to a trustee.

The recommended course where there is a conflict is for the trustee to withdraw from the room during the discussion and decision. However, some existing constitutions or protocols might provide that the trustee may speak but not vote on the matter, may not speak on the matter, or must withdraw from the meeting during the discussion. Unless the constitution provides otherwise the withdrawal might affect whether the meeting is quorate. In the view of OSCR, if the trustee in question remains during the deliberation and vote, it is incumbent on the charity trustees to justify the decision to allow them to remain, whatever role—or none—they play. Whichever course is adopted, the minutes should record[54]: 5–83

---

[51] Charities and Trustee Investment (Scotland) Act 2005 s.66(1)(c).

[52] See, generally, the Scottish Law Commission Discussion Paper on Breach of Trust (Scot. Law. Comm. No.123) re acting as "auctor in rem suam" (acting in their own interest) and at paras 4.1–4.6.

[53] See the OSCR, "Guidance and Good Practice for Charity Trustees" (June 2016).

[54] See the OSCR, "Guidance and Good Practice for Charity Trustees" (June 2016).

- which trustee was affected;
- when the conflict was identified and declared;
- what was discussed about it and decided;
- who withdrew;
- if the affected person was not required to withdraw, why that step was considered to be in the best interests of the charity; and
- whichever course was adopted, how the decision was made in the best interests of the charity.

5–84 A practical issue might be thought to arise where a charity trustee is a member of the same group as a class, or potential class, of beneficiary. An example might be the congregational trustees of a church who will have been chosen from the congregation because of a particular affinity. Any close connection with a particular class of beneficiary may require consideration at the point when a decision affecting that class has to be taken and it is probably best for the trustee in question not to participate in the determination. Many church trustee meetings are now held in public and these issues should be worked out in advance in discussions between the chair and the trustee.

5–85 A different sort of issue might arise where a trustee is in possession of information that is confidential to the stakeholder that has appointed them but which is also of great importance to a deliberation of the charity. If such a trustee failed to disclose the information to their co-trustees they might be in breach of fiduciary duty as a trustee; but on disclosing to the other trustees might be in breach of a duty of confidentiality, for example, to an employer. It might even be suggested that such a trustee, even if not participating in deliberations by reason of a conflicts protocol is still under a duty of disclosure to fellow trustees. In such circumstances, and because the trustee is appointed by the body to which they owe the duty of confidentiality, it should be possible to proceed by way of a specific confidentiality agreement between the charity and the sponsoring body.

Role of the chair and office bearers

5–86 The role of the chair is key to good governance (and often to the success of the charity) and although the trustees' authority comes from collective decision-making, the chair plays a critical role in providing leadership to the trustees both in identifying possible projects or appraisals and in assisting the trustees to bring forward possible initiatives. The chair, together particularly with the secretary or administrator trustee should also seek to ensure that each trustee has a meaningful role to play in the operation of the charity, and to monitor the fulfilment by each trustee of their duties and responsibilities for the proper governance of the charity. The chair should also support and where appropriate challenge any chief executive and aim to ensure that the board as a whole works in partnership with any executive staff.

5–87 The chair has an accepted authority in respect of many practical matters. The dates of meetings must be arranged in accordance with their availability. Together with the secretary, the chair will set the principal items for the agenda. At meetings the chair will have charge as to how long individuals may speak for and at what time a meeting should conclude. The chair will decide how to deal with unexpected business between meetings. It is sometimes thought helpful for the chair, secretary and a non office-bearer trustee to form an administrative group to meet between trustee meetings: (a) to confirm what has to be done following the preceding meeting; and (b) to set the items for the next agenda.

However, the chair may also have to be able to play a mediating role in helping all trustees to perform their duties. This can range among cajoling a trustee whose attendances from meetings have become irregular, explaining the existence of a conflict of interest and assisting a trustee to bring forward a valuable proposal. **5–88**

The chair or administrative secretary may also be the public face of the trustees and the charity. The question as to whether the chair or chief executive officer (CEO) fronts the public face of the charity often depends on the nature of the charity and, sometimes on the nature of the message being given. In any meetings with third parties the chair or secretary acts on behalf of the board of trustees and is accountable to them. However, no individual trustee, including the chair, has authority to bind the board unless specifically acting on behalf of the board and with the delegated authority, implied or specifically given, of the board. **5–89**

Employees

Larger charities will have employees to implement the decisions and strategy of the trustees. More complex charities will generally employ a chief executive, finance director and chief operating officer (often referred to as the executive or senior management team). No matter the size of the charity, proper governance and practice dictates that all employees have job descriptions that appropriately reflect what is required of them and terms of reference that set out clearly their role and responsibilities in relationship with the trustees. **5–90**

Executive staff will have significant powers to operate the charity but it should be remembered by the trustees that the exercise of these powers should be to give effect to the strategic decisions of the trustees rather than staff being allowed to take strategic decisions. Here it is crucially important that there be an effective and respectful firm relationship between the chair and the CEO, with the chair understanding that the CEO must take the business decisions and the CEO understanding that policy emanates from the trustees. **5–91**

UNDERSTANDING THE ROLE OF MEMBERS

A charity's legal form will determine who—out of all those closely involved—are indeed the charity trustees and how they interact with any other members. **5–92**

An important distinction is as between charities that have members and those that do not have members separate from the charity trustees themselves. Guarantee companies and SCIOs will have members[55] (who may also be the trustees). **5–93**

[55] See Ch.3.

5–94 Unincorporated associations will inevitably have members because these are essentially members' organisations, that is, they consist of a group of individuals who wish to act together with some common charitable purpose. In contrast, charitable trusts have no legal requirement for a separate category of "members" and operate simply through trustees; although there may well be members of an organisation who feel that they have a direct interest in the decisions of the trustees. An example is a church congregation.

5–95 The rights that members may have will vary from charity to charity, both in terms of law and under the terms of the particular constitution of individual charities. To take the church congregation example, the meeting of the trustees may be open to all members of the congregation, or indeed the public, and there may be a stated annual meeting at which all views may be expressed.

5–96 Members, acting as a group, may be able to exercise a number of important rights in relation to a charity. These can include rights to alter the charity's constitution, appoint and remove its charity trustees and wind the charity up and distribute its surplus assets for similar charitable purposes, and in some cases to approve the annual accounts and to appoint the auditors or independent financial examiners.

5–97 The rights of members derive from the legal form the charity takes so, for example, the members of a charitable company are granted these rights under the Companies Acts. The members of other charitable entities may have rights as a consequence of the provisions in the charity's constitution (for example, a SCIO) and the provisions of the 2005 Act.

5–98 Whilst the relationship between trustees and members will vary from charity to charity, there are certain models that are encountered more often than others. Outwith the provisions of these models, it is important to be aware that groups constituting "friends", "supporters"[56] (which may be informal or have their own constitution), an "advisory committee" or an "executive committee" have no binding power whatsoever over the actions of the trustees or board who, alone, are directly responsible in law for the operation of the charity.

The single-tier structure

5–99 This structure applies to the charitable trust (that has no members) and the guarantee company (where its trustees are also its only members) and the single-tier SCIO (where its trustees are its only members too). The key feature of this structure is that the members are the same people as the trustees. A consequence of this is that, subject to the 2005 Act and the provisions of any trust deed, it gives the trustees an absolute discretion to control the charity with no question of involving any third parties in the governance arrangements.

5–100 The single structure most closely reflects the fact that the trustees are responsible for managing the charity's operations and may be held liable if they fail to do so properly.

[56] See para.5–105 below.

However, the single structure may not work for a charity that is likely to need members in order to ensure that it can operate effectively and retain support. **5–101**

The two-tier structure

The key feature of the two-tier structure is that, in addition to the trustees, there is a group, or sometimes groups, of members capable of exercising some oversight and control over the activities of the trustees. **5–102**

An advantage is that it gives members a say in the operation of the charity and allows them, for example, to elect some or all of the trustees, approve the accounts and make constitutional changes. The members provide a democratic element to operating a charity and may be seen as the custodians of a particular ethos or approach inherent in the way the charity operates. **5–103**

A potential disadvantage of the two-tier structure is that it may impede the effective operation of a charity. The members may not appreciate or understand the operational circumstances to which the charity trustees are required to respond. Operating a two-tier membership structure may bring additional costs in terms of management time and legal requirements in meeting obligations of members and member expectations. It is worthwhile bearing in mind that the current or future operation of a charity may be affected because of healthy debate among members or between the body of members and the body of trustees. **5–104**

Supporters' charity

An alternative to the one- or two-tier models, which gives control of a charity to its trustees whilst allowing others (supporters) to be involved, may be achieved by the constitution providing for "supporters" or "friends" (who may or may not have their own constitution) who will not having voting rights. Such supporters may be consulted with regard to strategic issues and there may be meetings of supporters to inform them of the charity's operation and strategy. Unless specifically granted in the constitution, such supporters have no legal right to control any aspect of the charity's governance. Examples are often found in arts and cultural organisations. **5–105**

Stakeholder members

Certain charities have private or public funding partners, sometimes known as or referred to as stakeholders, who hold some type of position as members. Charities with stakeholder members may face particular governance issues because these third parties, often local authorities or other charitable bodies, may have a particular interest, often financial, in the work of the charity. **5–106**

A stakeholder member will often have the right to appoint an individual (usually referred to as an "authorised representative") to act on its behalf, sometimes as a full trustee. The charity's constitution must provide expressly for this and set out the mechanism by which such individuals are appointed and removed. Otherwise, **5–107** the stakeholder has no power to participate with the trustees in the operation of the charity. A standard provision allows the charity to agree to work in partnership with another body and accept as a charity trustee any individual which the partner body may nominate, in accordance with the terms of any partnership agreement or memorandum of understanding. Again it is standard to provide that such a nominee must subscribe to the ethos of the organisation. The way in which that representative and the trustees work together should be agreed in the partnership agreement or memorandum of understanding. For example, the representative may be allowed a power of veto over certain types of decision, or may be allowed to vote only on certain matters.

5–108 Having a stakeholder as a member of a charity requires careful management, especially as regards the potential for a conflict of interest between the charity and the interests of the stakeholder.[57]

Federal, branch and umbrella arrangements

5–109 Charities are sometimes set up as part of a federation of charities, generally operating in different localities. The aim is usually to carry out the work of the charity in particular geographical areas but under the influence of a national headquarters charity that may provide support and assistance to the local charity (perhaps in the form of a standard constitution, assistance with governance arrangements, etc.). The degree of affiliation between the local and the national bodies will vary from case to case. From the point of view of good governance, it is essential that the relationship between the two entities is clearly established. In practice, this will mean ensuring that the constitution of the local charity expresses with clarity the nature and degree of control that the national charity can exercise over the local.

5–110 A branch structure is different. There is no legal definition of a "branch" for this purpose. The key point is that the activities carried out locally are the activities of the national charity, but are carried out by individuals on the charity's behalf usually on the basis of delegated authority. Typically, a local subcommittee of the board of trustees of the main charity will have delegated authority to carry out all of the charity's activities in a particular area. Often the delegation will impose a number of restrictions on their ability to operate, including, for example, their ability to spend the charity's funds or to incur significant liabilities.

5–111 The principal governance issue that can arise is whether the branch is to be a separate charity from the national charity or will operate as a committee of the national charity. The relationship between a parent charity and its branches must be carefully expressed in the constitution of the national charity. If there is to be the possibility of establishing separate branch charities that must be specified. Whether there may be separate branch charities or individuals are to operate as a subcommittee, there must be clear written acceptance by the local individuals of the areas of responsibility accepted, any parameters, and lines of management.

[57] See paras 5–77 to 5–84 above.

There are also "umbrella" charities that have other charities as its members that share a common area of operation. **5–112**

ADMINISTRATION

Administration compliance

One of the responsibilities of each charity trustee is to ensure the proper administration of their charity. Charity trustees must ensure that the charity complies with the requirements imposed by relevant legislation. Such legislation includes health and safety law regulations, company law (in the case of charitable companies), data protection law and employment law if employing staff. **5–113**

References to charitable status

The way in which charities in Scotland refer to their charitable status is governed by: **5–114**

- the 2005 Act;
- the Charities References in Documents (Scotland) Regulations 2007 (the 2007 Regulations);
- the Charities References in Documents (Scotland) Amendment Regulations 2008 (the Amendment Regulations); and
- the Scottish Charitable Incorporated Organisations Regulations 2011 reg.9.

The 2005 Act and the 2007 Regulations introduced new requirements for charities entered in the Scottish Charity Register. The 2007 Regulations apply to all charities entered in the Scottish Charity Register apart from SCIOs, including those charities that are also registered as charities in another country or territory. **5–115**

Information that must be included on documents

All charities entered in the Register must clearly state the following information on all relevant documents (hard copy and electronic) issued or signed on behalf of the charity: **5–116**

- the charity's name as entered in the Register;
- any other name by which the charity is commonly known; and
- the charity's Scottish charity number allocated to it at the time of registration.

Additionally, a charity whose name does not contain the word "charity" or "charitable" must also state on documents the fact that it is a charity. This can be done in a number of ways, and one of the following terms may be used: **5–117**

- charity;

- charitable body;
- registered charity; and
- charity registered in Scotland.

5–118 Charities entered in the Register that are established under the law of Scotland, or which are managed or controlled wholly or mainly from Scotland, are also permitted to use one of the following descriptions:

- Scottish charity; and
- registered Scottish charity.

5–119 Any organisation that describes itself as a charity by using one of these terms or in any other way without being entered in the Register—unless it is entered to refer to itself as a charity in another country and meets the requirements outlined in s.14 of the 2005 Act—will be considered to misrepresent itself as a charity. OSCR may issue a direction to such a body under s.31(5) of the 2005 Act to stop it from representing itself as a charity.[58] It is an offence to breach such a direction.

5–120 The 2007 Regulations outline the information required to be included on the specified documents, but they do not govern where such information should be placed. Good practice, however, would dictate that the information should be placed in a prominent position, for example, on the first page of a statement of account or at the foot of the charity's letter headed notepaper or at an appropriate place in websites and emails.

5–121 The 2007 Regulations affect a number of specified documents which are "issued or signed on behalf of the charity". As the primary aim of the 2007 Regulations is to provide clarity to the general public regarding whether or not a body has charitable status, OSCR's view is that the 2007 Regulations apply only to external communications and documents intended for circulation outwith the charity.[59] If emails are used as a principal means of communication, the information should be given on those too.

5–122 The following documents must, not more than six months after the date of the charity's entry in the Scottish Charity Register, incorporate the information set out in para.5–117 above. Guarantee companies must also state the information required by the Companies (Registrar, Languages and Trading Disclosures) Regulations 2006.

- business letters and emails;
- advertisements, notices and official publications;
- any document that solicits money or other property for the benefit of the charity;
- promissory notes, endorsements and orders for money or goods;
- bills rendered;
- invoices, receipts and letters of credit;

[58] Any such direction may be to the charity itself or the person representing the body as a charity.
[59] Scottish Law Commission, *Report on Trust Law* (Scot. Law Comm. No.239), paras 13.2–13.29.

- statements of account prepared in accordance with regs 8, 9 or 14 of the Charities Accounts (Scotland) Regulations 2006[60];
- educational or campaign documentation;
- conveyances that provide for the creation, transfer, variation or extinction of an interest in land;
- contractual documentation; and
- bills of exchange (except cheques).

Contracts

When a charity is entering into contracts it must follow the requirements to publicise the fact that it is a charity.[61] In the case of unincorporated charities, the charity trustees should make clear to any third party that they are contracting only as trustees to prevent personal liability.[62] **5–123**

Publicly available documents

A charity is required to make certain documents available to the public. **5–124**

If requested, a charity must provide a copy of its governing document and a copy of its latest accounts.[63] But, in individual circumstances, charity trustees ought to consider whether a beneficiary is entitled to seek any additional information.[64] **5–125**

A charity is able to charge a fee for making these documents available, as long as the fee does not exceed the cost of supplying the copies (or any fee Scottish Ministers may decide upon).[65] The cost of supply does not include the cost of preparing accounts, as there is a statutory requirement for the charity to maintain records, prepare accounts and supply these to OSCR and the public. **5–126**

Insurance

It is a legal requirement for all charities that certain insurances are obtained in particular circumstances. The most common insurances required by charities are public liability insurance and employer's liability insurance. **5–127**

Trustee indemnity insurance is often obtained. Trustees are permitted to obtain trustee indemnity insurance although there is a degree of personal benefit to them. Charities may purchase trustee indemnity insurance in order to protect all **5–128**

---

60 Charities Accounts (Scotland) Regulations 2006 (SI 2006/218).

61 See the Charities References in Documents (Scotland) Regulations 2007 (SSI 2007/203) and the Charities References in Documents (Scotland) Amendment Regulations 2008 (SSI 2008/59).

62 Scottish Law Commission, *Report on Trust Law* (Scot. Law Comm. No.239), paras 13.2–13.29.

63 Charities and Trustee Investment (Scotland) Act 2005 s.23.

64 See *Schmidt v Rosewood* [2003] 2 A.C. 709.

65 Charities and Trustee Investment (Scotland) Act 2005 s.23(2).

and not just some of the charity trustees.[66] However, the limitation of liability for those engaged in guarantee companies or SCIOs may reduce the amount of cover required.

Data protection

5–129 Where a charity holds and processes information about individuals, including employees or suppliers, they are legally obliged to protect that information. Under the Data Protection Act a charity must:

- only collect information that is needed for a specific purpose;
- keep the information secure;
- ensure the information is relevant and up to date;
- only hold as much information as needed and only for so long as it is required;
- allow the subject of the information to see it on request;
- if it handles personal information, register with the Information Commissioners Office (ICO) as a data controller; and
- as notification is a statutory requirement every organisation who processes personal must notify the ICO unless they are exempt. Failure to notify is a criminal offence.

5–130 Where a charity handles personal information it may need to register with the ICO.[67] Notification is a statutory requirement and every organisation that processes personal information must notify the ICO unless they are exempt. Failure to notify is a criminal offence.[68]

Freedom of Information Act

5–131 Charities themselves are not generally subject to the Freedom of Information Act and therefore do not normally have to respond to a request for information under the Act. However, freedom of information (FOI) is a valuable resource for charities.[69] It provides a right to see the information held by Scottish public authorities. Organisations that receive funding from Scottish public authorities are not covered by the law.[70]

---

[66] Public Services Reform (Scotland) Act 2010 s.127.

[67] *https://ico.org.uk/* [Accessed 24 May 2016].

[68] Data Protection Act 1998.

[69] FOI has been used to access information on a huge range of issues, from the availability of services for disabled people, to the rationale behind the funding decisions made by central or local government. For more information see the website of the Scottish Information Commissioner (*http://www.itspublicknowledge.info/home/ScottishInformationCommissioner.aspx* [Accessed 25 May 2016]).

[70] While voluntary organisations are not covered by FOI, they will have legal responsibilities under the Data Protection Act if they hold personal data (*http://www.scvo.org.uk/running-your-organisation/legislation-regulation/data-protection/* [Accessed 25 May 2016]).

Health and safety

It is the responsibility of the charity trustees to ensure the health and safety of employees, volunteers and visitors to the charity's premises.[71] Health and safety policies should be a paramount requirement. Given the way that many charities now operate, particular information may be required for lone workers and home workers.[72] **5–132**

Confidentiality

From time to time trustees will be involved in activities either at board meetings or on behalf of the board that call for tact, discretion and above all confidentiality. Some of the more obvious examples of this include staff and employment issues or the appointment of new members of staff. The proceedings of all such meetings are confidential to those taking part. Those parts of trustee meetings at which such matters are discussed should also be treated as confidential.[73] Breaches of such confidentiality cause distress to the individuals concerned. Any serious breach should be dealt by the board with a view to considering whether the individual concerned should be asked to resign or be removed (if such a power exists). It will generally be appropriate to adopt a confidentiality policy.[74] **5–133**

Equality

The Equality Act 2010 provides protection from unlawful discrimination in relation to age, disability, gender reassignment, marriage and civil partnership, pregnancy and maternity, race, religion or belief, sex and sexual orientation. That Act makes it unlawful to discriminate against anyone on the basis of any of these "protected characteristics" in a wide range of areas, including employment and the provision of services.[75] **5–134**

There are a number of exceptions that may be relevant to charities. **5–135**

- Charities are allowed to restrict benefits to people with a particular "protected characteristic" even though this may exclude people with other protected characteristics if certain conditions are met.[76]
- Men or women only fundraising, where participation in activities to support or promote charities can be restricted to one sex only.

---

[71] See the Health & Safety at Work Act 1974, as amended.

[72] For more information and support see the Health and Safety Executive website (*http://www.hse.gov.uk//index.htm* [Accessed 25 May 2016]) where you can find an example risk assessment and health and safety policy, information for lone workers and home workers, and a charity shop risk assessment tool. Healthy Working Lives (*http://www.healthyworkinglives.com/* [Accessed 25 May 2016]) provides free health and safety advice for organisations in Scotland, including free workplace visits and a free helpline 0800 019 2211.

[73] See para.5–48 above.

[74] See para.5–30 above.

[75] See para.1–123 and following.

[76] See the Charity Commission, *Equality Act: Guidance for Charities* (February 2013).

- Admission to education, where schools and further and higher education institutions are allowed to admit students based on gender where the school or institution is single sex.

5–136 Charities that employ people, that have volunteers and that provide services, goods or facilities should consider explaining in an equality and diversity policy how they will make sure that they will treat people fairly and arrange any desirable training. Detailed guidance on the application of the Equality Act and exceptions can be found on the following websites:

- OSCR: Interim guidance on charities and equality.
- Charity Commission (*http://www.charitycommission.gov.uk*).
- Equality and Equality and Human Rights Commission (*http://www.equalityhumanrights.com*).
- Governance Equalities Office (*http://www.gov.uk/government/organisations/government-equalities-office*).

Bribery

5–137 Bribery is just as important a concern for charities operating in the UK as it is for those that have operations in other jurisdictions.

5–138 It is an offence to:

- offer, promise or give a bribe;
- request, agree to receive or accept a bribe;
- bribe a foreign official; or
- in the case of a company or other incorporated body, or a partnership carrying on business (principally in the UK), fail to prevent bribery (a corporate offence).[77]

5–139 An incorporated charity (e.g. a company limited by guarantee, SCIO and certain other legal forms) can be liable if a trustee or senior employee commits any of these offences, which can be attributed to the charity itself. The trustee or employee would also be personally liable, whether the charity is incorporated or unincorporated. An incorporated charity can also be liable for failing to prevent bribery committed by any of its trustees, employees or agents acting on its behalf (the corporate offence). However, the charity will have a full defence if it can show that it has adequate procedures in place to prevent bribery. These procedures should be proportionate to the risk of bribery, but are likely to include risk assessments, employee and trustee training and a bribery policy. It is mandatory for an incorporated charity to have a bribery policy (often included within a combined anti-bribery policy and anti-fraud policy) and it is good practice for an unincorporated charity to have a bribery policy.

[77] Bribery Act 2010 ss.1–7.

Risk management

Risk assessment is a crucial aspect of governance for charity trustees. Considering risks (including reputational risk) should form part of the annual cycle of trustee meetings. This should embrace the risk of an event occurring, the anticipated damage and any agreed approach to limitation of any damage. It is usually desirable for larger charities to operate with a subcommittee established to assess and audit risks. **5–140**

The risks that a charity faces depend very much on the size, nature and complexity of the activities it undertakes and also on its finances. By managing risk effectively, trustees can help ensure significant risks are known and monitored, enabling trustees to make informed decisions and take timely action. Risk management should direct a charity's strategy enabling a charity's aims to be more successfully achieved. **5–141**

If OSCR becomes involved in investigating a charity, one of its first questions is whether the charity has a risk management process in place. **5–142**

Complaints

This is dealt with in Ch.2, which look at the handling of complaints from the standpoint both of OSCR and charities. All charities should have a complaints policy. **5–143**

OSCR requirements

Charity trustees are required to ensure that their charity complies with any direction, requirement, notice or duty imposed on it by the Act.[78] Not to do so (for example, by not sending annual accounts or OSCR's annual return) is a breach of charity trustee duty, may result in a finding of misconduct and the removal of trustees.[79] **5–144**

OSCR is authorised to make inquiries, generally or for a particular purpose, of a charity, a body controlling a charity, a body representing a charity or a person representing such a body.[80] Compliance with this requirement is a statutory duty. **5–145**

Charity trustees are responsible for ensuring that the details on the Scottish Charity Register remain accurate and the charity must notify OSCR of changes to the details on the Register or to the constitution of a charity.[81] **5–146**

---

[78] Charities and Trustee Investment (Scotland) Act 2005 s.66(2).

[79] Charities and Trustee Investment (Scotland) Act 2005 s.66(4) and 66(5).

[80] Charities and Trustee Investment (Scotland) Act 2005 s.28; and see Ch.2.

[81] Charities and Trustee Investment (Scotland) Act 2005 s.17.

Sustainability

5–147 The charity trustees as a body have a collective general duty of care for the charity and the charitable assets. Charity trustees are expected to act together to realise the values and purposes of the charity and to comply with legislative and regulatory requirements. This means that there is also a duty to keep in view the sustainability of the charity. In other words, a stage might be reached when the costs of running the charity outweigh the benefits of operation: for example, the costs of trying to find beneficiaries or projects as against the sums expended on those projects. The assets of the charity are dedicated to charitable purposes, not to the purpose of administration. Trustees should always keep in mind the performance of the charity as against its purposes.

CHAPTER 6

CHARITY FINANCE

Victoria JW Simpson

INTRODUCTION

Charitable giving is an area of the law that is subject to constant review and change. The UK Government announced in the 2014 Budget that it will continue to promote charitable giving by encouraging more donors to use gift aid on eligible donations and by making it easier to donate online or by text. They will also seek to encourage more small charities to claim all the tax reliefs that they are entitled to receive. We will now consider some of the tax advantages and other practicalities that charities should be aware of in relation to charitable giving. 6–01

MAKING USE OF GIFT AID

Donations by individuals, partnerships and limited liability partnerships (LLPs)[1]

The gift aid scheme benefits both the donor and the charity concerned.[2] For our purposes, the tax treatment of cash donations made by an individual, partnership or LLP in the hands of a charity remain the same.[3] Where the cash donation is made to a charity under gift aid, the recipient charity can reclaim basic rate tax (at 20 per cent) from HMRC on the amount of the donation. It makes no difference if the donor is treated as being a basic rate or a higher rate tax payer at the time of the donation, because the amount the charity can reclaim will remain unchanged. 6–02

A gift aided payment therefore means that for every £1 donated, a charity can reclaim 25p (£1 x 20/80), making the actual value of the gift to the charity £1.25. It doesn't matter how big or small the donation is, because the gift aid provisions can apply to a donation of any amount. 6–03

---

[1] See the Income Tax Act 2007 ss.413–430.

[2] See HMRC's "Guidance Notes for Charities", Ch.3 on "Gift Aid", updated on 27 April 2016 for guidance.

[3] Donations from a partnership or LLP are eligible for gift aid in exactly the same way as an individual gift aid donation. The donation will be treated as being made by each of the partners or LLP members, split equally between them, unless the partners/LLP members agree that it should be split otherwise. Up to 5 April 2016, the donation could be made on the same declaration form. From 6 April 2016, each partner must complete their own gift aid declaration providing their full name and address and confirming the amount of their share of the donation.

6–04 For the donation to qualify under the gift aid provisions, the donor must be a UK taxpayer. The charity can make the tax reclaim because the donor is treated as having made the donation net of basic rate tax. Charities can encourage individual donors to make a donation under gift aid by explaining that they will receive tax relief at the donor's highest marginal rate of tax (whether in the form of income tax or capital gains tax relief). The fact that a charity can reclaim the tax paid on the donation also means that the donor can give less if they wish, knowing what the value of the final donation will be. This can act as a real incentive to make a charitable donation.

6–05 The donor must have paid or will pay an amount of income tax and/or capital gains tax in the same tax year as their donation (i.e. between 6 April–5 April) that will be equal to the amount of basic rate tax that the charity will seek to reclaim under gift aid. If insufficient tax has been paid, the donor's personal allowances can be restricted accordingly, failing which if there is still a shortfall the donor will be liable to pay the difference. The charity is not affected by this.

6–06 The donor should inform the charity that they are a UK taxpayer and that they would like gift aid to apply on their donation. The charity can then ask the donor to complete a gift aid declaration form. The gift aid declaration form can also be included on collection envelopes, etc. For convenience, the declaration is usually made at the same time as the gift, although it can be made up to four years afterwards.

6–07 This declaration can be made in writing, orally either in person or over the telephone, by email, fax, over the internet or by text message. An electronic declaration on the website of a charity is treated as being a written declaration. If it is made orally, and the charity doesn't keep a voice recording of oral declarations, the charity must send the donor a written confirmation of their declaration containing the information set out in para.6–09. An oral declaration is not effective until this written confirmation is sent out stating the date they made their oral declaration. The donor must also be advised that they can cancel their gift aid declaration in writing within 30 days of the date of the charity's letter.

6–08 It is important that each charity keeps proper records for audit purposes of all its gift aid declarations linked to the individual donations for HMRC review if required.[4] Written declarations can be kept in paper form, or scanned in, so the originals can be destroyed. For oral declarations this will include a record of the number of written confirmations issued and any cancellations received. HMRC may check to see whether the gift aid requirements set out in para.6–09 are correctly met on all or a sample of the declarations, that a valid gift aid declaration is held for each gift aid claim made and that any donor benefits given are within the accepted donor benefit limits as set out in paras 6–18—6–23. Inadequate records can invalidate a gift aid declaration meaning the charity has to repay all tax reclaimed under that declaration to HMRC, with interest (and possiby penalties).

[4] See HMRC, "Guidance Note for Charities" on "Gift Aid", paras 3.27–3.30 for details of the records to be kept, how they can be stored and the time limits for keeping records (updated on 27 April 2016).

HMRC have recently updated their style gift aid declaration forms and guidance following the introduction of Charities Online filing.[5] These model styles cover gift aid declarations for one off donations to a named charity, enduring declarations to one or more charities covering all past, present and future donations and also sponsored events. 6–09

A gift aid declaration must contain at least the following information;

- the name of the applicable charity or charities (if there is more than one, the declaration should show how the donation is divided);
- the donor's full name, including as a minimum their first initial and their full surname;
- the donor's full postal address;
- the gift or gifts to be covered by the declaration;
- confirmation that the donor wishes gift aid to apply to the donation, e.g. by stating "please treat the enclosed gift as a gift aid donation" and by ticking a box;
- a clear statement that the donor will pay an equivalent amount of tax (income tax or capital gains tax) to the amount being reclaimed by the charity for the year of the donation (the gift aid declaration will be invalid without this statement, with the result that the charity may need to repay tax to HMRC, so this is absolutely essential). It is easier to include this statement on the gift aid declaration form, although it can also be done separately. It should be explained that other taxes, such as council tax or VAT do not apply for these purposes; and
- the charity can also include any other additional information it requires, e.g. bank mandate details, data protection disclaimers, the period the declaration will apply from such as "all the donations I make from this date until further notice", or "all the donations I have made for the four years prior to this tax year", etc.

Although the HMRC styles provide guidance only and are not enforceable, it is recommended that all charities ensure that their own gift aid declaration forms comply by 6 April 2016 to prevent any later difficulties when the charity seeks to reclaim the tax. Stocks of material showing the old gift aid declaration wording, such as on collection envelopes that are printed or ordered before 21 October 2015 can still be used after 6 April 2016 if required, but evidence showing the date the printing order was made should be kept for audit purposes. 6–10

The declaration doesn't have to be signed or even dated, unless it relates to a one off donation. However, the charity may prefer to ask donors to sign to emphasise the commitment they are making. Dating the declaration is helpful to show the period that gift aid will apply. Spouses, civil partners or individuals living together can make a joint gift aid declaration on the same form for convenience, provided that they each meet the qualifying criteria for gift aid. 6–11

---

[5] See *http://www.hmrc.gov.uk/charities/new-model-declarations.htm* and *http://www.hmrc.gov.uk/news/new-guide-giftaid.htm* [Accessed 26 May 2016]. This guidance was updated on 7 March 2016.

6–12 An enduring gift aid declaration can be cancelled at any time, in whatever form suits the donor. It is easier for audit purposes however to have this in writing, and a record should be kept of the cancellation date. The cancellation will not affect any gift aid donations that have already been claimed, only future donations.

6–13 Gift aid only applies to monetary donations. The donation can be made in the form of cash, by cheque, direct debit, standing or postal order, using a credit card or debit card payment, etc. It cannot be subject to any repayment conditions in order to qualify as a gift aid payment, it must be a voluntary donation. A charity can only provide benefits in return for the donation up to the permitted donor benefit limits that are discussed in paras 6–18 to 6–23. In addition it cannot be conditional upon the charity acquiring property from the donor or anyone associated with them.

THE TAX DEFINITION OF A CHARITY

6–14 The Finance Act 2010 introduced a new definition of a charity for tax purposes. Gift aid can now apply to any UK, EU, Norwegian or Icelandic charity that is registered as a charity in its own country.[6] To qualify under the tax definition these bodies must be established for charitable purposes only, i.e. it meets the English and Welsh definition of a charity or community amateur sports club (CASC) as set out in the Charities Act 2011. It must meet the charity registration conditions of the country in question and be registered with the appropriate charity regulator for their country. In addition, all persons having control and management responsibilities within the charity itself must be what are referred to as "fit and proper persons", and meet the fit and proper person test. It is necessary for all these parts of the test to be satisfied in order to qualify for UK gift aid or other tax reliefs.[7]

6–15 Please see the HMRC website for further details about the fit and proper persons test and the procedures that will apply.[8] It should be noted that there is no definition of a "fit and proper person". The onus is on the charity concerned to satisfy itself that all those within a managerial role who control and manage the administration of the charity are suitably appointed to hold this role, particularly if they are in a position where they are able to exert control over the charity's finances. The onus is on the charity to carry out whatever checks it considers necessary for this purpose and to satisfy themselves. As a matter of good practice,

---

[6] These changes were made to reflect the judgments of the European Court of Justice in *Centro di Musicologia Walter Stauffer v Finanzamt Munchen fur Korperschaften* (ECJ C386/04) delivered on 14 September 2006 and *Hein Persche v Finanzamt Ludenscheid* (ECJ C318/07) delivered on 27 January 2009. Please also see the changes made in the Finance Act 2010 s.30 and Sch.6; Taxes (Definition of Charity) (Relevant Territories) Regulations 2010 (SI 2010/1904); Finance Act 2010, Schedule 6, Part 1 (Further Consequential and Incidental Provision etc.) Order 2012 (SI 2012/735); and Finance Act 2010, Schedule 6, Part 2 (Commencement) Order 2012 (SI 2012/736). Please also see the Income Tax Act 2007 s.989.

[7] From 1 April 2012 this tax definition was extended to include all forms of tax relief applicable to charities.

[8] Please see *http://www.hmrc.gov.uk/charities/guidance-notes/chapter2/fp-persons-test.htm* [Accessed 26 May 2016].

the charity should ask all those who fall within this category to complete a fit and proper persons declaration form to be retained as part of the charity's records.

This means that to register as a charity in Scotland, not only is it necessary to satisfy the requirements of the Office of the Scottish Charity Regulator (OSCR), but in order to obtain a tax reference number for use in all repayment claims, it is also necessary to demonstrate to HMRC that the charity meets the requirements of the English and Welsh charities test as set out in the Charities Act 2011 in terms of both its charitable purposes and the public benefit test. It must also satisfy the requirements of the fit and proper persons test. **6–16**

GIFT AID DONATIONS BY COMPANIES

Companies can also make a charitable donation under gift aid. Because, however, companies pay corporation tax rather than income tax, they are not treated as having made a "net" donation in the same way as an individual, the payment is made gross. So, a charity cannot claim a tax repayment on a corporate cash donation. The amount donated therefore remains unchanged in the charity's hands. Charities can, however, encourage companies to make a charitable donation by explaining that the company will benefit by being entitled to deduct the full amount of the donation from its total profits for that accounting period before calculating the corporation tax payable. The company will pay less corporation tax as a result. It is important that the charity keeps a proper record of all company donations to be included in the tax return and accounts. **6–17**

THE RELEVANT VALUE TEST

It is only to be expected that a charity may wish to thank the donor for their donation. It is perfectly acceptable for the charity to write to the donor to express their thanks and to send them further information about the charity, a newsletter, or to provide them with a small gift or other acknowledgement, e.g. a name plaque. These are not regarded as being a benefit. Be careful with this. Other types of gift, e.g. free tickets can have a monetary value which counts as a benefit for these purposes.[9] **6–18**

HMRC recognise the following permitted donor benefit limits, known as the relevant value test. Provided that the benefit given to the donor by the charity falls within these limits, the gift can still qualify as a gift aid donation. These limits cannot be exceeded. **6–19**

These rules will also apply to anyone connected with the donor, including their spouse, partner, child, parent or grandparent or a company controlled by the individual or by a connected person. **6–20**

---

[9] See HMRC's updated "Guidance Note for Charities", updated on 27 April 2016 on "Gift Aid", paras 3.20–3.23 for examples.

6–21 An unrestricted right of admission to premises owned by the charity for at least a year in return for a donation is not treated as being a benefit for these purposes in certain circumstances (this is discussed in more detail in paras 6–38—6–42).

6–22 In addition, if the donor makes more than one donation to the same charity in the same tax year, the total value of the benefits received by the donor cannot exceed £2,500 for donations made on or after 6 April 2011 (this is known as the aggregate value test). If the value of the benefit received under either the relevant value test or the aggregate value test are exceeded, the gift aid is lost, unless the split payment provisions can apply.[10]

6–23 The current permitted donor limits are as follows:

Donation amount	Maximum value of benefit or gift provided by the charity (per donation)
Up to £100	25% of the donation
£101 to £1,000	£25 maximum
Over £1,000	5% of the value of the donation (up to a maximum of £2,500 in one year (if made on or after 6 April 2011))

GIFTING SHARES, LAND AND PROPERTY

6–24 A charity can also accept gifts of shares, land and property owned by an individual, partnership, LLP or a company, and this has now been extended to include grants of leases to charity.[11] The value of the gift in the charity's hands will be the actual asset or market value at the transfer date. The charity is unable to make any tax reclaim on this value. Once again, charities can encourage such donations by making the donor aware that in the case of an individual, such a disposal should qualify for tax relief in the form of income tax relief or as an exemption from capital gains tax. Companies can claim a corporation tax deduction.

6–25 It is important that the charity advises the donor to seek their own advice on how to obtain and maximise the tax relief. There should be nothing to suggest that the charity is in any way offering financial advice. In addition, charities should not feel obliged to cover any incidental costs that may be incurred by the donor in

[10] See HMRC's "Guidance Note for Charities", updated on 27 April 2016 on "Gift Aid", para.3.25 on split payments for examples. Under the split payment provisions, the donor can divide their payments into two parts, one part to cover the cost of the benefit they receive, the second part to be treated as being the gift for gift aid purposes. The cost of benefit is deducted from the donor's payment. Only the remaining payment is treated as being the donor's gift for gift aid purposes provided that the benefit can be bought separately and the donor knows the value of the benefit at the time they make the donation.

[11] See the Income Tax Act 2007 s.433(4).

making the gift, such as stockbrokers fees or registration dues, as these can be taken into account by the donor when calculating their own tax relief.

In the case of shares, a charity may be asked whether they would prefer to receive the shares directly, or the cash proceeds of the shares if the donor decides to sell them first. This is entirely a matter of choice for the charity, based upon whatever is most convenient. If the donor decides to sell them first for their own tax reasons, they may request the charity concerned to agree to the arrangement in writing in advance of the sale including their acceptance of the gift under the gift aid provisions for HMRC purposes. It is perfectly acceptable for the charity to do this. **6–26**

As with any donation of land or property, it is for the charity concerned to consider the practical implications of this and to carry out their own due diligence or other checks if required before deciding whether or not to accept the gift. The charity must also consider whether any conditions attached to the gift are acceptable. For example, an outright gift of a house with a condition that the donor be permitted to reside there for the rest of their life, or be entitled to rental income for the rest of their life might put an unacceptable burden on the charity. **6–27**

TAINTED DONATIONS

Charities should be alert to the so called "tainted donation" provisions, which can apply to a donation of any amount. These rules will apply when a donor has entered into an "arrangement" to obtain a financial advantage from the charity for themselves or for some other person involved in the arrangement, in return for their donation. **6–28**

If the donation is deemed to be a tainted donation, then any tax relief which the donor has claimed on the amount of the donation under the gift aid provisions will be lost.[12] Charities can in these circumstances, however, continue to reclaim the basic rate tax due on the donation from HMRC (provided that it was otherwise eligible under the gift aid rules). This means that an income tax charge will arise, equal to the amount of the tax repayment. The liability for this tax charge would normally fall on the donor, any person connected to the donor or any other person who benefits from the arrangement. It would not fall on the charity, unless it can be shown that the charity was either a party to or was fully aware of the arrangements put in place to obtain a financial advantage. **6–29**

To determine whether the tainted donation provisions apply, the legislation considers the "purpose" of the donation and applies a purpose test. This test considers the circumstances in which the donation is made and its effect. In order for a donation to be treated as being a tainted donation, three conditions must each apply as follows[13]: **6–30**

[12] See the Income Tax Act 2007 ss.809ZH–809ZR for further information. This replaces the previous "substantial donors" rules (which applied to donations of £25,000 or more in one year or to a donation of £150,000 over a six year period).

[13] See HMRC guidance notes on charitable giving Annex 8 dealing with tainted charity donations for further information.

(1) **Condition A:** the donor makes a donation to charity and enters into an arrangement with the charity or with another linked person that is connected to the donation. For these purposes, an arrangement will include any scheme, arrangement or understanding of any kind, whether formal or informal that can involve one or more transactions.[14] Making a donation is not in itself an arrangement. There must be a reasonable assumption that the donation and the terms of the arrangement are dependent upon each other.

(2) **Condition B:** Either the main purpose, or one of the main purposes of the arrangement is for the donor (or a connected person) to receive a financial advantage in return for the donation, whether directly or indirectly from the charity. "Financial advantage" isn't defined in the legislation but can be taken to mean that the effect of the arrangement is to give the donor or connected person a greater benefit than might reasonably be expected from an arm's length transaction, while the charity receives the lesser benefit.

(3) **Condition C:** the donation is not made by a trading company that is wholly owned by the charity (and makes payments under gift aid to the charity) nor by a relevant housing provider (that would normally donate to linked charities within a particular housing group).

THE CULTURAL GIFTS SCHEME AND ACCEPTANCE IN LIEU SCHEME

6–31 A charity can also benefit from pre-eminent works of art and objects of historical, architectural, scientific or scenic interest that have been donated to the nation during a donor's lifetime under the cultural gifts scheme. The government minister concerned can then loan or give the objects to appropriate institutions such as a museum or charity for safe keeping and subject to allowing the public access. Gifts made under the cultural gifts scheme are exempt from inheritance tax (IHT) and capital gains tax and the donor will also receive tax relief on their UK tax liability.

6–32 Similarly, charities can also benefit from acceptance in lieu schemes[15] for IHT purposes, where certain assets are acceptable to the Secretary of State in satisfaction of an IHT liability. These include: pre-eminent works of art, prints, pictures, books, manuscripts and scientific or other objects which the Secretary of State agrees are pre-eminent for their national, scientific, historic or artistic interest, any land (if accepted and it can be used for the public benefit) and certain objects that are or have been kept within a particular building and where the Secretary of State considers it desirable for these objects to remain associated with the building. Once again these items can be either donated or loaned by the Government to a charity.

---

[14] See Income Tax Act 2007 s.809R(1) and the Corporation Tax Act 2010 s.99(1)(d).

[15] See the Arts Council (England) guidance note on the acceptance in lieu scheme the FOI published on 29 September 2015 for further information on the scheme.

PROCEEDS OF GOODS SOLD BY A CHARITY ON A DONOR'S BEHALF[16]

As we have seen, only cash gifts qualify for gift aid. A charity or its trading company can agree with a donor that the charity will sell an item of the donor's on their behalf, and that the donor can then agree to give the sale proceeds to the charity under gift aid. In this respect the charity is acting as an agent to the donor, and the item will belong to the donor until the point that it is sold. On informing the donor of the sale price, the donor is then free either to keep the cash or to voluntarily gift aid it to the charity. Gift aid is available on the net sale proceeds, if they are eligible for gift aid (see paras 6–02—6–13). **6–33**

Under this type of arrangement, HMRC will expect the charity to have a written agreement in place with the donor setting out these arrangements in full. This will include a gift aid declaration, which should be in place before the point of sale. It is also acceptable for the agreement to say that the charity will act in accordance with the donor's earlier instructions to gift aid the proceeds unless they hear from the donor to the contrary within a set time scale, not less than 21 days. **6–34**

The charity is entitled to claim gift aid on the proceeds being gifted to them, but not on any commission charge for dealing with the sale. **6–35**

CLAIMING GIFT AID ON THE PROCEEDS OF DONATED GOODS SOLD BY CHARITY SHOPS

This is an optional process for donors and charity shops, introduced in the Finance Act 2012. It allows donors to authorise that up to £100 of the sale proceeds from their donated goods sold by a charity that operates a charity shop directly, or £1,000 of sales proceeds for goods sold by the trading subsidiary company of a charity can be treated as being a gift for gift aid purposes, without the need for the shop to seek the donor's permission to claim the tax relief. The charity is only required to write to the donor when the sale proceeds exceed this amount. Please also see the detailed guidance on the retail gift aid scheme published by HMRC.[17] **6–36**

It is hoped that these provisions will considerably ease the administrative burden on charities and if utilised, should result in a significant cost saving. **6–37**

IS IT POSSIBLE TO GIFT AID ADMISSION CHARGES TO CHARITY PROPERTY?

Generally speaking, admission charges to a property owned by a charity do not qualify for gift aid. But they can qualify in certain circumstances where one of the following conditions is met[18]: **6–38**

---

[16] See HMRC's "Guidance Note for Charities" on "Gift Aid", para.3.42.3, updated on 27 April 2016.

[17] See HMRC's Guidance Note for Charities on "Gift Aid", para.3.42, particularly paras 3.42.6–3.42.18, updated on 27 April 2016.

[18] See HMRC's Guidance Note for Charities on "Gift Aid", para.3.39, on "A right of admission to view charity property".

- the visitor agrees to make a donation that is at least 10 per cent more than the standard admission charge and in return the charity gives the donor and/or their family an equivalent right of admission (i.e. the same right of admission that would apply to any member of the public) that could apply for any period up to 12 months. The whole amount paid (not just the extra 10 per cent) will qualify for gift aid; or
- a donation is made and, in return, the charity gives the donor and/or their family unlimited admission to the property for a 12 month period, during the times that the property is ordinarily open to the viewing public. It is up to the charity to decide what the minimum level of donation must be. The full amount donated will qualify for gift aid. If the charity provides that the first visit is free but a reduced admission charge will apply on subsequent visits, then only the initial donation will qualify for gift aid.

Free admission under both the above mentioned conditions must be offered by the charity to any donor on the same terms, even if the donor states that they do not want gift aid to apply, or if they are not eligible for gift aid.

6–39 The full amount of the donation qualifies for gift aid (if a gift aid declaration is made) because the value of the benefit to the donor provided by the charity in giving free admission is disregarded for the purpose of the gift aid rules. This will apply even if the charity gives the donor a small gift in return, provided that it falls within the donor limits discussed in paras 6–18 to 6–23. These provisions will apply to family admission tickets, but not to general group tickets.

6–40 These gift aid rules can also apply to donations giving the donor the right of admission to more than one property owned by one or more charities. If so, there must be a joint admission arrangement between the charities and it must be made clear to the donor how much of their donation will go to each charity. This division must also be reflected on the gift aid declaration form.

6–41 These gift aid rules can apply where a charity charges admission to view any property that is looked after by a charity in accordance with its purposes (i.e. the charity is responsible for the preservation, upkeep and maintenance of the property). It will include admission to the ground and buildings, plants, animals, works of art, artefacts and property of a scientific nature. The gift aid rules will not apply to admission charges that cover admission to view a specific performance within the property, unless the performance is incidental to viewing the property, e.g. a historical re-enactment is being carried out at a castle during normal visiting hours that is relevant to the history of that castle.

6–42 Some charities will, as a matter of course, ask every visitor whether or not they wish to make an additional donation in order to maximise the gift aid opportunities. This is fine provided that the individual is a UK taxpayer, they are advised of the normal admission charge, they are told that the donation is entirely voluntary and the gift aid conditions as previously discussed apply (see paras

6–04 to 6–06). For a more detailed explanation of the rules and examples, please see HMRC's guidance notes on this matter.[19]

CAN GIFT AID BE CLAIMED ON ADMISSION TO EVENTS OR TICKETS TO A CHARITY DINNER/CONCERT, ETC.?

A payment made in exchange for something else, such as when an individual purchases a ticket to attend a specific event, is not regarded as being a donation and will not qualify for gift aid. Gift aid only applies to voluntary donations. **6–43**

If, however, a donation is made in addition to the payment of the ticket price, then the excess can be treated as a gift aid donation provided that the usual gift aid conditions apply as previously discussed (see paras 6–04 to 6–06). The donor must be aware that the donation is entirely voluntary. For example, a charity states that to attend a charity concert an individual must pay the ticket price of £50 and a minimum donation of £25. Gift aid will not apply because the individual can only attend the concert by paying £75. For gift aid to apply, the charity must instead state that the individual should pay the ticket price and can also if they wish pay an additional suggested donation of £25. It must be clear on the ticket that £25 is only a suggested donation and that admission to the concert can be obtained by paying the ticket price only. **6–44**

If the donation is substantial and considerably exceeds the ticket price and the ticket price falls within the permitted donor benefit limits (see paras 6–18 to 6–23), then the whole payment, including the ticket price can be treated as being a gift aid donation. **6–45**

MEMBERSHIP SUBSCRIPTIONS

Generally speaking, membership subscriptions do not normally qualify for gift aid relief. They can qualify, however, if the payment does no more than provide basic membership rights to the charity, such as the right to vote, attend the annual general meeting, receive a newsletter, etc. In addition, the payment should not provide the right to any personal use of the services or premises provided by the charity. Any benefits provided by the charity will be subject to the normal donor benefit rules considered in paras 6–18—6–23.[20] **6–46**

[19] HMRC, *Guidance Note for Charities*, on "Gift Aid", particularly para.3.39, "Gift aid on donations that attract a right of free admission to charity property", updated on 27 April 2016.

[20] For further information and examples, see HMRC, "Guidance Note for Charities" on "Gift Aid", para.3.37 (updated 27 April 2016).

CAN GIFT AID RELIEF BE CLAIMED ON CHARITY AUCTION PAYMENTS?[21]

6–47 Generally speaking, it cannot. The payment is being made in order to purchase an item at auction, it is not a gift to the charity concerned. HMRC, however, do accept that some individuals are prepared to pay more than the item is worth in the context of a charity auction in order to benefit the charity.

6–48 If the individual is aware at the time they make a successful bid that they could buy the item elsewhere and what the standard retail price is, then if they voluntarily decide to pay more, the excess can be treated as being a gift aid payment provided that it meets the usual gift aid conditions and benefit rules. In order for gift aid to apply, the charity would need to make the standard retail price known before the bidding starts.

6–49 Some items ordinarily have a standard retail price, but this value could be commercially enhanced if, for example, the item was owned by a celebrity and donated to the auction for sale. In this case, the market value for gift aid purposes will be the auction price, not the standard retail price.

6–50 If the item doesn't have a standard retail price or is not commercially available—for example, an individual buys a day out with a celebrity, then its value is the price paid at auction. Gift aid will therefore apply on the full purchase price.

SPONSORSHIP PAYMENTS

6–51 Many charities now seek to raise funds by means of encouraging donors to take part in charity sponsored events or challenges. Most charities cover the costs of third party insurance, travel, food, and accommodation if required, etc. but ask the donor to pay a non-refundable deposit or registration fee or to raise at least a minimum amount of sponsorship in return for attending the event.[22]

6–52 So, any additional amount donated by the participant will not normally qualify for gift aid, unless the participant has paid the full cost of the event (at absolutely no cost at all to the charity).

6–53 In addition, any sponsorship payment made by a person connected to the participant (spouse, civil partner, relative and their spouse/partner or a company controlled by the participant or by a connected person) will not qualify for gift aid because of the benefit rules, unless the participant has paid the full cost of the event as described above.

6–54 HMRC suggest that all charities take reasonable steps to ensure that gift aid payments are not received from connected persons.[23] The event literature and

---

[21] See HMRC's Guidance Note for Charities on "Gift Aid", para.3.40 (updated 27 April 2016).

[22] The participant, therefore, receives a benefit from the charity that equals the cost of the event, less any amount they have contributed. Gift aid isn't available where the value of the benefit exceeds the limits set out in paras 6–18—6–23.

[23] See HMRC, "Guidance Note for Charities" on "Gift Aid", paras 3.38.12, updated on 27 April 2016.

sponsorship form should therefore state that that the participant and connected persons cannot make their donations by gift aid unless the participant has paid the full cost of the event. It should also explain what a "connected person" is.

The sponsorship form should contain a box that can be ticked by sponsors to confirm that they wish gift aid to apply to their donation. It should also prominently display all the usual information contained on a standard gift aid declaration form as previously discussed (see paras 6–06—6–09). **6–55**

HMRC published their amended instructions on 22 March 2014 on how to complete the gift aid schedule spreadsheet with the details of donations received from a sponsored event. The purpose of the amendments is to allow more sponsored event donations to be eligible for gift aid. The spreadsheet gives the details of the donations received for which a gift aid repayment is being claimed and should be attached to the charity's online repayment claim.[24] **6–56**

PAYROLL GIVING

Donors can also be encouraged to donate under payroll giving, which is a very easy way of making a charitable donation. All that a charity needs to ensure is that the donor's employer has registered with a payroll giving agency (PGA) and that the donor is subject to PAYE. A PGA is a registered charity in its own right that transfers the donations from the employer to the charity or charities of the donor's choice. **6–57**

Under payroll giving, the donor's employer sets up a payroll giving scheme that enables the donor to make a charitable payment that is deducted from their gross pay (before income tax is deducted) but after deducting national insurance. The charity receives this gross amount, so there is no requirement to reclaim basic rate tax (as would happen under the gift aid provisions) saving time and expense. **6–58**

The donor benefits by receiving the tax relief immediately at their highest marginal rate of tax. Charities should inform the donor to complete a mandate form instructing their employer of the amount to be deducted. Although there is no need to inform the employer of the actual charity if the PGA has the necessary details, some charities may prefer this. **6–59**

There is no limit on the number of charities that can benefit in this way. Any UK, EU, Norwegian or Icelandic charity can benefit under payroll giving, provided that it satisfies the conditions discussed previously paras 6–14—6–16. Once the donation has been deducted from the donor's salary, the employer must pass it to the PGA every month. The PGA must then pass the donation to the charity within 35 or 60 days of receipt. Most PGAs aim to do so within one month.[25] **6–60**

[24] See HMRCs gift aid guidance for further detail of the amendments to the gift aid schedule spreadsheet instructions. These instructions were published on 22 March 2014 and by press release dated 17 April 2014. Please also see the updated HMRC guidance at *https://www.gov.uk/government/publications/charities-detailed-guidance-notes/chapter-3-gift-aid* [Accessed 26 May 2016].

[25] Please see HMRC's amendments to the *Guidance Note for Charities* on "Payroll Giving", updated on 27 April 2016.

6–61 Charities should be aware that the PGA will make a small charge to the employer to cover the cost of administering the scheme.

MAKING A CHARITABLE LEGACY OR BEQUEST

6–62 Legacy income is very valuable to the charity sector. A charitable donation can be made on an individual's death through their will, codicil or under a deed of variation within two years of the date of death. A bequest could take many forms, it could be a gift of cash or a particular asset or even all or part of the residue of the estate.

6–63 Charities that seek to encourage their supporters to remember the charity in their will, should remember that this is an issue to be handled with care and great sensitivity. Reference should be made to the guidance issued on this matter and on effective communication with supporters by the Charity Commission and the Institute of Fundraising.[26]

6–64 The Charity Commission suggests that no one connected with the charity should prepare the will itself or act as a witness when the will is signed. This may help to reduce the risk of any later legal challenge.[27] Charities should suggest that the individual use their own solicitor for this purpose. This is particularly important if the charity are contributing towards the legal costs of putting the will in place. It is also good practice from a risk management point of view for each charity to put clear written procedures in place on legacy fundraising and will drafting and how it should be dealt with appropriately, which may help to minimise the risk of later challenge from the supporter's family.

6–65 This is particularly relevant in light of several recent English cases. In *Gill v RSPCA*,[28] Mrs Gill's will left the residue of her estate (worth £2.35 million)—her husband having predeceased—to the RSPCA. This was challenged by her daughter, Dr Gill, in the High Court. Dr Gill argued that her mother had been forced to make her will in these terms by her domineering husband and that without his influence, she would have wanted Dr Gill to benefit instead. The High Court upheld Dr Gill's argument. The RSPCA thereafter sought to challenge this without success. The RSPCA said that it had a duty to fight the ruling "to uphold the wishes of those that choose to bequeath it a legacy".

6–66 In *Ilott v Mitson*,[29] Mrs Jackson had disinherited her estranged daughter Mrs Ilott in her Will in favour of the Blue Cross, the RSPB and the RSPCA. Mrs Ilott challenged this. The Court of Appeal ruled that Mrs Jackson had failed to make

---

[26] Charity Commission, *Wills and Charitable Legacies* and the Institute of Fundraising's legacy fundraising guidance called "Using communication channels appropriately" and "Other relations with supporters, pledgers and legators".

[27] Charity Commission, *Wills and Charitable Legacies*, p.1.

[28] Also known as *Gill v Woodall* [2011] Ch. 380.

[29] This case was first reported in 2007 where the decision was opposed by the charities concerned leading to two further appeals in the English Court of Appeal, last reported on 27 July 2015. Please see *Ilott v Mitson* [2009] EWHC 3114 (Fam); *Ilott v Mitson* [2014] EWHC 542 (Fam) (3 March 2014); and *Ilott v Mitson* [2015] EWHC Civ 797. Permission to appeal was granted by the Supreme Court in February 2016.

reasonable financial provision for Mrs Ilott under the terms of the Inheritance (Provision for Family and Dependants) Act 1975, given Mrs Ilott's difficult financial circumstances at the time. The judge's decision took the view that although Mrs Ilott had no expectation that she would inherit from her mother's estate owing to the long term estrangement, the charities concerned also had no expectation that they would benefit under the will. The charities did not know about the will and had little involvement with Mrs Jackson during her lifetime. The judge therefore gave Mrs Ilott's interests a higher priority than those of the charities.

The lawyer acting for each of the three charities said at the time: **6–67**

> "This case raises serious questions about whether people have the freedom to choose who they want to leave money to in their Will."[30]

Although this is an English case, a similar principle applies in Scotland whereby a surviving spouse or civil partner can make what is known as a legal rights claim on the estate of their deceased spouse or partner. Children can also make a legal rights claim on the estate of a deceased parent.[31]

This clearly has enormous potential implications for the charity sector as a whole. Charities need to be aware that we may now see an increase in the number of challenges and/or claims being made to the terms of a will in which the charity concerned benefits, adversely affecting the amount the charity expects to receive. It also demonstrates the importance of ensuring that charities handle the issue of legacies correctly.[32] **6–68**

Charities should also highlight that leaving a charitable legacy can be tax efficient, particularly if the individual's estate will be subject to IHT at 40 per cent. A charitable legacy/bequest is exempt from IHT, reducing the amount of IHT payable if the estate exceeds the IHT threshold.[33] From April 2012, if more than 10 per cent of an estate subject to IHT is left to charity, then the applicable rate of IHT is reduced to 36 per cent. Charities should also note that if the deceased intends to give 4 per cent of their net estate to charity, the beneficiaries could use a deed of variation if possible to increase the value of the gift to 10 per cent without causing any reduction in their own share of the estate. It simply **6–69**

---

[30] Please see the comments of James Aspden following the final Court of Appeal judgment issued in the press on 27 July 2015.

[31] For further information about legal rights, please see the Succession (Scotland) Act 1964. Legal rights currently only apply to moveable (not heritable) assets. Currently a spouse/civil partner can claim up to a one-half share of the moveable estate if there are no children/issue and a one-third share if there are. Children can make a claim to one half of the moveable estate if there is no surviving spouse/civil partner or otherwise a one third share if there is, divided equally between them. Legal rights are currently under review and there are proposals to extend them to heritable property under the Scottish Law Commission, "Succession" (Scot. Law Comm. No.215).

[32] *Gill v Woodall* [2011] Ch. 380.

[33] Currently £325,000 for the 2015–2016/2016–2017 tax year for an individual or £650,000 for a combined estate passing to the surviving spouse or civil partner.

means that less tax is payable as a result.[34] It is up to the charity concerned to decide whether or not it wishes to raise this, given that it may come at a time when the family are grieving.

THE GIFT AID SMALL DONATIONS SCHEME (GASDS)

6–70 From 6 April 2013, the GASDS[35] allows charities and CASCs to claim a gift aid style top up payment on cash donations of £20 or less, on up to £5,000 of donations per year without the need to collect gift aid declarations. As GASDS relief is paid at the same rate as gift aid, this means that the maximum amount each charity can reclaim is a top up payment of £1,250 per year. This is ideal for small cash donations, such as those collected in a church or as part of a public collection where the donor may be either unwilling or doesn't have time to complete a gift aid form. The claim must be made using HMRC's Charities Online.

6–71 There are some important eligibility criteria as follows:

- the donor must not receive any benefit from the charity, such as a small gift in return;
- the charity or CASC must be recognised as such by HMRC and have a tax reference number;
- the charity or CASC must have existed for at least two complete tax years; and
- the charity or CASC must have a successful track record in dealing with and making gift aid claims, having made successful gift aid claims in two of the last four tax years without incurring any kind of penalty on either gift aid or GASDS.

6–72 The last-mentioned criterion is necessary in order to establish an audit trail. For these purposes, it is therefore necessary for a charity that receives regular amounts in cash, such as a church collection, to have some form of system in place that can demonstrate to HMRC the donations have been received. Not surprisingly. however, the GASDS has been criticised as unfairly prejudicing charities and CASCs who have not previously claimed gift aid.

6–73 The amount claimed under the GASDS must also be matched with the claims made under gift aided donations in the same tax year. So, for every £1 of gift aid claimed, GASDS top up payments can be made of £10, subject to the £1,250 limit. This means that if a charity or CASC claim on the maximum amount of £5,000 of small donations, they must have successfully claimed gift aid on at least £500 of donations in the same tax year.

6–74 In addition where the charity or CASC is part of a wider group structure, the maximum relief is still restricted to £1,250 for the entire group.

34 Please see HMRC's guidance on the reduced IHT rate for some worked examples of this.

35 See HMRC guidance on "The Gift Aid Small Donations Scheme". The GASDS was introduced in the Small Charitable Donations Act 2012, which received Royal Assent on 19 December 2012 after being announced in the 2011 Budget.

To date the GASDS rules appear to have caused some confusion. It is not possible to claim both gift aid and GASDS on the same donation, although a number of charities have tried to do so. The GASDS should only be used for small cash donations where there is no gift aid declaration in place. **6–75**

A GASDS claim should be made within two years of the end of the tax year in which the charity receives the donations. **6–76**

BORROWING

It is now becoming increasingly common for charities to consider taking out debt finance. Many different options and levels of risk are available depending upon a charity's specific needs; from a short term bridging loan while awaiting known funding or over a longer term basis to cover large upfront capital outlays such as the sums required to get a community renewables project up and running. The charity trustees must consider the best mix of funding to achieve the required end result, so debt finance may be a way of providing at least part of a charity's funding needs. **6–77**

Charity trustees must demonstrate, as part of their statutory duty of care and financial prudence, that they have exercised all appropriate care when borrowing funds for a charity and that it is in the charity's best interests to do so. **6–78**

The trustees should consider the following checklist: **6–79**

- That the charity's constitution contains the necessary powers to borrow funds, and, if applicable, to grant a security for a loan over the charity's assets. If not, it may be necessary to amend the constitution in the usual way. These powers are conferred automatically on all trusts under the Trusts (Scotland) Act 1921,[36] unless the trust deed states that it does not apply and also on Scottish Charitable Incorporated Organisations (SCIO) even if there is no express power to do so contained in the SCIO's constitution. There is no requirement under the Charities and Trustee Investment (Scotland) Act 2005 (the 2005 Act) to obtain OSCRs prior consent to borrow funds. The loan will be detailed in the notes to the accounts on the balance sheet in due course.
- Is a loan necessary? This sounds obvious, but it is worth considering whether or not it is possible to implement cost saving measures that could avoid this step or at least reduce the amount required. This will also depend upon a number of other factors, such as the timescales involved (this may be harder to achieve if a short term loan is required quickly), and the size and reasons for taking out the loan. If time allows, the trustees may wish to consider holding a specific fund raising campaign instead, in order to raise all or part of the required funds.
- Is taking out a loan in the best interests of the charity? There will be interest charges, possible arrangement fees and late payment penalties. The trustees must be satisfied that it is absolutely necessary and that the charity will

[36] Trusts (Scotland) Act 1921 s.4(d).

have sufficient resources or budgeted income to meet the repayment terms. The trustees must also bear in mind the possibility of a rise in interest rates, and the impact of any provision entitling the lender to call up the loan for immediate payment.

- The trustees have a duty to ensure that the loan agreement is on the most favourable terms that can be negotiated for the charity and that the repayment terms are reasonable. This can be demonstrated by comparing the terms and rates offered in the loan agreement to those offered by other lenders.
- The use of professional advice will be almost inevitable. Given that most loans will be a significant future financial commitment, taking legal and financial advice will probably be essential for the trustees in making their decision and in helping them to negotiate the most favourable terms possible in the circumstances. The trustees must be satisfied that they understand the terms of the loan documentation and that there are no hidden surprises.
- Is the risk level appropriate? An unsecured loan, for example, charging a higher interest rate may pose a greater risk to the charity. The trustees must be comfortable that the risk level is appropriate.
- If there is already an existing loan facility in place, can it be extended or can its terms be revised to cover the additional funds required without penalty? This may be easier and more cost effective than taking out a further loan.

6–80 If the trustees wish to borrow funds in order to invest, the constitution ought to contain the power to borrow for investment purposes. The trustees must be satisfied that the overall investment return is justified when compared to the risk profile of taking out a loan. As an investment decision, the trustees should consider taking professional advice.[37]

6–81 As a matter of good practice, the trustees should ensure that all of their discussions regarding the loan including any concerns they may have and their reasons for proceeding are fully minuted and that the loan arrangements are thereafter kept under close review.

SOCIAL IMPACT BONDS (SIBS)

6–82 SIBs are also growing in popularity as an alternative to taking out loan finance, particularly if social investors are prepared to fund what may be regarded as a potentially higher risk charitable project. Charities can offer a lower interest rate on a bond when compared to a conventional company issuing first time bonds, because although investors are looking to get a return on their capital, they may be prepared to accept a below market return from a charity. The bonds are also listed, so they are easier to buy and sell. The capital on the bond also doesn't have to be repaid for at least five years.

[37] See the Trusts (Scotland) Act 1921 s.4A(2).

There is an element of risk attached to SIBs. The return is based on the successful performance of the project in question. If the project outcome does well there can be a good return. If the project is not a success then the investor may receive no return at all. Other disadvantages could potentially include an important investor (carrying a greater degree of the risk) seeking to obtain a degree of control within the charity, such as by becoming a trustee, which the trustees will need to take a view on. 6–83

Sources of potential SIB funding include the Government Social Outcomes Fund launched in November 2012 and the Big Lottery Fund Commissioning Better Outcomes Fund that is intended to encourage more innovative projects.[38] 6–84

DO THE TRUSTEES FACE ANY PERSONAL RISK IN TAKING OUT A LOAN?

This can depend upon the charity's structure. An incorporated body will borrow funds in the charity's name because it has its own separate legal identity. Personal liability, if any, will be limited to the minimal amount set out in the constitution, unless fraud, gross negligence or criminal charges, etc. should apply. 6–85

There is a greater risk of potential personal liability if a loan is taken out by trustees on behalf of an unincorporated body such as a charitable trust or unincorporated association, if circumstances should later change with the result that the trustees find that the charity's funds are insufficient to cover the loan repayments. Trustees should not enter into personal guarantees. 6–86

ACCOUNTING REQUIREMENTS

Introduction

This section is intended to provide a general overview of the accounting and reporting requirements of Scottish registered charities. Charities who think it necessary should seek further professional advice and also consider the various OSCR guidance on accounting requirements.[39] 6–87

A charity's annual report and accounts make its affairs open and transparent. It allows a charity to demonstrate to the wider public, their funders, OSCR, donors, supporters and to potential new donors how it has applied its charitable purposes and funds during the financial year; together with providing a summary of its activities, what the charity hopes to achieve and its financial position at the year end. The annual report should tell the "story" of the accounts and the charity and can be used to promote the charity. 6–88

---

[38] Please see *http://biglotteryfund.org.uk* [Accessed 26 May 2016] for more details.

[39] See OSCR, *Scottish Charity Accounts: An Updated Guide to the 2006 Regulations* (2011) and the Charity Commission, "Charity Reporting and Accounting: the Essentials" (CC15), published in January 2013. OSCR and the Charity Commission have produced a number of factsheets on the FRS 102 SORP, which also help users determine which of the new SORPs should be followed if fully accrued accounts are used.

6–89 The relevant legislation, which applies to all Scottish charities, is the 2005 Act,[40] the Charities Accounts (Scotland) Regulations 2006, the Charities Accounts (Scotland) Amendment Regulations 2007, the Charities Accounts (Scotland) Amendment Regulations 2010 and the Charities Accounts (Scotland) Amendment Regulations 2014 (the Regulations). Charitable companies are also subject to the requirements of the Companies Act 2006.

6–90 If accrued accounts are required, then the additional provisions of the statement of recommended practice (SORP)[41] will also apply. A SORP is intended to improve the financial reporting standards of charities. SORP information sheets are also available for guidance from OSCR explaining how the SORP and its recommendations should be applied. Registered social landlords and further and higher education bodies are also subject to their own sector specific SORP.

6–91 The two new SORPs came into effect on 16 July 2014, these are the Charities SORP (FRS102) (FRS102 SORP)[42] and the Financial Reporting Standard for Smaller Entities 2015 (FRSSE SORP). Both SORPS apply to all accounting periods beginning on or after 1 January 2015. The FRSSE SORP will only apply to smaller charities that use accrued accounts and which meet two out of the following three criteria: they have an annual income of less than £6.5 million, their total assets are less than £3.26 million and they have fewer than 50 employees.

6–92 It is currently proposed that the FRSSE SORP will be withdrawn and be replaced by the Financial Reporting Standard for Micro-Entities (FRSME), which doesn't apply to charities. We are still awaiting the details of the recent OSCR consultation regarding the changes that will therefore need to be made to the FRS102.

Keeping proper accounting records

6–93 All charities must keep proper accounting records.[43] This means keeping a detailed record of all of the charity's financial transactions to enable the annual statement of account and report on activities to be prepared for each financial year.[44] In general terms, this means that a charity must keep all record books (whether written or computerised records or spreadsheets) in which daily transactions are entered showing the funds received and spent as well as recording assets and liabilities. It will also include bank statements and

---

[40] Charities and Trustee Investment (Scotland) Act 2005 ss.44–48 inclusive.

[41] Each SORP is produced by OSCR and the Charity Commission as the joint SORP making body alongside the sector based SORP committee representing a wide spread of professionals operating in this field, such as charity advisers, charity directors, charity auditors, etc.

[42] This replaces the Accounting and Reporting by Charities: Statement of Recommended Practice 2005 (the 2005 SORP) as amended by the 2008 SORP.

[43] Charities and Trustee Investment (Scotland) Act 2005 s.44(1)(a), for charitable companies, the Companies Act 2006 s.386 and the Charities Accounts (Scotland) Regulations 2006 s.4, as amended.

[44] Charities and Trustee Investment (Scotland) Act 2005 s.44(a) and 44(b).

reconciliations, receipts, invoices, vouchers, gift aid records, etc. These records should be sufficiently clear to show the financial position of the charity at any time.

Accounting records must be kept by the charity for six years from the end of the financial year in which they are made.[45] This will override the requirement that charitable companies must keep their accounting records for only three years.[46] Records regarding gift aid payments with donor details must also be kept for HMRC purposes for six years. The trustees must decide as a matter of good practice whether these minimum periods are sufficient, or if they require the accounting records to be kept for a longer period. **6–94**

Any interested person can request a copy of a charity's constitution and latest accounts directly from the charity.[47] The charity must provide this information in the form requested, if they consider the request to be reasonable. The charity can also charge a small fee for doing so, but this cannot exceed the cost of providing the material and postage.[48] **6–95**

WHICH FORM OF ACCOUNTS SHOULD BE USED?

Charity accounts must be prepared either as receipts and payments accounts, or as fully accrued accounts, both of which are considered below. The following criteria will apply in deciding whether receipts and payments accounts or fully accrued accounts should be used: **6–96**

- Does the charity have gross annual income that exceeds £250,000? If yes, then fully accrued accounts must be used.
- If the gross annual income is £250,000 or less, receipts and payments accounts may be used instead, unless any of the following points apply:
    - If the constitution or governing statute directs that fully accrued accounts must be used, then this will apply, unless the charity can amend its constitution.
    - If the charity is a company, a registered society, a friendly society, a registered social landlord or a higher or further education institution, then it must use fully accrued accounts.
    - The charity trustees may prefer to prepare the accounts on a fully accrued basis. Funders, for example, may prefer to see fully accrued accounts. If this is the case, then the charity trustees should also consider the additional cost implications of preparing fully accrued accounts before deciding whether or not receipts and payments accounts will suffice.

---

45 Charities and Trustee Investment (Scotland) Act 2005 s.44(2) and as seen in the FRS102 SORP.

46 Companies Act 2006 s.355(2).

47 Charities and Trustee Investment (Scotland) Act 2005 s.23.

48 Charities and Trustee Investment (Scotland) Act 2005 s.23(2).

RECEIPTS AND PAYMENTS ACCOUNTS

6–97 This is the most straightforward form of accounting. For full details, reference should be made to OSCR's detailed guidance, CD guide and workpack for these accounts.[49] As noted above, not all charities may use receipts and payments accounts.

6–98 Receipts and payments accounts summarise the following:

- *All funds received during the financial year* whether from donations, investment income, bank interest, grants, rental income, etc.
- *All payments made during the financial year.* This will include expenditure in furtherance of the charitable objectives, governance costs, general expenses, salaries and the purchase of assets or investments.
- *A statement of balances held.* This reconciles the cash and bank balances held at the start and end of the financial year with any surplus or deficit being shown in the receipts and payments statement. It will also include details of any funds and investments held, any other assets held by or gifted to the charity and an estimate of total liabilities at the financial year end.
- *The trustees annual report.* Smaller charities that are not subject to an audit do not need to provide the same level of detail in the annual report as audited charities. The annual report however gives a good opportunity to provide important information about the charity and show the public what it does. The trustees should therefore provide as much information as possible by including a summary of its general performance, the nature of the charity, its reserves policy, its successes and challenges over the last financial year, how it has carried out its charitable purposes, its main activities and plans for the future and how it can achieve these.

6–99 Both the statement of balances and the trustees' annual report must be approved and signed by at least one trustee on behalf of the charity and dated. In addition, receipts and payments accounts must also contain either an independent examiner's report or an audit report as discussed further below.

FULLY ACCRUED ACCOUNTS

6–100 Fully accrued accounts are more complex than receipts and payments accounts and will show when the charity becomes entitled to the receipts in question (which may not be the same date that they are actually received) and when the liability for the expenses is incurred (which again, may not necessarily be the same date that the payment is made).

---

[49] Please see the OSCR guide to Scottish Charity Accounts, *An Updated Guide to the 2006 Regulations* (referring to the Charities Accounts (Scotland) Regulations 2006 as amended), Pt 2 of which deals with receipts and payments accounts in detail and provides a sample set of accounts in the appendix. OSCR have also produced a CD guide and workpack that is available on request and which provides further guidance and templates. See also the Charities Accounts (Scotland) Regulations 2006 s.9 as amended.

Fully accrued accounts must contain the following[50]: 6–101

- *A statement of the charity's financial activities* providing a true and fair view of the charity's income and its application during that financial year. This must differentiate between the categories of restricted, unrestricted and endowment funds. Further details will be included in the notes to the accounts to explain the charity's accounting policies in relation to these funds.
- *The balance sheet:* this gives a true and fair view of the financial affairs of the charity at the year end.[51] This must be approved by one of the trustees.
- *Cash-flow statement* with a comparison to the last financial year for information.[52]
- *Trustees' annual report:* FRS102 SORP aims to ensure that, in the interests of transparency, a detailed picture of the charity and its activities are presented in the annual report. This means providing a certain amount of mandatory information, with greater detail required for larger charities (defined in the FRS102 SORP as being charities that are required to have an audit under charity law[53]). The trustees are also now responsible for both preparing and approving the annual report.

Mandatory information under the FRS102 SORP includes the following: 6–102

- a statement on the charity's reserves policy, the amount held in reserves and how this compares to the charity's policies;
- all trustees who have acted during that financial year should be identified[54];
- the charity must explain its social investment policies. The charity must also explain the financial effect of any significant events and report on its principal charitable activities[55];
- the charity must provide a description of the principal risks faced by it and its subsidiaries, together with the trustees' strategies for managing these risks; and
- the charity must disclose the pay and remuneration arrangements for key employees and any benchmarks used in setting their pay.

In addition, the annual report of larger charities that are subject to audit must also contain the following[56]: 6–103

---

[50] See the Charities Accounts (Scotland) Regulations 2006 reg.8.

[51] FRS102 SORP has made no significant changes to the SORP 2005 requirements for these purposes.

[52] See OSCR, *Scottish Charity Accounts: An Updated Guide to the 2006 Regulations, Part Three*.

[53] See the Companies Act 2006 ss.477 and 478. Section 477 provides that a company is exempt from the requirements of the Companies Act 2006 in relation to the auditing of accounts if the company qualifies as a small company in that financial year, its turnover in that year does not exceed £5.6 million and its balance sheet total for that year is not more than £2.8 million.

[54] Under the 2005 SORP no more than 50 trustees' names could be disclosed.

[55] See Ch.9 dealing with investments.

[56] See the Charity Commission, "Charity Reporting and Accounting—the Essentials" (January 2013) p.21 onwards.

- the name of the chief executive officer and other key staff responsible for the daily management of the charity;
- the name and address of the charity's bankers, accountants, solicitors, etc.;
- the policies and procedures for the induction and training of trustees;
- how decisions are made in the context of the organisational structure;
- the relationship and operational structure of the charity with any related parties, such as subsidiaries, an umbrella structure, etc.;
- a far more detailed business activities report (the "strategic report"), which also includes the charity's strategies for achieving its objectives and its main targets for the year, details of grant making policies if any, information regarding use of volunteers and a detailed review of its significant activities;
- a more detailed report on the achievements and performance of the charity and its subsidiaries if any, including a review of the charity's performance against its set objectives, a detailed review of the fundraising activities and strategies considering performance against set objectives, etc.; and
- an additional financial review, reviewing the financial position of the charity and its subsidiaries and its principal financial management policies, how its expenditure has supported the purposes and its investment policy and objectives.

6–104 Accrued accounts must also contain either an independent examiner's report or an audit report as discussed below.

THE INDEPENDENT REVIEW OF ACCOUNTS

6–105 All charity accounts, regardless of whether they are prepared on a receipts and payments basis or on a fully accrued basis must go through a further external and impartial examination before they can be approved and signed off by the trustees.[57] This is referred to either as an independent examination or an audit.

6–106 An independent examiner or auditor must have no connection with the management of the charity or the charity trustees for these purposes. They cannot be a charity trustee or connected to them (such as the spouse, civil partner, partner, close relative or business partner of a trustee), involved in the charity's administration (whether as an employee or as a volunteer), or be a major donor or beneficiary of the charity.

6–107 An independent examination is a less onerous form of examination of the accounts than a formal audit. It can be carried out by a full or associate member of the Association of Charity Independent Examiners, a qualified accountant whether retired or currently in practice, or by any other professional or person with financial expertise.[58] The charity trustees will decide who to appoint as their independent examiner according to the complexity of the charity's affairs. It

[57] Charities and Trustee Investment (Scotland) Act 2005 s.44(1)(c).

[58] See the full list of recognised professional bodies in the Charities Accounts (Scotland) Regulations 2006 reg.11 as amended.

follows that the more complex the arrangements, or if accrual accounts are used, the more experienced the independent examiner should be.

An audit must follow the International Standards on Auditing for the UK and Ireland as well as the UK Auditing Practices Board's ethical standards. It must be carried out by a registered auditor, by the Auditor General for Scotland or by an auditor appointed by the Accounts Commission for Scotland following UK audit standards in accordance with the 2005 Act. If it is a larger company, the auditor must be appointed in accordance with the requirements of the Companies Act 2006.[59] 6–108

The Regulations provide that independent examiners and auditors can ask to see any documents, papers, records or books that they require in order to complete their examination.[60] They are also entitled to speak to trustees and employees, including former employees and trustees. 6–109

THE INDEPENDENT EXAMINER'S REPORT AND THE AUDIT REPORT IN THE CONTEXT OF RECEIPTS AND PAYMENTS ACCOUNTS

The accounts on their own cannot provide a completely true and fair view of the financial affairs of the charity. The purpose of the independent examiners or audit report is to provide a reasonable assurance that no concerns have been identified in the appraisal of the accounts. Examples might be finding that proper accounting records have not been kept, that the accounts do not reconcile with the charity's records, that there is any material expenditure or action that falls outside the charity's objectives, that requested information has been deliberately withheld or if there appears to be a material difference between the accounts and the statements in the annual report. 6–110

Both the independent examiner's report and the audit report are carried out in accordance with the requirements of the 2005 Act.[61] An audit report will also state whether in the auditor's opinion the statement of account complies with the Regulations which cover receipts and payments.[62] 6–111

Both an independent examiner's and an audit report will state whether the accounts properly present the receipts, payments and the statement of balances at the year end. An auditor will, however, carry out a more detailed examination than an independent examiner. 6–112

The report is signed either at the same time as, or after the trustees have approved and signed the accounts. 6–113

[59] Companies Act 2006 s.1212.
[60] See the Charities Accounts (Scotland) Regulations 2006 reg.13 as amended.
[61] Charities and Trustee Investment (Scotland) Act 2005 s.44(1)(c).
[62] See the Charities Accounts (Scotland) Regulations 2006 reg.10(4)(e)(i).

THE INDEPENDENT EXAMINER'S REPORT AND THE AUDIT REPORT IN THE CONTEXT OF FULLY ACCRUED ACCOUNTS

6–114 In addition to the information contained in the report for receipts and payments accounts mentioned above, an audit report will contain a statement whether, in the auditor's opinion, the statement of account complies with the regulations dealing with fully accrued accounts and gives a true and fair view of the charity's financial year end, as well as the income and expenditure for that financial period.[63]

6–115 By its nature, an audit is a far more detailed investigation. The auditor will carry out whatever investigation is required in order to enable them to form a proper opinion on the accounts.

6–116 The report is signed either at the same time as, or after the trustees have approved and signed the accounts.

THE DUTY OF THE INDEPENDENT EXAMINER OR AUDITOR TO REPORT TO OSCR

6–117 The 2005 Act provides that if any independent examiner or auditor becomes aware of any matter relating to the activities or affairs of a charity (or of a connected organisation, such as a trading company) that they have reasonable cause to believe is likely to be of "material significance" to the charity and to OSCR in carrying out its functions, they must immediately report this matter to OSCR.[64] All trustees should be aware that mistakes cannot be hidden. If the trustees do discover that a mistake has been made, they should immediately seek professional advice from an accountant or their legal adviser to establish how the error has occurred and how it can be dealt with and corrected going forward.

6–118 Matters of "material significance" will include finding evidence of the following[65]:

- the misuse or theft of a charity's funds or assets by anyone concerned with the charity, such as the trustees, senior management, agents, employees or volunteers that hasn't been reported to the police;
- if a trustee is disqualified from acting as a trustee but continues to act;
- that someone connected with the charity has knowingly provided false or misleading information to OSCR;
- the honesty or integrity of any charity trustee;

---

[63] Charities Accounts (Scotland) Regulations 2006 reg.10(4)(e)(i).

[64] Charities and Trustee Investment (Scotland) Act 2005 s.46(2). See also OSCR's guidance on "Notifiable Events" under OSCR's targeted regulatory changes that came into effect from 1 April 2016. The trustees must also decide whether the event could have a potentially significant impact upon the charity and should therefore report it to OSCR as soon as possible after discovery. OSCR will want to know the steps taken by the trustees to resolve the matter and establish how it occurred, and in the case of fraud/theft, etc. whether it has been reported to the police.

[65] These examples are set out in the OSCR, "Scottish Charity Accounts; An updated guide to the 2006 Regulations", Pt 1, p.14.

- serious legislative breach;
- acting outside the scope of the charitable purposes; and
- if information or records which they have requested have not been provided.

Even if the matter does not appear to the independent examiner or auditor to be of material significance, but they reasonably consider that it is likely to be relevant to OSCR, they *may* report it to OSCR.[66] This could include the following[67]: **6–119**

- serious problems in the management and control of charitable funds, particularly if the charity trustees are seen to be reckless in their actions, perhaps by taking unnecessary risks;
- if it appears that the trustees are not running the charity properly;
- if it is unclear who the charity trustees are;
- evidence of theft or dishonesty by charity employees or volunteers that has already been reported to the police; and
- evidence of the trustees knowingly making significantly inaccurate or misleading claims about the charity to the public in any way.

It is important to note that, even if the independent examiner or auditor ceases to act for the charity for any reason, this statutory duty remains.[68]

Finally, if an auditor takes the view that their concerns about the charity mean they must cease to act, the auditor must also give OSCR a copy of any report they have sent to the trustees setting out their reasons for leaving and any circumstances they wish to draw to the charity trustees' attention. This duty does not apply to independent examiners. **6–120**

TYPE OF ACCOUNTS AND FORM OF EXTERNAL SCRUTINY: EXCLUDING CHARITABLE COMPANIES AND SCIOS

The following considerations will apply in determining what form of external scrutiny is appropriate for the charity concerned: **6–121**

- *Gross annual income of the charity is below £25,000*
  - (a) The charity can prepare either receipts and payments accounts or fully accrued accounts.
  - (b) There is no requirement to have the accounts independently examined or audited, unless the constitution provides for this.
- *Gross annual income of the charity is between £25,000 and £250,000*
  - (a) Accounts can be prepared either on a receipts and payments basis or on a fully accrued accounting basis.

---

[66] Charities and Trustee Investment (Scotland) Act 2005 s.46(3).

[67] These examples are set out in the OSCR, "Scottish Charity Accounts; An updated guide to the 2006 Regulations", Pt 1, p.14.

[68] Charities and Trustee Investment (Scotland) Act 2005 s.46(4).

(b) An independent examination or audit can be used, unless the constitution directs which form should be used.

- *Gross annual income of the charity is between £250,000 to £500,000 inclusive and its total assets do not exceed £3.26 million*

(a) Fully accrued accounts must be used in accordance with the regulations and the FRS102 SORP.

(b) An independent examination or audit can be used, unless the constitution directs which form should be used.

- *Gross annual income of the charity exceeds £500,000 or its gross income exceed £250,000 and its gross assets exceed £3.26 million*

(a) Fully accrued accounts must be used.

(b) The accounts must be audited.

In addition, charities with subsidiaries (whether they are charitable or not) preparing group accounts where the gross income after deducting consolidated adjustments exceeds £500,000 must also prepare fully accrued accounts. The accounts must be audited.

TYPE OF ACCOUNTS AND FORM OF EXTERNAL SCRUTINY: CHARITABLE COMPANIES

6–122 Charitable companies must produce fully accrued accounts and are also subject to the accounting requirements of the Companies Act 2006.

- The Companies Act 2006 provides that charitable companies are no longer exempt from the audit requirements that apply to all companies: i.e. a charitable company will therefore be treated in exactly the same way as any other company for audit purposes. This means that a charitable company only requires an audit under the Companies Act 2006 if it exceeds the threshold set out in the Companies Act 2006.[69] Small charitable companies and small charitable company groups made up of a parent charity and subsidiaries are now therefore covered by the audit exemption.

  The audit exemption will not apply to larger charitable company groups where the gross income for the group exceeds £500,000, so an audit will be required in this case. If an audit is not required under the Companies Act 2006, the accounts must state that the charitable company is exempt from the requirements for a Companies Act audit.

- *Gross income does not exceed £500,000 or if the gross income exceeds £250,000 but the gross assets do not exceed £3.26 million*

(a) The accounts can be independently examined, unless the articles provide for an audit to be carried out, or unless the trustees prefer that the accounts are audited.

[69] See the Companies Act 2006 ss.477 and 478. Section 477 provides that a company is exempt from the requirements of the Companies Act 2006 in relation to the auditing of accounts if the company qualifies as a small company in that financial year, its turnover in that year does not exceed £5.6 million and its balance sheet total for that year is not more than £2.8 million.

- *Gross income exceeds £500,000 or if the gross income exceeds £250,000 and the gross assets also exceed £3.26 million*
  (a) The accounts must be audited.

TYPE OF ACCOUNTS AND FORM OF EXTERNAL SCRUTINY: SCIOs

- *Gross income of the SCIO is less than £250,000* 6–123
  Receipts and payments accounts may be used, unless the trustees prefer otherwise.
- *Gross annual income exceeds £250,000*
  Fully accrued accounts must be used.
- *Gross annual income does not exceed £25,000*
  An independent examination or audit is not required.
- *Gross annual income is below £500,000, or if gross annual assets do not exceed £3.26 million or if gross annual income exceeds £250,000*
  An independent examination will be sufficient unless the constitution provides otherwise or unless the trustees prefer the accounts to be fully audited.
- *Gross annual income exceeds £500,000, or if gross annual assets exceed £3.26 million and its gross annual income exceeds £250,000*
  A full audit is required.

THE ACCOUNTING REFERENCE DATE

Every Scottish registered charity must decide upon the date of its financial year 6–124
end, to which the accounts will be made up. This information will also appear in the Scottish charity register. The following considerations apply:

- charities that are set up in Scotland and which are not a company can choose a date not less than six months and not more than 18 months from the date it was entered onto the charity register;
- charitable companies can choose a date not less than six months and not more than 18 months from the date that it was incorporated;
- charities established outside of Scotland and seeking Scottish registration, can choose a date not less than six months and not more than 18 months from the date after it was established; and
- if the charity has obtained OSCR's consent to wind up or merge or amalgamate with another charity, then the accounts will be made up to the date that this event takes place.

CHANGING THE ACCOUNTING REFERENCE DATE

It is straightforward to change the accounting year end date for the current 6–125
financial year or for the immediately preceding financial year provided that the charity does so in time, i.e. provided that the financial year has not exceeded 18 months and that the charity does not have three or more financial years exceeding

12 months in any five year period. Charitable companies must also ensure that any change to their financial year end also complies with the requirements of the Companies Act 2006.

6–126 Remember to notify OSCR within three months of the date of the change, so that the charity register can be updated. Charitable companies must also notify Companies House within 14 days of the date of the change.

DUAL REGISTERED CHARITIES

6–127 It should be noted that dual registered charities that are registered with both OSCR and the Charity Commission, do not need to prepare separate accounts for each regulator. One form of compliant accounts will suffice for both. OSCR will, however, expect the trustees' annual report to cover the charity's UK wide activities and should also clearly set out the charity's particular activities in Scotland.

REPORTING TO OSCR AND THE MONITORING PROCESS

6–128 As part of its monitoring role, and in order to keep the Scottish charity register up to date, OSCR require all Scottish registered charities to submit an annual return and accounts to it.

6–129 OSCR has now simplified the annual return form and got rid of the supplementary monitoring return. Charities will now be required to complete different sections of the annual return according to their annual income level. Charities with an income of £25,000 or above and £250,000 or above will have to complete some additional sections.[70] OSCR now reviews a sample of annual returns and annual accounts, chosen both at random and taking a risk-based approach, rather than review the annual return and accounts for every charity. The nature of their review will also change, with more emphasis being placed upon the quality of the trustees' annual report.

6–130 As part of OSCR's review on the regulatory process and to increase transparency and accountability,[71] it will now publish the annual reports and accounts for all charities with an income of £25,000 or above and for all SCIO's with effect from 1 April 2016 on the Charity Register. The details of the trustees' signatures and the names and addresses of the independent examiner/auditor will be removed, however, for reasons of confidentiality. Charities can also send OSCR a link to their own website if they publish their accounts, which will be published on the Charity Register. This is a useful way of providing the public with greater information about the charity. OSCR does not presently publish nor provide the names of the charity trustees.

[70] These changes take effect from 29 March 2016.

[71] See the OSCR, "Targeted regulation of Scottish charities—progressive, preventative and proportionate—A summary of the consultation proposals" published on 5 August 2014. Please also see *http://oscr.org.uk/hot-topics/publishing-charity-accounts* [Accessed 26 May 2016].

The annual return and annual accounts must be submitted to OSCR within nine months of the charity's financial year end. These can now be lodged online, or by hard copy. If it is by hard copy, OSCR require the original signed documents, photocopies will not be acceptable. OSCR's online service has proved to be a great success and the majority of Scottish registered charities now prefer to file directly online. **6–131**

THE OSCR REVIEW PROCESS

OSCR will not accept accounts as fully compliant: **6–132**

- for receipts and payments accounts: if the statement of receipts and payments, statement of balances or independent examiner's or auditor's report are not in the correct form;
- for fully accrued accounts: if the statement of financial activities, balance sheet or auditor's report are not in the correct form; and
- if OSCR identifies a problem in the accounts and has had to write to the charity regarding breaches in the accounting provisions at least three times within consecutive years.

Should this be the case, the charity must resubmit fully compliant accounts within 60 days of OSCR's letter or within nine months of its year end, whichever is the later.

OSCR has also identified various triggers that they will look out for on the annual return, such as a possible trustee remuneration issue.[72] If a trigger is activated, then the accounts and constitution will be scrutinised more closely. OSCR may, of course, also request further information in order to resolve any outstanding queries. If these queries cannot be resolved, then the matter will normally be referred to OSCR's compliance and investigations team. **6–133**

From a practical point of view, it is also usually the case that, where a charity has undergone an investigation in the recent past, or is the subject of current public or press interest, the accounts may also be scrutinised more closely. This provides a further good reason for ensuring that the charity's housekeeping and accounting records are all kept in good order. **6–134**

Once OSCR is satisfied that the annual return and accounts are in order, it will update the charity register accordingly. **6–135**

Likewise it will record whether any charity has been late in filing its annual return and accounts, or whether it is under investigation. This is highlighted in red on the register. It is therefore possible to tell immediately from a check of the charity register what the current position of the charity is and whether or not its filing is up to date. **6–136**

[72] OSCR, "An Updated Guide to the 2006 Regulations", Pt 1, p.18.

CONSOLIDATED ACCOUNTS

6–137 Consolidated accounts and a consolidated trustees report should be produced and submitted annually to OSCR where the charity is part of a group structure (such as a parent charity with subsidiary charities), or where there are one or more trading subsidiaries or community interest companies, and their combined gross income is at least £500,000 after deducting consolidation adjustments.

6–138 In addition, each charity within the group must also prepare their own individual accounts, which must also be submitted to OSCR annually. They are not, however, required to prepare a separate trustees' report. It is sufficient for the accounts to confirm that a consolidated trustees' annual report has been prepared and is available.

FINAL ACCOUNTS

6–139 In the event that the trustees have sought and received OSCR's consent to wind up the charity, whether as part of a reorganisation exercise, takeover, merger or amalgamation, final accounts up to the termination date must be prepared, independently examined or audited and submitted to OSCR. OSCR will not remove the charity from the charity register unless satisfied that everything is in order and the charity's funds are properly accounted for.

6–140 Final accounts up to the date of removal are also required from charities that OSCR has removed from the charity register. Thereafter, for as long as the former charity continues to hold assets or receive income, it remains under a duty to apply these assets and any income from them in accordance with its former charitable purposes,[73] unless the Court of Session approves a scheme allowing OSCR to direct that these assets should pass to another charity. In the meantime, the body is still required to submit an annual statement of account to OSCR, in compliant form, for as long as they continue to hold these assets.

[73] Charities and Trustee Investment (Scotland) Act 2005 s.19.

CHAPTER 7

CHARITY FUNDRAISING AND DONATIONS

Victoria JW Simpson

TRUSTEES DUTIES AND RESPONSIBILITIES IN RELATION TO FUNDRAISING AND DONATIONS

Fundraising can provide an essential source of income, and the development of an effective and appropriate fundraising strategy can be crucial to any charity that is seeking to diversify its income stream and develop new sources of income. As part of the trustees' overall responsibility for managing the charity's affairs, the financial management plan will normally include a budget for the charity's fundraising strategies and will set target income projections over both the short and longer term. When considering any fundraising issue, the trustees have a responsibility to act in the best interests of the charity. Let us further examine trustees' duties of care and prudence in relation to fundraising and the considerations that they must apply. **7–01**

Trustees should first of all ensure that the constitution allows the charity to carry out fundraising or other profile raising activities, to accept donations of all kinds, to delegate fundraising where required and to meet fundraising expenses using the charity's funds. If there is not, the constitution should be updated accordingly[1] to allow this. **7–02**

There are no legal requirements or recommended good practice regarding the minimum or maximum expenditure that the trustees can authorise in relation to any fundraising initiative. It all comes down to what the trustees consider to be reasonable, justifiable and proportionate after taking into account the following considerations, which are discussed in more detail in this chapter: **7–03**

- The charitable purposes and values of the charity. Does the fundraising activity fall within the charitable purposes or do the purposes need to be amended?[2] Is it in the best interests of the charity to undertake this particular fundraising activity? Are there any ethical fundraising issues to take into account?
- The size of the charity and its funds—is the proposed fundraising activity justified? Does it fall within the current budget or if not, is there scope to widen the budget?

---

[1] See paras 5–09—5–19 for further information on this.

[2] See Chs 12 and 13 for further information on this.

- The charity's financial risk profile and a consideration of any possible risks resulting from the proposed fundraising campaign.
- Do the fundraising methods to be used fit in with the charity's values and portray and promote the charity in a favourable way?
- The charity's current public profile and maintaining a good public image.
- The objects of the campaign in terms of both fundraising targets and as a profile raising exercise.
- Whether the funds are intended to be used for a particular fundraising project or whether it will be for the charity's general charitable purposes.
- The intended time scales for the campaign and how it will be conducted, i.e. by the charity itself and its staff, by volunteers or by using a professional fundraiser or commercial participator.
- Do the fundraising methods comply with all relevant legislation and other regulations?
- The anticipated likely financial return.

7–04 It is important that the trustees keep detailed records of their decision-making process throughout the fundraising initiative, and take legal and/or accounting advice where required. This helps to demonstrate that the trustees have properly exercised their duties of care and diligence, good management and financial prudence.

7–05 The importance of good record keeping is demonstrated in the Office of the Scottish Charity Regulator (OSCR) investigation report issued under s.33 of the Charities and Trustee Investment (Scotland) Act 2005 (the 2005 Act) into the Royal Zoological Society of Scotland (the RZSS).[3] As part of their investigation, OSCR were required to consider whether or not the trustees had potentially exposed the RZSS to an unnecessary degree of financial risk by signing a lease agreement for the two giant pandas from China. The trustees were able to provide OSCR with their detailed minutes recording their discussions in full, including the pros and cons of proceeding. The trustees recognised that the lease was not without risk to the RZSS, but considered that the benefits far outweighed the risks. Before coming to a decision the trustees had also taken appropriate legal advice. In doing so, OSCR were satisfied that the trustees had properly considered the matter, had met their statutory duties of care and responsibility and had acted in what they considered to be in the best interests of the RZSS and in accordance with its charitable purposes.

7–06 Any type of fundraising activity will bring the charity and its fundraisers into contact with the wider public, perhaps for the first time. It is the trustees' responsibility to ensure that the charity is represented properly at all times by well trained, knowledgeable and committed staff, volunteers or other professionals who understand that this first crucial impression must be a good one. Winning new supporters as well as retaining long term supporters is also essential. The trustees must always be careful about the way in which the charity is portrayed to the public.

---

[3] This case was published on the OSCR website on 14 February 2012.

A controversial fundraising campaign, perhaps displaying distressing images, using unwelcome fundraising methods or allowing the perception that fundraising standards have fallen can cause serious harm to any charity and risks losing public trust, supporters and confidence in the charity. It emphasises the responsibility placed upon the trustees to ensure that they get every aspect of their fundraising campaigns right and that they choose an appropriate fundraising method. **7–07**

Trustees should remember that, even where the daily running of fundraising activities has been delegated to staff or other agents, it is the trustees who will always bear ultimate responsibility and accountability for the decisions, fundraising strategies and methods that are adopted. Any delegated remit regarding fundraising matters should be clearly set out in writing and reviewed regularly by the trustees and updated when necessary. There should be a good reporting structure put in place so that the trustees are kept well informed of all fundraising progress and developments, and can closely monitor costs against the fundraising budget. If it looks likely that costs may exceed the proposed budget, the trustees should review this and decide whether or not to authorise the additional expense, minuting their reasons for doing so. Whilst fundraising budgets and targets should be realistic, the trustees should also be flexible if it becomes clear that a proposed strategy isn't working and the strategy or business plan needs to be modified. **7–08**

The trustees must also keep a close eye on the way in which funds are collected. We shall look at this in the context of public collections later in this chapter. In addition the trustees must ensure that wherever money has been collected, the charity receives all the funds to which it is entitled.[4] **7–09**

The trustees must be satisfied that, whatever the fundraising method used, the charity complies with all the necessary legal requirements in doing so. Finally, trustees also have a duty to ensure that any fundraising agreement entered into as discussed in more detail below is in the best interests of the charity and is on the best possible terms. Failure to do so could be regarded as a breach in their duty of care. **7–10**

REFUSING DONATIONS

Both the Charity Commission and the Institute of Fundraising (IOF) have produced guidance relating to England and Wales which is useful to consider in relation to Scottish fundraising activities, advising trustees on when it may be **7–11**

---

[4] See the case of *Moonbeams*. Moonbeams was a children's cancer charity based in Edinburgh. Following court action in the Court of Session on 14 October 2003 brought about by the then Scottish Charities Office (the precursor to the 2005 Act and OSCR), it emerged that although the charity had received over £3million in income over the last four years, only £70,000 was applied in accordance with its charitable purposes. The Court of Session suspended the directors and appointed a judicial factor to run the charity's operations. Thereafter, steps were taken to liquidate the charity. There was no evidence of substantial fraud, it was more a case of a poorly administered charity whose income was largely consumed in running costs. See also the case of *Breast Cancer Research (Scotland)*, another charity that collapsed in 2003 after it was found that only £1.5m of the £13m it raised went to charity.

appropriate to refuse a donation.[5] It suggests that trustees should exercise particular care when deciding whether it is necessary to refuse a donation for practical reasons and because they consider that it is in the best interests of the charity to do so, as discussed below. There is no legal procedure set out in the 2005 Act whereby trustees can seek OSCR's consent before refusing a donation. Trustees are recommended, however, to first consider taking legal advice to ensure that they have met their duty of care under s.66(1) of the 2005 Act.

7–12 As a matter of good practice, trustees should be able to demonstrate that they have reasonable grounds to believe that accepting the donation could be detrimental to the charity in some way. Perhaps the potential donor has attached certain conditions to the donation that the trustees consider to be contrary to the charity's purposes, or that would require the trustees to carry out some ultra vires act, or that the trustees generally view as being unreasonable.[6] Receiving a donation of a significant amount of money or property from an unknown or unverified source that could potentially be from a "tainted" source, is also a notifiable event under OSCR's targeted regulatory changes, which came into effect from 1 April 2016.[7]

7–13 Alternatively, the trustees could take the view that there is a risk that the donation is being made for money laundering purposes or from the proceeds of a criminal activity. The charity can minimise this risk by having appropriate policies and procedures in place and by ensuring that all staff and volunteers know to look out for suspicious donations.[8]

FUNDRAISING MATERIAL

7–14 The trustees must also ensure that any promotional or fundraising material that is available to the public complies with all the requirements of the Charities References in Documents (Scotland) Regulations 2007 as amended.[9] This must show that it is a charity, give its name, any other name that it may trade under or be known by, its charity number and whether it is a Scottish or dual registered charity. A charitable company or Scottish Charitable Incorporated Organisation (SCIO) must in addition give the registered office address. Charitable companies must also give their company number.[10]

---

[5] See the IOF "Acceptance and Refusal of Donations Guidance", under the section dealing with Scotland headed "Refusing a donation in Scotland" and Charity Commission general guidance on "Charity Fundraising: A Guide to Trustee Duties" (CC 20) (7 June 2016).

[6] See the IOF guidance on "Acceptance and Refusal of Donations" guidance under the section dealing with Scotland headed "Refusing a donation in Scotland".

[7] See OSCR's "Guidance on Notifiable Events" published in March 2016. The trustees must decide whether the event could have a potentially significant impact upon the charity and should therefore report it to OSCR as soon as possible after discovery. OSCR will want to know the steps taken to identify the funding source and also any particular concerns the trustees have.

[8] See the Charity Commission guidance on "Trustees and Fundraising", Ch.6, "Protect your charity's reputation, money and other assets".

[9] Charities References in Documents (Scotland) Regulations 2007 (SSI 2007/203).

[10] See the Charities References in Documents (Scotland) Regulations 2007 as amended for further information.

All fundraising material should also be checked to ensure that the information is accurate and that the charity and fundraising appeal have been portrayed correctly. It cannot be misleading in any way and should be transparent and respectable. If it is for a particular appeal, does it explain openly to the public what the appeal is for and how the funds will be applied? Does it say how the excess funds will be used if the appeal targets are exceeded, or what will happen if the appeal funds fall short of the target? The charity does not want to be in the difficult position of having to return donations because it didn't provide an alternative use. Make it clear that the charity's general funds will benefit in this event. Remember to keep any money collected for a particular appeal separate from general funds.[11] **7–15**

THE SELF REGULATORY FUNDRAISING SYSTEM—A NEW LANDSCAPE OF ENHANCED REGULATION

It is important to maintain public confidence in the charity sector and to be able to demonstrate that charities are seeking to fundraise in a way that is responsible, legal, open, transparent, honest and respectful. Trust in charity fundraising remains high in Scotland, but did fall in 2015.[12] This was primarily due to the UK-wide adverse press coverage of matters such as the death of Olive Cooke,[13] the collapse of high profile charities such as Kids Company, the row over senior executive pay and also criticism over the Kiltwalk.[14] Trust was also lost due to some of the negative fundraising methods experienced by the general public, such as street fundraising and telephone fundraising. **7–16**

This led to a UK-wide review of the current self regulatory system of fundraising (discussed in more detail below) by the National Council for Voluntary Organisations (NCVO) for England and Wales commissioned by the UK **7–17**

---

[11] See the IOF information on "Honesty in Fundraising" for further information: *http://www.institute-of-fundraising.org.uk/guidance/about-fundraising/honesty-in-fundraising/* [Accessed 26 May 2016].

[12] Please see the SCVO report on "The effectiveness of the self-regulation of fundraising in Scotland: an informal review": (*http://scvo.org.uk/long-form-posts/fundraising-in-scotland-survey-report/* [Accessed 26 May 2016]) issued in September 2015.

[13] Olive Cooke was a pensioner whose suicide in 2015 was linked by the media to the large number of charity fundraising letters she had received that she was reported to have found overwhelming. The FRSB's investigation following her death stated that during her lifetime she had given to at least 88 charities, 48 of them regularly. She had also been a long-term volunteer for the Royal British Legion. Of the 1,442 charities that took part in the investigation, over 99 charities had her details on file. Twenty four of these charities had passed her contact details on to other organisations without her express consent in breach of the Data Protection Act 1988 and the Privacy and Electronic Communications (EC Directive) Regulations (SI 2003/2426). Mrs Cooke's details were therefore held on the donor lists maintained by 22 commercial data suppliers. Many of the charities sending Mrs Cooke mail didn't make it easy for her to opt out of the mailings. Please see the FRSB report on the Olive Cooke investigation published on 20 January 2016.

[14] In June 2015 four of the Kiltwalks' official charity sponsors (CLIC Sargent; Cash for Kids; Aberlour and Edinburgh Sick Kids Friends Foundations) withdrew their support over concerns about the amount of money reaching them from the Kiltwalk. In June 2015 the latest accounts showed that of the income of £1.6 million, £780,000 was spent on running costs, which was more than the amount of £776,000 received by each charity. The entire board was replaced as a result.

Government, known as the Etherington Report.[15] This was followed by the Scottish Government that has devolved powers over charity regulation who asked the Scottish Council for Voluntary Organisations (SCVO) to carry out its own informal review of the system in Scotland.[16] Both reports were now been published in autumn 2015. Their proposals are outlined below:

THE ETHERINGTON REPORT

7–18 This recommended a number of changes. These included replacing the Fundraising Standards Board (the FRSB) with a new body, "the Fundraising Regulator", which came into operation on 7 July 2016 and covers England and Wales. The Fundraising Regulator will set its own standards of fundraising practice by adopting and developing the existing Code of Fundraising Practice as provided by the IOF. It will report to the Public Administration and Constitutional Affairs Committee of the UK Parliament and will be funded by the charity sector. It will prioritise the public interest and better protect vulnerable people.

7–19 The Fundraising Regulator will oversee a new "fundraising preference service" in England and Wales that will allow the public to opt out of receiving fundraising literature or phone calls. One request to opt out will mean that the individual concerned is opting out of all fundraising efforts from any charity. The individual will need to actively opt in to the charities that they wish to support in order to hear from them.

THE SCVO REPORT

7–20 This recognised that while public trust in Scotland over charity fundraising had fallen, the overall trust still remained high. It stated that

> "most expressed a wish that the review is not a knee-jerk reaction in response to negative media coverage. Respondents want the review to take a long-term, supportive view that recognises that fundraising is carried out responsibly for the most part".[17]

The report recommended that self regulation should remain in place but that the system needed to be improved.[18]

---

[15] Please see the Etherington Report for further details: *https://www.ncvo.org.uk/about-us/media-centre/press-releases/1033-tough-new-fundraising-regulator-to-ensure-high-standards-review* [Accessed 26 May 2016]) published in September 2015.

[16] See the SCVO report on "The effectiveness of the self-regulation of fundraising in Scotland: an informal review": (*http://scvo.org.uk/long-form-posts/fundraising-in-scotland-survey-report/*) issued in September 2015.

[17] See the SCVO, "The effectiveness of the self-regulation of fundraising in Scotland: an informal review", s.2.2.

[18] See the SCVO, "The effectiveness of the self-regulation of fundraising in Scotland: an informal review", s.2.3.

SUMMARY

The SCVO established the Scottish Fundraising Working Group to consider three new options for self-regulation, which went out to public consultation. The options were: **7–21**

(1) a model that followed the Etherington Report proposals, so that fundraising in Scotland would become part of the UK-wide system subject to a UK-wide fundraising regulator;
(2) a similar to option (1) above, but with a new Scottish fundraising regulator; and
(3) a model that would more closely follow the SCVO report, so that the existing self-regulatory system would be strengthened and OSCR would be given greater powers. There would not be a new fundraising regulator.

Consultation on the report closed on 31 March 2016. The results showed that the third option had the most support, so the Scottish Fundraising Working Group has recommended that this be adopted in Scotland. **7–22**

WHAT ARE THE MAIN PROPOSALS MADE BY THE SCOTTISH FUNDRAISING WORKING GROUP

The main proposals by SCVO[19] reflect the findings set out in SCVO's earlier report and are as follows: **7–23**

- that a new Scottish fundraising hub be established,[20] which now takes effect from 7 July 2016 to tie in with the launch of the Fundraising Regulator in England and Wales. The hub is intended to be the first port of call for the public to express their views about charity fundraising or to make a complaint about a particular charity;
- that a UK-wide approach is adopted to developing the new fundraising standards. A new Scottish Independent Standards and Adjudication Panel (the "Independent Panel") will be put in place by autumn 2016. This body will work closely with the Fundraising Regulator to adopt, develop and improve the existing IOF Code of Fundraising Practice. The Independent Panel will be made up of the public, donors, charities, fundraisers, OSCR and the Scottish Government. All charities will be subject to the new fundraising regime and must now adhere to the Code of Fundraising Practice. Previously it was up to each individual charity to decide whether or not to become a member of the IOF and sign up to the Code of Fundraising Practice. Non-member charities were therefore not regulated. It has been suggested that this arrangement be reviewed in 12 months time

[19] See the SCVO report "Clear, confident and connected: An enhanced system of charity fundraising regulation for Scotland" (June 2016).
[20] The hub can be contacted on telephone number 08081642520 or by accessing the website on *http://www.fundraisingcomplaints.scot* or by email on scottishfundraisingcomplaints@scvo.org.uk.

to see how it is working and decide whether or not it is necessary to develop any separate Scottish fundraising standards;

- that an improved complaints procedure is introduced for all charities and that all charities should have a robust complaints procedure in place. This is discussed in more detail below. Any complaint directed to the new charity hub will be passed to the charity concerned in the first instance to deal with. Complaints relating to fundraising in dual registered charities will be resolved using the "lead regulator model", i.e. by being passed to the Fundraising Regulator;
- it is strongly recommended that the Fundraising Regulator's board has at least one Scottish representative to ensure that Scotland's interests are represented when the Fundraising Regulator sets the new standards for UK-wide fundraising practice;
- that all Scottish charities ensure that their donors have access to a straightforward process to opt out of fundraising communications if they choose to do so. The Scottish Fundraising Working Group has not recommended at this stage that Scotland adopt the Fundraising Preference Service mentioned above;
- that the Independent Panel should be able to choose its own non statutory sanctions that will be in line with those available to the Fundraising Regulator;
- that a new "fundraising guarantee" should be developed that will be available to the public, setting out the values, culture and practices that all charities operating in Scotland should follow;
- that all fundraisers should receive suitable training and if necessary that a new qualifications system should be developed;
- that the new fundraising regulatory system should report annually to the Scottish Parliament that will also oversee these developments;
- it is also anticipated that all charities will be required to contribute to the cost of supporting the enhanced self regulatory system going forward. SCVO will fund the Scottish fundraising complaints hub for the first 12 months;
- as explained above, the new system for self regulated fundraising came into operation in Scotland on 7 July 2016. The Scottish Fundraising Working Group has suggested that it reform again after 12 months to consider how the system is working and to suggest any further improvements. In the meantime, an implementation group is being set up in Scotland to recruit the Independent Panel which is intended to be in place by autumn 2016. The implementation group will also look at the remit, of the Indpendent Panel, how it will be funded in the long term, what powers it should have, the working relationship it will have with OSCR and how fundraising complaints should be handled; and
- it is also anticipated that further primary legislation will be required for OSCR to properly fulfil its role as an enhanced regulator and to enable it to impose proportionate and appropriate civil or interim sanctions. OSCR can presently only impose criminal sanctions under the 2005 Act.

THE SELF REGULATORY FUNDRAISING SYSTEM

The principles and standards of fundraising in a responsible, legal, open, transparent, honest and respectful way are set out in the Code of Fundraising Practice. This was initally developed by the IOF and will now be adopted and developed by the Fundraising Regulator and the Independent Panel. The Code represents a benchmark standard of good fundraising practice. **7–24**

The IOF is the professional body representing fundraising in the UK. By becoming a member of the IOF, charity trustees demonstrate that their charity is following the Code of Fundraising Practice when carrying out their fundraising activities. The IOF also produces some helpful guidance on good fundraising practice which is available on their website. **7–25**

The IOF differs to the Public Fundraising Association ("PFRA"), which is the standards and membership body for organisations carrying out street and door to door fundraising.[21] **7–26**

COMPLAINTS PROCEDURE

All charities should have a written complaints procedure in place to deal with any complaints they receive about the charity's fundraising methods/practices and the individuals concerned. It should be made available to the public on request and must be clear and transparent. This procedure should be reviewed regularly and kept up to date. It should be followed closely by the charity as soon as a complaint is received in order to minimise any potential reputational damage and to protect the charity's good name. **7–27**

The procedure should set out the time scales involved for dealing with the complaint and the charity should aim to deal with it as quickly as possible. In doing so, the charity can also identify any problems arising in their fundraising strategies, learn from them and do their best to ensure that they do not happen again. It is important that the charity can demonstrate that all such complaints are dealt with efficiently and promptly. **7–28**

If the charity is unable to resolve the complaint to the satisfaction of the individual concerned, then larger charities should have a two tier complaints process whereby the matter can then be referred to the trustees. **7–29**

If the complainer is still not satisfied having gone through the charities complaints procedure, the complaint can now be referred to the Independent Panel.[22] The Independent Panel will be able to decide whether or not the charity has breached the Code of Fundraising Practice and will be able to tell the charity what steps to take to correct this. **7–30**

Where the Independent Panel identifies any regulatory concerns while investigating the complaint, such as any concerns about the breach of trustees' duties, any **7–31**

---

[21] See their website *http://www.pfra.org.uk* for further information and advice.

[22] See the SCVO report "Clear, Confident and Connected; An Enhanced System of Charity Fundraising Regulation" published in June 2016 for further information.

misconduct or mismanagement in the administration of the charity that could potentially jeopardise the charity's assets and damage the charity's reputation and public trust, then the Independent Panel can refer the matter to OSCR under its current inquiry powers. The Scottish Fundraising Working Group have recommended that the Independent Panel and OSCR work closely together to provide a clear and proportionate fundraising complaints system for charities in Scotland.

BENEVOLENT FUNDRAISING

7–32 There are statutory regulations[23] that deal with fundraising and apply to any form of benevolent body that has been set up for charitable, benevolent or philanthropic purposes; so it does not necessarily have to be a charity. OSCR will, however, only have a remit over benevolent bodies that are also Scottish charities and these are examined here. We will first consider how these regulations will apply to a charity that wishes to use a commercial partner in its fundraising activities.

ENTERING INTO A FUNDRAISING ARRANGEMENT WITH A COMMERCIAL PARTNER

7–33 The charity could decide to enter into a fundraising arrangement with what the regulations refer to as either a professional fundraiser or a commercial participator. What is the difference? A professional fundraiser[24] is defined as being a person or company that carries out a fee charging fundraising service.

7–34 A commercial participator is a company that undertakes a promotional venture, advertising that part of their profits will be donated to one or more charities,[25] such as a bank promoting an affinity credit card or the sale of charity Christmas cards.[26] Let's consider the implications of this further.

7–35 It can be advantageous to the charity to use a professional fundraiser, who will have the expertise, staff and facilities to initiate and carry out a large scale fundraising appeal that a charity may not necessarily have. A professional fundraiser may also agree to bear some of the financial risk of failure, helping to mitigate some of the risk to the charity, although the charity will always bear the higher degree of risk.[27]

---

[23] The legal requirements are set out in ss.79–83 of the Charities and Trustee Investment (Scotland) Act 2005 and the Charities and Benevolent Fundraising (Scotland) Regulations 2009 (SI 2009/121). Please also see OSCR's guidance on the Regulations, called "Benevolent Fundraising Guidance", published June 2009.

[24] Charities and Trustee Investment (Scotland) Act 2005 s.79(1).

[25] Charities and Trustee Investment (Scotland) Act 2005 s.79(1).

[26] See the OSCR guidance on the Charities and Benevolent Fundraising (Scotland) Regulations 2009 (SI 2009/121), glossary re "Commercial Participators".

[27] See also Charity Commission guidance on "Charity Fundraising: A Guide to Trustees duties" (CC 20) (7 June 2016), s.6.1 "Protect your charity's reputation" and s.5 "Supervise your Fundraisers", subs.5.3.

The trustees do, however, need to carefully consider any risk to the charity in entering into the arrangement. The charity is allowing the professional fundraiser to use the charity's name and logo and in some cases the professional fundraiser's staff will represent the charity to the public (see the comments below regarding protecting the charity's reputation in para.7–37). The trustees must be satisfied with the techniques and methods that the fundraisers will use to engage the public and with the way that the charity is portrayed. **7–36**

An arrangement with a commercial participator gives a charity the opportunity to significantly raise their public profile. If handled sensibly, the arrangement can provide a good marketing opportunity for both the company and the charity. The trustees must ensure that the charity's reputation, name, brand, logo and values are protected at all times, particularly as a commercial participator may wish to include the charity's branding on some of its own products. The trustees must be satisfied that there is no unauthorised or inappropriate use of the charity's brand and agree how the charity's name, brand and logo will be used. **7–37**

Using a commercial participator rather than a professional fundraiser can provide a lower degree of risk, provided that the charity is satisfied with their ethical choice of company and the way in which the charity brand will be promoted or associated with that particular product or service. The trustees should seek as far as possible to minimise any risk of being associated with a company that could later be discredited owing to inappropriate or criminal practises by fully researching the company before entering into any agreement, particularly if it is a non-UK based company that is not subject to the requirements of UK law.[28] **7–38**

PUTTING A WRITTEN FUNDRAISING AGREEMENT IN PLACE

The regulations[29] make it a criminal offence for a commercial partner to fundraise for a charity without first having a written agreement put in place. For a professional fundraiser this means that the charity must put a written fundraising agreement in place before the professional fundraiser can seek money or any promises of money (i.e. direct debit arrangements, etc.) on behalf of the charity. For a commercial participator, this means putting a written agreement in place before the commercial participator informs the public that all or part of the proceeds in a promotional venture are for a particular charity. This agreement must be signed by both the charity and commercial partner concerned. **7–39**

The written agreement must include the following information[30]: **7–40**

- the date the agreement was signed;
- the period it will cover;
- any terms regarding the variation or termination of the agreement before the agreed expiry date;

[28] Charity Commission guidance on "Charity Fundraising: A Guide to Trustees duties" (CC 20) (7 June 2016), s.6.1 "Protect your charity's reputation" and s.5 "Supervise your Fundraisers", subs.5.3.
[29] Charities and Trustee Investment (Scotland) Act 2005 s.81 and the Charities and Benevolent Fundraising (Scotland) Regulations 2009 reg.7(1).
[30] See the Charities and Benevolent Fundraising (Scotland) Regulations 2009 reg.2.

- the objectives of the agreement and the fundraising methods to be used;
- if the agreement covers more than one charity, how the charities will split the funds between them;
- how the remuneration and expenses of the commercial partner will be calculated; and
- for commercial participators only, the proportion of the proceeds to be received by the charity and the amount of donations the commercial participator will make to the charity as a result of the sales.

7–41 It is also helpful to provide that the funds will be transferred to the charity as soon as possible. The onus is on the commercial partner to ensure that the agreement is drawn up correctly because otherwise it cannot be enforced against the charity without seeking a court order. Likewise a commercial partner cannot reclaim their expenses if there is no provision to do so in the agreement.[31]

7–42 As a matter of good practice, the trustees should consider taking legal advice before entering into the agreement. The trustees have a duty of care to the charity to ensure that the charity receives the best possible return under the arrangement, that the terms are in the charity's best interests and that the remuneration/ expenses payable are reasonable. The agreement should be kept under regular review.

7–43 It is also a criminal offence for the commercial partner to refuse to make available on request its books, records, documents or other records relating to the agreement. This is to enable the charity to monitor the funds collected and ensure that the funds are handed over as per the agreement.

WHAT INFORMATION MUST FUNDRAISERS GIVE TO THE PUBLIC UNDER THE REGULATIONS?

7–44 This information is set out below. It varies depending upon who carries out the fundraising and how it is done. Interestingly, the regulations do not cover the information to be provided by charity volunteers, although OSCR suggests that as a matter of good practice volunteers should make it clear to the public which charity they represent and the fact that they are volunteers.[32]

7–45 **For fundraising carried out by the charity's own fundraisers/ employees**

- the charity's name;
- if more than one charity is to benefit, how the funds will be divided; and
- for oral fundraising, that they are an employee and remunerated by the charity. The precise amount does not need to be disclosed.

7–46 **For fundraising carried out by professional fundraisers**

- the charity's name;

[31] See Charities and Trustee Investment (Scotland) Act 2005 s.81(5) and 81(6).

[32] See OSCR, "Guide to the Charities and Benevolent Fundraising (Scotland) Regulations 2009" s.4.1.

- if more than one charity is to benefit, how the funds will be divided;
- whether they are to receive any remuneration and how it will be calculated. They must disclose the actual amount if known, otherwise an estimate should be provided; and
- for both oral and written appeals that the information on remuneration is available in writing and will be provided upon request.

For fundraising carried out by commercial participators 7–47

- the charity's name;
- if more than one charity is to benefit, how the funds will be divided;
- whether they are to be remunerated and if so, how it is calculated. The following must be stated if known:
  - (a) the actual/estimated proceeds received for the goods or services provided;
  - (b) the actual/estimated proceeds received from the promotional venture; and
  - (c) the level of donations to the charity in relation to the goods/services provided.
- for both written and oral fundraising appeals, that information on remuneration is available in writing and will be provided upon request.

PROVIDING INFORMATION ABOUT THE RIGHT TO RECEIVE A REFUND OR TO CANCEL AN AGREEMENT

Commercial partners must also inform potential donors in an oral appeal of their right to seek a refund or to cancel their agreement to make a charitable payment if they have either paid £100 or more by debit or credit card in response to a television or radio appeal, or if they have paid £100 or more by any means in response to a telephone/video email appeal. 7–48

Failure to provide this information is a criminal offence. The refund or cancellation request must be made in writing within seven days of the request to the commercial partner. It is also a criminal offence for the commercial partner to fail to meet the request as soon as reasonably possible. The refund can only be refused if services or goods have already been provided in return for the donation, unless the donor returns the goods. The commercial partner is also entitled to deduct their reasonable administrative costs from the refund. 7–49

Please note that the right to a refund only applies to oral fundraising appeals carried out by a commercial partner, not to those carried out directly by a charity or its trading company. OSCR suggests however that as a matter of good practice that *all* fundraisers (including charity employees) meet *any* request for a refund within seven days of the request, if practical to do so.[33] 7–50

[33] OSCR, "Guidance on the Charities and Benevolent Fundraising (Scotland) Regulations 2009" s.3.

7–51 Finally, it is a criminal offence[34] for the commercial partner to fail to transfer the money or promises of money to the charity as soon as possible and within at least 28 days of receipt.[35]

PREVENTING UNAUTHORISED FUNDRAISING

7–52 A charity should take steps to prevent any unauthorised fundraising (whether by an individual or any other body) in order to protect its name and brand and to prevent any adverse publicity or reputational damage. The legal process that the charity should go through is as follows[36]:

- It should serve a notice on the person or body, requesting that they immediately cease to fundraise on behalf of the charity. The notice must state that if they fail to do so, the charity will seek an interdict. It is recommended that the notice is sent by recorded delivery.
- If the person or body continues to fundraise regardless of the notice, then after 28 days the charity can apply to the court seeking an interdict.
- If the person or body stopped fundraising after receiving the notice, but started again after the 28 day period has elapsed (but within 12 months of the date of the notice), the charity can immediately apply for an interdict. No further notice is required.

7–53 Instances of this may be unusual, but there is no quick solution to this problem and it is unfortunate that the charity concerned may have to incur the costs of seeking court intervention at all. The charity may also need to consider other ways of minimising any reputational damage in the meantime, such as a press release. More serious cases may even require police involvement. As a matter of good practice the charity can also inform OSCR. It is worth noting that there can also be serious implications for the fundraisers concerned.[37]

---

[34] All references to a criminal offence in this section are to a fine not exceeding level 5 on the standard scale, which is currently £5,000.

[35] See the Charities and Benevolent Fundraising (Scotland) Regulations 2009 reg.6.

[36] See Charities and Trustee Investment (Scotland) Act 2005 s.82.

[37] OSCR can, under the Charities and Trustee Investment (Scotland) Act 2005 s.31, direct that a person or body stop acting for a charity, or cease holding themselves out as representing a charity and "within such period as the direction may specify" pay over the proceeds to the charity. Although there is no time limit specified within the legislation to deal with this, as OSCR need to carry out an inquiry under s.28 of the 2005 Act first, it is unlikely to be within the 28 day time scale mentioned in this section.

PUBLIC BENEVOLENT COLLECTIONS

The new local authority and OSCR-led system for licensing public benevolent collections are not yet in force.[38] We are also awaiting the more detailed regulations governing public benevolent collections under the 2005 Act.[39] 7–54

For the time being therefore, the law dealing with public benevolent collections remains: the Civic Government (Scotland) Act 1982 (the 1982 Act); the Public Charitable Collections (Scotland) Regulations 1984 (the 1984 Regulations); and the Public Charitable Collections (Scotland) Amendment Regulations 1988 (the 1988 Regulations). 7–55

We will therefore consider the current position regarding public benevolent collections and the proposed changes as set out in the 2005 Act. 7–56

WHAT IS A PUBLIC COLLECTION?

A public collection is defined as being a collection of money from the public that is carried out in a public place or by means of visits from place to place (such as house to house) for charitable purposes.[40] "Charitable purposes" is defined as being any charitable, benevolent or philanthropic purpose, so it doesn't necessarily need to be for a Scottish registered charity. 7–57

Once the new legislation under the 2005 Act comes into force,[41] this definition will be extended to include collections of both cash and promises of money, such as a direct debit. This means that fundraisers looking to sign up individuals in a public place to give a direct debit to a charity will also require to be licensed. 7–58

A "public place"[42] under the 2005 Act will include any road or other place to which the public have the right of free access at the time of the collection. This definition will therefore apply to a privately owned building or area such as a shopping centre, train station, airport or shop entrance. 7–59

Private collections such as those carried out within a "members only" association or club (not accessible by the general public), or within a family group carried out on private premises are not covered by these regulations.[43] The collectors should still however have regard to the regulations and guidelines issued by the IOF regarding the Code of Fundraising Practice, and make sure that the charity knows about the collection so that the cash can be properly accounted for. 7–60

[38] These new provisions are set out in the Charities and Trustee Investment (Scotland) Act 2005 ss.83–92. These sections of the 2005 Act will cover both street collections and door to door collections.

[39] These can be issued under the Charities and Trustee Investment (Scotland) Act 2005 s.90, which will be open to public consultation before coming into force.

[40] See the Civic Government (Scotland) Act 1982 s.119(16).

[41] See the Charities and Trustee Investment (Scotland) Act 2005 s.84, which is not yet in force.

[42] See the Charities and Trustee Investment (Scotland) Act 2005 s.84(3), not yet in force.

[43] In particular they are not covered by the Civic Government (Scotland) Act 1982.

WHAT CONSENTS ARE REQUIRED TO HOLD A PUBLIC COLLECTION?

7–61 Charities must currently obtain a licence to hold a public collection (whether it is a street collection or door to door) from the appropriate local authority for that area. Most local authorities require a minimum of at least one month's notice, which the charity should check.[44] Some local authorities may require longer notice periods. It is an offence to hold a public collection without obtaining the permission to do so.[45]

7–62 In addition, if the collection is being held on privately owned property, such as a shopping centre or train station, the charity should also seek the consent of the owner or manager.

7–63 Once the new legislation comes into force,[46] a written application must be submitted to the local authority concerned at least two months in advance of the proposed collection date (up to a maximum of 18 months advance notice). The local authority will be obliged to consult with the chief constable and can make such other inquiries as it considers necessary before making a decision. The local authority will be able to impose such conditions as it sees fit, such as the date, time or frequency of the collection, where it can take place; and regulate the way in which the collection is conducted in terms of the types of collection boxes to be used, collectors' identification badges, etc.

7–64 The local authority will have various grounds upon which they may refuse the licence, which include the following[47]:

- if the date, time, frequency of the collection or the proposed location will cause undue public inconvenience;
- if they have already consented to another collection taking place in that area either on the same day, or on the day before or after;
- if it appears that the collected funds to be applied for charitable or benevolent purposes will be inadequate when compared to the size of the likely collection, which is understood to mean that the costs of the collection are disproportionately high;
- if the organiser has failed to provide any additional information which the local authority request; and
- if the organiser has previously committed an offence under the 2005 Act, such as holding a collection without a licence, or any other offence involving dishonesty.[48]

7–65 The local authority will still be able to withdraw its consent once issued, vary its terms or impose additional terms no later than one day before the proposed collection date if it believes that there has been a change in circumstances, so that

[44] Please also see s.119 of the Civic Government (Scotland) Act 1982 for further information about the procedure to be followed.

[45] Civic Government (Scotland) Act 1982 s.119(1). If convicted, a fine can be imposed.

[46] Charities and Trustee Investment (Scotland) Act 2005 s.86.

[47] Charities and Trustee Investment (Scotland) Act 2005 s.86(6).

[48] Charities and Trustee Investment (Scotland) Act 2005 ss.85(1), 90(3) or 91(3).

one or more of the above mentioned grounds of refusal now apply or there is likely to be a breach of any imposed condition.[49]

The local authority must give the organiser the reasons for its decision, which the organiser can appeal against by making a summary application to the sheriff.[50] An appeal can only be made regarding the granting of consent subject to conditions, refusing consent, withdrawing or varying a consent. A decision about the date of the proposed collection cannot be appealed.[51] **7–66**

THE EXEMPT PROMOTERS SCHEME

For charities that currently carry out significant fundraising activities over all or part of Scotland, the process is made much easier by applying to OSCR to become an exempt promoter.[52] Exempt promoter status is not held by the charity itself. It is, instead, held by an employee acting on behalf of that particular charity. This, of course, can cause practical difficulties if the individual leaves the charity and the charity has to start the process again. **7–67**

The obvious advantage of being an exempt promoter is that they do not need to obtain local authority consent before organising a public collection. This is particularly useful if collections are being held over a wide area covering a number of different local authority areas. However, the exempt promoter must still give the local authority three months notice of their intention to hold the collection and must also adhere to all other regulatory requirements. **7–68**

In order to become an exempt promoter for a specific charity, the individual concerned has to demonstrate the following to OSCR[53]: **7–69**

- that they have collected over at least five different local authority areas in Scotland during the charity's three financial years preceding the application;
- that every year each collection has produced a reasonable sum;
- that their expenses incurred in organising the public collections have not exceeded more than 30 per cent of the amount collected; and
- they must submit the report and accounts for the charity in question for the last three financial years and any written agreement the charity may have with a commercial fundraising partner.

49 Charities and Trustee Investment (Scotland) Act 2005 s.86(7) and 86(8).
50 Charities and Trustee Investment (Scotland) Act 2005 s.88.
51 Charities and Trustee Investment (Scotland) Act 2005 s.88(2).
52 See the Civic Government (Scotland) Act 1982 s.119(11).
53 See OSCR's guidance note on "Public Charitable Collections".

7–70 If OSCR is satisfied with this information, it will issue a direction confirming that exempt promoter status has been awarded to that individual. To maintain exempt promoter status, exempt promoters must also submit the following information to OSCR annually[54]:

- an audited breakdown of the public charitable collections that have been carried out;
- a breakdown of the amounts collected and the expenses incurred for each local authority area;
- signed statements from both the promoter and the auditor of the charity in question, in the prescribed form set out in the Schedule to the 1984 Regulations; and
- a copy of the notice summarising the audited collection accounts published in a newspaper with a national circulation throughout Scotland. This must be published within one month of the date that the above mentioned information is submitted to OSCR.

7–71 OSCR will examine this information and, if all is in order, issue a formal letter confirming that exempt promoter status remains in place.

DESIGNATED NATIONAL COLLECTORS

7–72 One significant difference under the 2005 Act[55] is that the charity itself will receive designated national collector status rather than it being an individual organiser, as per the current exempt promoters scheme. OSCR will be able to grant and withdraw designation as a national collector,[56] replacing the current exempt promoters scheme. OSCR will also be able to specify the criteria to be met for the purpose of obtaining and retaining designated national collector status and will be required to consult on this.

7–73 A designated national collector that proposes to hold a public collection must inform the local authority no earlier than 18 months and no later than three months before the proposed collection date.

7–74 The local authority will be entitled to prevent the collection taking place if it considers that it is likely to cause undue public inconvenience (such as another collection being held on the same date and at the same time and place). If so, it must inform the designated national collector of the reasons for its decision and inform them of their right to appeal.[57]

54 This information has been taken from OSCR, "Public Charitable Collections". Please also see the Public Charitable Collections (Scotland) Regulations 1984 and the Public Charitable Collections (Scotland) Amendment Regulations 1988 for further information.
55 Charities and Trustee Investment (Scotland) Act 2005 s.87 (not yet in force).
56 Charities and Trustee Investment (Scotland) Act 2005 s.87 (not yet in force).
57 Charities and Trustee Investment (Scotland) Act 2005 s.88.

THE COLLECTION OF GOODS

The public collection of goods for charitable or benevolent purposes is not currently regulated.[58] The 2005 Act[59] makes provision for the Scottish ministers to issue such regulations as may be required. Contravention of these regulations will be an offence.[60] **7–75**

The collection envelope or materials must clearly state the name of the charity and who will be carrying out the collection, as well as containing all the usual information about the charity.[61] Please refer to the OSCR guidance on "Charity Doorstep Collections" and the IOF's "Clothing Collections Guidance", both of which contain information for charities and donors about the legitimacy of goods collections and ensuring that the donation is properly collected. **7–76**

Local authorities must have regard to any guidance issued by OSCR and liaise with OSCR regarding the exercise of their functions in relation to public benevolent collections or the collection of goods.[62] **7–77**

We will now consider the practical controls that the charity should put in place to ensure that collections are properly monitored and carried out. **7–78**

THE COLLECTORS

Only adults over the age of 16 are allowed to conduct a public or house to house collection as there are obvious child protection issues. The charity should take reasonable steps to ensure that all collectors are suitable to collect and represent the charity in a professional, courteous and informed way, without causing any public inconvenience or obstruction. Donors or potential householders/site holders should never be pressurised. Proper training if required should be given to the collectors before they commence work, explaining the legislative requirements and the charity's procedures for handling and paying over cash. **7–79**

All collectors must have an identity badge and a certificate of authority which must be shown to the householder/site holder. These should both contain the following: **7–80**

For the identity badge: **7–81**

- the charity's registered name and any other name it is known by;

---

[58] Under either of the Public Charitable Collections (Scotland) Regulations 1984 and the Public Charitable Collections (Scotland) Amendment Regulations 1988.

[59] Covered under the Charities and Trustee Investment (Scotland) Act 2005 s.91. It covers the requirement that the organiser of the collection should notify the local authority of the area to be included, allows the local authority to prohibit the collection and regarding the dates, times, places and frequency with which the collection can be carried out, keeping and publishing records of the collection and seeking to prevent public inconvenience.

[60] This could result in being liable under summary conviction to a fine not exceeding level 5 on the standard scale.

[61] As per the Charities References in Documents (Scotland) Regulations 2007 as amended, also discussed in para.7–14.

[62] Charities and Trustee Investment (Scotland) Act 2005 s.92.

- the charity's status, i.e. registered in Scotland or dual registered; and
- the charity number.

7–82 **For the certificate of authority:**

- all the above mentioned information;
- the collector's name and address;
- where the collection is to be held;
- the authorised collection dates; and
- it must be signed by both the collector and by or on behalf of the charity.

7–83 It is also good practice to include the contact details of the fundraising organisation where relevant. Reference should also be made to the Public Fundraising Regulatory Authority (PFRA) for further guidance and best practice in dealing with the public on a face to face basis and the applicable regulations.[63] The PFRA runs compliance checks and has a self accreditation process for members.

7–84 In addition the IOF also suggests that collectors are issued with written instructions[64] setting out the following:

- clear guidelines on how to conduct the collection;
- emergency contact details in case there are any problems;
- the need to comply with the IOF guidance;
- the precise collection area;
- the dates and times they can collect (not after 9pm);
- the materials they will be issued with as set out above, which are to be returned on completion; and
- if a professional fundraiser is used, a briefing on the charity so they are well informed and knowledgeable.

CONDUCTING A CASH COLLECTION

7–85 Each collector should be issued with either collection boxes, buckets, tins or collection envelopes. These should all be numbered and contain the charity's name, address and charity number.

7–86 All collection boxes, buckets or tins (including freestanding ones sitting on a counter or bar, etc.) should be securely made out of plastic, wood or metal and either sealed or locked and then covered with a tamper proof seal. Freestanding collection boxes or tins should also be secured to the floor or counter to reduce

---

[63] See *http://www.pfra.org.uk* [Accessed 26 May 2016].

[64] See the IOF guidance on "Public Collections" section on "conduct of collections". Also see the guidance on "conduct of fundraisers/agents" on the "face to face fundraising" section of "conduct of collections".

the likelihood of theft. At present, freestanding collection boxes and tins fall outside the scope of the Regulations,[65] but they remain a popular form of fundraising.

The following practical considerations will apply when carrying out a cash collection, although reference should be made to the extensive guidance issued by the IOF.[66] The charity must ensure that it has proper written procedures and controls in place which comply with the Regulations and deal with all aspects of the collection including counting, security, banking and the audit trail. The IOF suggest nominating a person within the charity or fundraising body to act as the principal promoter to whom the collectors can report directly. The principal promoter can closely monitor the collection process, ensure compliance with the charity's procedures and ensure that the collection boxes are emptied and securely counted on a regular basis, particularly freestanding boxes. **7–87**

Proper records must be kept of: **7–88**

(i) the full name, address and contact details of the collector;
(ii) the date and collection area to be covered;
(iii) the number of collection boxes or envelopes that are issued to each collector;
(iv) the individual numbers of the collection boxes if any;
(v) the amounts collected by each collector; and
(vi) the dates on which the cash and cheques are handed over or paid into a bank account in the charity's name (which must be within 28 days of receipt).

A record of any expenses and fees incurred by the collector must be kept separately, and should not be deducted from the proceeds before they are paid in. Because only sealed collection boxes or envelopes can be used,[67] the donated amount is, to the collector, anonymous, and so it follows that collectors are not normally required to provide a receipt. **7–89**

An independent cash reconciliation should be carried out between the banked cash and cheques and the charity's income summaries as soon as possible. The principal promoter is also responsible for ensuring that proper accounting records and receipts are kept up to date with the particular appeal and that every payment, expense and fee can be traced back to the particular collector and the collection box/envelope. All such donations will also appear in the annual accounts and during the accounting period in question. **7–90**

At the end of the collection, each collector must return their identity badge, certificate of authority and any unused envelopes or collection boxes to the charity and the details and date of return should be recorded. **7–91**

---

[65] See the Public Charitable Collections (Scotland) Regulations 1984 and the Public Charitable Collections (Scotland) Amendment Regulations 1988.

[66] Also see the IOF guidance on "Handling of cash and donations".

[67] See the Public Charitable Collections (Scotland) Regulations 1984 and the Public Charitable Collections (Scotland) Amendment Regulations 1988 for further information.

DATA PROTECTION ISSUES

7–92 Data protection issues apply as soon as a charity records personal details, such as a supporter or donor's name, contact details, or credit and debit card details. Every charity and its fundraisers should therefore be familiar with the requirements of the Data Protection Act 1998 (the DPA). Stored information should only ever be used in an agreed manner and permission should be obtained to contact supporters or donors. A charity can also only share personal data with the supporter or donor's consent. The charity may also wish to consider putting data protection policies and procedures in place covering the specific requirements of the DPA. Please see the DPA for further details.

ONLINE FUNDRAISING

7–93 Charities can include details of their fundraising activities and donations page on their main website, or on a separate microsite, if it is for a particular fundraising campaign. Individuals fundraising on behalf of a charity may also set up a "JustGiving" page.[68] The site should also include all the usual information which a charity is required to disclose, as previously discussed.[69] The IOF also suggests that, as a matter of good practice, the charity also include easily visible contact details.

7–94 The website should deal with the following[70]:

- the charity's DPA procedures when using personal details and data, including their own privacy statement;
- how supporters can unsubscribe from the site;
- the charity's policies on the use of website cookies (which store a supporter's personal data), which must be clearly stated in a prominent part of the website. A supporter must consent to the use of cookies. Please also see the requirements of the Privacy and Electronic Communication (EC Directive) Regulations 2003 as amended, as discussed in more detail in para.7–100;
- details of the Direct Debit Guarantee if a direct debit is being set up under a credit card payment. A charity may also provide their bank account and sort code details for payments to be transferred electronically to the charity's bank account; and
- for other card transactions, the requirements of the Payment Card Industry Data Security Standard (PCI DSS) will apply. This means ensuring that all donations are processed using a secure payment gateway that is PCI DSS compliant, particularly if it is necessary to take the card security code (CSC), the three or four digit number on the back of the card. The CSC cannot be kept.

---

68 Please see the JustGiving campaign website for further information.

69 Under the terms of the Charities References in Documents (Scotland) Regulations 2007 as amended, referred to in para.7–14.

70 Please see the IOF guidance on "Digital Media" for further information.

FUNDRAISING OVER THE TELEPHONE

Before starting any form of telephone fundraising campaign, charities should provide the fundraiser with a policy statement setting out the following[71]: 7–95

- the purpose of the call;
- the target audience and how it is to be selected;
- how the calls are to be conducted in terms of the information to be provided, setting the right tone, being polite, friendly, sensitive and professional and dealing with queries. Many charities prefer to issue an approved script for this purpose;
- explaining how a donation can be made; and
- explaining how a donor's details will be held and passed back to the charity if relevant.

It is important to remember that all the points discussed above will apply regarding setting out the nature of the contract between the charity and the fundraiser, the information to be provided and the circumstances in which a refund can be made. 7–96

Calls should not be made after 9pm unless the potential donor requests this. After explaining the reason for the call, the potential donor should be asked to confirm whether they are happy for the call to continue. If they are not a more convenient time should be arranged. If it is a first time cold call, the potential donor should confirm whether they consent to being contacted by the charity. If they do object, they should not be called again. The IOF suggests that before making a cold call, it is better to send a "pre-call letter".[72] This gives the potential donor the opportunity to decline the call if they wish. Any such request should be respected to avoid making a nuisance call, discussed in more detail below. 7–97

Where marketing messages are sent to a mobile telephone, a clear means of opting out must also be provided. 7–98

The costs of using a premium rate telephone call service must also be clearly explained to the potential donor at the outset.[73] 7–99

THE PRIVACY AND ELECTRONIC COMMUNICATION (EC DIRECTIVE) REGULATIONS 2003[74] (THE PECR REGULATIONS)

The PECR Regulations cover the sending of unsolicited marketing material by telephone, fax, broadcast, email, text, video/picture messaging and by bluetooth. They resulted in the Telephone Preference Service (TPS), which allows 7–100

[71] Please see the IOF guidance on "Preparation and Procedure" in connection with telephone fundraising for further details.

[72] Please see the IOF guidance on "Preparation and Procedure".

[73] Please see the IOF guidance on "Digital Media", s.9.6 dealing with mobile devices and SMS and MMS for further information.

[74] Please see *http://www.legislation.gov.uk/uksi/2003/2426/contents/made* [Accessed 26 May 2016] as amended.

individuals or partnerships who do not want to receive unsolicited marketing or sales calls in any capacity to register their telephone number. Companies and other public bodies can use the Corporate TPS (CTPS). The PECR Regulations should be consulted for further details.

7–101 A charity should not make a direct marketing call to an individual or body registered with the TPS or CTPS, unless that individual or body has confirmed to the charity that they are happy to be contacted, such as by providing their telephone number or by opting in to receive calls and marketing materials. This confirmation is dependent upon there having been a prominent statement in the charity's literature explaining the implications of opting in.

7–102 It should be noted that the PECR Regulations do not apply to a call made for administrative purposes only. The TPS/CTPS register should always be checked before making any calls to a target donor.[75] Only adults over the age of 16 should be contacted.

7–103 The PECR Regulations include the following requirements:

- Potential donors should not be called by using an automated dialing system (which dials a series of numbers and plays a pre-recorded message) unless they have already consented to this, or by using random digit calling in any form.
- The charity must identify itself when making a direct marketing call and provide their contact details and business address.
- A charity should take care not to be perceived as making "nuisance calls". It must leave at least 72 hours before calling again if the individual concerned hung up or was unable to take the call, unless, of course, the individual has specifically asked not to be contacted again.[76]
- Charities should not play a pre-recorded message before the individual is passed to the charity.

7–104 Failure to adhere to the regulations on a persistent and regular basis can result in a substantial fine from Ofcom.

FUNDRAISING EVENTS—SOME PRACTICAL CONSIDERATIONS

7–105 There are many different ways in which a fundraising event can be organised. In recent years there have been a large number of charities advertising events such as sponsored challenges or treks in the UK and abroad, as well as charity dinners, dances, fundraising galas, coffee mornings, etc.

7–106 If alcohol is to be sold at the event, the premises will require a drinks licence. The IOF also produce some helpful guidance relating to the sale of food and

[75] See the IOF guidance called "Telephone Fundraising" and the section on "Key Legal Points" when dealing with telephone fundraising.

[76] For this see Ofcom, *Revised statement on the persistent misuse of an electronic communications network or service* (2008).

non-alcoholic drinks at such events.[77] Any food that is sold should comply with all the necessary regulations.[78] Although it is not necessary to label food that isn't prepared as part of a business or food sold at one off events, the IOF suggest that it is good practice where possible to state whether the ingredients may contain anything that could cause a possible allergic reaction (or have been prepared alongside food that could). If in doubt, the charity can contact the trading standards department of the local authority or the Food Standards Agency before an event to find out what regulations will apply,[79] if any.

Check to see whether there are adequate insurance arrangements in place, particularly public liability insurance cover if relevant. Make sure that all accessible facilities such as toilets, changing rooms, refreshments, first aid, etc. are well signposted. Check that there are sufficient staff/volunteers available to help the event to run smoothly on the day, that they are all clear about their roles, that they know who is in charge and supervising and who can deal with any problems that may arise. 7–107

A full risk assessment should be carried out beforehand for all endurance-type events. The charity should also consider asking participants to sign a disclaimer form where relevant stating that the charity will not be held liable for any injury or accident that the participant may suffer during the event and that they take part at their own risk. 7–108

All participants must be informed in advance of the event what it will involve and the suggested fitness levels or skills required to deal with this, any possible risks and how to be properly prepared in terms of the clothing or equipment they will need to bring. 7–109

LOTTERIES AND RAFFLES

The law relating to lotteries is complex, so charities should take care when holding any form of raffle, sweepstake, traditional lottery or tombola, all of which are types of lottery (referred to here as "lotteries") to which the Gambling Act 2005 (the GA 2005) may apply.[80] A lottery is any game where there is at least one prize on offer, where participants pay to enter and where the winner is selected at random. 7–110

Free draws, by their nature, are exempt from the GA 2005 as participants don't pay to enter.[81] Prize competitions will not be treated as being a lottery and can also fall outside the scope of the GA 2005 in certain circumstances, if it can be 7–111

---

[77] See the IOF guidance on "Event Fundraising".

[78] Please see the Food Safety Act 1990 and the Food Safety (General Food Hygiene) Regulations 1995.

[79] Please see the Food Safety Act 1990 and the Food Safety (General Food Hygiene) Regulations 1995.

[80] Please refer to the Gambling Act 2005 and the guidance on the Gambling Act 2005 issued by the Gambling Commission called "Prize competitions and free draws: The requirements of the Gambling Act 2005" (December 2009) and the IOF for further information.

[81] See the Gambling Act 2005 Sch.2, which sets out what is considered to be a "Payment to enter" and will therefore qualify as a free draw.

shown that it is a competition requiring a degree of skill, judgement or knowledge that is therefore open to a limited number of participants. Please see the GA 2005 for further details about when prize competitions can fall with the GA 2005.[82]

7–112 Lotteries that are typically held at a small fundraising event to raise funds for the charity, such as a raffle held at a fete or fundraising dinner are considered to be incidental, non-commercial lotteries.[83] A charity can organise this without the need to be licensed by the Gambling Commission or to be registered with the local authority. But the charity should still identify one senior person to be responsible for the overall conduct of the lottery, such as the chief executive or a trustee.

7–113 The tickets for this type of lottery can only be sold at the event and the winner will also be drawn at that event. It cannot included any rollover prize. All the proceeds must be applied for the charity's purposes. The prizes cannot exceed £500 in value, regardless of whether they have been bought or donated. The deductible costs cannot exceed £100.[84] Please refer to the GA 2005 for further details about the requirements that apply when issuing the ticket and conducting the lottery itself.

7–114 Most other forms of lottery, depending upon its size, will be required to register with the local authority; and in some cases, will also require a licence from the Gambling Commission or even a personal management licence. It is suggested that professional advice is taken before proceeding further with substantial lotteries and that reference is made to the GA 2005 for details of the different categories of lottery and the specific legal requirements that apply to each category.[85]

AUCTIONS

7–115 Charity auctions are covered by the Trade Description Act 1968. Each item must be described and valued accurately. If the auction is held online, other legislation also applies.[86]

7–116 The IOF suggests that the charity should consider an appropriate reserve price that they wish to place on each item, in consultation with the auctioneer.[87] For a high profile event with an item of moderately high value, it is also good practice for the charity to have an agreed procedure in place for dealing with known risks,

[82] See the Gambling Commission guidance on the Gambling Act 2005 called "Prize competitions and free draws: The requirements of the Gambling Act 2005" (December 2009) and the Gambling Act 2005 s.14.

[83] See the Gambling Act 2005 on incidental lotteries. These must comply with the conditions set out in the Gambling Act 2005 Sch.11 and the Gambling Act 2005 (Incidental Lotteries) Regulations 2016 (SI 2016/239) and the Legislative Reform (Exempt Lotteries) Order 2016 (SI 2016/124).

[84] See the Gambling Act 2005 (Incidental Non-Commerical Lotteries) Regulations 2007.

[85] See the Gambling Act 2005 and the Gambling Commission general guidance for details on private society lotteries and large society lotteries.

[86] The Consumer Protection (Distance Selling) Regulations 2000 and the Consumer Protection from Unfair Trading Regulations 2008.

[87] See the IOF guidance on "Auctions".

such as a prize being suddenly withdrawn or ceasing to exist after being advertised, or where the purchaser changes their mind after successfully bidding on the item.[88]

The use of gift aid when dealing with charity auctions is dealt with separately in Ch.6 under gift aid. **7–117**

[88] See the IOF guidance on "Auctions".

CHAPTER 8

USE OF ASSETS

Simon A Mackintosh

FUNDAMENTAL RULES

Section 7 of the Charities and Trustee Investment (Scotland) Act 2005 (the 2005 Act) provides that a body meets the charity test if: **8–01**

(a) its purposes consist only of one or more of the charitable purposes; and
(b) it provides (or, in the case of an applicant, provides or intends to provide) public benefit in Scotland or elsewhere.

An extended list of charitable purposes follows, which is covered in Ch.1.[1]

The public benefit rules are covered in Ch.1.[2] The charity must, therefore, apply its assets, in line with its purposes, in the provision of public benefit. **8–02**

Section 7 of the 2005 Act also contains restrictions on the use of assets. The simpler one is that a charity's purposes must not include the advancement of a political party.[3] The other restriction is that its constitution must not allow the charity to distribute or otherwise apply its property (on being wound up or at any other time) for a purpose that is not a charitable purpose. **8–03**

This means that any entity that has a purpose, or definition of charitable purposes—that is not charitable under the 2005 Act—cannot be a Scottish charity. The word "charitable" in this context means charitable under the 2005 Act.[4] Any broad reference to charitable purposes must, therefore, refer to and be limited by the charitable purposes set out in the 2005 Act. The issue often arises in respect of how assets could be used in the event of a charity being wound up. It needs to be addressed at the registration stage of a new charity. **8–04**

This can give rise to difficulties in respect of a charity established before the 2005 Act came into force. Very often, the constitution of such older charities will refer to charitable purposes as defined for UK-wide taxation purposes. These are not exactly the same as the 2005 Act, but adopting the alternative approach of defining charitable purposes with reference only to the 2005 Act, means that the charity tax test is not precisely met. **8–05**

---

[1] See paras 1–11—1–63.
[2] See paras 1–77—1–132.
[3] Charities and Trustee Investment (Scotland) Act 2005 s.7(4)(c).
[4] Charities and Trustee Investment (Scotland) Act 2005 s.106.

8–06 The Office of Scottish Charity Regulator's (OSCR) 2015 publication "Meeting the Charity Test: Guidance" states

> "to pass the charity test and to qualify for charitable tax relief, an organisation's governing document must allow its property to be used only for purposes that are charitable both in Scots law and in UK tax law".[5]

8–07 Suitable "hybrid" definitions of charitable bodies and purposes are as follows:

- "Charitable body" shall mean a body on the Scottish Charity Register that is also regarded as a charity in relation to the application of the Taxes Acts.
- "Charitable purpose" shall mean a purpose which is a charitable purpose in terms of the Charities and Trustee Investment (Scotland) Act 2005 and that is also regarded as charitable in relation to the application of the Taxes Acts.

8–08 Issues with the use of assets in connection with the definition of charitable purposes could arise during the lifetime of an existing charity, when it is a general grant giving charity with broad purposes or for charities reviewing existing activities or considering new ones. They may also arise on the winding up of a charity, where very often a winding up clause will authorise distribution of a charity's assets to some other body. The purposes of such other body may be tightly defined or may be defined with reference only to charitable purposes chosen by the trustees or directors of the winding up body. To meet the tax and Scots charity law tests, any winding up, however remote its possibility, must be to a body which meets (or has purposes which meet) both tests.

8–09 Apart from issues relating to the definition of charitable purposes, the winding up clause of a charity needs to be examined to ensure that there is no possibility of its assets being shared out or given to its members on a wind up. If there were any circumstances in which this might happen, the charity test would be failed.

8–10 It is not a requirement of charity law in Scotland that on the winding up of a charity, assets must pass to another charity: it is only a requirement that the recipient body will be under an obligation to apply the assets for charitable purposes.[6]

WHEN THE ASSETS ARE APPLIED

8–11 Turning to the basics of charity tax reliefs and assessment of potential benefit, the time when assets are put to charitable purposes needs to be considered.

8–12 Section 524 of the Income Tax Act 2007 and s.478 of the Corporation Tax Act 2010 explain when certain income received by a charity is exempt from income tax and corporation tax. The profits of a charitable trade are exempt where the profits are applied to the purposes of the charitable trust only. A charitable trade is one exercised in the course of carrying out a primary purpose of the charitable

---

[5] OSCR, "Meeting the Charity Test: Guidance for applicants and existing charities" (2015), p.94.

[6] Charities and Trustee Investment (Scotland) Act 2005 s.7(4)(a).

trust; or where the work in connection with the trade is mainly carried out by beneficiaries of the charitable trust. The relevant point here is that the exemption is for profits from trade where applied to the purposes of the charitable trust.

There is a similar point in relation to the 2005 Act and OSCR's "Apparently Inactive Charities" published in October 2009. In that guidance, OSCR looks at the status of charities that are not apparently carrying out activities, but that expect to carry out activities in the future. Do they provide the public benefit without which a body cannot be a Scottish charity? The potential issue is not using the charity's assets for charitable purposes. **8–13**

Charities that are accumulating income[7] need to be aware of these requirements and be ready to explain to HMRC how they are applying funds for charitable purposes; and to OSCR how they are providing public benefit. Examples might be accumulating funds for a capital project; creating a sinking fund for anticipated repairs; replenishing reserves. **8–14**

APPLICATION OF INCOME AND CAPITAL TO CHARITABLE PURPOSES

Given the requirements of UK tax laws and Scottish charity law to apply funds for charitable purposes, charity trustees should normally expect to be distributing the charity's income. Whether they must distribute all income, or may carry forward some unspent income, or accumulate surplus income, depends on the governing document. Whether or not they are able to distribute capital will also depend on the specific powers in their governing document in respect of capital generally, and in respect of specific funds. It may also depend on the terms on which donors have given funds to the charity. Paragraph 8–33 covers this in more detail. **8–15**

Restrictions on income generally will flow from any restrictions imposed on the underlying capital fund as to the purposes to which that capital can be put. **8–16**

From a trust law perspective, the question for both permanent endowment and restricted funds is what powers to spend (or not) do the trustees have and what restrictions are there as to the purposes to which this particular fund of capital, and income generated by it, can be put? **8–17**

PERMANENT ENDOWMENT AND RESTRICTED FUNDS

"Permanent endowment" is not a defined term in the 2005 Act: it is a term that comes from the accounting requirements imposed on Scottish charities. In essence, it is a fund the charity is not free to spend: it is a fund with spending restrictions attached.[8] **8–18**

In contrast "restricted funds" are defined in s.43D of the 2005 Act to mean **8–19**

---

[7] See paras 8–33—8–42.

[8] Normally to be held indefinitely.

> "property (including money) given to a charity for a specific purpose and in respect of which conditions have been imposed as to its use".

8–20 These two separate types of restriction should be kept in mind when viewing a fund for disbursement and when making up accounts.

REDIRECTING THE USE TO WHICH ASSETS CAN BE PUT

8–21 Since 2012, Scottish charities have been able to apply to OSCR to reorganise restricted funds, in the same way as they have, since 2007, been able to apply to OSCR for consent to reorganise their constitutions.[9] This is covered in Ch.12.

8–22 A permanent endowment can be seen as a type of restricted fund. The permanent endowment could be unrestricted as to purposes or restricted as to purposes, but it is not spendable. In contrast, a restricted fund could be restricted as to its purposes, but could be wholly spendable.

8–23 Before discussing the circumstances in which restricted funds can be reorganised, by application to OSCR, the general rules relating to these funds should be considered.

8–24 OSCR's guidance on this topic[10] is helpful as it does indicate the difficulty in establishing, sometimes, whether a fund is indeed restricted and exactly how that restriction has arisen. The available evidence may be sketchy or lost in time.

8–25 If a charity has received funds on conditions that are impossible to fulfil, then the funds should be returned to the donor. Once accepted, the general principle in relation to restricted funds is that, as the restriction is imposed by a donor, the donor may also lift that restriction.

8–26 If a charity has received funds for a restricted purpose, which has been fulfilled, or has become, for example, now impossible or non-charitable to fulfil, the charity should refer to the donor to seek to have the restrictions lifted.

8–27 It is only if the donor cannot be contacted for consent, that the reorganisation provisions in the 2005 Act come into play. The general principle, though, is that charities must respect and adhere to the terms on which funds are given to them, unless the donor lifts the restrictions or an application is made to OSCR.[11]

8–28 Assuming the application to be such as OSCR may approve, OSCR must be satisfied that the proposed reorganisation will enable the resources of the restricted funds to be applied to better effect for charitable purposes consistently with the charity's constitution; and that the charity is unable to ascertain the wishes of the donor.

8–29 "Donor" is defined to mean such person or body who may vary the purpose of, or any conditions imposed in relation to, restricted funds as may be specified by

---

[9] See para.12–45—12–101.

[10] OSCR, "Reorganisation of Restricted Funds; Guidance for Charity Trustees and their advisers" (2012), p.2.

[11] See para.12–45 and following.

regulations made by Scottish ministers.[12] This has been specified as the person or body who gave the restricted funds to the charity.[13]

The competent reorganisation is either: (a) the variation of the purpose for which restricted funds may be used; or (b) the variation or removal of any condition imposed on the charity in relation to the use of restricted funds. **8–30**

OSCR may itself apply to the Court of Session for a restricted funds reorganisation, under similar conditions and with the same objectives in mind. **8–31**

OSCR's guidance points out that the legislation does not permit applications to directly transfer or wind up restricted funds, which will always continue to exist but with amended conditions of use or purposes.[14] However, an amendment to the conditions of use might permit the charity to exhaust the funds and thus, in effect, wind up the fund. **8–32**

ACCUMULATION OF INCOME

The question of whether to accumulate income arises when a charity generates more income than it needs to spend in a particular period; where it is saving up for a future project; or, possibly, where it adopts a "total return" approach to investment.[15] **8–33**

Where income is accumulated and added to capital, and is not merely saved for future use, being carried forward as income, it becomes part of the charity's capital fund. Of course, the charity trustees may have power to spend capital, either generally, or restricted to previously accumulated income. **8–34**

Charities that are accumulating or saving income should bear in mind the points made at paras 8–12—8–14 above as to requirements to satisfy both OSCR and HMRC that the charity's funds are being applied for charitable purposes. **8–35**

Where a charity adopts a "total return" approach to investment that is likely to involve at different times spending income and capital or capital gains, this implies that the charity has the legal power both to carry forward or accumulate income, and to spend capital, at different stages of the cycle of investment. **8–36**

The present trust law on accumulations of income (applicable to lifetime trusts and will trusts) is contained in the Trusts (Scotland) Act 1961 s.5 and the Law Reform (Miscellaneous Provisions) (Scotland) Act 1966 s.6. Any one of the following periods for accumulation of income may apply: **8–37**

(1) the life of the grantor;
(2) a term of 21 years from the death of the grantor;
(3) the duration of the minority or respective minorities of any persons living or in utero at the death of the grantor;

[12] See Charities and Trustee Investment (Scotland) Act 2005 s.43D.

[13] See the Charities Restricted Funds Reorganisation (Scotland) Regulations reg.3.

[14] OSCR, "Reorganisation of Restricted Funds; Guidance for Charity Trustees and their advisers" (2012), p.6.

[15] See paras 9–20—9–23.

(4) the duration of the minority or respective minorities of those who would, if of full age, be entitled to that income;

(5) 21 years from the date of the making of the settlement or other disposition; and

(6) the minority or respective minorities of any persons living or in utero at the date of making the settlement or other disposition.

8–38 In practice, for charities, any period of accumulation selected is likely to be number (1), (2) or (5).

8–39 The Scottish Law Commission's *Report on Trust Law*[16] contains a full review of the existing law and recommends (proposal 93) that the existing rules restricting accumulation should be repealed, but not in respect of public trusts which are charitable trusts, for which the existing law should remain in force.

8–40 OSCR and HMRC will approve charity constitutions in which accumulation of income is authorised. Where accumulation is permitted in respect of a charitable trust, the assumption should be that these permitted periods of accumulation of income will be the only ones authorised for Scots law charities.

8–41 Even if the restriction on accumulation periods were lifted, remember that the principal purpose of charities and the funds under their control should be seen as application of funds for charitable purposes and for the public benefit.

8–42 Where a charitable trust is varied, it is possible that a fresh period for accumulation of income will be triggered. The question in any variation is whether the provisions of the original trust are superseded to such an extent as to constitute a new trust. That will be a question of fact in each case—is the reorganisation of a trust so substantial as to be fundamentally equivalent to the making of a new trust or transfer of funds to a new trust?[17]

LENDING

8–43 Charity trustees often make loans. This is covered at para.6–76 onwards under "borrowing". In making loans they should be very clear why they are considering doing so—what are their motives? If these are purely commercial then the transaction should be treated as a commercial one with appropriate securities and sanctions. If it is not a commercial loan then it is still right to consider whether interest should be payable and whether security is appropriate. If no security is taken then the charity trustees must, as a minimum, be very clear as to the circumstances in which repayment is expected, and fully document these.

[16] Scottish Law Commission, *Report on Trust Law* (Scot. Law Comm. No.239) (August 2014).
[17] *Aikman, Petitioner*, 1968 S.L.T. 137, 141.

What sort of consideration might charity trustees have in mind?

They may make a loan purely as an investment decision and on a commercial basis. Some mixed motivation might come in to a decision to make an apparently commercial loan to those, possibly within the charity's beneficiary population, who might otherwise not easily obtain commercial funding. There might be a loan on obviously non-commercial terms—a "soft loan" to support the charitable objectives of the charity. **8–44**

The charity trustees must first consider their governing document to ensure that there is power to carry out the loan transaction in the way in which they wish to do so. Very often, there will be express powers to lend with or without security and to do so either commercially or charitably. **8–45**

If not, are any such powers implied?

For trusts, the general powers of trustees are in s.4 of the Trusts (Scotland) Act 1921 (the 1921 Act) as extended by the 2005 Act. The question for the trustees will be whether the loan can be classed as an investment within the power "to make any kind of investment of the trust estate (including an investment in heritable property)". If on a commercial basis, it might qualify. If merely to provide assistance to someone in the beneficiary population it might not qualify as an investment. **8–46**

The Scottish Law Commission *Report on Trust Law*[18] proposes the repeal of s.4(1) of the 1921 Act and its replacement by a provision that confers on trustees in their dealings with the trust property **8–47**

> "power to exercise all of the powers of administration and management that a natural person of full age and capacity would have in respect of his or her own property".

This power is proposed to apply to all trusts, whenever created, unless the trust deed expressly provides otherwise.

For trusts there may, therefore, be some considerable extra flexibility from this proposed legislative change. The making of a loan would be clearly within that extended power. **8–48**

For charitable companies, registered societies and Scottish Charitable Incorporated Organisations (SCIOs) it will be relatively straightforward to add power to make loans through amendment to their constitutions. **8–49**

SOCIAL INVESTMENT

The Charities (Protection and Social Investment) Act 2016 (the 2016 Act) adds specific powers under the [English and Welsh] Charities Act 2011 in relation to "social investment". **8–50**

---

[18] Scottish Law Commission, *Report on Trust Law* (Scot. Law Comm. No.239) (August 2014).

8–51 Section 15 of the 2016 Act introduces new s.292A of the 2011 Act, which provides that:

> "A social investment is made when a relevant act of a charity is carried out with a view to both—
> (a) Directly furthering the charity's purposes; and
> (b) Achieving a financial return for the charity."

8–52 A "relevant act" is either an application or use of funds or other property; or taking on a commitment in relation to a liability of another person (such as a guarantee) that puts the charity's funds or other property at risk of being applied or being used.

8–53 New s.292B then provides that an incorporated charity has, and the charity trustees of an unincorporated charity have, power to make social investments. This is subject to restrictions imposed upon the particular funds being applied or by the constitution.

8–54 Section 292C then provides duties in relation to social investments that are similar to those applying to other investment decisions.

8–55 The description of social investment mirrors the type of loan described in para.8–46, but unless and until similar legislation is introduced in Scotland, it should not be assumed that all Scottish charities have appropriate powers to make social investments.

8–56 Constitutions may require to be amended to achieve appropriate powers.

LOANS OF CHARITABLE ASSETS

8–57 It is arguable that if there is power to make capital grants for charitable purposes, then a loan, with expectation of repayment, is a lesser disposal of charity assets and power to make a loan ought therefore to be implied within powers to make capital grants.

8–58 If making charitable loans is seen as a way of creating a rotating core of charity assets which can, in effect, put the same money to use several times over to help, this can be an extremely effective charitable operation. It is more sustainable than making a series of grants, which are not repayable, and minimises depletion of the capital of the charity while recognising that not all beneficiaries of such loans will see things working out to the extent that they will be able to repay. It is a model which has been put to effective use by a number of charities.

8–59 If a charity which is a trust is contemplating this type of activity, and if the powers to do so are truly lacking, then an application could be made to OSCR[19] to add in such power to the trust.[20]

---

[19] By virtue of the Charities and Trustee Investment (Scotland) Act 2005 s.42(2)(d).

[20] See para.12–45 below.

Charity trustees contemplating making loans must refer back to their general duties under s.66 of the 2005 Act to seek to ensure that the charity acts in a manner consistent with its charitable purposes. **8–60**

WASTING ASSETS

Charity trustees may sometimes hold assets that are wasting assets. If a charity holds an asset as an investment it is done with the aim of making a financial return from it. How does this fit with holding a wasting asset, which is expected to diminish in value over time, possibly even to the extent of extinction? Examples of wasting assets include a lease of land (which may have been acquired for a premium); moveable property such as plant and machinery. These are assets that have a short predictable life (for capital gains tax purposes, this is taken as less than 50 years). Why would a charity hold such an asset? **8–61**

One reason might be that the asset is held or applied in a particular way that, of itself, helps to achieve the purposes of the charity—a property or asset that is made available to beneficiaries or to achieve charitable purpose such as public access for purposes of recreation or culture. **8–62**

Such an asset may have been received by way of gift or inheritance or may have been acquired by the charity by application of other funds. Where such an asset is held with the aim of direct implementation of the charity's purposes, the charity trustees need to be entirely clear of their reason for holding wasting assets. Holding such assets needs to be carefully approached against the background of trustee duties which are generally stated to be to preserve the trust estate, which is not possible in the context of an asset which by its nature diminishes. By retaining a wasting asset, the charity is in effect spending capital or applying income towards a capital loss. In the case of any charitable entity, no matter what its legal form, the charity trustees need to be clear that their powers permit them to do so; and if there are wide enough powers, the trustees need to be satisfied that holding the wasting asset is a proper application of charitable funds implementing those powers. **8–63**

USE OF ASSET FOR TRADING PURPOSES

It is a fundamental principle explained in para.8–02 above that a charity's assets must be applied for charitable purposes. Practical issues often arise in connection with the initial funding and continued support of a trading activity. As to a charity trading generally, see Ch.10. **8–64**

In addressing this issue from the point of view of appropriate application of charitable funds, the first question must be whether the charity has sufficient powers to carry out trading activities. In trusts, such a power is often but not inevitably conferred upon the trustees. Even where there is a power, when entering into trading activities through the medium of a trust, the trustees need to **8–65** be very alive to the issues of potential personal liability.[21] For this reason, and again if powers permit, trusts that determine to engage in trading activity will often do so through the medium of an incorporated trading subsidiary.[22]

8–66 For charities constituted as companies, registered societies or SCIOs, powers to engage in trading activity will routinely be included in the constitution.

8–67 If the charity trustees have the appropriate powers, they must then decide whether it is in the best interests of the charity to engage in the trading activity, with a view to either generating funds to support the charity's other activities, or further the charitable purposes by the carrying out of some trading activities. The charity trustees must be entirely clear as to the specific aims they have in mind in engaging in charitable activity, how the application of the charity's assets towards the trading activities will help achieve the charity's aims, and the extent of the assets they are prepared to apply towards trading activities.

8–68 Trustees may have mixed motivations in engaging in these activities, partly commercial and partly charitable purposes, but should be clear in their decision as to what those motivations are.

8–69 A charity owning land and buildings may do so purely as an investment, but may also apply them more directly for its operations. It will very often be the case that they are applied partly for charitable purposes (for example, public access to national heritage such as the built environment or environmentally significant sites) and partly towards trading activities (for example, visitor facilities such as tea rooms and restaurants and shops) and possibly even activities like corporate hospitality to raise funds for the charity.

8–70 The premises of a school or university may be held primarily for the purposes of carrying out educational purposes of the institution which owns the premises, but may also be made available free or at discounted rates to other bodies or for charitable purposes within its own charitable purposes. Alternatively they may be met for commercial purposes to earn money to support the charity's activities.

8–71 These are examples of assets that are held or applied in a particular way because of themselves they help to achieve the charitable purposes of the charity. There may be land and buildings, the preservation of which is, in itself, the charitable purpose, or land of outstanding natural beauty held for the purpose of environmental protection or allowing public access for purposes of recreation.

8–72 Such property may be held for combined motives of preservation and also of making a financial return.

8–73 Charity trustees need to be clear about their motivations and aims in all such dealings with land.

8–74 Land may have been transferred to a charity subject to a "no sale" restriction. If the charity is unable to use it for its own purposes but lets the property to an entity with purposes aligned with the owning charity's aims then that is an appropriate use of that asset. Charity trustees might consider that a lease at under

[21] See para.4–80—4–91.

[22] See Ch.10.

value or at peppercorn rent to another charity or body that seeks to achieve aims similar to the owning charity's purposes would be an appropriate use of their assets. Alternatively, there might be imposed restrictions on the use of the land when donated, which the trustees would be bound to comply with. These might well also apply to any subsequent proceeds of sale.

A more general example is of a charity with general charitable purposes that owns property surplus to requirements, or specifically acquired for this purpose, and lets the property out on favourable terms to one or more operating charities. Provided that these activities are undertaken in accordance with the charitable purposes of the property-owning charity, these are examples of appropriate use of assets for motivations which range from straightforward financial return of the owning charity to direct achievement of charitable purposes. **8–75**

When applying assets for charitable purposes, the specific rules on charity trading for tax purposes should be considered as it is not the case and must not be assumed that all such income will be exempt from income or corporation tax.[23] **8–76**

[23] See Ch.10.

CHAPTER 9

INVESTMENT

Gavin McEwan

INTRODUCTION

A proper understanding of the duties in investing trust monies is essential for each and every charity trustee. The areas that must be kept in mind are: (i) general duties; (ii) ordinary investment issues; (iii) using advisers; and (iv) ethical and other special investment issues. **9–01**

GENERAL DUTIES

Investment, here, can be said to be the employment of money in the purchase of anything from which interest or profit is expected.[1] **9–02**

The general common law duty is to invest a charity's funds to the extent that they are not required in the short term for carrying out the charity's purposes. This will have differing impacts on grant-making trusts that hold a large investment portfolio used to produce funds for distribution, and on charities which may be holding substantial funds for an extended period. **9–03**

The powers of charitable vehicles vary. Generally speaking, charitable companies, registered societies, Scottish Charitable Incorporated Organisations (SCIO) and unincorporated associations have the same flexible powers of investment as a natural person so long as there is nothing in their constitution which would otherwise create a restriction. **9–04**

For charitable trusts, trust deeds will normally give express and wide powers of investment to the charity trustees. Otherwise, charity trustees can rely upon the statutory power to make any kind of investment of the trust estate (including an investment in heritable property).[2] **9–05**

Where charity trustees are relying upon that statutory power of investment it is incumbent upon them to have regard to the suitability to the trust of the type of **9–06**

---

[1] See *Re Wragg* [1919] 2 Ch. 58. Also, a good and very full source of discussion on trustee investment duties can be found in *Trustees' Powers and Duties* (1999) Law Com. No.260; Scot. Law Comm. No.172, and that is a useful place to begin if more detailed coverage is required.

[2] Trusts (Scotland) Act 1921 s.4(1)(ea) as inserted by the Charities and Trustee Investment (Scotland) Act 2005 s.93(2).

investment proposed, to have regard to the need for diversification of investments of the trust in so far as is appropriate to the circumstances of the trust, and often to obtain and consider advice.[3]

9–07 Those powers of investment always have to be applied within the wider context of the charity trustees' duties to act in the interests of the charity, consistently with the charity's purposes and applying the relevant standard of care and diligence.[4]

Maintaining an investment policy

9–08 To help ensure that charity trustees adhere to their investment duties and remain aligned with proper investment motives, every charity ought to consider the creation of an investment policy as a matter of good practice. This should be the case even if investment decisions will be taken by the charity trustees themselves and not in the context of an investment policy that is designed to guide investment managers instructed on the trustees' behalf.

9–09 Indeed the current Charity Statement of Recommended Practice (SORP) for charity accounts[5] places an expectation upon charity trustees that disclosures will be made in the body of their written report each year on investment performance against objectives where there are material financial investments held, on significant events that have impacted upon financial performance and on the extent to which social, environmental or ethical considerations are taken into account.[6] Having a formal investment policy in place can help to inform the structure of these parts of the trustees' report and provide a focus for the trustees when measuring performance against agreed benchmarks.

9–10 While an investment policy need not exist as a standalone document and could instead be a series of principles agreed at trustee meetings, where investments form a material part of a charity's assets trustees should consider the creation of a separate investment policy that is then subject to regular review. The creation of an investment policy can also help charity trustees to ensure that the policy they have devised is consistent with their charitable objectives and the overall investment motive which they consider to be appropriate in their own circumstances.

9–11 Investment policies should be tailored to suit the charity's own needs, but in general terms should include an overview of the charity's aims and objectives, the investment powers that are available to the charity trustees, a commentary on cash flow and the extent to which cash requirements are (or may be) met from

---

[3] Trusts (Scotland) Act 1921 s.4A as inserted by Charities and Trustee Investment (Scotland) Act 2005 s.94, and paras 9–24—9–27 below.

[4] Charities and Trustee Investment (Scotland) Act 2005 s.66.

[5] Charities SORP FRS 102, "Accounting and Reporting by Charities: Statement of Recommended Practice applicable to charities preparing their accounts in accordance with the Financials Reporting Standard applicable in the UK and Republic of Ireland" (2015).

[6] Charities SORP FRS 102, "Accounting and Reporting by Charities: Statement of Recommended Practice applicable to charities preparing their accounts in accordance with the Financials Reporting Standard applicable in the UK and Republic of Ireland" (2015), para.1.47.

income yield or capital growth or both, the degree of risk the charity trustees consider is appropriate, any ethical or other considerations the trustees consider to be binding upon them and/or their investment managers, and the degree of liquidity that is required at any one time. Some investment policies also include a statement on the charity trustees' expectations regarding the level of income yield and capital growth which may be achieved.

The investment policy ought also to set out who is managing the investments on behalf of the trustees, how performance is to be measured (usually in relation to income yield and capital growth expectations, as mentioned above at para.9–11) and which trustees or senior managers, if appropriate, have authority to give instructions to the investment managers. **9–12**

ORDINARY INVESTMENT ISSUES

The degree to which types of investment are permitted for individual charities is nowadays primarily dictated by the tax treatment of those investments[7]; although particular restrictions may apply because of the terms of a charity's constitution. But subject to any other restriction or exclusion that might be imposed by a specific statute, no terms contained in a post-August 1961 trust deed has effect as restricting or excluding the power of investment.[8] For commentary on social investment issues, see paras 8–50—8–56. **9–13**

Since charities will generally be at pains to preserve as much of their tax effectiveness as possible, the approach taken to qualifying investments in the Taxes Acts will be material to any investment decisions. The tax definition of "approved charitable investments" under the Income Tax Act 2007 (the 2007 Act) is very wide[9] and includes in broad terms: **9–14**

- securities listed in s.559 of the 2007 Act;
- common investment funds;
- common deposit funds;
- similar collective funds established purely for the benefit of charities;
- interests in land (other than as security for a debt);
- bills, certificates of tax deposit, savings certificates and tax reserve certificates issued by the UK government;
- Northern Ireland treasury bills;
- units in a unit trust scheme or other recognised scheme;
- deposits with banks, building societies, national savings and mutual credit institutions; and
- other certificates of deposit.

A similar definition applies under the Corporation Tax Act 2010 (the 2010 Act).[10] **9–15**

---

[7] See paras 9–14 to 9–16.

[8] Trusts (Scotland) Act 1921 s.4(1D) as inserted by the Charities and Trustee Investment (Scotland) Act 2005 s.93(3).

[9] Income Tax Act 2007 s.558.

[10] Corporation Tax Act 2010 s.512.

9–16 Where investments do not fall within the definition of "approved charitable investments" in terms of s.558 of the 2007 Act, or s.512 of the 2010 Act, any amounts expended on such investments will normally be treated as non-charitable expenditure, resulting in a restriction of the tax relief available to the charity in relation to those investments. It may however be possible in terms of the legislation to satisfy HMRC that any investment that falls outwith the definitions was nevertheless made "for the benefit of" the charity and "not for the avoidance of tax", whether by the charity or by any other person.

Collective investment schemes

9–17 As mentioned above, participation by charities in Scotland in collective investment schemes (described in the relevant legislation as "common investment funds" and "common deposit schemes"—see para.9–18 below) falls within the range of permitted investments under both charity and tax legislation, although the primary non-tax provisions are contained in the (English and Welsh) Charities Act 2011 (the 2011 Act). Such schemes can help charities to spread investments more widely across a range of assets than could be achieved if investing directly, thus reducing risk and increasing diversification. They achieve this by pooling the assets of a number of investors in order to achieve the desired degree of overall diversification across all of the participating investors' funds. It is still incumbent upon charity trustees to have regard to risk and diversification and the suitability of the collective investment schemes selected: participation in collective investment schemes does not of itself relieve the trustees of those duties.

9–18 The Charity Commission for England and Wales is specifically enabled to create common investment funds and common deposit schemes (the two most common types of collective investment schemes used by charities) in terms of ss.96–104 of the 2011 Act. These schemes are treated as if they were themselves charities: they are regulated by the Charity Commission and appear on the English charity register. In terms of s.97(3)(a), "Scottish recognised bodies" are entitled to participate in common investment funds, with a matching provision in s.101(3)(a) for common deposit schemes.

9–19 For these purposes, a "Scottish recognised body" is one established under the law of Scotland, or is managed or controlled wholly or mainly in or from Scotland, and

> "to which HMRC have given intimation, which has not subsequently been withdrawn, that tax relief is due in respect of income of the body which is applicable and applied to charitable purposes only".[11]

[11] Charities Act 2011 s.104.

"Total return" policy

A total return policy is one where both income yield and capital growth can be relied upon to generate funds for the fulfilment of a charity's objectives. This may be especially helpful where economic conditions mean that income yield is very low but the growth in capital values is high. 9–20

The position in England and Wales for some considerable time was that an approach had to be made to the Charity Commission for permission to invest on a total return basis, but that has been changed by statute. The ability of charities in Scotland to invest on a total return basis is broadly a matter for charity trustees to decide in each individual case, unless the constitution imposes restrictions that might prevent the use of capital. 9–21

Until recently, however, many charity trustees felt constrained to focus on income yield as they doubted whether a total return approach was valid. Modern judicial authority supports the notion that, whilst investments held by trustees must be used to further the purposes of the trust, where they are held to generate money the purposes of the trust will best be served where trustees can obtain from their investments the maximum return, whether that is from income yield or capital growth.[12] 9–22

Where the restrictions of a constitution on use of capital are so strict as to prevent the adoption of a total return policy, and where the result is that charity trustees consider that this prevents the most efficient use of their assets, it may be possible for an application to be made for a reorganisation scheme in order to relax or replace any restrictions on investment policy.[13] 9–23

USING ADVISERS

Trustees of trusts properly so-called are under statutory duties to take advice as follows[14]: 9–24

(1) Before exercising the power of investment, a trustee shall have regard to—
  (a) the suitability to the trust of the proposed investment, and
  (b) the need for diversification of investments of the trust, in so far as is appropriate to the circumstances of the trust.

(2) Before exercising that power of investment, a trustee shall (except where paragraph (4) below applies) obtain and consider proper advice about the way in which the power should be exercised.

(3) When reviewing the investments of the trust, a trustee shall (except where paragraph (4) below applies) obtain and consider proper advice about whether the investments should be varied.

---

[12] See *Harries (Bishop of Oxford) v Church Commissioners* [1992] 1 W.L.R. 1241, 1246.

[13] Charities and Trustee Investment (Scotland) Act 2005 ss.39–42 and para.12–45 following below.

[14] Trusts (Scotland) Act 1921 s.4A as inserted by the Charities and Trustee Investment (Scotland) Act 2005 s.94.

(4) If a trustee reasonably concludes that in all the circumstances it is unnecessary or inappropriate to obtain such advice, the trustee need not obtain it.

(5) "Proper advice" means the advice of a person who is reasonably believed by the trustee to be qualified by the person's ability and practical experience of financial and other matters relating to the proposed investment.

9–25 These provisions make clear that the duty is to "obtain and consider" the advice. This does not mean that the advice must be followed. However, where charity trustees decide not to follow proper advice that has been obtained from a suitably qualified person, they should as a matter of course minute carefully that advice has indeed been obtained and considered, and they should narrate on what basis the advice has been rejected. This will demonstrate that the trustees have fulfilled their statutory duty and will provide a suitable record for future trustees (or for any third party, which could include the Scottish Charity Regulator) of the reasons for departing from the advice obtained and considered.

9–26 The exception contained in s.4A(4) of the 1921 Act allows trustees to avoid the expense of obtaining advice, where they consider the obtaining of advice to be unnecessary or inappropriate. The trustees have to reach a "reasonable conclusion" that advice should not be obtained and, as with the rejection of advice obtained and considered, it would be sensible for trustees to minute the basis on which the reasonable conclusion was reached. The conclusion could reasonably be reached, for instance, where all or some of the trustees are sufficiently skilled in investment matters, or where the decision required relates to an investment so immaterial that it would not be worthwhile obtaining advice. The onus will be on the trustees, however, to demonstrate that they have nevertheless adhered to the standard investment criteria set out in s.4A(1) of the 1921 Act as regards suitability of the investment and the need for diversification. Where trustees cannot demonstrate that, they open themselves to potential difficulty.

9–27 If trustees are to demonstrate to their fullest ability that the statutory duty has been followed and proper advice obtained, it would make sense for trustees to obtain investment advice in writing, although the legislation does not specifically require written advice. At the very least, trustee minutes that serve the purpose of recording the advice given should be kept, perhaps also recording how it was given, and setting out the trustees' decisions whether in reliance upon or in rejection of that advice.

Discretionary investment advice

Until recently concern was sometimes expressed that trustees could not appoint advisers to act on a discretionary basis because of the rule that those to whom a power was delegated could not themselves delegate that. Statute now specifically provides[15] that trustees have the power, subject to any specific restriction 9–28

> "... to authorise an agent to exercise any of their investment management functions at the agent's discretion or in such other manner as the trustees may direct".

Advisers

Identifying the right people to give advice is stated in the statutory duty to be a matter for the trustees' reasonable belief. If trustees consider themselves to be qualified to take investment decisions without the need for external advisers, they ought as a point of best practice to consider whether they meet the test set out in s.4A(5) of the 1921 Act—namely, whether or not they are qualified by their own ability and practical experience of financial and other matters. 9–29

Needless to say, if trustees fail to adhere to the statutory duty, they lay themselves open to potential liability in the event that their decision is taken negligently or recklessly. Taking advice in compliance with the statutory duty, on the other hand, should mean that if investment advice obtained turns out to be seriously wrong, someone else ought to be liable and not the trustees themselves. 9–30

The suitability of investment managers to any one charity will depend upon that charity's specific needs. When selecting investment managers for appointment, charities may wish to consider the relative size of their own portfolio when considered against the managers' funds under management and the extent to which the managers have experience of investing for the charity sector. 9–31

Other factors will be relevant including the extent to which the investment managers are willing or able to accommodate particular ethical considerations or restrictions contained in the charity's investment policy. Charity trustees will want to be clear about the style and frequency of reporting that will be provided by the investment managers and whether that will meet the charity's needs. They will often also want to ensure that their investment manager is accessible and is willing to attend occasional meetings of the trustees, and that is also a point to raise at the appointment stage. 9–32

Investment management firms have different styles and approaches and it may be worth trustees knowing ahead of a beauty parade what they are looking for and to state this clearly in any tender document. Trustees may wish to consider these and other additional considerations: 9–33

- Do the trustees want active or passive management?

[15] Trusts (Scotland) Act 1921 s.4C as inserted by the Charities and Trustee Investment (Scotland) Act 2005 s.94.

- Do the trustees have a preference for a portfolio consisting of direct equities, collective investment funds or a combination?
- Do the trustees want a segregated portfolio or would they be happy to be invested in a pooled fund?
- Do the trustees want to set any asset allocation guidelines or are they happy for the investment manager to propose these based on the trustees' specific objectives?
- Do the trustees have any ethical or socially responsible criteria or other exclusions, and are those criteria or exclusions relevant to the charity's investment policy overall?
- Might the trustees consider more than one investment manager if a number of specialist mandates are required? (This would normally only be for larger portfolios as this approach could bring additional costs and administration.)

9–34 The normal process for appointing investment managers is to begin by drawing up a shortlist of those who are known to work in the charity investment sector. It is not essential that there is a specialist charity investment department, as not all investment managers will work in that way, but experience in the charity sector is certainly essential. The shortlist can then be used as a list of those whom the charity will invite to submit a written proposal on how the charity's investments might be managed by them. Once written proposals are received, the charity trustees should, either alone or with external assistance, decide which of the investment managers who have submitted proposals they would like to meet, and conduct a form of interview to explore more of the detail of a potential appointment. Appointing on the basis of the written proposal alone is generally to be discouraged.

9–35 Charity trustees often create a complex tender process that goes beyond any formal legal duty imposed upon them: unless a charity is also a public body or carries out a substantial degree of public functions, it is unlikely to have to go through a formal procurement process. That is not to say that a selection process is to be avoided. The charity trustees should still be able to demonstrate that they have exercised some degree of independent judgement when selecting and appointing investment managers.

Contract with adviser

9–36 It should be self-evident to charity trustees that the relationship between them and any investment manager they appoint should be set out in writing. Indeed, this is almost certainly a requirement imposed upon the investment managers themselves under the regulatory regime overseen by the Financial Conduct Authority.

The statutory provisions relating to the appointment of nominees[16] create a useful model for the creation of an appointment in the absence of any other pre-existing model, but care should be taken not to restrict any contractual terms only to the nominee relationship itself. **9–37**

The broad requirements of charity law nevertheless provide that charity trustees must, when entering into any contract, be satisfied that it is in the charity's best interests (compare s.66 of the 2005 Act) and the rules on references in documents must also be adhered to, which will involve disclosure of the charity's full legal name and registered charity number as a minimum. **9–38**

The contract with the investment managers ought to refer to any investment policy statement which the charity trustees have drawn up (while admitting that it may be changed from time to time), the details of any benchmark identified against which the investment managers' performance may be measured, and include provisions for the termination or review of the contract. Many charities approach charity investment nowadays on the basis of a time-limited appointment (often for three to five years), with the possibility of reappointment thereafter should performance have met satisfactory levels. **9–39**

Nominees

The use of custodians or nominees is generally an essential part of modern day investment management, particularly where discretionary investment managers are appointed. There is now a specific statutory power to appoint nominees.[17] **9–40**

It is worth setting out the power to appoint nominees in full as the section contains detailed provisions relating to the contractual terms which must be entered into on creating a nominee appointment. Although the legislative provision relates only to trustees of trusts, the procedure that is created may be considered to be best practice for all charity trustees in the absence of any other overriding requirement. **9–41**

The wording of the section is: **9–42**

> **"4B Exercise of power of investment: power to appoint nominees**
>
> (1) The trustees of a trust may, for the purpose of exercising the power of investment under section 4(1)(ea) of this Act—
> (a) appoint a person to act as their nominee in relation to such of the trust estate, heritable as well as moveable, as they may determine, and
> (b) take such steps as are necessary to secure the transfer of title to that property to their nominee.
>
> (2) A person may not be appointed as a nominee unless the trustees reasonably believe—
> (a) that the appointment is appropriate in the circumstances of the trust, and
> (b) that the proposed nominee has the skills, knowledge and expertise that it is reasonable to expect of a person acting as a nominee.
>
> (3) The power to appoint a nominee is subject to any restriction or exclusion imposed by or under—
> (a) the trust deed, or

[16] See paras 9–40—9–42 below.

[17] Trusts (Scotland) Act 1921 s.4B as inserted by the Charities and Trustee Investment (Scotland) Act 2005 s.94.

(b) any enactment (within the meaning of the Scotland Act 1998 (c.46)).

(4) An appointment as a nominee shall—

(a) be made in writing,

(b) be subject to the trustees' retaining power to—

(i) direct the nominee, and

(ii) revoke the nominee's appointment, and

(c) subject to subsection (4), otherwise be on such terms as to suitable remuneration and other matters as the trustees may determine.

(5) The trustees may not appoint a nominee on any of the following terms unless it is reasonably necessary for them to do so—

(a) a term permitting the nominee to appoint a substitute,

(b) a term restricting the liability of the nominee, or of any substitute, to the trustees or to any beneficiary,

(c) a term permitting the nominee, or any substitute, to act in circumstances capable of giving rise to a conflict of interest.

(6) While a nominee continues to act for the trust, the trustees shall—

(a) keep under review the arrangements under which the nominee acts and how those arrangements are being put into effect,

(b) if circumstances make it appropriate to do so, consider whether there is a need to exercise their power—

(i) to direct the nominee, or

(ii) to revoke the nominee's appointment, and

(c) exercise either or both of those powers if they consider that there is a need to do so."

Review and monitoring

9–43 Throughout the duration of the appointment of investment managers, the ultimate responsibility for the investment of the charity's assets remains with the charity trustees. This does not necessarily mean that the charity trustees will be liable for the negligence of the investment managers, but it does mean that the charity trustees must be seen to respond to inadequacies or failings on the part of the investment managers, either by requiring an improvement in performance, or by effecting a change in the appointment to new managers in serious cases or where performance has not improved despite a review.

9–44 It is always important to understand how and why an investment manager is underperforming or outperforming. Poor performance can often be the catalyst for a change in investment manager. However, studies have shown that a change in manager can result in worse performance in the ensuing years than if no change had been made. In part this reflects the way in which different investment styles move in and out of favour and that performance, even in the best investment firms, can ebb and flow.

9–45 Trustees may feel that an investment manager who is underperforming because their usually successful investment style is currently out of favour should be allowed more time to demonstrate an adjustment in style or a change in performance. On the other hand a manager with a high level of staff turnover, an unpremeditated change in investment philosophy or a significant change in service or fee levels may be a more worthy candidate for change.

9–46 Where major underperformance against a set benchmark has arisen, trustees may need to consider whether the benchmark was in fact appropriate in the first place, and this also requires a discussion with the investment managers. Nevertheless, if benchmarks have been departed from, whether with or without good justification, the trustees will wish to understand why. Where there is a lack of adherence to a benchmark, it can be more difficult for charity trustees to monitor how well their portfolio is performing relative to the wider market. That may not in itself be fatal to the relationship between the charity trustees and their investment managers, but it should lead to a discussion between both parties so that there is a clear understanding of what is happening and why. The charity trustees are ultimately responsible for acting upon any such discussion, whether that is to agree a new benchmark with the investment managers, insist upon adherence to an existing benchmark, or review the appointment as a whole.

ETHICAL INVESTMENTS AND OTHER SPECIAL INVESTMENT ISSUES

The potential issues attending ethical and other special investments require particular consideration. As noted at the beginning of this chapter, the starting point for an assessment of appropriate investment is the employment of money to produce interest or profit in order to further the charity's purposes. In particular, the private views of trustees are not a proper basis for acting. In the conduct of their own affairs trustees are free to abstain from making investments in, say, certain countries or certain companies concerned with alcohol, tobacco or armaments. But if, as a trustee, the individual is aware that investments of that type would be more beneficial to the beneficiaries than other possible investments, the trustee must not refrain from making such investments by reason of the personal views held.[18] **9–47**

Further, as a general rule, whilst trustees are required to show no higher degree of diligence than a person of ordinary prudence, it is the duty of the trustee to confine themselves to the class of investments permitted by the trust and to avoid all investments of that class that may be hazardous.[19] On the other hand, trustees do not have an unqualified duty simply to rubber stamp the advice of an investment adviser or to invest in the most profitable investment available.[20] **9–48**

For some time, therefore, charity trustees have felt constrained in their ability to invest in an ethical or socially responsible way. **9–49**

The broad direction now is that circumstances can exist where the maximising of funds at all costs is not in the charity's best interests.[21] There are thought to be five particular types of circumstance. They should not be viewed as exhaustive, but may be so in practice. **9–50**

First, there may be particular types of investment that are in conflict with the charity's purposes. The classic example is the case of a cancer research charity investing in shares in a tobacco company. If the charity trustees are clear that investing in a particular business presents a conflict with their charitable objectives then they may consider such an investment to be impermissible. **9–51**

---

[18] *Cowan v Scargill* [1985] Ch. 270, 287–288.

[19] *Learoyd v Whiteley* (1887) 12 L.R. App. Cas. 727, 733.

[20] *Martin v City of Edinburgh District Council*, 1988 S.L.T. 329, 334.

[21] *Harries (Bishop of Oxford) v Church Commissioners* [1992] 1 W.L.R. 1241, 1247.

9–52 Secondly, there may be circumstances where investing in particular assets would cause a charity's beneficiaries to become unwilling to receive aid from the charity. This type of scenario has arisen for many charities in recent times where donations from potentially "tainted" donors were proposed—charity trustees have felt that to receive a donation from a prolific criminal (for example) would not be acceptable, even if that meant declining substantial financial support. Charity trustees may quite legitimately avoid investments that would cause a charity's supporters or beneficiaries to feel alienated from the charity's cause. Charity trustees should weigh up the loss of support or of profile against the financial loss which could be suffered: the charity trustees alone would then have to decide what they felt, on balance, was in the charity's best interests.

9–53 Thirdly, the charity's constitution itself contains a restriction or exclusion.

9–54 Fourthly are cases where particular investments might bring the charity into disrepute. This is similar in some ways to the second circumstance in as much as the end result may be the same—a loss of influence amongst supporters or beneficiaries. When assessing the possibility of reputational damage, charity trustees must not be seen to make personal moral judgements if those would be made at the charity's expense. Some charity trustees would, for example, consider a holding in a munitions company to be morally repugnant, while others would take an opposing view. If the charity trustees are not satisfied that the charity might be at risk of significant financial detriment through holding such shares, their personal moral views should be set aside.

9–55 Fifthly is that charity trustees should be free to take into account the views of third parties on whether particular investments would conflict morally with the charity's purposes, provided that this would not give rise to significant financial detriment.[22]

9–56 There may be other sets of circumstances. Apart from a formal constitutional barrier, the issue is likely to be one of balancing moral, ethical or other social factors against the financial benefit or detriment that particular investments might bring.

Donor community

9–57 The extent to which the views of a charity's donor community can be taken in to account when making investment decisions is important to consider.

9–58 The Scottish Charity Appeals Panel case of *St Margaret's Children and Family Care Society*[23] dealt with charitable purposes and their interaction with equality legislation. One relevant factor for the charity was considered to be the impact on the charity's donor community had the charity been forced to amend its purposes. The suggestion was that donors would choose no longer to support the work of

[22] See the Scottish Charity Appeals Panel case of *St Margaret's Children and Family Care Society v Office of the Scottish Charity Regulator* (Case ref: APP 02/13).

[23] *St Margaret's Children and Family Care Society v Office of the Scottish Charity Regulator* (Case ref: APP 02/13).

the charity with the result that the charity would lose income to such an extent that it would have to close. That, in turn, would lead to a loss to the wider community.

While the *St Margaret's* case is not directly in point when dealing with questions of charity investment, and while its decision must be viewed on the particular facts that applied in the case, the decision is consistent with that in *Harries* considered at paras 9–50—9–56 above. **9–59**

Guidance

The Charity Commission for England and Wales in its guidance document number CC14 on "Charities and investment matters: a guide for trustees" says that: **9–60**

> "Trustees of any charity can decide to invest ethically, even if the investment might provide a lower rate of return than an alternative investment. Ethical investment means investing in a way that reflects a charity's values and ethos and does not run counter to its aims. However, a charity's trustees must be able to justify why it is in the charity's best interests to invest in this way. The law permits the following reasons:
>
> - a particular investment conflicts with the aims of the charity; or
> - the charity might lose supporters or beneficiaries if it does not invest ethically; or
> - there is no significant financial detriment."

The guidance goes on to state: **9–61**

> "Trustees must ensure that any decision that they take about adopting an ethical investment approach can be justified within the criteria above. They must be clear about the reasons why certain companies or sectors are excluded or included. Trustees should also evaluate the effect of any proposed policy on potential investment returns and balance any risk of lower returns against the risk of alienating support or damage to reputation. This cannot be an exact calculation but trustees will have to assess the risk to their charity."

This guidance, originating as it does from England and Wales, is not technically binding in Scotland, but it provides a summary framework that may be considered to be persuasive in Scotland. This is particularly so given that OSCR has been known to refer Scottish charities to CC14 as representing OSCR's views on the subject of charity investment.[24] **9–62**

The Charity Commission approach does also influence the SORP, which is a creation of both the Charity Commission for England and Wales and OSCR. In relation to ethical investments in particular, the SORP states: **9–63**

> "Investment decisions may be subject to the ethical, socially responsible or mission related investment policies adopted by a charity. The adoption of ethical, socially responsible or mission related investment policies does not create a separate class of investment asset that is presented separately in a charity's balance sheet. However, investment policies must be explained in the trustees' annual report and the value of investments held in pursuit of particular ethical investment policies may be identified separately in the note to the accounts analysing investments."

[24] See also *Martin v City of Edinburgh District Council*, 1988 S.L.T. 329.

Programme related and mixed motive investment

9–64 Some additional guidance from CC14 is helpful in setting out in summary terms the definitions of programme related investment and mixed motive investment.

9–65 Both "programme related investment" and "mixed motive investment" are focused at least in part on non-financial return. The driving factor may be a combination of financial gain and performance of objectives for the public benefit. In deciding whether or not to engage in programme related or mixed motive investment, charity trustees have to weigh up the possibility of financial loss with the performance of charitable aims. The degree to which one outweighs the other will depend on each charity's view on the proper deployment of its assets—some will adhere to the desire to generate income and capital growth for the purposes of making grants to third parties; others will consider that the charity's assets can be directly employed in the furtherance of benefiting others without the same degree of financial gain.

9–66 Programme related investment is defined by the Charity Commission in CC14 as

> "the use of expendable resources by a charity in a way which may generate a financial return but is principally for the furtherance of the charitable purpose or purposes of a charity".

The Commission gives examples such as loans or loan guarantees. The emphasis is on "social impact or return rather than a financial return".

9–67 To justify programme-related investment, charity trustees are encouraged to consider the extent to which the aims of the charity will be furthered by the proposed investment, whether and to what extent any private benefit might arise, whether external advice should be obtained and what the tenor of that advice is, the degree of risk attached to the proposed investment, and the governance and contractual arrangements required in order to put the investment into place and to monitor it properly.

9–68 Mixed motive investment, on the other hand, is investment which carries with it features of "both financial investment and programme related investment", according to CC14, but in a context where the investment cannot be classified as wholly one or the other.

9–69 For such an investment to be justified, CC14 places more focus on the need for professional advice. Charity trustees would need to be satisfied that:

- the investment is in the best interests of the charity;
- the investment "can be justified by the dual nature of the return", i.e. part financial return and part contribution to the charity's aims; and
- there is no other reason for making the investment, including creating unauthorised private benefit to some or all of the charity trustees or persons connected with the charity trustees, or creating unacceptable private benefit to other third parties.

Positive ethical investment policies

We have already considered the possibility of negative ethical investment policies: that is to say, policies where the charity trustees decide not to invest in particular stocks for particular ethical or moral reasons, even although this may result in a lower potential return for the charity. 9–70

Positive ethical investment policies, on the other hand, arise where a charity decides to exercise its powers (usually exercising voting powers as an investor) in order to influence a change in the policies of the companies it invests in. CC14 provides a helpful definition of "positive screening": it is described as the investment or all or part of a portfolio in "companies or sectors which reflect a charity's values". Those values could relate to areas such as employment rights, human rights, matters of environmental or health protection, reduction of carbon footprint, or in some other aspect of good corporate governance or corporate social responsibility. 9–71

Charity trustees need to be clear that in doing so, they are acting in the interests of the charity, as influencing policy change in a company could in theory lead to a lowering of the company's overall profits. But that could nevertheless be in line with the ethical or moral stance the charity trustees take in the context of their wider charitable aims and objectives. 9–72

On the other hand, positive investment can influence corporate policy in order to engender financial return, particularly where improved governance results in a company becoming better managed or more socially responsible. In this case, it is easier to justify the positive investment choices: but where loss might result, the charity trustees need to be clear that there is some higher beneficial objective which may result, which would be aligned with the charity's own purposes. Advocating policy change that could result in loss and that is not aligned with the charity's own purposes, however, is not permitted. 9–73

Many investment managers will now offer a system of positive screening to charities and non-charities alike as part of their standard investment approach. 9–74

Derivatives

Derivatives take the form of contracts. The value from derivatives does not come from the contract in itself, but from the performance of an underlying entity, which could be an asset or an interest rate or index. They are frequently used in order to hedge (insure) against price movements and they are therefore speculative types of investment, relying as they do on fluctuations in the value or price of the underlying entity. Depending on the form they take, derivatives are generally not treated as investments, but in some fixed circumstances CC14 considers that they could be entered into for gain and could therefore qualify as investments from the point of view of charity trustees. 9–75

Essentially, for the use of derivatives to be appropriate for charity trustees, the purpose of the derivative must be to manage or mitigate risk in an investment transaction or must be designed to manage transaction costs as part of the 9–76 investment process, or conceivably both. However, CC14 suggests that a derivatives transaction must be economically appropriate and the regulatory view is that only a very small proportion of a larger fund of assets could at any one time be used to invest in derivatives. Because they are higher risk, they must be treated with extra care: derivatives ought not to be used as investment vehicles by charity trustees without professional advice.

9–77 There is considerable risk that investing in derivatives would be treated not as an investment but as a trade, and this is another reason why charity trustees must treat derivatives with additional caution. Commentators in the United States have gone as far as to suggest that charities wishing to trade in derivatives would have to register first with the local futures trading commission. If this approach were borne out, it would suggest that few, if any, charities would wish to go down this route, not least because of the difficulty it could cause in relation to restriction of charity tax reliefs. Even without additional regulatory registrations, the risk of inadvertent non-primary purpose trade through investing in derivatives—and the resultant restriction of charity tax reliefs—means that charity trustees must seek advice from investment managers before investing in these vehicles.

Heritage assets and works of art

9–78 Heritage assets represent another category of asset which may in some cases be treated as investments. For many charities, heritage assets are the means by which some or all of their charitable objectives are performed. The SORP describes a heritage asset as

> "a tangible or intangible asset with historical, artistic, scientific, technological, geophysical or environmental qualities that is held and maintained principally for its contribution to knowledge and culture".

Where a heritage asset falls outwith that category, it is more likely to have to be classified as a tangible fixed asset or investment.

9–79 It may well be open to argument whether any one asset falls within the category of heritage asset. An ancient parish church, for example, may hold several sets of communion silver. One or two of those sets may be in regular use during religious ordinances, whereas others may be considered too valuable or fragile to be brought into regular use. A decision has to be made (normally in consultation with the charity's auditors) as to whether those lesser used sets of vessels may be treated as a heritage asset or should be treated as a "working asset" of the charity, albeit one that is not in daily use. There may be a time when a line is crossed and the asset becomes an investment—retained only for its intrinsic financial value—rather than an item that will ever be given practical use. Analogies can easily be drawn with artefacts in libraries, museums, galleries, historic houses and the like.

9–80 The difficulty that heritage assets present is primarily in accounting terms. It can be difficult to obtain an appropriate valuation for some heritage assets and even where a valuation can be obtained, the cost of obtaining the valuation may be prohibitive. This is likely to lead to further disclosures in a charity's accounts on why the asset has not been valued and what policies are in place for the management, conservation and disposal of such assets.

In addition to accounting difficulties, there is also the question of insurance of such items. If a heritage asset is to be treated as an investment, but its age, design or other quality make it prohibitively expensive to insure (or otherwise properly to conserve it), then a question must arise for the charity trustees as to whether that asset should properly be retained any longer. This, therefore, points once again to the general investment duties to have regard to suitability, risk and diversification, and potentially the need for professional advice. **9–81**

Land and buildings

As with any other type of investment property, direct investments in land and buildings should be considered by charity trustees only after having regard to their suitability to the charity, and having regard to risk and diversification. Direct investments in land and buildings can, however, bring additional concerns for charity trustees particularly in relation to practical issues such as management, maintenance, conservation and leasing. The employment of land agents or factors can relieve charity trustees of the day to day burden of these practical issues, but care needs to be taken that the costs of managing land and buildings do not begin to outweigh the potential investment benefits. As with all other investment types, having regard to suitability, risk and diversification should be the rule for charity trustees, combined with the need for professional advice. **9–82**

[illegible]

[illegible]

Land and buildings

[illegible]

CHAPTER 10

TRADING

Jandy Stevenson

INTRODUCTION

Trading by a charity will normally fall into one of two broad categories: **10–01**

- The first is activity carried out in pursuit of the primary objectives of the charity and would include, for example, a school that charges school fees or a nursing home that charges for care where the entities are charities and not for profit. This is known as primary purpose trade.
- The second category is that of a charity that engages in a trade in order to generate funds for the charity. An example of this would be the sale of new goods to generate a profit but could also be, for example, sponsorship deals. This type of activity is more likely to be commercial. Such activity must fall within the charity's purposes.

Seeking new and innovative ways of funding a charity is a constant pressure and may give rise to activities which are more akin to commercial trading. **10–02**

Where charities receive funding other than by straightforward donation or investment income the possibility of such income sources being treated as trading income has to be considered as there are risks associated with trading which need to be managed. The principal risks with trading income are: **10–03**

(i) reduction in value of charitable assets if the trading does not go well and the charity has to give support to the enterprise;
(ii) tax being levied and reducing the sums available to the charity; and
(iii) trading by the charity could adversely affect its charitable status if found not to fall within the charity's purposes.

The first step in managing any risks associated with trading is to identify any activities carried on within the charity that could be considered as trading activities. Having done so, the trustees should consider whether the activities could give rise to a commercial risk to the charity as one of their principal duties is to safeguard the assets of the charity. This type of risk may arise because there is a deficit arising from the activity that has to be met from other charitable resources or because the nature of the activity presents a risk from which the charity should be protected. It is important that trustees ask themselves what they **10–04** are trying to achieve, whether they have appropriate resources to undertake the activity, and whether this is the most appropriate way forward.

10–05 In addition to the commercial risks to the charity carrying out activities that might be a trade, HMRC may seek to tax any profits arising and, if exemptions are not available, restructuring, by creating a trading subsidiary, for example, to ring fence the activity, should allow the charity to manage any tax leakage.

10–06 Charity trustees should bear in mind that some activities carried out by the charity may amount to taxable trading income but are, in fact, making a loss. Charity trustees should consider carefully whether such activity should continue. Evaluating the results from the trade in so far as the financial contribution enhances the ability to the charity to further its purposes is very important and the existence of losses should not be dismissed lightly (see also para.10–41). Such a tax loss would not be regarded as charitable expenditure. If the trade was carried out on a commercial basis but had made a loss due to difficult trading conditions there would be no liability to tax on the non-charitable expenditure. However, HMRC guidance says that if a charity makes a loss year on year they will take the view that the trade is not carried out on a commercial basis and the equivalent of the amount of the loss on the trading activity will be deemed taxable.

DEFINITION OF TRADE

10–07 An activity that constitutes a trade is usually thought of in terms of selling goods or services to customers but it can also cover one-off activities including some fundraising arrangements. Neither the dictionary definition of a trade as "buying, selling or exchange of goods" nor the Taxes Act definition[1] that defines trade as "trade includes every trade, manufacture, adventure or concern in the nature of a trade" is very useful.

10–08 However, the courts have amplified this over the years by establishing eight "badges of trade" that can be applied to particular activities. Meeting any one of these criteria may be enough to establish the activity as a trade. The badges are:

(1) *A profit seeking motive*: An intention to make a profit is not in itself conclusive but fundraising activities by a charity carried out with a view to making a surplus are likely to be trading.

(2) *The number of repeat transactions*: A single transaction can be treated as a trade but is less likely than if the transaction is repeated.

(3) *The nature of the asset*: The test here is whether the asset could be used for personal enjoyment or whether it is the sort of asset that can only be enjoyed by selling it. An asset that can only generate profit by being sold is likely to be a trading asset.

(4) *Existence of similar transactions*: If an entity carries on other related activities this could add weight to the view that the activity is trading.

[1] See the Income and Corporation Taxes Act 1988 (c.1).

(5) *Enhancements made to the asset to improve possible profit*: If assets are repaired or improved with a view to selling at a profit this could be indicative of trade.
(6) *The way in which the sale is made*: Was this typical of a trading enterprise or just a need to realise some cash?
(7) *How it is financed*? Financing arrangements may help to determine the nature of the transaction.
(8) *The interval between purchase and sale*: The quicker the realisation the more akin to trading.

Some examples of activities undertaken by charities and applying the above badges of trade: **10–09**

- *Sale of Christmas cards.* **10–10**
  These:
  — are sold to make a profit (badge 1);
  — are sold over a period of weeks (badge 2);
  — are for use by others who buy them (badge 3); and
  — are often bought in for resale (badges 6, 7, 8)

Sale of Christmas cards is a trading activity.

- *Development of a building formerly used by the charity for other commercial purposes in order to realise a profit:* **10–11**
  — profit seeking motive (badge 1);
  — enhancement made to asset to improve possible profit (badges 3 and 6); and
  — financing of the improvement works likely to be indicative of trade (badge 7).
  This is likely to be a trading activity.

An agreement that sets out the services to be provided by the charity and which may also set out the performance standards expected is known as a service level agreement (SLA). The document sets out the service required and that any surplus can be retained by the charity and any deficit must be met by the charity: **10–12**

- profit (surplus) seeking motive is possible (badge 1); and
- there are likely to be repeat transactions in carrying out the services (badge 2).

This could be trading but if for the primary purpose of the charity would be exempt from tax.[2]

[2] See para.10–15 below.

COMMERCIAL RISK

10–13 When considering new and innovative ways of raising funds the possibility of commercial risk to the charity assets should be considered by the charity trustees. In example (b) above there could be considerable risk. The development of the property may cost more than expected and the ultimate sale be insufficient to cover costs and loan repayments, or something happens during the development which gives rise to a claim against the charity. When entering into any new contract the risks associated with it should be evaluated with a view to managing and reducing risk wherever possible. In some cases trustees may be of the view that the risks to the charity are too great and should be avoided altogether. In undertaking any activity there are risks that, if the enterprise is to be taken forward, cannot be avoided altogether. The importance of understanding those risks and the mechanisms in place for managing them are very important and cannot be taken lightly.

TAX EXEMPTION

10–14 Having examined the characteristics of the possible trading income and considered commercial risk management, the next step—if activities could be treated as trading—would be to consider whether there are tax exemptions available.

10–15 Not all trading transactions carried out by a charity are necessarily taxable. There are four types of activity where there are specific tax exemptions. These are:

- primary purpose trading and ancillary trade;
- trading activities mainly carried out by the charity's beneficiaries;
- small trading exemption; and
- exemptions in respect of certain fundraising activities.

Primary purpose trade

10–16 Primary purpose trades are those carried out to pursue the purposes of the charity as reflected in the constitution. Example of such activity would be schools who charge fees for the provision of education, the holding of an exhibition by a gallery or museum where an entry fee is charged, or charges by a healthcare establishment for accessing the services.

Ancillary trade

10–17 Some activities carried out by charities do not fit exactly with the primary purpose laid down in the constitution but may be so closely aligned with the purposes that they are treated as falling within the exemption for primary purpose trade. Examples of this would be provision of catering facilities to a school or care home where the primary purpose would be the provision of education and advancement of health respectively. The key question in determining whether the activity is ancillary to primary purpose trade is whether there is an obligation to provide such facilities. If the answer is yes then the activity is likely to be exempt as an ancillary activity to the primary purpose trade.

Work done by the beneficiaries

This exemption was introduced after the First World War to encourage disabled beneficiaries to participate in trading activities. Sheltered workshops are a prime example of this activity but it would also cover trades ancillary to the primary purpose such as the provision of a café run by members of a charitable youth club or church organisation.[3] Where beneficiaries are reimbursed for their work they are subject to normal employment tax rules on their earnings. **10–18**

Small trading exemptions

This exemption applies where the trading income by a charity is below the limit as set out in the following table: **10–19**

Charity's gross annual income	**Maximum permitted small trading turnover**
Under £20,000	£5,000
£20,001–£200,000	25% of your charity's total annual turnover
Over £200,000	£50,000

If the accounting period is less than 12 months the limits are reduced proportionately.

Exemptions in respect of fundraising activities

(1) *Activities that are not taxable*: **10–20**

Where a charity receives a donation for which it has to do nothing in return, the funds raised will not be taxable. Examples of this type of activity are:

- house to house and street collections;
- sponsored walks and other activities;
- legacies;
- offerings such as freewill offerings in a place of worship; and
- charity auctions or shops where the sale is of donated goods only.

(2) *Activities that are or could be taxable*:

[3] See para.10–16 above.

Where a charity is providing something in return for the activity then there is a likelihood that tax will be a factor in considering risks arising from the activity. Types of activity that come into this category are as below.

Fundraising events

10–21 An event that is organised and promoted primarily to raise money for the charity could be subject to tax but there is an exemption if there are fewer than 15 events of the same kind at any one location in the charity's financial year. If the limit is exceeded none of the events qualify for exemption. If small scale events are held where gross takings from all similar events such as coffee mornings do not exceed £1,000 a week these small scale events do not count towards the total. Small scale events carried out more than once or twice a week are likely to be trading activity and not eligible for exemption.

10–22 Social events that make a profit do not fall within the exemption unless the people attending are aware of the primary fundraising purpose.

Charity shops

10–23 Problems can arise where the shops do more than sell donated goods. Either they bring in goods for resale or they make significant change to the goods to sell them for a better profit and this activity is not undertaken by the beneficiaries.

10–24 Gift aid does not apply to goods donated to charity shops because for gift aid to be applicable the donation has to be of cash. The way round this is for the charity to enter into an arrangement by which it offers to sell the goods on the donor's behalf as their agent. The donor is then asked if they will require the proceeds or whether they will donate the proceeds to the charity. Letters to potential donors will often state that the charity will presume it can keep the proceeds if it does not hear from the donor within a reasonable period.[4]

10–25 Sales of donated goods are taxable at the zero rate for VAT but goods sold on behalf of a third party (e.g., a donor) are non-business and this reduces the VAT recovery on costs.

10–26 Where the shop sells goods on behalf of the donor for a commission (which itself is subject to standard rate VAT) and the donor then donates the balance of the monies raised to charity under the gift aid arrangements, commission income will be trading income unless it falls within the small trade exemption.

Christmas cards

10–27 Christmas cards and other gifts sold in retail premises (shops or special centres) or by mail order are not usually within the primary purposes of the charity and are likely to be treated as taxable income unless one of the other exemptions can be

[4] See paras 6–33—6–37.

evoked, such as small trading exemption. If the charity is registered for VAT these sales will be taxable at the standard rate of VAT.

Sponsorship

The terms detailed in a contract with the sponsor will determine whether or not any arrangement would be liable for tax. **10–28**

Where a business makes a sponsorship deal with a charity and receives either nothing in return or only a small amount of publicity (such as a single acknowledgement of support) from the arrangement the income is not likely to be taxable as trading activity. **10–29**

Sponsorship becomes a trading activity when what is returned to the sponsor is of greater value. This might be the case where the publicity amounts to advertisements for the business sponsor. This would normally be the case where there is a large and prominent display of the sponsor's corporate colours or a description of the products and services sold by the sponsor. It may also be that such advertisements are used in conjunction with the premises of the charity when hosting promotional activities for the sponsor. **10–30**

Another example of this type of sponsorship trading activity would be the use of an affinity credit card carrying the sponsor's logo where the aim of the sponsor will be to recruit new users of the credit card from amongst the members and supporters of the charity. The attraction to the supporters of the use of the card is the benefit which the use of the card could bring to the charity. **10–31**

Lotteries and competitions

Social lotteries promoted by a charity are specifically exempt under the legislation. Other competitions or quizzes designed to raise funds may not fall within the specific exemption. In these cases the small trading exemption might be of assistance in avoiding a tax charge if the overall activities fall within the limits. **10–32**

Letting income

The letting of excess space by the charity without any other services should be exempt from tax. Letting income may become taxable where the services provided with it turn it into a trade. Examples would be provision of conference facilities or of overnight accommodation in addition to the hire of the premises. **10–33**

For VAT purposes, letting income in commercial property is exempt from VAT unless an option to tax is made. **10–34**

THE NEED TO MANAGE RISK

10–35 The Office of the Scottish Charity Regulator's (OSCR) view is that trading, other than that carried out to fulfil its purposes, involves risk to the charity assets and that risk must be managed. The first question for trustees and OSCR is whether the activity is permitted within the constitution. If it is permitted OSCR will normally accept that the activity can be carried out within the charity. If it is not permitted then clearly the activity should not be carried on within the charity. In cases where the activity is not permitted by the purposes or falls within the tax regime and trustees consider that the activity is appropriate to achieving the objectives for the beneficiaries, the charity should look to carrying out these activities through a trading subsidiary to minimise risks.

SETTING UP A TRADING SUBSIDIARY

10–36 The first step towards mitigating the risks is to consider setting up a trading subsidiary which can operate the commercial activities. A trading subsidiary will normally be a limited company all of the shares in which will be owned by the charity. As a wholly-owned subsidiary company a trading subsidiary can gift aid its profit to the parent charity to minimise the tax payable on the trading profits. Carrying out activities through a trading subsidiary should protect the charity from any commercial forces which might adversely affect it although care must be taken to ensure that the charity's assets are not put at risk because of a need to support the trading company. The charity receives distributable profits from the subsidiary under gift aid and can use them in furtherance of the purposes of the charity. However, because the activities of the subsidiary are unlikely to be charitable, the charity cannot give its money directly to the subsidiary. There may, however, be ways by which the charity can assist—see para.10–43. Whilst the principle is simple the success of such an arrangement depends on establishing the subsidiary on a sound commercial basis and initial investment which should be made only if it is in line with the charity purposes and should be sufficient to underpin the work of the subsidiary.

10–37 Custom and practice has been for companies that are wholly owned subsidiaries of charities to donate all taxable profits to the parent charity and to claim tax relief on the whole amount.[5] This approach was endorsed by the Charity Commission in their guidance note CC35 issued on 1 April 2007. In October 2014 ICAEW sought counsel's opinion on whether or not such a payment was a distribution in company law and obtained confirmation that in counsel's view it was a distribution under the Companies Act definition. This opinion is important in cases where the gift aid donation exceeds distributable profits as determined by company law and has now been endorsed by HMRC and the Charity Commission, who, on 24 February 2016, issued a revised guidance incorporating this view and noting:

---

[5] Under the Corporation Tax Act 2010 Pt 6 s.189 and following.

> "Parent charities with wholly-owned trading subsidiaries must bring their operations into compliance with this revised position for any accounting period starting on or after 1 April 2015."[6]

As a result of this legal interpretation, the extent by which the gift aid donation exceeds distributable profits will be unlawful and the charity would be liable to repay the excess and the directors of the subsidiary at the time the payment was made could be liable. Where taxable profits in the trading subsidiary exceed the distributable profit the trading company may be liable to a tax charge. **10–38**

HMRC published detailed guidance[7] on gift aid in October 2015. It explains the impact where a trading subsidiary has taxable profits in excess of the amount it can distribute. HMRC also confirms that a company that makes a qualifying donation to a charity or Community Amateur Sports Club can set out the amount paid against profits for corporation tax purposes. In addition, HMRC note that charitable donations cannot be used to create or add to a company's trading losses, nor can excess charitable donations be carried forward or back although they may be surrendered for group relief. **10–39**

The importance of the trading company producing profits arises both from the point of view of distributable profits discussed above but also to ensure that it does not need further support from the charity parent that could be seen as an inappropriate use of charity assets. **10–40**

Capital allowances are the allowances permitted by tax law on fixed assets in place of depreciation (which is the amount by which accounts will normally reflect the provision for asset replacement during its useful life). As the rates of capital allowances are seldom the same as the rates of depreciation adopted by an entity when setting its accounting policies, the capital allowances available to the subsidiary can be less than the accounting allowance for depreciation. The result of this is that taxable profits are higher than distributable profits and may mean that some profits remain taxable in the subsidiary because they cannot be distributed in full. Trading subsidiaries should carefully consider both claims for capital allowances and the need to hold fixed assets within the trading entity to address this difficulty. One way around this would be for fixed assets to be held by the charity that could make a charge for their use that can be beneficial to the charity as a means of improved cash flow. Trustees should be aware this charge could be liable to VAT depending on the overall VAT position of the charity and appropriate advice should be sought to ensure the charity proceeds in the most beneficial way. If the charity is already registered for VAT there would be a requirement to charge VAT but the additional income liable to VAT may enhance the charity's ability to obtain relief for input VAT on expenditure. **10–41**

Although the arrangement of putting trading activities into a subsidiary and stripping out profit by way of gift aid is a neat mechanism for ensuring maximum flow of funds to the charity, it does make it difficult for the trading subsidiary to **10–42**

---

[6] The Charity Commission, "Trustees, trading and tax: How charities may lawfully trade" (CC35) (February 2016).

[7] HMRC, *Charities: detailed guidance notes*, see *http://www.gov.uk/government/publications/charities-detailed-guidance-notes* [Accessed 3 June 2016].

deal with any periods where it struggles to make a profit or wishes to expand the work it does and needs working capital. Having gift aided its profits and depleted reserves it may look to the parent to provide funds to assist.

10–43 The parent may look to provide funds by:

(i) purchasing more shares in the subsidiary;
(ii) intercompany loan; and
(iii) intercompany current account,

but may find that any of these routes can be difficult. If the trading subsidiary has previously made gift aid payments to the charity and then looks to the charity for support, there is a risk that HMRC will invoke the gift aid benefit rules. To avoid this pitfall the charity needs to be able to show that the provision of funding is clearly required for an identifiable purpose not associated with the earlier provision of gift aid payment.

10–44 Purchasing more shares is unlikely to be an acceptable option. OSCR will expect that any investment in a trading subsidiary by way of share capital should be kept at a minimum as there is less security for the charity should the trading subsidiary fail.

10–45 HMRC will look to see if further investment in the trading subsidiary could be classed as "non-qualifying expenditure"[8] as defined. The consequence of any investment or loan being treated as non-qualifying expenditure is to restrict the tax exemption for trading activities. To avoid this difficulty the loans or investment must be made on a commercial basis but it may be difficult to show that without proper back up documentation such as business plans and forecast of the activities of the trading company.

10–46 HMRC have a non-statutory clearance procedure under which they will provide written confirmation of their view where the taxpayer remains uncertain about the likely HMRC interpretation of a transaction and they try to respond within 28 days. However, in some circumstances HMRC will decline to give advice where, for example, they consider there are no points of uncertainty or the purpose of the transaction is to avoid tax. Where the charity wishes to increase funding to the trading subsidiary they may wish to avail themselves of this procedure.

10–47 An intercompany loan, which arises when the charity lends money (or other assets) to its subsidiary, should be subject to a commercial rate of interest which the trading company should pay and not simply allow to build up unpaid. Trustees should have a formal loan agreement setting out the market rate of interest on the loan, any fixed or floating charge over the assets of the trading subsidiary and the term over which the capital is to be repaid.

10–48 Where there is current account movement between the charity and the trading subsidiary, for example, where the charity has paid for some of the subsidiary's

[8] Definitions are given in the Income Tax Act 2002 (c.3) ss.558–561 and Corporation Tax Act 2010 (c.4) ss.511–514.

trading stock on its behalf, the subsidiary should be able to repay any indebtedness on normal commercial terms and not treat it as some form of longer term advance that is interest free.

HMRC accept that a charity may wish to make a number of small investments in a trading company rather than one large investment in order to reduce risk. However, to avoid loss of tax exemptions it is important to be able to demonstrate that the investment being made is of benefit to the charity, that terms and conditions are in place on how the trading subsidiary will repay the investment and that the charity gets a fair return that is actually paid. **10–49**

Monies given to the charity have special treatment for tax purposes and should not be advanced into the commercial entity without attracting a rate of interest commensurate to the commercial risk. Advancing money to a trading subsidiary without the prospect of repayment would be inappropriate use of charity assets and the trustees could be challenged by the Charity Regulator and HMRC were this to be the case. The capital underpinning of the subsidiary should be sufficient to allow it to carry out its activities successfully. Sometimes the issued share capital is not enough to achieve this and the charity has to consider acquiring more shares (rather than advance further loans) as this approach would support the entity in the longer term. If purchasing more shares the trustees should be clear that there is prospect of the subsidiary producing a return on the investments for the charity. If the creation of a trading subsidiary was a good idea, but which cannot subsequently achieve commercial success, then trustees should take advice on whether or not to wind it up. In looking at both the creation of a trading subsidiary in the first instance and at the continuation of support, trustees should have financial information available to them to appraise the position. **10–50**

SHOULD A TRADING COMPANY BE CREATED?

Trustees require some basic information when considering the creation of a trading company. These include: **10–51**

- understanding the risks that accompany commercial activities;
- the business plan;
- the company structure and governance;
- financing of the company; and
- routes by which profit will be transferred to charity.

The business plan

A trading subsidiary is set up by a charity to carry on non-primary purpose trade: it is likely to be done where there is significant risk and planning is essential. The objectives of creating a trading subsidiary are threefold: **10–52**

(i) to manage the significant risks arising through commercial trading and to protect charity assets;

(ii) to avoid payment of tax on profits that are intended to be used by the charity; and
(iii) to minimise any adverse reputational risk in the event of the subsidiary failing.

10–53 Setting up a trading subsidiary should not be entered into without careful consideration. There are costs associated with the running of the trading subsidiary and it might be that those costs outweigh the benefits otherwise achieved. It is important to ensure that there is a sound business plan that considers the viability of the entity. There is little point in entering an arrangement that will continue to need financial or other support where the activity is non-primary purpose and not within the purposes of the charity. The need for that support may put charity assets at risk by, for example, an inability to repay working capital lent by the charity or placing a strain on human resources available within the group.

10–54 A failure of a trading subsidiary may also present the charity with a reputational risk. In some cases there can be pressure to pay liabilities incurred by the subsidiary in order to protect the position of the charity. If there is a significant overlap of those who are the directors of the subsidiary and also trustees of the parent charity, and if the strategy of the subsidiary is broadly set by the parent charity board, then such "intermingling" would make it more likely that a creditor could be successful in suing both the subsidiary and the parent charity in order to access the funds of both to meet the sum or any damages claimed against the subsidiary. Payment of liabilities incurred by the trading subsidiary would be an inappropriate use of charity money; but anxiety about protecting the good name of a charity may tempt trustees to make such payments in the hope of improved trading enabling refund. Normally done by way of intercompany loan, trustees should evaluate the likelihood of repayment before making any advance.

10–55 The starting point for all these considerations is thus a well-thought-through business plan that sets out the vision for the running of the business and tests the robustness of the decisions with sensitivity analysis and an appraisal of the likelihood of success. The headings in the plan would be as below.

Revenue streams

10–56 Where will sales come from? Will there be a lot of competition for the funds and, if so, what is your unique selling proposition? (Important for sponsorship, for example.) When a charity attracts sponsorship but the activity has to be carried on by a trading subsidiary, what is the position about the use of the charity name? Sponsors will normally want to use the charity name so a licensing agreement between the charity and the trading entity may be a requirement to protect the revenue stream.

Cost of sales

What costs will have to be incurred to access the revenue stream? This might be costs of buying assets for resale or labour costs and property costs. Is special equipment or know-how required to carry out trading activities successfully? **10–57**

Human resources

How many people will be required to do this? What emoluments will have to be paid and what on-cost will be incurred? Who will line manage the activity on a day to day basis? If it is expected that existing staff will be involved, will the additional workload be a barrier to the carrying out of the main objectives of the charity because there is insufficient time and resource available? **10–58**

The market

Is the market you have identified already crowded with suppliers or is it a niche? Will people buy from you? **10–59**

Financing the operation

How much will the charity have to provide to finance the business? Is such provision appropriate in the light of its charitable purposes? Can others help finance it? Will commercial borrowing be required and, if yes, how easy will it be to access and what will the cost be? If there are loans from the charity to the trader what will the rate of interest be? If money is advanced only to assist with working capital when will it be repaid? Is it likely that a return can be achieved from the capital underpinning? If provision of external finance is advanced on condition that the charity offers guarantees to the lender, trustees should ask themselves whether to do so would be acting in the interests of the charity and consider the position of the charity were such a loan to be called up. The assets of the charity could be put at risk and such guarantees should be avoided. **10–60**

Developing the business/plans for the future

If the business grows or a new product line is to be added what additional costs will be incurred and how will they be funded? What other resources will be required? **10–61**

Sensitivity analysis

Figures used in the business plan will include some estimates and a change in value of those figures will affect the outcomes. Sensitivity analysis seeks to determine what happens if figures are different. A major question to ask is what if **10–62** sales do not materialise and a loss is made? Over what timescales and at what level would such a loss be acceptable, if at all? What action would be needed to address any shortfalls?

SWOT analysis

10–63 Be sure of the strengths, weaknesses, opportunities and threats to the business before you embark on creating a trading subsidiary. Work out what the likely effect of these characteristics will have on the business. For example, if a strength is seen to be high demand for this type of activity, does it mean that pricing is difficult because there is a lot of competition? Low margins demand high volume sales—can this be achieved?

Governance

10–64 Charity boards and executives are not always best placed to run commercial enterprises. Who will be on the board of the trading subsidiary and how will it account to the charity? It is important that the trading activities are not at variance with the purposes of the charity. You would not, for example, expect the trading subsidiary of an anti-smoking charity to sell cigarettes. Directors of trading subsidiaries should include amongst their number at least one person with experience of commercial activity.

10–65 The ultimate test will be whether, having considered the business model carefully, the trade(s) contribute to the overall ability of the charity to enhance its work with its beneficiaries or whether the whole project is a distraction which will not produce the desired result.

RUNNING THE TRADING SUBSIDIARY

10–66 Once the subsidiary is up and running it needs to be monitored to ensure that it produces the required contribution for the ultimate benefit of the charity's beneficiaries. The board of the trading subsidiary will monitor progress and report back to the charity on the success or otherwise of the enterprise. At a minimum the monitoring process by the trading subsidiary board should include a review of monthly management accounts with variance analysis to enable the board to get a proper understanding of the financial position and any stresses the trading entity is facing. It must be armed with the information to make decisions to improve profits for the ultimate benefit of the charity that owns it.

10–67 The existence of a trading company may well mean that the charity and trading entity together are over audit threshold and audited consolidated accounts need to be prepared. As noted in the OSCR report on "One Plus: One Parent Families",[9] there is value in obtaining independent third party advice; and auditors whose prime responsibility is to consider whether, in their opinion, the accounts show a

[9] OSCR, "One Plus: One Parent Families: A Report from the Office of the Scottish Charity Regulator under section 33 of the Charities and Trustee Investment (Scotland) Act 2005" (2008).

true and fair view, can also provide helpful insight—through management letters that highlight matters of concern and issues connected with systems and controls within the audited entities. OSCR has the right to examine the accounts and activities of the subsidiary even though the subsidiary is not itself a charity.

Discussing the financial statements with an independent examiner or auditor, as appropriate, can assist the trustees in understanding any issues that are affecting the success of the organisation and its parent charity. This consideration will extend to the working of the trading subsidiary. **10–68**

STRUCTURE AND GOVERNANCE OF THE SUBSIDIARY

Classic model

To be suitable for both the transfer of profits to the charity and to ensure that control rests with the charity, the vehicle should be a company, limited by shares, of which the charity will own 100 per cent of the voting shares to ensure it has control. Control arises where there is a power to govern the financial and operating policies of an entity in order to obtain benefit from its activities. A parent charity will be deemed to have control where it has: **10–69**

- directly or indirectly more than half the voting rights;
- power over more than half the voting rights by virtue of agreement with other investors;
- power to govern the financial and operating policies of the entity either by statute or by agreement;
- the power to appoint or remove the majority of the members of the board of directors or equivalent governing body and control of the entity is by that board or body; or
- the power to cast the majority of votes at the meetings of the board of directors or equivalent governing body and control of the entity is by that board or body.

Where a charity exercises control as an owner or investor it does so to benefit from the cash flows and financial return on investment.[10] **10–70**

Subsidiary part-owned by the charity

In some cases the subsidiary is not owned 100 per cent by the charity and there are outside investors who provide finance. Where there are outside shareholders in the trading subsidiary the charity needs to ensure that it still has control (para.10–69 above) and the outside investors do not try to take the trading company in directions which are not within the purposes of the charity. **10–71**

---

[10] Charities SORP FRS 102, "Accounting and Reporting by Charities: Statement of Recommended Practice applicable to charities preparing their accounts in accordance with the Financials Reporting Standard applicable in the UK and Republic of Ireland" (2015), paras 24.14–24.23.

Joint venture vehicles

10–72 In some instances the charity may have an interest in a company as part of a consortium or which is a joint venture. An example of joint venture would be where a building company offers to develop a property owned by the charity and the development is carried out via a joint venture vehicle under an agreement by which the charity has a share of the profits. Any contract with another commercial organisation should look to minimise the exposure to losses falling on the charity's subsidiary.

Consortium

10–73 An example of a consortium arrangement might be one where two or more charities decide that they will share an interest in a trading entity. Each charity must protect its own interests. The legal agreements between all the parties must, as a minimum, identify the source of funds and any residuary risks and how they are to be managed, how the governance arrangements will work so that the entity is properly controlled and how rewards will flow back to each of the charities. It may also need to set out the working practices so that if each organisation makes a demand at the same time there is an agreed mechanism for determining whose interests are looked after first.

Trading company board, directors and management

10–74 The trading company needs to be comprised of individuals who will be able to drive the business and have the right skills mix. Those individuals should also be aware that the trading company should not operate in a way that cuts across the purposes of the charity that controls it. A board comprised of some members of the charity board, and some other individuals so as to ensure that there are sufficient skills to run the business for the ultimate benefit of the charity, is advisable but care needs to be taken to avoid "intermingling"[11] if there is a wish to try to separate risk between the charity and its subsidiary (or between one subsidiary and another).

10–75 With effect from 6 April 2016 all UK companies (except companies listed on the Stock Exchange or AIM List) are required to keep a register of "persons with significant control". For this purpose significant control is met by a person who meets at least one of the five conditions that they:

(i) directly or indirectly hold more than 25 per cent of the nominal share capital;
(ii) directly or indirectly control more than 25 per cent of the votes at general meetings;
(iii) directly or indirectly be able to control the appointment or removal of a majority of the board;

[11] See para.10–54.

(iv) actually exercise, or have the right to exercise, significant influence or control over the company; or
(v) actually exercise or have the right to exercise significant influence or control over any trust or firm (which is not a legal entity) which has significant control (under one of the four conditions above) over the company.

From 30 June 2016, the information from the Register will require to be made available at Companies House as part of the new confirmation statement regime which will replace annual return. New companies will be required to send a statement disclosing any persons with significant control when applying to Companies House for incorporation. Further guidance can be obtained from the government website.[12] **10–76**

There can be occasions of conflict between the charity and the trading company and to manage this there should be members of the trading subsidiary board who are not also trustees of the charity. All individuals can participate in the debate but only those who are not conflicted should be making the decisions. **10–77**

A chief executive of the trading company must both understand the business and have sufficient time to devote to it if it is to be successful. At the beginning this may be a member of the charity management team but if the trading company grows this may not be the best person to run the subsidiary on a day to day basis and an appropriately qualified person may need to be employed for the purpose. **10–78**

Trading companies should be producing budgets, management accounts and forecast cash flows for their business as well as statutory accounts. To do this, adequate financial skills need to be available. **10–79**

If these skills are to be drawn from the charity finance staff, consideration needs to be given to the effect of these demands on existing staff. Can the need be met adequately or should staff be recruited for the purpose? The ability to recruit separate staff may be dependent on the success of the trading company but, equally, an inadequate human resource dedicated to the running of the trading enterprise may act as a barrier to success. Careful cost control will need to be exercised against the requirement to be adequately resourced for success. If a business is carried on at a distance from the finance staff, it will require good communication between the entity and the finance staff to ensure adequate controls and safeguards in the trading company and a clear picture of the financial position of the business. **10–80**

ROUTES BY WHICH PROFIT WILL BE TRANSFERRED FROM THE SUBSIDIARY TO THE CHARITY

There are three possibilities for transfer of profit to the charity: **10–81**

(i) gift aid;

[12] *https://www.gov.uk/government/publications/confirmation-statement/confirmation-statement* [Accessed 7 July 2016].

(ii) management charge and cost sharing; and
(iii) dividends.

Gift aid

10–82 A trading company can make a gift aid payment to a charity and the payment must be made without deducting tax. Where the trading company is owned by the charity and it is gift aiding its profits to the charity there are special rules that allow it to make the payment up to nine months after the year end but claim the relief in the earlier year. A gift aid payment is a charge on income for tax purposes and normally tax relief would only be given for payments made within the accounting period.[13]

10–83 By gift aiding profits to the charity parent the trading subsidiary minimises its tax liability and maximises the amount available to the charity.

Management charges and cost sharing arrangements

10–84 Where a trading subsidiary shares costs with the parent charity, for example in occupying the same property, a charge can be made by the parent for the provision of facilities. This management charge may be subject to VAT if there is no group registration and the business income in the subsidiary exceeds the VAT registration threshold.

10–85 Payroll costs may also come into this category where the payroll is paid by the charity in the first instance and then has to be reclaimed from the subsidiary. In some cases employees may have responsibilities in their contracts of employment to both entities and the payroll cost can simply be shared on an appropriate basis. Setting up the arrangement so that it does not constitute a management charge but simply a cost sharing needs care to ensure that VAT complications are not an issue.

Dividends from the limited company trading subsidiary

10–86 Another way of transferring monies from trading subsidiary to the parent charity is by dividend. This is not tax advantageous as there is no deduction for the dividend payment in the subsidiary and tax remains payable on the profit and dividends can only be paid where there are distributable[14] profits.

VAT

10–87 VAT is chargeable on taxable business activity and, in particular, the supply of goods or services in the UK. Business activity is not the same as trading and the VAT rules are detailed and not covered in depth here. Where charities are making

[13] See para.10–37 above.
[14] See para.10–36 above.

a supply of goods or services they need to be clear whether the activity is subject to VAT, and, if so at what rate, or is exempt from VAT or outwith the scope of VAT. The distinctions between these categories is very important in managing VAT liability risk.

Just as there is no useful definition of a trade the VAT legislation does not define what it means by business activity. However, the Court of Session has considered whether the absence of a profit motive meant that charges by a charity for pupil accommodation were made in the course of business.[15] Lord Cameron gave a definition of business in the following terms[16]: **10–88**

> "It has every mark of a business activity; it is regular, conducted on sound and recognised business principles, with a structure which can be recognised as providing a familiar constitutional mechanism for carrying on a commercial undertaking, and it has as its declared purpose the provision of goods and services which are of a type provided and exchanged in course of everyday life and commerce. Not only so, but to some extent the association is necessarily competing in the market with other persons and concerns offering precisely similar services to the same clients and customers."

New forms of contract for the provision of services can be problematic. These SLA contracts can be more than a grant and potentially subject to VAT. Care must be taken to ensure that contractual terms do not give rise to a liability to VAT or, if they do, that the charity structures its activities so as to minimise the impact of the tax charge. In some cases, it may suit both parties for the supply to be taxable—it is, therefore, vital that both parties consider the VAT aspects of any agreement at an early stage so that matters can be arranged as VAT-efficiently as possible. **10–89**

---

[15] *Customs & Excise Commissioners v Morrison's Academy Boarding Houses Association*, 1977 S.C. 279; [1978] S.T.C. 1.

[16] *Customs & Excise Commissioners v Morrison's Academy Boarding Houses Association*, 1977 SC 279, 289.

CHAPTER 11

CROSS-BORDER ISSUES

Simon A Mackintosh and Gavin McEwan

INTRODUCTION

This chapter is intended as a simple guide for charities based in other jurisdictions operating in Scotland, and for Scottish charities operating outside Scotland. The piecemeal system of recognition and regulation of charities throughout the UK means that very often a charity will fall under the jurisdiction of a "domestic" and "foreign" regulator. This chapter is intended to operate as a form of checklist for such charities, and will make use of cross-referencing to other chapters in this book for further detail. **11–01**

Charities operating in more than one jurisdiction are very often referred to as cross-border charities, a term we will use in this chapter. Where we use the word "foreign" to refer to a charity or other body, we are referring to charities or bodies which are established in a jurisdiction other than Scotland. **11–02**

REGISTRATION OF NON-SCOTTISH CHARITIES

Most non-Scottish charities which are cross-border are English and Welsh charities, registered with the Charity Commission for England and Wales (CCEW) as their home regulator. They are, on the whole, at the larger end of the scale, as demonstrated by Office of the Scottish Charity Regulator's (OSCR) own statistics relating to the Scottish charity sector, which show that of the largest 10 per cent of Scottish charities by turnover, roughly 26 per cent are CCEW-registered. **11–03**

This raises the question of why these charities are required to register with OSCR and be placed on the Scottish Charity Register at all. The answer lies in the policy behind the Charities and Trustee Investment (Scotland) Act 2005 (the 2005 Act), which sought to regulate all charitable activity in Scotland, not merely Scottish-based charities. The policy memorandum issued by the Scottish Government at the time that the 2005 Act was first introduced made clear that the aim is to regulate all charities with significant operations in Scotland. **11–04**

The 2005 Act achieves this aim in part by regulating the use of descriptions implying that an entity has charitable status, and restricting this use largely to bodies on the Scottish Charity Register. **11–05**

A body established under the law of a country or territory other than Scotland that is entitled to refer to itself as a "charity" (by any means or in any language) in **11–06** that country or territory, that is managed or controlled wholly or mainly outwith Scotland, and that does not occupy any land or premises in Scotland or carry out activities in any office, shop or similar premises in Scotland may refer to itself in Scotland as a charity.[1] However, it must refer to its having been established under the law of a country other than Scotland.

11–07 Put in a more direct manner, this means that if a foreign charity:

(1) makes it clear that it is registered outside Scotland; and
(2) does not occupy any premises in Scotland,

then it may refer to itself as a "charity", but may not refer to itself as a "Scottish charity". If a foreign body is registered with OSCR, then it would be entitled to use the descriptions "charity", "charitable body", "registered charity" or "charity registered in Scotland". The terms "Scottish charity" or "registered Scottish charity", however, are reserved for charities that are established in Scotland or that are managed or controlled wholly or mainly in Scotland.

11–08 If a foreign charity meets the exemption requirements, then registration with its domestic regulator is sufficient to allow the limited use of the approved terms implying foreign charity status. The fact that a charity may be registered with CCEW or the Charity Commission for Northern Ireland (CCNI) does not absolve it of the exemption requirements.

REGISTRATION WITH OSCR

11–09 There is no "foreign charity" section of the Scottish Charity Register and so the registration of a foreign charity with OSCR involves the same registration requirements as apply to a purely domestic Scottish charity.

11–10 Taking as an example the most common case, one of a CCEW-registered charity operating in Scotland, it might be expected that meeting the English charity test and the similarity between the definitions of charitable purposes north and south of the border[2] might mean that there are relatively few practical difficulties in achieving OSCR registration. Unfortunately, that is not always the case.

11–11 To achieve registration as a Scottish charity, an entity must meet the Scottish charity test[3] in addition to meeting the requirements of the entity's home charity test.

11–12 In short, this requires:

(1) the provision of public benefit in Scotland or elsewhere—usually demonstrated in the case of applicants by a business plan, and in the case of existing bodies by a report on their current and planned activities;
(2) charitable purposes which fall within the list set out in s.7 of the 2005 Act;

---

[1] Charities and Trustee Investment (Scotland) Act 2005 s.14.
[2] Charities and Trustee Investment (Scotland) Act 2005 s.7 and Charities Act 2011 s.3.
[3] See, in more detail, para.1–10 and following.

(3) that there is no ministerial control of the body;
(4) that there are no party political purposes; and
(5) that the constitution of the body does not permit the body's assets to be applied for non-charitable purposes.

Even if the principal charitable purposes are entirely in line with one or more of the extended list in s.7 of the 2005 Act, it is this final prohibition that has caused practical problems for foreign charities seeking to register in Scotland. **11–13**

A typical winding up clause of a charity, particularly in charities established prior to the creation of OSCR, might read as follows: **11–14**

> "If, in the opinion of the Trustees, the purposes for which this [Trust] has been established are no longer capable of fulfilment, the Trustees shall pay and make over the [Trust Fund] to such body charitable in law as the Trustees may in their sole discretion select."

In this case, charitable purposes will need to be interpreted in accordance with the entity's domestic law. In this example, let us imagine that consideration is being given to an English charity, or one that defines its charitable purposes as falling within the definition of "charity" for tax purposes. Some charity winding up clauses will make an explicit connection to the tax definition and a typical formula for this is: **11–15**

> "For the purposes of this [clause/deed], 'charitable in law' has the same meaning as the phrase 'charitable purposes' has for the purposes of the Taxes Acts."

However, the 2005 Act requires that a charity's constitution prohibits distribution for anything other than charitable purposes. In the case of entities seeking to register in Scotland, this means charitable purposes according to s.7(2) of the 2005 Act. (See the 2005 Act s.106.) **11–16**

Because there is a small but identifiable difference between the 2005 Act definition and the English Charities Acts/Taxes Acts, a charity that allows distribution only in line with the differing (English) definitions of charity would fall foul of the Scottish charity test, because its constitution would technically allow for potential distribution for non-Scottish charitable purposes. The differences can be summarised as follows: **11–17**

- the 2005 Act includes the advancement of public participation in sport, whereas the English definition refers to the advancement of amateur sport;
- the 2005 Act refers to "sport" as sport that involves physical skill and exertion, whereas the English definition refers to sport or games that promote health by involving physical or mental skill or exertion;
- the 2005 Act includes the provision of recreational facilities, or the organisation of recreational activities, with the object of improving the conditions of life for the persons for whom the facilities or activities are primarily intended, whereas the English definition does not contain matching wording;
- the 2005 Act treats as analogous to the advancement of religion the advancement of philosophical belief (whether or not involving belief in a

god), while the English definition uses subtly different references to religion which involves belief in more than one god and religion which does not involve belief in a god; and
- the English definition includes the promotion of the efficiency of the armed forces of the Crown, or of the efficiency of the police, fire and rescue services or ambulance services, whereas the 2005 Act does not include that wording (although OSCR has stated that it would consider such purposes to be analogous to the advancement of citizenship or community development).

11–18 The Scottish registration requirement means that English and Welsh charities registering with OSCR must amend their winding up clauses to restrict the charitable purposes available on distribution to those which also fall within the Scottish list.

11–19 A suitable form of wording approved by OSCR/HMRC for an appropriate definition of the term "charitable" is:

> "The expression 'charitable purpose' shall mean a charitable purpose under section 7 of the Charities and Trustee Investment (Scotland) Act 2005 which is also regarded as a charitable purpose in relation to the application of the Taxes Acts."

REGULATION OF CROSS-BORDER CHARITIES BY OSCR

11–20 Having ensured that a cross-border charity's constitution meets the Scottish charity test, satisfied OSCR as to public benefit, and achieved registration in Scotland, a number of other issues then arise. A charity registered with OSCR requires OSCR's consent to certain actions, and requires to report some actions to OSCR, as well as submitting an annual report and accounts.

Actions that require OSCR's consent

11–21 A number of actions can only be taken in relation to charities with the prior consent of OSCR.[4] Consent for such actions must be sought by foreign charities listed on the Scottish Charity Register as well as by charities established in Scotland. The relevant actions are set out in ss.11 and 16 of the 2005 Act, and are covered in detail in Ch.2. They include, in summary:

- changing its name;
- amending its constitution so far as it relates to its purposes;
- amalgamating with another body;
- winding itself up or dissolving itself; and
- applying to the court in relation to any of the above actions;

11–22 Note that these actions require at least 42 days' notice to be given in advance to OSCR.

[4] See also the detailed coverage at paras 12–28—12–35.

An amendment to a charity's purposes may only be undertaken with OSCR's positive consent, but consent may be assumed after a period of 28 days' notice in the case of a change of name, a charity merger or winding up, and an application to the court to achieve any of the s.16 actions. 11–23

Actions that require notification to OSCR

Foreign charities that appear on the Scottish Charity Register must also give notification to OSCR of certain actions.[5] They include: 11–24

- any change in the principal office of the charity;
- any change in the name and address of a charity trustee specified in the Scottish Charity Register;
- any change to any other details in the charity's Register entry;
- any change to its constitution;
- any merger, winding up or application to the court for a s.16 change;
- any administration order or an order for winding up made by the court in respect of the charity; and
- the appointment of a receiver in respect of any of the charity's property.

All of the above actions must be notified to OSCR within three months of the date of the action taking place, with the exception of administration orders or appointment of a receiver, which must be notified to OSCR within a month of the relevant order or appointment. 11–25

Regulatory oversight by OSCR and CCEW

All of OSCR's regulatory powers in respect of domestic Scottish charities apply to cross-border charities registered with OSCR. These include power to intervene substantially in the management of a charity, including power, for example, to make inquiries, suspend trustees, issue directions and restrict transactions that may be undertaken. These regulatory powers are covered in paras 2–13—2–37. 11–26

A protocol has been agreed between OSCR and CCEW (the other regulator most frequently involved in cross-border charities), which provides for areas of operational liaison between the two regulators. 11–27

The main areas where OSCR and CCEW will liaise in relation to cross-border charities are: 11–28

- where it becomes evident during the registration process that a charity is cross-border, OSCR will advise CCEW and vice versa, although it is not the responsibility of CCEW to ensure that a cross-border charity registers

[5] These are set out in the Charities and Trustee Investment (Scotland) Act 2005 s.17 and are covered in detail at paras 12–36—12–44.

with OSCR. OSCR and CCEW undertake to consult with each other where a cross-border charity seeks to change its name or constitution or to merge or wind up;

- where possible, OSCR and CCEW will reach a common position on the charity test, both in relation to differences in the definition of charitable purposes and in the application of the public benefit test;
- OSCR and CCEW will seek to ensure that larger charities are enabled to follow consistent financial reporting procedures and, where possible, will work together to standardise the format and content of receipts and payments accounts for smaller charities; and
- OSCR and CCEW will consult each other about any complaint or allegation of serious misconduct in relation to cross-border charities. If appropriate, a joint inquiry, intervention and reporting may be considered. Both regulators will provide information to each other where abuse results in a formal investigation into a charity by either regulator, and both will liaise with the police where such abuse raises issues of a criminal nature.

REPORTING TO OSCR

11–29 Cross-border charities require to submit annual reports and accounts to OSCR within nine months of the end of the year to which they relate, and to prepare accounts that comply with Scottish requirements in the 2005 Act and the Charities Accounts (Scotland) Regulations 2006 and the Charities Accounts (Scotland) Amendment Regulations 2007 and 2010.

11–30 For larger charities, accounts will in any event be SORP-compliant[6] and so will be expected to comply with the Scottish regulations applicable to larger charities. The SORP is jointly produced by OSCR and CCEW and is intended to promote consistency across the UK, although thresholds for audit, for example, can and do change independently in each jurisdiction from time to time. Where the accounting or audit thresholds differ between Scotland and England, charities may require to take a different accounting approach from others in their jurisdiction in order to comply with the requirements of the two regulators.

11–31 The latest guidance published on charity accounting rules (November 2014) states that "OSCR would expect to see some narrative in the trustees' annual report referring to activities in Scotland" but this is not a formal regulatory requirement.

11–32 OSCR's plans to adjust its reporting requirements will lead to additional requirements imposed on all charities, including cross-border charities. One particular change that smaller English charities will wish to be alert to is the intention of OSCR to publish charity accounts on its website as part of the online version of the Scottish Charity Register. The process to publish accounts is developing gradually and is focused initially on Scottish Charitable Incorporated

[6] Charities SORP FRS 102, "Accounting and Reporting by Charities: Statement of Recommended Practice applicable to charities preparing their accounts in accordance with the Financials Reporting Standard applicable in the UK and Republic of Ireland" (2015).

Organisations (SCIOs) and charities within incomes of £25,000 or over, but the intention is to move to a position where all charity accounts are available online. This would include cross-border charities whose accounts are not presently published online by CCEW.

DISCLOSURE OF CHARITABLE STATUS

Section 15 of the 2005 Act enables Scottish ministers to make regulations about the disclosure of charitable status. These are contained in the Charities References in Documents (Scotland) Regulations 2007 as amended by the Charities References in Documents (Scotland) Amendment Regulations 2008. **11–33**

The regulations are very broad in scope and are covered in detail in Ch.5,[7] to which all charities registered with OSCR should make reference. In brief, they require the charitable status of a Scottish charity to be disclosed in a range of documents, including all contracts, headed notepaper and emails, publicity materials, and on charity websites. In principle, these regulations require an English charity registered with OSCR and operating outside the UK to disclose their Scottish charitable status in contracts entered into anywhere in the world. **11–34**

STANDARD OF CARE

The standard of care for charity trustees (defined as those in control of the management and administration of the charity in terms of s.106 of the 2005 Act) is stated as follows in s.66 of the 2005 Act: **11–35**

> "A charity trustee must, in exercising functions in that capacity, act in the interests of the charity and must, in particular … act with the care and diligence that it is reasonable to expect of a person who is managing the affairs of another person."

The law relating to this is covered in more detail in paras 4–60—4–79. **11–36**

To the extent that the Scottish requirement is in any way a higher standard of care than applies in a cross-border charity's home jurisdiction or than is applied by its constitution, the Scottish standard of care will apply. The general position in England, for example, is that a trustee must use their skills and experience to inform decision-making and benefit the charity concerned. The Trustee Act 2000 says that trustees of unincorporated charities must "exercise such care and skill as is reasonable in the circumstances", and different standards are applied in the case of charitable companies and charitable incorporated organisations (CIOs). **11–37**

Failure to meet the Scottish standard of care is treated as misconduct in the administration of a charity, and opens the door to a range of potential regulatory action.[8] **11–38**

---

[7] See paras 5–114—5–122.

[8] Charities and Trustee Investment (Scotland) Act 2005 s.66(4) and Ch.2.

REMUNERATION OF TRUSTEES

11–39 Section 67 of the 2005 Act adopted a regime that permits remuneration of charity trustees where certain conditions are met. These are covered in para.4–120 and following. They apply to all Scottish charities including cross-border charities, and remuneration can be paid, broadly, when not prohibited by the charity's constitution or by its home jurisdiction.

FUNDRAISING

11–40 The initial emphasis on fundraising regulation across the UK has been on self-regulation. The memorandum of understanding between OSCR and CCEW records that both regulators will support the development of good practice in fundraising. Both regulators broadly supported the Institute of Fundraising's development of the Code of Fundraising, and the Fundraising Standards Board's approach to applying that Code. Changes to how the Code will be maintained and applied will arise once the reviews of fundraising regulation are complete north and south of the border.[9]

11–41 Despite the initial emphasis on self-regulation, there is nevertheless a body of law that must be complied with in both jurisdictions. Part 2 of the 2005 Act applies to a wide range of fundraising practices for benevolent bodies. The definition of benevolent bodies includes charities that are listed on the Scottish Charity Register, but also includes other bodies that are established for "benevolent, charitable or philanthropic purposes" and therefore extends to cross-border charities which are not entered on the Scottish Charity Register.

11–42 The sections of Pt 2 of the 2005 Act that had been brought into force up to 2015 include sections on solicitation statements and arrangements for the appointment of professional fundraisers and entering into contracts with commercial participators. Sections relating to public benevolent collections are not yet in force and cross-border charities must therefore comply with the requirements of the Civic Government (Scotland) Act 1982 and the Public Charitable Collections (Scotland) Regulations in the same way as any other Scottish charity. Further detail on the fundraising regulations can be found in Ch.7.

PUBLIC BENEFIT

11–43 Section 7 of the 2005 Act is quite clear that public benefit arising from a Scottish charity's activities may be provided in Scotland or elsewhere. While the provision of public benefit according to OSCR's interpretation and application of the 2005 Act is crucial to any cross-border charity's Scottish registration, the requirements of the charity's home regulator must also be met.

[9] This is expected to mean the abolition of the Fundraising Standards Board and the transfer of responsibility for maintaining the Code to the new Charity Fundraising Regulator for English and Welsh purposes. How Scottish aspects of the Code will be maintained had not, at the time of publication, been determined.

CCEW places greater expectations on English charities in terms of trustee reporting disclosures on public benefit, including a statement that the charity trustees have had regard to the CCEW guidance on the subject. There are no matching obligations in Scotland, although OSCR is keen to see further discussion about public benefit in charity trustees' reports. Cross-border charities should consider the CCEW requirements as the minimum standard required for accounting purposes. HMRC generally applies the English charity test and public benefit test when granting charity tax reliefs, which make the CCEW guidance equally useful reading for Scottish-only charities. **11–44**

SCIOs

Cross-border charities established outwith Scotland will not be created as SCIOs, since by definition a SCIO is recognised and registered by OSCR under the provisions of the 2005 Act as a body established under Scots law. However, CIOs registered with CCEW can and do register with OSCR where they operate cross-border. Only a very small number of CIOs is registered with OSCR, but the number is likely to grow over time. **11–45**

The introduction of CIOs in England has undoubtedly helped their slightly older Scottish counterparts, SCIOs, to become recognised as legal vehicles—a point that had concerned the charity sector at the point of their introduction. There are still potential issues around the recognition of CIOs and SCIOs outside the UK, and these issues are likely to continue until the vehicle becomes better understood in more jurisdictions. **11–46**

TRUSTS, FOREIGN ACTIVITIES AND LIABILITY

A key issue for charity trustees of charitable trusts properly so called is the question of when there may be limitations on the trustees' liability. This often gives rise to a heightened perception of risk where charitable trusts are operating on a cross-border basis. The Scottish Law Commission has already commented on whether there are effective legal limits on trustee liability and how trustees can protect themselves.[10] Normally liability will be limited to the trust funds where it is clear that the charity trustees are acting in that capacity, but much will depend on the contractual arrangements that are in place and the liability in question. **11–47**

There is some doubt as to whether the law as it stands matches the general expectation of creditors. Most creditors probably believe that they are contracting with the trust as a legal entity (regardless of the technical legal position) and their expectation will therefore often be that they can only look to the trust funds in the event that they need to be paid. Some foreign jurisdictions limit liability for trustees (including, for example, Jersey,[11] Guernsey[12] and the United States of **11–48**

[10] See para.5–123.

[11] See, for example, *In the matter of the representation of C* [2015] J.R.C. 031 (Clyde-Smith, Commissioner).

[12] See the Trusts (Guernsey) Law 2007 s.42 (as amended).

America) where the trustees have acted within their powers and the third party knows that the trustees were acting in that capacity. Personal liability for trustees arises in such cases only where the trustees' capacity was not disclosed or where the trustees expressly undertook personal liability.

11–49 The Scottish Law Commission has proposed that there should be formal limits of liability for trustees, so that personal liability would not be incurred. Trustees would only be liable to the extent of the trust funds. It is open to question whether such limits on liability will always be recognised in foreign jurisdictions and if foreign law applies to a particular contract or liability, this could still open up issues of liability for trustees of cross-border charities.[13]

11–50 It is suggested that where a charity is established as a trust, the charity trustees should review carefully how best to structure their cross-border activities. In some cases, cross-border activities may usefully be managed through an incorporated subsidiary in order to deal with potential liability issues flowing from foreign activity. This approach might also be considered where the "head charity" is a SCIO if there are any concerns about the recognition of SCIOs as legal vehicles outside Scotland.

SUMMARY

11–51 When a cross-border charity has registered with OSCR, it has to recognise that it must comply with regulatory requirements in Scotland in addition to those of its home jurisdiction and regulator. This can have substantial potential implications for, say, a UK-wide charity that is considering a merger or winding up, or even a straightforward change of name. Compliance with the requirements of the 2005 Act, and the notice periods required, must be built into any timetable for such actions.

11–52 The regular reporting requirements to OSCR in the form of an annual report and accounts, and the timetable for that, must also be taken into account. If a charity is required to undertake or is considering undertaking activities which will require it to register with OSCR then an early review of its constitution is necessary in order to enable steps to be taken to meet the Scottish charity law definition of "charitable purposes".

[13] See *Investec (Guernsey) Ltd v Glenalla Properties Ltd*, 18 I.T.E.L.R. 30 (but subject to an appeal to the Privy Council).

CHAPTER 12

VARIATION, REORGANISATION AND AMALGAMATION

Colin Liddell

INTRODUCTION

The trustees of a charity may at times wish to vary its constitution,[1] or may find that they have to do so in order to comply with changes in the law or to take account of other social or economic changes, or changes within the charity itself. Indeed, it is good governance for trustees regularly to review their charity's constitution, and to consider whether it should be varied as a result of such review. **12–01**

Examples of when trustees may choose to do so include: **12–02**

- an awareness or discovery that the charitable purposes may no longer reflect what the charity does, or wishes to do;
- a wish to change the charity's name;
- a need to vary the length of time a trustee may remain as a trustee;
- responding to a change or update in relevant legislation; or
- a prompt, perhaps from the charity's professional advisers, that a constitutional review should be carried out.

When a charity is imagined and created this is the start of its journey. Its founders may have a vision of the direction of that journey, and they will plan the terms of its constitution accordingly. It is quite common though that the route of that journey turns out differently than planned. This may, for example, be because of: **12–03**

- changing priorities;
- new funding opportunities;
- introducing new or changed activities;
- the transition between the founders (with the initial ideas and enthusiasm) and the trustees who succeed them (with the skills needed to manage the charity efficiently in the longer-term); or
- changes in society, or socio-economic changes.

It can also be, all too often, that a charity has chosen, or simply been given, an "off-the-shelf" constitution, either from the internet, or from a seemingly helpful adviser, and thus receives a one-size-fits-all solution, only for its trustees to discover in time the benefit of, if not the need for, a tailor-made constitution. **12–04**

---

[1] See, for example, para.3–09.

12–05 Any difference between what a charity was envisaged or designed to be and what it has become will almost certainly require to be bridged. Such a void should not be left unattended, because a charity is confined by its charitable purposes and must adhere to the administrative requirements of its constitution. Thus, the terms and scope of its constitution have to be—and to continue to be—relevant to what the charity's activities are and how it conducts its governance in practice.

12–06 Some seem to consider it an embarrassment or an admission of drafting errors to see on the cover of a constitution that it has been reviewed at least once or more often since inception. However, quite the opposite is almost always the case, because such changes are part and parcel of an ever-evolving charity whose trustees have ensured that its constitution evolves too, to remain relevant and topical, as well as embracing legislative changes and current good practice. There are lots of constitutions which have not (yet) been reviewed and updated to take account of the Charities and Trustee Investment (Scotland) Act 2005 (the 2005 Act) or, if a guarantee company,[2] of the Companies Act 2006, let alone of current good practice. The trustees of such charities would be well advised to consider doing so.

12–07 The purpose of this chapter is principally to explain the practical processes involved in any change a charity wishes to make after its inception (including each type of variation, reorganisation, or amalgamation), but is also to encourage regular constitutional review.

12–08 The methodology of all but one type of change a charity can make will depend upon the terms of its constitution, as explained below.[3] That one exception is a change in the charity's name, which, therefore, will be considered first.

12–09 Whatever change is intended, it is prudent to read the relevant guidance,[4] to consider the steps which need to be followed, including those involving formal decisions to be taken by the trustees and/or members of the charity, and to prepare relevant documentation as much as one can before embarking on the process itself.

CHANGE OF NAME—2005 ACT S.11

12–10 The provisions of s.10 of the 2005 Act have been explained earlier with regard to selecting a charity name, and in avoiding an "objectionable" name.[5]

12–11 A charity, which is registered as such in Scotland, may wish, or be required,[6] to change its name. If it does so, and wishes only to change its name (without any other constitutional change), the procedure is as follows:

---

[2] Described in para.3–12.
[3] See paras 12–22—12–27.
[4] *http://www.oscr.org.uk* [Accessed 4 June 2016].
[5] See para.3–33.
[6] Charities and Trustee Investment (Scotland) Act 2005 s.12 gives OSCR the power to require a charity to change its name either if it is "objectionable" in terms of Charities and Trustee Investment (Scotland) Act 2005 s.10 or if it is "too alike" the name of another charity.

Preliminaries

(1) for the trustees to reach a decision in principle to change the name of the charity; and **12–12**

(2) to check:

(a) that there is no existing Scottish charity on the Scottish Charity Register maintained on the Office of the Scottish Charity Regulator's (OSCR) website[7] with too similar a name, or that the proposed name is not likely to be "objectionable" in terms of s.10 of the 2005 Act[8];

(b) on the internet to see if the proposed name could cause an issue with an existing internet name or website address;

(c) if a guarantee company, that there is no existing company listed in the Register of Companies with a name which would be considered too similar; and

(d) if a guarantee company, that the new name does not include any word considered by Companies House to be "sensitive".[9]

Application

(3) to send to OSCR: **12–13**

(a) a completed and signed application for Consent to Change the Name of Your Charity,[10] in order to seek OSCR's consent in terms of s.11 of the 2005 Act to the proposed name, providing OSCR with at least 42 days prior notice of the date of change[11];

(b) a copy of the charity's current constitution; and

(4) to receive OSCR's decision, which, if in consent, enables the process to be concluded formally (if OSCR has not responded within 28 days of the charity's lodging its application, it is taken to have given its consent)—however, please note that if OSCR does not give its consent, the charity cannot proceed further with the application, but can seek a review.[12]

Post consent

(5) to give requisite notice of and to convene a formal meeting of the decision-makers (the trustees if a single-tier charity, or the members if a two-tier charity), to take place at least 42 days after the application was lodged with OSCR, with a special resolution duly passed by the requisite special majority[13]; **12–14**

---

[7] *http://www.oscr.org.uk* [Accessed 4 June 2016].

[8] See para.3–34.

[9] See guidance on company names at *http://www.companieshouse.gov.uk* [Accessed 4 June 2016].

[10] Available at *http://www.oscr.org.uk* [Accessed 4 June 2016].

[11] In the case of an unincorporated association this will be the date of the formal meeting at which the new name is to be adopted; in the case of a guarantee company, this will be the date of issue by Companies House of a Certificate of Incorporation on Change of Name.

[12] See para.12–102.

[13] See para.5–53.

(6) to obtain two copies of either a notification[14] of the passing of the special resolution or of the minutes of the relevant meeting, in either case signed by two trustees of the charity;

(7) to prepare an amended constitution to show the new name where relevant—in doing so it is advisable to state on the cover of the constitution "formerly known as … "[15];

(8) if a guarantee company, to send to Companies House:
   (a) a Form NM01, signed by one of the trustees or the company secretary, with the requisite fee[16];
   (b) if the change of name also includes a removal of the word "Limited" from the previous charity name, a Form NE01, also signed by one of the trustees or the company secretary;
   (c) if the new name includes any "sensitive" words,[17] any explanation and/or letter of support as required by Companies House in terms of its current guidance; and
   (d) one of the signed notifications of the special resolution or of the signed minutes of the relevant meeting.

(9) if a guarantee company, to receive from Companies House the new Certificate of Incorporation on Change of Name;

(10) to send to OSCR (in terms of s.17 of the 2005 Act):
   (a) one of the signed notifications of the special resolution or of the signed minutes of the relevant meeting;
   (b) a certified copy of the amended constitution to show the new name; and
   (c) if a guarantee company, a copy of the Certificate of Incorporation on Change of Name.

   OSCR will acknowledge in due course in completion of its process.

(11) to notify all trustees, members, the independent financial examiner, HMRC, the charity's Bank, and all others connected with the charity of the new name, by providing them with a copy of the amended constitution, or a link to an electronic version if it is placed on the charity's own website.

12–15 If OSCR does not give consent at step (4) above, it will instead refuse consent and issue a direction[18] to the charity directing the charity not to change its name. In doing so, OSCR will give its reason(s) as to why it considers the proposed name to be "objectionable".[19] If the charity disagrees with OSCR's reasoning it may, within 21 days of the date of the direction notice, require OSCR to review its decision.[20]

---

[14] A notification is simply a written statement confirming that the wording of the special resolution(s), as laid out in full in the notification, has been passed either unanimously, or at least by the requisite special majority, at the particular meeting, which is signed by two trustees of the charity

[15] See para.12–17.

[16] Forms NM01 and NE01 are available from *http://www.companieshouse.gov.uk* [Accessed 4 June 2016], which also confirms the current fee due to accompany the NM01.

[17] See guidance on company names at *http://www.companieshouse.gov.uk* [Accessed 4 June 2016].

[18] Under the Charities and Trustee Investment (Scotland) Act 2005 s.11(3).

[19] In terms of the Charities and Trustee Investment (Scotland) Act 2005 s.10.

[20] See para.12–102.

Should a change of name be introduced at the same time as other constitutional change, as often may be the case, the procedure listed above will need to be blended with the relative procedure for either a change of charitable purposes, other constitutional change, a reorganisation scheme and/or an amalgamation, each as explained later in this chapter. **12–16**

In considering and achieving a change of name for the charity, thought must also be given to continuity. This relates both to continuity of contracts and to continuity of identity. **12–17**

In relation to continuity of contracts, intimation of the change of name should be given to all contracting parties, such as: **12–18**

- landlords;
- employees;
- bankers;
- funders;
- stakeholders;
- service providers;
- bodies to whom the charity provides services; and
- utilities.

In relation to continuity of identity, change needs to be made to all stationery, publicity material, website, etc. **12–19**

Also in relation to identity consideration has to be given to continuity of donations and especially of legacies. Unfortunately, unlike the Charity Commission of England and Wales, OSCR neither has, nor intends to, provide a register of mergers. However, even a register of mergers would not cater for a simple change of name where there is no merger. It would be good if OSCR were to provide an historical database of former names and of mergers and amalgamations, but in the absence of this a charity is left to protect its own continuity of identity. **12–20**

Whilst the same Scottish Charity Number will be retained by a charity which has simply changed its name, which is effective evidence of continuity, it is nonetheless recommended upon a change of name to publicise that change, not only amongst members, stakeholders, known supporters and donors, but also more widely in appropriate geographical, sectoral or national publications. As stated above,[21] continuing with the "formerly known as" link for a period of time will also help in publicising a transition from a former name to a new one. **12–21**

CLAUSES OF VARIATION AND DISSOLUTION

Where a charity's constitution contains either a variation clause or a dissolution clause (and if it has one it will usually, but not always, have both), it is able, within the parameters of those clauses, to carry out its own variation and/or dissolution. **12–22**

[21] See para.12–14 at step (7).

12–23 However, in doing so, a charity must still comply with the terms of s.16 of the 2005 Act (where OSCR's prior consent is required) and/or s.17 of the 2005 Act (where notification has to be given to OSCR) as explained later in this chapter.[22]

12–24 A variation clause enables a charity to vary its constitution. This may be subject to restrictions, usually in relation to whether and by how much the charitable purposes can be varied. It will also confirm whether a resolution to change the constitution requires a special resolution by a special majority vote,[23] although that is the default position for most types of organisation, especially an unincorporated association, guarantee company or Scottish Charitable Incorporated Organisation (SCIO), but not trusts.[24]

12–25 A dissolution clause enables a charity to be dissolved.[25] It should specifically state what is to happen to any surplus belonging to the charity upon its dissolution. Usually it will specify that such surplus must be transferred to one or more other charities and may additionally state that such charity or charities must have the same or similar charitable purposes.

12–26 This is important, especially in relation to changes in legal form or in amalgamations (as we shall see),[26] where the whole assets, liabilities and undertaking of the charity being dissolved need to be transferred to the successor charity. As in the case of a variation clause, a dissolution clause will also confirm whether a resolution to change the constitution requires a special resolution by a special majority vote,[27] although that is the default position for most types of organisation, especially an unincorporated association, guarantee company or SCIO, but not trusts.[28]

12–27 Provided, therefore, that a charity has a variation clause and/or a dissolution clause, and follows closely the parameters of these, it can make relative changes but, as indicated above, in doing so the charity must adhere to the terms of ss.16 and 17 of the 2005 Act, which will each now be considered in turn.

VARIATIONS REQUIRING OSCR'S CONSENT—2005 ACT S.16

12–28 Even if it has a variation clause and/or a dissolution clause, there are some matters which a charity, registered as such in Scotland, cannot do without first obtaining OSCR's consent. These are listed in s.16(2) of the 2005 Act, as follows:

> (a) amending its constitution so far as it relates to its purposes;
> (b) amalgamating with another body;
> (c) winding itself up or dissolving itself;
> (d) applying to the court in relation to any action set out in paragraphs (a) to (c).

---

22 Respectively in paras 12–28 onwards and para.12–36 onwards.
23 Described in Ch.6.
24 Unincorporated associations, guarantee companies and SCIOs are described in Ch.3.
25 Detailed in Ch.13.
26 Respectively in paras 12–166 onwards and para.12–148 onwards.
27 Described in Ch.6.
28 Unincorporated associations, guarantee companies and SCIOs are described in para.3–12.

Amalgamation (2005 Act s.16(2)(b)) and dissolution (2005 Act s.16(2)(c)) are dealt with in detail later.[29] 12–29

Amending charitable purposes

If a charity wishes to amend its charitable purposes, even if its constitution gives it express power to do so without restriction, the terms of s.16(2)(a) mean that it must first obtain OSCR's prior consent. Thus, the procedure is: 12–30

Preliminaries

(1) for the trustees to reach a decision in principle to amend the charitable purposes; 12–31

(2) to ensure that the new charitable purposes:
  (a) reflect accurately the charity's current and prospective activities;
  (b) fall exclusively within one or more of the heads of charity listed in s.7(2) of the 2005 Act; and
  (c) will continue to provide public benefit in terms of s.8 of the 2005 Act.

Application

(3) to send to OSCR a completed and signed application for Consent to Amend the Constitution (so far as it relates to its purposes) of a Charity,[30] providing OSCR with at least 42 days prior notice of the date of the formal meeting at which the new charitable purposes are to be adopted; 12–32

(4) to receive OSCR's response, which if giving consent, enables the process to be concluded formally—however, please note that if OSCR refuses its consent to the application, the charity cannot proceed further but can seek a review.[31]

Post consent

(5) to give requisite notice of and to convene a formal meeting of the decision-makers (the trustees if a single-tier charity, or the members if a two-tier charity), to take place at least 42 days after the application was lodged with OSCR, with a special resolution duly passed by the requisite special majority[32]; 12–33

(6) to obtain two copies of either a notification[33] of the passing of the special resolution or of the minutes of the relevant meeting, in either case signed by two trustees of the charity;

---

29 Respectively in para.12–148 onwards and Ch.13.

30 Available at *http://www.oscr.org.uk* [Accessed 4 June 2016].

31 See para.12–102.

32 See para.5–38 onwards.

33 A notification is simply a written statement confirming that the wording of the special resolution(s), as laid out in full in the notification, has been passed either unanimously, or at least by the requisite special majority, at the particular meeting, which is signed by two trustees of the charity.

(7) to prepare an amended constitution to show the new charitable purposes (and, where relevant, any other constitutional changes then made);

(8) if a guarantee company, to send to Companies House:
  (a) one of the signed notifications of the special resolution or of the signed minutes of the relevant meeting; and
  (b) a copy of the amended constitution to include the new charitable purposes;

  Companies House will not acknowledge receipt;

(9) to send to OSCR:
  (a) one of the signed notifications of the special resolution or of the signed minutes of the relevant meeting;
  (b) a copy of the amended constitution to include the new charitable purposes; and
  (c) if, as is often the case, there have been other constitutional changes, a notification in terms of s.17(1)(c) of the 2005 Act.[34]

  OSCR will acknowledge receipt;

(10) to notify all trustees, members, the independent financial examiner, HMRC and all others connected with the charity of the amended constitution by providing each with a copy, or a link to an electronic version of it if it is now placed on the charity's own website.

12–34 It is important to reiterate that, owing to the terms of s.16(5) of the 2005 Act, a charity cannot proceed beyond step (4) unless and until OSCR gives its consent.

12–35 If OSCR does not give consent at step (4) above, the charity may, within 21 days of the date of OSCR's decision letter, ask OSCR to review its decision.[35]

VARIATIONS NOT REQUIRING OSCR'S CONSENT—2005 ACT S.17

12–36 There are other variations by a charity, registered as such in Scotland, which do not require OSCR's consent, but of which OSCR must be given due notification. These are listed in s.17 of the 2005 Act, as follows:

> (a) any change in—
>   (i) the principal office of the charity; or
>   (ii) where it does not have such an office, the name or address of the charity trustee specified in the Register (or which would, but for s.3(4), be so specified),
>
> (b) any change in any other details set out in its entry in the Register;
> (c) any change to its constitution;
> (d) any action set out in s.16(2)(b) to (d) which the charity has taken;
> (e) any administration order or an order for winding up made by the court in respect of the charity; and
> (f) the appointment of a receiver in respect of any of the charity's property, setting out the date on which the change, action, order or appointment took effect.

12–37 Notification to OSCR under subss.(a)–(d) above must be made by the charity within three months of the change or action.

---

[34] See para.12–40.

[35] See para.12–102.

Notification to OSCR under subss.(e)–(f) must be made by the charity within one month of the event. 12–38

The provision which concerns us at this juncture is s.17(1)(c) which for a charity relates to "any change in its constitution". 12–39

This provision requires a charity to give notice of the change to OSCR, within three months of the date of the change. That change refers to "any change in its constitution" and therefore includes any change in the charitable purposes. In other words, just because OSCR has given specific consent under s.16(2)(a) to a change in a charity's charitable purposes, that of itself is not enough; the charity still has to provide subsequent notice to OSCR in terms of s.17(3) that the charitable purposes have indeed been changed, within three months of the date of the formal meeting at which the change was adopted. 12–40

This is why step (9) is included at para.12–33. 12–41

Similarly, s.17(1)(b) states that a charity must give notice to OSCR in terms of s.17(3) of "any change in any other details set out in its entry in the Register". This will include a change in the charity's name in terms of s.11 and, indeed, any other change in relation to its principal or registered office, year end date, etc. 12–42

In the case of a change of name, this is why step (10) is included in para.12–14. 12–43

In this respect, it is important to note that it is the charity's responsibility, not OSCR's, to ensure that the details set out in its entry in the Scottish Charity Register on OSCR's website[36] are correct. There have been times when due notice of a change has been given by a charity to OSCR, but the relative change on the charity's entry in the Register has not been updated accordingly. It is therefore recommended that a month after a charity has submitted a notice to OSCR under s.17 it should check its entry in the Register and, if the notified change has not yet been reflected there, to write again to OSCR specifically to request that the relevant change be made to the charity's entry in the Register. 12–44

REORGANISATION SCHEMES—2005 ACT SS.39, 41–43

We have seen[37] how a charity registered as such in Scotland may vary its constitution, albeit with prior consent from and/or due notification to OSCR, where the terms of its constitution permit it to do so. 12–45

We now need look at the situation where the constitution of a charity registered as such in Scotland is silent in this respect, without either or both of a variation clause or a dissolution clause. 12–46

There is, however, one exception to this silence. This is where a charity, formed by a deed of trust, has explicit power that all of its capital can be expended. This effectively is equivalent to a power to dissolve by virtue of transferring all capital to an appropriate other body which, upon denuding the trust of any assets, would cause it to be dissolved. However, whilst this would mean that no reorganisation 12–47

[36] *http://www.oscr.org.uk* [Accessed 4 June 2016].

[37] At para.12–22 onwards.

scheme would be required in such circumstances, the trust, in transferring all of its capital to another body, would still need to make a formal application to dissolve to OSCR, so that OSCR can be satisfied either that the recipient body is a charity with appropriate charitable purposes, or otherwise, if the recipient body is not a charity, that the terms of s.19 of the 2005 Act would be brought into play.

12–48 Before the advent of the 2005 Act, there was only one option for a Scottish charity, the constitution of which contained no variation and/or dissolution clause, wishing to invoke a variation or dissolution. This sole option, and an expensive one at that, was to petition the Court of Session for a Cy-près scheme. A Cy-près scheme enables[38] the Court to alter the purposes of a public charitable trust where they would otherwise be impossible to carry out, or where there is a compelling case of expediency[39]; "cy-près" comes from the French, meaning "so near" or, more understandably in this context, "as near to", thereby enabling change but with a result still as near to the original as possible. These schemes are, of course, still to be found as forming the current constitution of a number of existing charities.

12–49 Additional help came, but only for public trusts and smaller charities, with the advent of the Law Reform (Miscellaneous Provisions (Scotland) Act 1990 (the 1990 Act).[40] Whilst not entirely satisfactory, the 1990 Act provided a useful way for a number of charities, locked into old and effectively unchangeable constitutions (because of the cost of a Cy-près scheme), to make a change. It was also the forerunner of and test-bed for the provisions in the 2005 Act, which now enable all charities to reorganise, by way of a reorganisation scheme, if and where their constitution does not permit them to make change. The provisions of the 2005 Act have been further enhanced by statutory amendments.[41]

Reorganisation scheme—preliminaries

12–50 Now, the 2005 Act (as amended), provides a ready mechanism for all charities, especially older ones, to consider reviewing original and often outdated constitutions and, where appropriate, to use these provisions to effect a reorganisation scheme and, thereby, to end up with a more modern, relevant and effective constitution for the present and future.

12–51 However, before embarking upon a reorganisation scheme, the starting point for any charity must be to check through its constitution to see if it is actually necessary. It is necessary only if the constitution does not give the charity power to make the change(s) it wishes to introduce.

---

[38] It is still an option to be used in certain specific circumstances—see para.12–60.

[39] *Trustees of the RS Macdonald Charitable Trust, Petitioners*, 2009 S.C. 6, [33].

[40] It still enables public trusts to apply to the Court of Session for a reorganisation scheme, and small trusts to vary their constitution, to amalgamate or to be dissolved by way of resolution, public advertisement and consent of the Lord Advocate.

[41] By Pt 9 of the Public Services Reform (Scotland) Act 2010 (asp 8).

Reorganisation scheme—steps

The next step is to look at the procedure for a reorganisation scheme so as to ensure that the charity is ready and able to embark upon this process. The procedure involves four main steps. These are: 12–52

(1) Step 1: reorganisation scheme—to establish that the proposed change falls within one of the three types (variation, transfer or amalgamation).
(2) Step 2: reorganisation conditions—to ensure that at least one of the statutory "conditions" applies to the proposed change.
(3) Step 3: required result—to demonstrate that the change achieves the relevant statutory "result".
(4) Step 4: reorganisation procedure—to follow the detailed procedure precisely.

Each of these steps is explained in turn below. It is unfortunate that the 2005 Act does not deal with these steps in a logical sequence, which is what is adopted here. 12–53

There are also some other aspects to be considered, which may be important in a number of cases; these relate to charities established by Royal Charter or which are educational endowments. Each of these is mentioned below,[42] whilst the variation of restricted funds is explained later.[43] 12–54

Step 1—Reorganisation scheme—2005 Act s.42(3)

Section 42(3) of the 2005 Act confirms that a reorganisation scheme can be used to effect three different types of change: 12–55

(a) variation of the constitution of the charity (whether or not in relation to its purposes);
(b) transfer of the property of the charity (after satisfaction of any liabilities[44]) to another charity (whether or not involving a change to the purposes of the other charity); or
(c) amalgamation of the charity with another charity.

As can be seen, a reorganisation scheme is intentionally versatile, in relation to variation, transfer of assets, and amalgamation. 12–56

Under s.42(3)(b) it is possible to use the reorganisation scheme as a method of transferring all the assets, liabilities and undertaking of the charity being reorganised to another charity without having to complete any other process of dissolution (but subject to demonstrating to OSCR that the transfer has been fully and properly completed following approval of the reorganisation scheme). This works where "another charity" is already in existence so that the transfer can readily take place between the charity being reorganised and "another charity". 12–57

However, where the plan is to transfer the assets, liabilities and undertaking of the charity being reorganised to a new charity (as in the case, for example, of a 12–58

---

[42] Respectively in paras 12–60 and 12–61.
[43] See para.12–108 onwards.
[44] To the extent these are not or cannot be transferred.

charitable trust, once reorganised, wishing to transfer its assets, liabilities and undertaking to a new guarantee company or SCIO, which has not yet been formed), then the reorganisation scheme should include the addition of a clause of dissolution, as a variation of its constitution under s.42(3)(a).

12–59 After the successful reorganisation scheme, a change in legal form process[45] can be undertaken to incorporate and register the new guarantee company or SCIO, to which the assets, liabilities and undertaking, of the charity being reorganised can then be transferred.

Charities established by Royal Charter or warrant or under any enactment

12–60 A charity constituted under a Royal Charter or warrant or under any enactment cannot use the reorganisation scheme provisions (s.42(5) of the 2005 Act refers). A Cy-près scheme to the Court of Session[46] is still permitted and indeed in some cases may be the only way of proceeding, whilst for others they may be obliged, depending upon their constitutional origin, to petition either the Privy Council, the Scottish Government or the Westminster Government.

Charities established as educational endowments

12–61 There are a number of charities which are "educational endowments".[47] OSCR originally interpreted s.42 of the 2005 Act (the terms of which are, on the face of it, less than clear) in such a way as to deny educational endowments an opportunity to use the reorganisation scheme to amend their constitutions.

12–62 However, in a test case,[48] OSCR accepted that it could not rely upon s.42(5) of the 2005 Act without taking account of s.42(6). Section 42(5) excludes from the reorganisation provisions of ss.39 and 40 of the 2005 Act "any charity constituted under a Royal charter or under any enactment". Section 42(6) confirms that ss.39 and 40 do indeed apply to an educational endowment if its governing body is a charity. This conclusion is reinforced by the terms of s.43 of the 2005 Act, where any educational endowment, the governing body of which is a charity, is expressly removed from the provisions of the Education (Scotland) Act 1980.

12–63 This means that any educational endowment to which s.42(6) applies can submit an application for a reorganisation scheme. As a result of the test case, many have now successfully done so.

Step 2—reorganisation conditions—2005 Act s.42(2)

12–64 Section 42(2) confirms that the reorganisation conditions are:

(a) that some or all of the purposes of the charity—

[45] See para.12–166 onwards.

[46] Charities and Trustee Investment (Scotland) Act 2005 ss.42(4) and 43B(6).

[47] As defined by the Education (Scotland) Act 1980 (c.44).

[48] Brought by the Aberlour Childcare Trust (SC007991).

(i) have been fulfilled as far as possible or adequately provided for by other means,
(ii) can no longer be given effect to (whether or not in accordance with the directions or spirit of its constitution),
(iii) have ceased to be charitable purposes, or
(iv) have ceased in any other way to provide a suitable and effective method of using its property, having regard to the spirit of its constitution,

(b) that the purposes of the charity provide a use for only part of its property,
(c) that a provision of the charity's constitution (other than a provision setting out the charity's purposes) can no longer be given effect to or is otherwise no longer desirable, and
(d) that it is desirable to introduce a provision (other than a provision setting out a new charitable purpose) to the charity's constitution.

In respect of its proposed reorganisation scheme, a charity must rely upon at least one of these reorganisation conditions (the last of which, now s.42(2)(d), was added in 2010[49]). **12–65**

Section 42(2)(a) and 42(2)(b) deal with a partial or complete frustration of the charitable purpose(s) of the charity. Most practitioners have encountered the Victorian wording of an old deed of trust, for example: **12–66**

- to provide coal supplies to the needy womenfolk of an old village, now a suburb of a new town, which has been rendered obsolete by today's economic circumstances, fuel provision and state funding; or
- to provide for a building to comprise a town library, where library services have been taken over by the local authority in another building, leaving the former library building empty and redundant of a purpose relating to the storage and lending of books.

These statutory provisions enable the trustees of such a charity locked into an obsolete purpose to reorganise, whilst retaining faith with the spirit of the original purpose, so as to create a modern set of charitable purposes which can ensure that charitable funds may once again be used positively and effectively for public benefit. **12–67**

An alternative to using a reorganisation scheme to modernise the charitable purposes may be to arrange instead for a transfer of the charity's undertaking to another or a new charity. This may still, of course, require a reorganisation scheme under s.42(2)(d) if the charity has no clause in its constitution permitting such transfer and/or dissolution. **12–68**

Section 42(2)(c) and 42(2)(d) deal with other constitutional aspects which are either no longer effective or desirable, or where it would be desirous or advantageous to introduce new constitutional provisions, for example where a trust deed which lists the trustees, each appointed by virtue of the position they hold, on an ex officio basis, but where none, or almost none, of those offices still exist, and where the clause narrating the recruitment of trustees needs to be redrawn. **12–69**

---

[49] By Pt 9 of the Public Services Reform (Scotland) Act 2010 (asp 8).

12–70 Provided that the charity trustees can demonstrate the problems caused by constitutional elements which are ineffective and/or undesirable, these statutory provisions enable constitutional refreshment, so as to provide a relevant and effective constitution for the charity to make it fit for purpose in the modern age.

12–71 The potential ambit of s.42(2)(d) is unclear, especially as its interpretation is in the hands of OSCR in the first instance. The concept of its being "desirable to introduce a provision (other than a provision setting out a new charitable purpose) to the charity's constitution"[50] might be thought sufficient to reflect the issues considered by the Court of Session in the decision in *The Trustees of the RS Macdonald Charitable Trust*,[51] but the current OSCR charity reorganisation guidance suggests a more restricted application. In *The Trustees of RS Macdonald Charitable Trust* the issues emerged through an extraordinary and unexpected expansion of funds by the exponential increase in the value of shares on the public takeover of a listed, but family-controlled, company. A restrictively expressed pool of charitable beneficiaries was inadequate to be sufficient recipients of the resultant funds, and expressions as to categories of beneficiaries, although not impossible to find, were outmoded partly as a result of advances in medical science. Thus, in the event that OSCR insist upon a more restricted interpretation of s.42(2)(d), a Cy-près scheme[52] may, as in the case of *The Trustees of RS Macdonald Charitable Trust,* offer a better alternative for reorganisation in cases of expediency.

12–72 However, s.39(1A) of the 2005 Act[53] makes it clear that any variation clause, which may be introduced by virtue of the power to do so within s.42(2)(d), will not be approved by OSCR where

> "the proposed provision would enable the charity to make amendments to its constitution which would not be consistent with the spirit of the constitution".

In other words, as in the case of s.39(1)(b), which we are about to consider, the spirit of the original constitution is paramount and must be maintained in some shape or form.

Step 3—required result—2005 Act s.39(1)(b)

12–73 Section 39(1)(b) confirms that the reorganisation scheme must achieve a required result. This is stated in the alternative, to ensure that the proposed reorganisation scheme will either:

> (i) where the condition satisfied is that set out in para.(a) or (b) of s.42(2), enable the resources of the charity to be applied to better effect for charitable purposes consistently with the spirit of its constitution, having regard to changes in social and economic conditions since it was constituted; or
> (ii) where the condition satisfied is that set out in para.(c) or (d) of that section, enable the charity to be administered more effectively.

---

[50] Charities and Trustee Investment (Scotland) Act 2005 s.45(2)(d).

[51] *The Trustees of RS Macdonald Charitable Trust*, 2009 S.C. 6.

[52] See para.12–48.

[53] Added by Pt 9 of the Public Services Reform (Scotland) Act 2010 (asp 8).

Subsection (i) above relates to those reorganisation schemes which seek to create a variation of the charitable purposes, where the required result is: **12–74**

(1) to ensure that the variation of the charitable purposes is consistent with the spirit of the original constitution, but allowing changes in social and economic conditions to be taken into account; and
(2) to enable the resources of the charity to be applied to better effect (which may therefore include a situation where there is to be a transfer of the charity's undertaking to another or a new charity).

Thus, the provision of coal supplies to the needy womenfolk of an old village, now a suburb of a new town, can be varied, for example, to enable: **12–75**

- the provision of financial assistance towards the cost of utility bills for the needy within a similar geographical area; or
- the transfer of the charity's undertaking to a charity with similar purposes which are still operable.

Subsection (ii) above relates to those reorganisation schemes which seek to vary other constitutional provisions or to introduce new constitutional provision (other than the charitable purposes), where the required result is to enable the charity to be administered more effectively. **12–76**

Thus, provision could be added to set out various governance aspects such as the recruitment and retention of trustees, the holding of meetings and so on. **12–77**

In respect of its proposed reorganisation scheme, the trustees must ensure that they can demonstrate the required result. **12–78**

Step 4—reorganisation procedure

The procedure for applying to OSCR for a reorganisation scheme is derived collectively from ss.39 and 42 of the 2005 Act and also from the relative regulations.[54] **12–79**

The procedure differs according to the size of the charity being reorganised. The current sizes and values[55] are as follows: **12–80**

(1) "large charity"—a charity with a gross annual income of £250,000 (as shown in the its most recent statement of account);
(2) "small charity"—a charity with a gross annual income of less than £250,000 (as shown in the its most recent statement of account);

[54] Currently the Charities Reorganisation (Scotland) Regulations 2007 (as amended by the Charities Reorganisation (Scotland) Amendment Regulations 2012), available at *http://www.oscr.org.uk* [Accessed 4 June 2016].
[55] The Charities Reorganisation (Scotland) Amendment Regulations 2012.

(3) "very small charity"—a charity with a gross annual income of less than £1,000 (as shown in the its most recent statement of account), and where the assets of which include neither any heritable property nor any shares in a private limited company.

These labels as to the size of a charity are used throughout this section.

Initial procedure—all charities

12–81 For all charities (large, small and very small—as described above), the process is:

Preliminaries

12–82 (1) to check that the charity's constitution does not include the requisite variation clause and/or dissolution clause, meaning that a reorganisation scheme is the only way[56] to effect change;

(2) for the trustees to reach a decision in principle:
   (a) to vary the charitable purposes;
   (b) to vary other provisions of the constitution; and/or
   (c) to include new constitutional provisions,

   (any one or more of which may be part of a process of transferring the original charity's undertaking to another or a new charity, ensuring therefore that the recipient charity is willing to receive the original charity's property and can use the original charity's property in keeping with the spirit of the original charity's constitution (as now to be amended if appropriate), if necessary by way of a restricted fund);

(3) to ensure that the proposed scheme complies with at least one of the reorganisation conditions (step 2 above); and

(4) to ensure that the proposed scheme will have the required result (step 3 above).

Application

12–83 (5) to send to OSCR:
   (a) a completed and signed Application for Approval of a Charity Reorganisation Scheme[57];
   (b) a copy of the existing constitution;
   (c) a copy of the proposed new constitution (or deed of variation or amendment);
   (d) a set of the most recent accounts; and
   (e) if a large charity, a copy of the draft advertisement and the name of the newspaper (or other publication) in which the charity intends to place the advertisement[58];

(6) to receive OSCR's acknowledgement, which must be given within 14 days.

---

[56] Except where a Cy-près scheme may still be preferable: see para.12–71.
[57] Available at *http://www.oscr.org.uk* [Accessed 4 June 2016].
[58] See para.12–87 onwards.

Remaining procedure—large and small charities

(7) to receive intimation from OSCR of the start of the "publication period", which they will provide at least seven days before it starts—the publication period lasts for between 28 and 42 days, and publication itself is provided in every case on the OSCR website (for a minimum of 28 days and a maximum of 42 days) and, if a large charity, in a local newspaper (or other publication or periodical relevant to the charity's charitable purposes) on one day within the first 14 days of the publication period; **12–84**

(8) if a large charity, to arrange for the advertisement to appear, once, in a relevant newspaper (or other publication or periodical relevant to the charity's charitable purposes) during the first 14 days of the publication period[59];

(9) if a large charity, to send to OSCR evidence of publication in terms of step (8) before the end of the representation period (as described in step (10) below);

(10) as representations[60] are permitted throughout the publication period and for 14 days thereafter (the "representation period"), which can be submitted by members of the public by post or email to OSCR, to hear from OSCR, after the expiry of the representation period, who will:

    (a) state whether there have been any representations received by OSCR (and, if so, OSCR will send copies or summaries[61] of these to the charity, to give its trustees an opportunity to comment—see step (12) below); and

    (b) ascertain whether any representations have been received by the charity;

(11) to send to OSCR copies of all representations inadvertently sent to and received by the charity—OSCR recommends that these be sent by registered letter, recorded delivery or email;

(12) to provide OSCR with the trustees' comments (if any) on any representations within 28 days of the date on which copies or summaries of any representations have been sent by OSCR to the charity;

(13) to receive OSCR's decision on the application, which it is obliged to provide to the charity within six months of the end of the representation period[62]; and

(14) if OSCR's decision is to approve the application, the charity can then proceed to implement the scheme (see below at para.12–86 at post consent)—however, please note that if OSCR does not approve the scheme, the charity cannot proceed further with the application, but can only seek a review.[63]

---

[59] See para.12–88.

[60] See para.12–91 onwards.

[61] Summaries are more likely where the application has been part of a charity's response to an ongoing investigation by or complaint to OSCR, by which OSCR may be able to withhold personal information or identification of complainers or informers.

[62] See para.12–99.

[63] See para.12–102.

Remaining procedure—very small charities

12–85 Applications relating to very small charities may continue instead with a simplified procedure by way of the following steps after step (6) above:

(7) where OSCR decides[64] to deal with the application under a simplified procedure, it intimates this to the charity within 14 days of OSCR's receipt of its application;

(8) applications under the simplified procedure for appropriate very small charities require no publicity at all;

(9) OSCR is obliged to issue its decision within 13 weeks of its receipt of the charity's application and must send a copy of its decision to the charity within seven days of the decision being made; and

(10) if OSCR's decision is to approve the application, the charity can then proceed to implement the scheme (see below from step (19) onwards at para.12–86 under Post consent)—however, please note that if OSCR does not approve the scheme, the charity cannot proceed further with the application, but can only seek a review.[65]

Post consent

12–86 (19) if the application is approved, for the charity to give requisite notice of and to convene a formal meeting of the decision-makers (the trustees if a single-tier charity, or the members if a two-tier charity), with a special resolution duly passed by the requisite special majority[66] to introduce the new constitution with the changes approved by the successful reorganisation scheme;

(20) to obtain two copies of either a notification[67] of the passing of the special resolution or of the minutes of the relevant meeting, in either case signed by two trustees of the charity;

(21) to prepare the amended constitution;

(22) to send to OSCR:

(a) one of the signed notifications of the special resolution or of the signed minutes of the relevant meeting; and

(b) a copy of the amended constitution.

OSCR will acknowledge receipt.

(23) if a guarantee company, to send to Companies House:

(a) one of the signed notifications of the special resolution or of the signed minutes of the relevant meeting; and

---

[64] OSCR has discretion as to whether an application by a charity that falls within the definition of a "very small charity" will be considered under the simplified procedure—in some cases OSCR may consider that the standard procedure (and publication) is appropriate.

[65] See para.12–102.

[66] See para.5–38 onwards.

[67] A notification is simply a written statement confirming that the wording of the special resolution(s), as laid out in full in the notification, have been passed either unanimously, or at least by the requisite special majority, at the particular meeting, which is signed by two trustees of the charity.

(b) a copy of the amended constitution.
Companies House will not acknowledge receipt.

(24) to notify all trustees, members, the independent financial examiner, HMRC and all others connected with the charity of the amended constitution by providing each with a copy, or a link to it on the charity's own website; and

(25) if the reorganisation scheme is part of a process to transfer the charity's undertaking to another or a new charity, additional steps will of course be required.[68]

Publication

Applications for a reorganisation scheme by a large or small charity (but not by a very small charity), as defined above, have to be publicised, as stated at step (7) in para.12–84 above, so that members of the public have an opportunity to respond with any representations in terms of step (10) above. At the least, these are published on the OSCR website. In this respect, OSCR creates a written summary, based on the information supplied by the charity within its application,[69] which it places on its website. This may be all the publicity required for a charity in relation to its application. **12–87**

However, additional publicity is required in relation to an application by a large charity. This additional publicity (see steps (7) and (8) in para.12–84 above), which must be arranged by the charity itself, is an advertisement to be placed in a newspaper, publication or periodical relevant to the work of the charity, that is, in relation to its activities and/or its geography. **12–88**

In most cases, the expectation is that the advertisement will be published in a national newspaper, but if the work of the charity relates to a specific geographical area, it may be possible to choose a local newspaper which is circulated throughout that same area. The charity should (as stated at step (5)(e) in para.12–83 above) advise OSCR of the newspaper (or other periodical or publication) in which it intends to place the advertisement so that OSCR can agree or comment upon this proposed choice. **12–89**

The advertisement needs to appear only once, but must comply with the required text (as specified in the OSCR guidance[70]). Evidence of publication must be submitted to OSCR (a copy of the original newspaper, periodical or publication, or a photocopy), to include the name of the newspaper, periodical or publication and its date—so it is sensible to send or copy to OSCR the entire page in which the advertisement appears. **12–90**

Public representations

Members of the public are entitled to make representations to any proposed reorganisation scheme. Representations can oppose the proposed scheme, may simply comment on the scheme, or can be in support of the scheme. **12–91**

[68] See para.12–148 onwards.

[69] This means that the detail supplied by the charity in its application should be clear and relevant.

[70] See *http://www.oscr.org.uk* [Accessed 4 June 2016].

12–92 Representations must be provided to OSCR (although some may inadvertently direct theirs to the charity, but should send them to OSCR by registered letter, recordered delivery letter or email) prior to the end of the representation period.[71] The latest date for receipt of representations is shown on the OSCR website in respect of the charity's proposed scheme.

12–93 Any representation must include the name and address of the sender, the name of the charity which is applying for the scheme, the nature of the representation and the reason or reasons for it. The identity of the sender will normally be given to the charity, unless the sender requests anonymity, with a suitable reason for doing so, and where OSCR considers that reason to be acceptable.

12–94 OSCR will consider any representation received. It does so by assessing the content of the representation in relation both to the stated reorganisation condition(s) and to the proposed reorganisation result. In its current guidance, OSCR says that it uses any representation received to "inform the process … but not to determine the outcome".

12–95 At the end of the representation period, OSCR will check with the charity whether it has inadvertently received any representations directly. If so, the charity should send these to OSCR—OSCR recommends that these be sent by registered letter, recorded delivery or email.

12–96 OSCR sends copies or summaries[72] of all representations received to the charity and also gives the charity an opportunity to comment upon any of them. If it wishes to do so, the charity must lodge these comments with OSCR within 28 days of OSCR's sending the copy representations to it.

12–97 After OSCR has made its decision whether to accept or decline the scheme (which it must do within six months of the end of the representation period), it will within seven days inform all those who have sent a representation, providing them with a copy of the decision notice. Those who have sent in representations have no right either to seek a review or of appeal.

12–98 Please be aware that a representation could also (whether intentionally or unintentionally) give other information to OSCR which, whilst not directly related to the application, may cause OSCR either to ask questions of the charity, or to investigate specific comments within the representation, or to treat part or all of the representation as a complaint (and therefore to arrange for its investigation team to conduct more detailed inquiries).

12–99 If OSCR decides, within six months of the end of the representation period, to approve the reorganisation scheme, the charity can proceed from step (15) in para.12–85 above.

12–100 If OSCR decides, within the time limit of six months from the end of the representations period, not to approve the reorganisation scheme, it will write to the charity to confirm this is its decision and to give its reasons why.

---

[71] See para.12–84 at step (10).

[72] Summaries are more likely where the application has been part of a charity's response to an ongoing investigation by or complaint to OSCR, by which OSCR may be able to withhold personal information or identification of complainers or informers.

In that event, if the charity disagrees with OSCR's decision, the charity may ask for a review of OSCR's decision.[73] **12–101**

REVIEW OF OSCR'S DECISION

In terms of s.74 of the 2005 Act, if a charity does not agree with a decision taken by OSCR, it can ask OSCR to review its decision. The charity must do so in writing (post, fax or email) to OSCR's review officer within 21 days of the date of OSCR's decision (not from the date of the charity's receipt of that decision), so it must act swiftly to comply with this time limit. **12–102**

OSCR will acknowledge the charity's request and will usually, as a matter of procedure, arrange for the review to be conducted by a member (or members) of its senior management team not involved in the original decision. **12–103**

There are four possible outcomes of such a review: **12–104**

(1) the decision is confirmed, and therefore remains the same;
(2) the decision is varied in some way;
(3) the decision is reversed, thereby approving the change being sought by the charity; or
(4) the decision is revoked, as though OSCR had not reached a decision at all, in which event the application is considered of new by a member or members of OSCR staff not previously involved in either the decision or the review, with the intention of a new decision being reached.

Notice of the outcome of OSCR's review, setting out its reasons, is notified to the person who requested the review (usually one of the trustees). **12–105**

If a charity remains dissatisfied with the outcome of OSCR's review, it may appeal to the Scottish Charity Appeals Panel[74] and, ultimately, to the Court of Session.[75] **12–106**

If a charity is faced with a situation where OSCR has not made a decision within the time limit specified by the 2005 Act, this does not enable its charity trustees to seek a review in terms of s.74, although they would be able to raise a service level complaint against OSCR. **12–107**

REORGANISATION OF RESTRICTED FUNDS—2005 ACT SS.43A–43D

A charity does not usually hold all of its money in one single fund. There may be a number of different funds, including, for example: **12–108**

- a reserves fund, retained as a "cushion" to meet outstanding obligations in the event of a dissolution;

[73] See para.12–102.
[74] Charities and Trustee Investment (Scotland) Act 2005 s.76 and Sch.2.
[75] Charities and Trustee Investment (Scotland) Act 2005 s.78.

- an endowment fund, to create ongoing revenue usually for general running costs;
- a development fund, to grow funding for a specific capital project;
- a designated fund, set aside by the trustees for a specific purpose; and/or
- one or more restricted funds (see below).

12–109 Funds which are set up and allocated by the trustees themselves, as a voluntary decision as part of good financial housekeeping, remain as unrestricted funds of the charity, all of which could be considered as designated funds (as opposed to restricted funds); this is because the voluntary allocation or designation could be changed by the trustees at any time in future, so that those funds could then become available for general (unrestricted) use by the charity.

Restricted funds

12–110 In contrast to unrestricted funds (whether designated funds or not), restricted funds[76] are established by a charity in order to set aside specific assets (which can include property and money) which are to be "ring-fenced" and kept separate from all its other assets. This is because the assets within the restricted fund have to be used for a specific purpose and subject to legally binding conditions imposed by the donor as to its use.[77] Examples include:

- a legacy where the maker of a will has specified that the money must be spent on a particular project;
- funds received from another charity which are to be spent only on the purchase of a particular item; or
- receipt of a flat from a donor which is to be used to provide a home for a disabled ex-serviceman.

Other funds

12–111 Each endowment fund or a development fund could therefore be a restricted fund if it holds assets which must be spent for the purposes of the endowment or development as a result of a condition imposed by the donor or because of the terms of a specific fundraising campaign. Examples include:

- money given specifically to be invested as an endowment, with only its income being available to offset running costs;
- money to be used only towards the maintenance of a specific building;
- money collected through the charity's own fundraising campaign to raise money for a specific project; or
- an asset which is to be held meantime until sold in specific circumstances in order to achieve a particular outcome.

---

[76] Charities and Trustee Investment (Scotland) Act 2005 s.43D.

[77] See also para.8–18 onwards.

Reorganisation of restricted funds—preliminaries

Evidence of the fact that a donation or fundraising campaign has to be ring-fenced may be easy to ascertain in certain cases, such as the terms of a will or a letter of gift. In other cases, it may be necessary to find other evidence such as within correspondence, in minutes of meetings or, particularly in the case of a fundraising campaign, by virtue of its name (such as the "Organ Repair Fund" or "The Defibrillator Appeal"). **12–112**

As in the case of a charity's constitution, so the terms of a restricted fund may require to be reviewed and amended from time to time. This can be achieved relatively simply, without involving OSCR, if the donor is still alive or in existence and agrees to a relevant change being made to the original conditions of gift. **12–113**

If the donor does agree to an amendment to the original conditions, this should be recorded in writing, be signed and dated by the donor, and be retained carefully by the charity. **12–114**

Indeed, the first step a charity must take, if wishing to amend the terms of any restricted fund, is to trace and approach the donor. This is crucial, because the reorganisation provisions referred to below can be invoked only if the charity can demonstrate to OSCR that, having taken reasonable steps, it cannot find or obtain instructions from the donor. **12–115**

If the donor is no longer alive or in existence, or cannot be contacted, or cannot give instructions, a specific procedure has been introduced, by virtue of ss.43A–43D of the 2005 Act[78] and relative regulations,[79] to enable OSCR to consider and approve the reorganisation of restricted funds. **12–116**

Reorganisation of restricted funds—steps

At the start, the trustees should look at the procedure for a restricted funds reorganisation scheme so as to ensure that the charity is ready and able to embark upon this process. With similarities throughout to a reorganisation scheme for a charity's constitution,[80] the procedure involves four main steps. These are: **12–117**

(1) Step 1: reorganisation scheme—to establish that the proposed change falls within one or both of the two types (change of purpose and/or change or removal of conditions).
(2) Step 2: reorganisation conditions—to ensure that at least one of these statutory "conditions" applies to the proposed change.
(3) Step 3: required result—to demonstrate that the change achieves the relevant statutory "result".

---

[78] Introduced by Pt 9 of the Public Services Reform (Scotland) Act 2010 (asp 8).

[79] Currently The Charities Restricted Funds Reorganisation (Scotland) Regulations 2012, available at *http://www.oscr.org.uk* [Accessed 4 June 2016].

[80] See para.12–50 onwards.

(4) Step 4: reorganisation procedure—to follow the detailed procedure precisely.

12–118 Each of these steps is explained in turn below. It is unfortunate that the 2005 Act does not deal with these steps in a logical sequence, which is what is adopted here.

Step 1—restricted funds reorganisation scheme—2005 Act s.43D

12–119 Section 43D confirms that a restricted funds reorganisation scheme is applicable to two different types of change (and can be used for either or both):

(a) the variation of the purpose for which restricted funds may be used; and
(b) the variation or removal of any condition imposed on the charity in relation to the use of restricted funds.

12–120 The 2005 Act (as amended) does not allow the restricted fund to be transferred or wound up and dissolved. As will be seen,[81] the outcome of the required result is always that the assets within the restricted fund continue to exist and be used in terms of the varied purposes and/or conditions. It is possible that those variations could allow the charity effectively to exhaust the restricted fund in due course.

Step 2—restricted funds reorganisation conditions—2005 Act s.43A(2)(a)

12–121 Section 43A(2)(a) confirms that the restricted funds reorganisation conditions are:

(a) that some or all of the purposes of the restricted funds—
  (i) have been fulfilled as far as possible or adequately provided for by other means,
  (ii) can no longer be given effect to (whether or not in accordance with the directions or spirit of the restricted funds' purposes),
  (iii) have ceased to be charitable purposes,
  (iv) have ceased in any other way to provide a suitable and effective method of using the funds, having regard to the spirit of the restricted funds' purposes,
(b) that the purposes of the restricted funds provide a use for only part of its property.

12–122 In respect of its proposed restricted funds reorganisation scheme, a charity must rely upon at least one of these restricted funds reorganisation conditions.

Step 3—restricted fund required result—2005 Act s.43A(1)(a)(ii)

12–123 Section 43A(1)(a)(ii) confirms that the required result of a restricted funds reorganisation scheme is

> "that the proposed reorganisation will enable the resources of the restricted funds to be applied to better effect for charitable purposes consistently with the charity's constitution".

---

[81] See para.12–123.

The required result is to allow funds unduly locked up within a restricted fund to be unlocked by the restricted funds reorganisation scheme and to be used to good effect. Thus, for example, a restricted fund designated for the purchase of a specific asset which has since been bought, but with money left over, can as a result be reorganised so that the surplus can be applied to better effect, for example, to provide further support related to the charity's use of that asset. **12–124**

Step 4—restricted funds reorganisation procedure

The process for applying to OSCR is derived collectively from ss.43A–43D of the 2005 Act and the relative regulations.[82] **12–125**

The procedure differs according to the size of the restricted funds being affected. The current sizes and values[83] are as follows: **12–126**

(1) "large restricted funds"—where they comprise property of more than £1 million, or have a gross annual income (as shown in the charity's most recent statement of account) of more than £100,000;
(2) "small restricted funds"—where they comprise property of £1 million or less, or have a gross annual income (as shown in the charity's most recent statement of account) of £100,000 or less; and
(3) "very small restricted funds"—where they do not comprise any heritable property or shares in a private limited company, and with a gross annual income (as shown in the charity's most recent statement of account) of less than £1,000.

Initial procedure—all restricted funds

For all applications the initial procedure is as follows: **12–127**

Preliminaries

(1) for the trustees to reach a decision in principle to vary the terms of the restricted fund; **12–128**
(2) to check that the donor is no longer in existence, or cannot be contacted, or cannot give instructions—if the donor can give a decision, then that decision will prevail[84];
(3) to ensure that the proposed scheme complies with at least one of the reorganisation conditions; and
(4) to ensure that the proposed scheme will have the required result.

---

[82] Currently the Charities Restricted Funds Reorganisation (Scotland) Regulations 2012, available at *http://www.oscr.org.uk* [Accessed 4 June 2016].
[83] In the Charities Restricted Funds Reorganisation (Scotland) Regulations 2012 (SSI 2012/219).
[84] See para.12–115.

Application

12–129 (5) to send to OSCR:

(a) a completed and signed Application for Approval of a Restricted Funds Reorganisation Scheme[85];

(b) a statement that the charity has been unable to ascertain the donor's wishes, including a description of the action taken by the charity to endeavour to obtain those wishes;

(c) a copy of the document which imposes conditions or restrictions upon the charity's use of the restricted fund, or a statement explaining the purpose and conditions relating to the restricted fund;

(d) a statement showing the balance in the restricted fund at the date on which the application is sent to OSCR together with, for the preceding financial year, a note of any incoming resources to or payments made from the restricted fund; and

(e) where relevant,[86] a copy of the draft advertisement and, where relevant, the name of the newspaper (or other publication) in which the charity intends to place the advertisement.

(6) to receive OSCR's acknowledgement, which must be given within 14 days.

Remaining procedure—large and small restricted funds

12–130 Applications relating to both large and small restricted funds, continue with the following steps after step (6) above:

(7) to receive intimation from OSCR of the start of the "publication period", which they will provide at least seven days before it starts—the publication period lasts for between 28 and 42 days, and publication itself is provided in every case on the OSCR website (for a minimum of 28 days and a maximum of 42 days) and, where relevant,[87] in a local newspaper on a day within the first 14 days of the publication period;

(8) where relevant,[88] to arrange for the advertisement to appear, once, in a relevant newspaper or publication during the first 14 days of the publication period;

(9) where relevant,[89] to send to OSCR evidence of publication in terms of step (8) before the end of the representation period (as described in step (10) below);

(10) as representations[90] are permitted throughout the publication period and for 14 days thereafter (the "representation period"), which can be submitted by members of the public by post or email to OSCR, to hear from OSCR, after the expiry of the representation period who will:

---

85 Available at *http://www.oscr.org.uk* [Accessed 4 June 2016].

86 See para.12–132.

87 See para.12–132 onwards.

88 See para.12–132 onwards.

89 See para.12–133 onwards.

90 See para.12–136 onwards.

(a) state whether there have been any representations received by OSCR (and, if so, OSCR will send copies of these to the charity, to give its trustees an opportunity to comment—see step (12) below); and
(b) ascertain whether any representations have been received by the charity.

(11) to send to OSCR copies of all representations inadvertently sent to and received by the charity—OSCR recommends that these be sent by registered letter, recorded delivery or email;
(12) to provide OSCR with the trustees' comments (if any) on any representations within 28 days of the date on which copies or summaries of any representations have been sent by OSCR to the charity;
(13) to receive OSCR's decision on the application, which it is obliged to provide to the charity within 26 weeks of the end of the representation period[91]; and
(14) if OSCR's decision is to approve the application, the charity can then proceed to implement the scheme—however, please note that if OSCR does not approve the scheme, or does not respond within six months of the end of the representation period, the charity cannot proceed further with the application, but can only seek a review.[92]

Remaining procedure—very small restricted funds

Applications relating to very small restricted funds, continue instead with the following steps after step (6) at para.12–129 above: **12–131**

(7) OSCR decides to deal with the application under a simplified procedure, and intimates this to the charity within 14 days of OSCR's receipt of its application;
(8) applications relating to very small restricted funds require no publicity at all;
(9) OSCR is obliged to issue its decision within 13 weeks of its receipt of the charity's Application and must send a copy of its decision to the charity within seven days of the decision being made; and
(10) if OSCR's decision is to approve the application, the charity can then proceed to implement the scheme—however, please note that if OSCR does not approve the scheme, the charity cannot proceed further with the application, but can only seek a review.[93]

Publicity

Applications relating to both large and small restricted funds have to be publicised, so that members of the public have an opportunity to respond in terms of step (10) above. All proposed schemes relating to both large and small restricted funds are published on the OSCR website. In this respect, OSCR **12–132**

[91] See para.12–141.
[92] See para.12–102.
[93] See para.12–102.

creates a written summary, based on the information supplied by the charity within its application, which it places on its website. This may be all the publicity required for a charity in relation to its application.

12–133 However, additional publicity is required in relation to an application by a charity which has large restricted funds. This additional publicity, which must be arranged by the charity itself, is an advertisement to be placed in a newspaper, publication or periodical relevant to the work of the charity, that is, in relation to its activities and/or its geography.

12–134 In most cases, the expectation is that the advertisement will be published in a national newspaper, but if the work of the charity relates to a specific geographical area, it may be possible to choose a local newspaper which is circulated throughout that same area. The charity should (as stated at step (5)(e) in para.12–129 above) advise OSCR of the newspaper (or other publication or periodical) in which it intends to place the advertisement so that OSCR can agree or comment upon this proposed choice.

12–135 The advertisement needs to appear only once, but must comply with the required text (as specified in the OSCR guidance).[94] Evidence of publication must be submitted to OSCR (a copy of the original newspaper, publication or periodical, or a photocopy), to include the name of the newspaper, publication or periodical and its date—so it is sensible to send or copy to OSCR the entire page in which the advertisement appears.

Public representations

12–136 Members of the public are entitled to make representations to any proposed restricted funds reorganisation scheme. Representations can oppose the proposed scheme, may simply comment on the scheme, or can be in support of the scheme.

12–137 Representations must be provided to OSCR (although some may inadvertently direct theirs to the charity, but should send them to OSCR by registered letter, recorded delivery letter or email) prior to the end of the representation period.[95] The latest date for receipt of representations is shown on the OSCR website in respect of the charity's proposed scheme.

12–138 Any representation must include the name and address of the sender, the name of the charity which is applying for the scheme, the nature of the representation and the reason or reasons for it. The identity of the sender will normally be given to the charity, unless the sender requests anonymity, with a suitable reason for doing so, and where OSCR considers that reason to be acceptable.

12–139 OSCR will consider any representation received. It does so by assessing the content of the representation in relation both to the stated restricted funds reorganisation condition(s) and to the proposed rorganisation result.

---

[94] See *http://www.oscr.org.uk* [Accessed 4 June 2016].

[95] See para.12–132 in relation to large and small restricted funds.

At the end of the representation period, OSCR will check with the charity whether it has inadvertently received any representations direct. If so, the charity should send these to OSCR—OSCR recommends that these be sent by registered letter, recorded delivery or email. 12–140

After OSCR has made its decision whether to accept or decline the scheme (which it must do within 26 weeks of the end of the representation period), it will, within seven days, inform all those who have sent a representation, providing them with a copy of the decision notice. Those who have sent in representations have no right either to seek a review or of appeal. 12–141

If OSCR accepts the scheme, the charity can proceed to effect the permitted change to its restricted fund. 12–142

If OSCR declines the scheme, all the charity can do is ask for a review of OSCR's decision.[96] 12–143

OSCR's power to apply for a charity reorganisation scheme or a restricted funds reorganisation scheme—2005 Act ss.40 and 43B

Apart from setting up and developing the framework for charities within the terms and scope of the 2005 Act, the Regulator's role is usually one of reaction—reacting to applications, information and complaints. Here are two instances where OSCR can be proactive although, at the time of writing,[97] it has not as yet chosen or been requested to invoke either. 12–144

Section 40 of the 2005 Act provides OSCR with the power, either of its own accord or on behalf of the charity's trustees, to apply to the Court of Session for the approval of its own reorganisation scheme. OSCR has to demonstrate that: 12–145

(1) at least one of the reorganisation conditions[98] applies;
(2) at least one of the required results[99] will occur;
(3) if OSCR relies upon s.42(2)(d) of the 2005 Act (the introduction of a new provision other than a provision setting out a new charitable purpose), the proposed new provision must not enable the charity to make amendments which would not be consistent with the spirit of its constitution[100]; and
(4) it has notified the charity in question at least 28 days before making its application to the court; the trustees may enter appearance as a party to the court proceedings.

Similarly, s.43B of the 2005 Act provides OSCR with the power, either of its own accord or on behalf of the charity's trustees, to apply to the Court of Session for the approval of a restricted funds reorganisation scheme. 12–146

[96] See para.12–102.
[97] June 2016.
[98] See para.12–64.
[99] See para.12–73.
[100] Charities and Trustee Investment (Scotland) Act 2005 s.40(2A).

12–147 OSCR has to demonstrate that:

(1) it has not been able to ascertain the wishes of the donor;
(2) at least one of the restricted funds reorganisation conditions[101] applies;
(3) the restricted funds required result[102] will occur; and
(4) it has notified the charity in question at least 28 days before making its application to the court; again, the trustees may enter appearance as a party to the court proceedings.

AMALGAMATIONS, MERGERS AND TAKEOVERS

Introduction

12–148 There are occasions when charities may choose to amalgamate or merge, or where one charity may take over another (all referred to as "amalgamation" in this section). There are a number of reasons for this, including:

- having collaborated successfully on various back office functions, two charities realise that they could be stronger acting together in all aspects;
- two similar charities choose to expand by joining forces; or
- a charity with stronger governance and/or funding streams takes over the activities and role of another similar charity, which may be smaller, weaker or less able to cope.

12–149 Amalgamation may be thought attractive when times are hard, but experience suggests that the amalgamation of two weak charities may be unlikely to create one stronger one. It is also vital to appreciate that an amalgamation involves not only a relevant and sound business case but also a cogent and sympathetic cultural case. The business case may be one of consideration of finances and strategy, whilst the cultural case involves consideration of vision, mission and values and of identity, brand and structure in relation to, and taking account of, the board, senior management, all other staff, volunteers, funders, and beneficiaries of each of the two charities.

12–150 It is important to appreciate that, in some cases, the business case could be quite complex, especially if there is any one or more of:

- another regulator involved other than OSCR[103];
- asset transfers which are significant in value or number;
- restricted funds;
- grants subject to outstanding conditions;
- uncertain liabilities;
- critical contracts;
- pensions (and especially potential pension deficits);

[101] See para.12–121.
[102] See para.12–123.
[103] Such as the Care Inspectorate.

- the need to preserve standing orders and direct debits; and
- the protection of future legacies.

With careful forward planning, these obstacles can usually be overcome.

Presuming that each of the business and cultural cases has been made, and that the appropriate planning, internal approvals and due diligence processes have been achieved, all charities registered in Scotland must, before amalgamating, secure OSCR's prior consent. **12–151**

An amalgamation involves one of the following two scenarios: **12–152**

- *Scenario 1*—one charity transfers all of its assets, liabilities and undertaking to the other charity and is then dissolved, leaving the other charity as the ongoing charity to operate with the combined undertaking (whilst this resembles a takeover, it is also the logical way to proceed for most amalgamations).
- *Scenario 2*—a new charity is formed (often with a new name, charitable purposes and brand), after which both existing charities transfer their respective assets, liabilities and undertaking to the new charity and then both existing charities are dissolved, leaving the new charity as the ongoing charity to operate with the combined undertaking.

Strictly speaking, scenario 1 is the dissolution of one charity[104] after it has transferred its assets and liabilities to the ongoing charity, and that is the appropriate procedure the applicants should adopt and which OSCR will follow. Thus, a true amalgamation relates only to scenario 2. **12–153**

Preliminaries

Before embarking upon an application to OSCR in relation to scenario 2, there are two preliminary legal checks in relation to process. **12–154**

The first preliminary check is to ascertain whether both charities have sufficient power either to transfer all assets and liabilities to another charity and/or to dissolve. If not, then either one or both of the charities may have to undergo a reorganisation scheme[105] in order to include one or both of these powers to enable the proposed amalgamation. If changes are required to only one charity's constitution, that may be a reason to retain that one as the ongoing charity under scenario 1 above (although if it lacks either the power to transfer and/or the power to dissolve, its constitution may be lacking also in other modern aspects of governance). **12–155**

The second preliminary check is to ascertain whether the charitable purposes of one of the charities are more restrictive than (or different from) those of the other. If so, one of the following outcomes is likely: **12–156**

[104] See Ch.13.

[105] See para.12–50 onwards.

(1) the charity with the more restrictive charitable purposes is chosen as the ongoing charity under scenario 1 above, so that the combined assets of both charities are available in future only in relation to those more restrictive charitable purposes;
(2) the charity with the less restrictive charitable purposes, if chosen as the ongoing charity under scenario 1 above, will need to ensure that the assets from the charity with the more restrictive charitable purposes are ring-fenced as a restricted fund to be applied only in relation to those more restrictive charitable purposes in the future;
(3) the charity with the more restrictive charitable purposes applies to OSCR, as a first step, to amend these in order to widen their scope[106];
(4) the two charities adopt scenario 2 above, as a true amalgamation, so that the charitable purposes of the new charity adopt the more restrictive charitable purposes; or
(5) the two charities adopt scenario 2 above with wider charitable purposes, so that the assets of the charity with the more restrictive charitable purposes would be held as a restricted fund by the new charity.

Application (except by SCIOs)

12–157 Except for SCIOs,[107] the procedure for all other types of charity which wish to adopt scenario 2[108] is mapped out in s.16(2)(b) of the 2005 Act, and involves sending to OSCR:

(1) an Application for Consent to Amalgamate a Charity with Another Body (available on OSCR's website),[109] providing OSCR with at least 42 days' prior notice of the date of the formal meeting at which the amalgamation is due to be formally agreed;
(2) the date on which amalgamation is proposed;
(3) a copy of both existing charities' current constitutions;
(4) the constitution of the new charity[110];
(5) details of other regulators, if any, from whom consent to the proposed amalgamation has to be obtained;
(6) a statement from each of the amalgamating charities that it approves the proposed amalgamation to form a new charity, with its proposed constitution, which is then to receive, hold and manage the assets of the amalgamating charities; and
(7) a statement from the new charity that it is prepared to accept the assets and liabilities from the amalgamating charities.

---

[106] See para.12–28.
[107] See para.12–160.
[108] See para.12–152.
[109] *http://www.oscr.org.uk* [Accessed 4 June 2016].
[110] Which may therefore involve the contemporaneous application to OSCR for a new charity.

Depending upon the nature of the proposed amalgamation, there may be other information which OSCR will require to see. If so, it would request this from the applicant charity or charities within five days of receiving the application to request it. 12–158

Within the 28 days after receiving the completed application (the date of OSCR's receipt of everything listed in para.12–157 and, if relevant, any further detail requested as explained in para.12–158), OSCR will notify the applicant charity or charities that it either: 12–159

(1) is consenting to the amalgamation—if giving consent, OSCR may attach conditions about the amalgamation itself or about the way in which the assets of either charity may be used by the new charity;
(2) is refusing consent—but, before doing so, OSCR will usually alert the applicant charity or charities and ascertain whether there is a way in which any perceived difficulty may be overcome (and if consent is refused, the only remedy for the applicant charity or charities is to seek a review of OSCR's decision[111]); or
(3) is issuing a direction to the applicant charity or charities not to take any action (this direction will apply for a specified period not exceeding six months)—this may simply be to allow time for any difficulty to be discussed to see whether on what basis it may be overcome—thus this option (3) may be applied by OSCR as part of the process of its applying either option (1) or (2).

Application by SCIOs

It is said by some commentators that a SCIO can amalgamate only with another SCIO, or that it can transfer its assets, liabilities and undertaking only to another SCIO. This is because s.59 and s.61 of the 2005 Act refer respectively to a situation where either two or more SCIOs may apply to be amalgamated or where one SCIO may resolve that its property rights and liabilities be transferred to another SCIO. What s.59 and s.61 of the 2005 Act actually do is to provide a special enabling procedure whereby SCIOs can amalgamate together or transfer assets, liabilities and undertakings between them in a way which avoids the need for formal transfer of leases, contracts, etc. These provisions are enabling (both sections use the word "*may*"), not prohibitive. They do not prohibit a SCIO from amalgamating with another type charity, nor to do they prohibit a SCIO from transferring its assets and liabilities to another charity (not being a SCIO). If a SCIO chooses to do so, it would use the normal process of dissolution and, if a new charity is being created as a result of amalgamation, there would then be an application process for the new charity (be it a SCIO or otherwise).[112] 12–160

The trustees of a SCIO wishing to transfer its assets to another SCIO as recipient should take the following steps: 12–161

[111] See para.12–102.
[112] See para.3–20.

(1) to check the consistency or otherwise of the charitable purposes of the SCIO with those of the recipient SCIO—see para.12–156 above;
(2) to convene a meeting of its members in order to pass a special resolution (by at least a two-thirds majority of those voting) to transfer its undertaking to a recipient SCIO;
(3) to arrange for the recipient SCIO to convene a meeting of its members in order to pass a special resolution (by at least a two-thirds majority of those voting) to confirm acceptance of the prospective transfer;
(4) to send to OSCR:
   (a) a completed Transfer of a SCIO's Undertaking form[113]; and
   (b) copies of the two resolutions passed in terms of (2) and (3) above.
(5) to receive OSCR's response, which if in consent of the application enables the transfer to proceed,[114] but if in refusal leaves the applicant charity with the only remedy of seeking a review of OSCR's decision.[115]

12–162 If consent is given for amalgamation, there is still much to do in:

(1) bringing into being the new charity;
(2) transferring the assets, liabilities and undertakings of the two amalgamating charities to the new charity;
(3) arranging the dissolution of the two amalgamating charities; and
(4) remembering that notification under s.17 of the 2005 Act has to be given to OSCR of each of these steps, within three months of each taking place.

DEMERGERS

12–163 As charities can amalgamate, so they can decide that the merger has not worked and that they therefore wish to demerge. Usually, one component part of the original merger will retain what was the merged charity, whilst a new charity will now be created, duly approved by OSCR as such, to which relevant assets and liabilities of the merged charity will be transferred, to enable the new charity to operate.

12–164 Alternatively, both component parts of the merged charity may decide to set up new charities, to which all assets and liabilities of the merged charity are transferred proportionately, after which the merged charity will be dissolved.[116]

12–165 The decision as to which alternative is chosen will depend on whether the name, brand and identity of the merged charity is readily agreed to be retained by only one component part of the demerger, or whether there needs to be complete change, or reversion to the status quo ante, by both component parts.

---

[113] See *http://www.oscr.org.uk* [Accessed 4 June 2016].
[114] See para.12–176, steps (12) and (13).
[115] See para.12–102.
[116] See Ch.13.

CHANGE IN LEGAL FORM

Introduction

As has been seen,[117] there are many types of organisation which can be registered as a charity in Scotland, each type with its own advantages and disadvantages, some of which provide limited liability and others which do not. Inevitably, and for differing reasons, a charity may at some stage wish to change from one type of organisation to another; these include: **12–166**

- a charity set up as an unincorporated association, which has developed its activities (and increased its risks, perhaps because it now enters into contracts with third parties) and therefore wishes to become a limited liability organisation[118];
- a charity attracted by the features of a SCIO when such an option was not available at the time of its creation;
- a charity finding it hard to attract trustees unless it changes from an unlimited liability organisation to a limited liability one; or
- a charity wishing to move from a two-tier structure to a single-tier structure and deciding at the same time to change legal type.

Usually, the change relates to a charitable trust or an unincorporated association (each with unlimited liability, the former with a single-tier structure and the latter with a two-tier structure) wishing to become either a guarantee company or a SCIO (each with limited liability and each capable of being either single-tier or two-tier). Since the advent of the SCIO, there are now some guarantee companies which wish to become a SCIO. The choice of type of legal structure, and the relative advantages and disadvantages of each are considered elsewhere.[119] **12–167**

Procedural options

Here, we consider the process, which technically involves: **12–168**

(1) the creation of the new charity (usually with the chosen new legal form of guarantee company or SCIO);
(2) the transfer of the assets, liabilities and undertaking of the original charity to the new charity; and
(3) the dissolution of the original charity.

As clarified above at para.12–160, a SCIO can transfer its assets, liabilities and undertaking to an organisation other than a SCIO, through dissolution.[120] **12–169**

---

117 See Ch.3.
118 Usually a guarantee company or a SCIO.
119 See Ch.3.
120 See para.13–41 onwards.

12–170 There are different application processes depending on whether the chosen new legal form is to be:

(1) a guarantee company; or
(2) a SCIO.

12–171 In making such an application a charity may choose also to change its charitable purposes and/or change its name and, if so, these elements can be included within this same process.

12–172 Before proceeding, forward planning is again essential, in considering the implications of a change in legal form. Whilst it may be thought that the end product is the same charity in different clothing, it is really and legally the transfer of assets and liabilities from one organisation to another. Some regulators and other bodies may try or choose to treat the change as being a new start-up,[121] with ensuing costs. If this is at all likely, it is advisable to ascertain and deal with such issues before deciding to proceed further.

Change from a charitable trust or unincorporated association to a guarantee company

12–173 For a change of legal form from a charitable trust or unincorporated association to a guarantee company, the procedure is as follows:

Preliminaries

12–174 (1) to check that the original charity has power to transfer its assets to another charity (the new guarantee company in this case) and to be dissolved—if not, it may as a vital preliminary step require to apply to OSCR to include these provisions by way of a reorganisation scheme[122];
(2) to check and list the identity, character and approximate current value of all the assets and liabilities of the original charity, so as to clarify what steps will need to be taken within the process for the successful transfer of all of these to the new guarantee company (and to have this information to hand to give to OSCR in due course)[123];
(3) to check that there are no restrictions on specific assets or restricted funds which may prevent their transfer to the new guarantee company—if there are, consideration may be required to see if the nature of such restriction can be changed by agreement of the donor (who applied the restriction) or whether a restricted funds reorganisation scheme[124] may be appropriate and necessary;

[121] For example, the Care Inspectorate has been known to treat the transfer to the new legal form as a start-up which requires a new registration.
[122] See para.12–45 onwards.
[123] See specific issues listed in para.12–176 step (12).
[124] See para.12–108 onwards.

(4) to check that the new guarantee company should meet the charity test[125];
(5) to check that the proposed name of the guarantee company does not include any word considered by Companies House to be "sensitive"[126] and that it is not likely to be "objectionable" in terms of s.10 of the 2005 Act[127];
(6) to prepare draft articles of association of the new guarantee company; and
(7) to hold a meeting of the members of the original charity and to obtain their formal approval to:
  (a) incorporation of a new guarantee company in terms of the draft articles of association, subject to OSCR's consent; and
  (b) the transfer of all the assets, liabilities and undertaking of the original charity to the new guarantee company, so that the original charity can be dissolved after such transfer has been effected.

Application

(8) to send to OSCR: **12–175**
  (a) a completed and signed New Charity application[128] for the guarantee company, which must have a different name to that of the original charitable trust or unincorporated association (it could, for example, simply add a year at the end of the existing charity name)—bearing in mind that, after the original charity has been dissolved (see below), it would be possible for the new guarantee company to apply to OSCR for its consent to a change of name (that change of name could be to the same name that the now-dissolved charity had)[129];
  (b) a copy of the proposed articles of association of the new guarantee company; and
  (c) trustee declaration forms[130] for the first trustees of the new charity.
(9) to receive OSCR's response, after it has checked the points raised at (1)–(3) above and that the elements relating to the proposed new guarantee company comply with the charity test, which if in consent, enables the charity to complete the process of bringing the proposed new guarantee company into being (that is, to hold an incorporation meeting of the trustees as subscribers, and then to obtain incorporation at Companies House)—however, please note that if OSCR does not give its consent, the charity cannot proceed further with the application, but can seek a review.[131]

---

125 See para.1–10.
126 See guidance on company names at *http://www.companieshouse.gov.uk* [Accessed 4 June 2016].
127 See para.3–34.
128 Available at *http://www.oscr.org.uk* [Accessed 4 June 2016].
129 Please note that if the new guarantee company is to retain a different name to the original charity's, careful consideration should be given to continuity—see paras 12–17—12–21.
130 Available at *http://www.oscr.org.uk* [Accessed 4 June 2016].
131 See para.12–102.

Post consent

12–176 (10) to send to OSCR an Application for Consent to Wind-Up or Dissolve a Charity[132] (which will also show all assets, liabilities and undertaking of the original charity to be transferred to the new guarantee company), together with:

   (a) a certified copy of the articles of association of the new guarantee company; and
   (b) a certified copy of its certificate of incorporation.

(11) to receive from OSCR notification that the new guarantee company has been entered on the Scottish Charity Register with its own Scottish Charity Number (as no two charities can have the same Scottish Charity Number concurrently) and with a cross-reference link between the original charitable trust or unincorporated association and the new guarantee company;

(12) to arrange the transfer of all the assets, liabilities and undertaking of the original charity to the new guarantee company on the date of transfer—this will involve a deed of transfer between the trustees of the original charity (as it does not have its own legal personality) and the new guarantee company, which lists all of the assets and liabilities; this deed may be sufficient to transfer certain of the assets (such as intellectual property rights, future legacies, furniture and computer equipment) but the transfer of other assets may require further legal documentation (such as specific notifications of change to suppliers, contractors and employees; assignations of leases, contracts, etc.; and/or a title deed of any heritable property), whilst bank accounts will in most cases involve the opening of new accounts for the new guarantee company to which the closing balance in each of the original charity's bank accounts can be transferred[133];

(13) to provide evidence to OSCR of the transfer of all assets, liabilities and undertaking of the original charity to the new guarantee company by way of:

   (a) a copy of the deed of transfer;
   (b) the final accounts of the original charity drawn up to a date after the date of transfer[134];
   (c) a copy of the final bank statement of the original charity, showing the resultant nil balance after transfer to the new guarantee company;
   (d) the bank statement of the new guarantee company showing the credit of the original charity's closing bank balance;

---

[132] Available at *http://www.oscr.org.uk* [Accessed 4 June 2016].

[133] Care must therefore be taken if standing orders and direct debits are to be preserved, with forward planning undertaken with the charity's bank.

[134] The charity being removed has to complete an OSCR annual return up until the final transfer of its assets (so charities changing legal form should ensure that they do so within 18 months of the last completed accounts, as otherwise they would have to complete another set of accounts and another annual return, and to do so they may need to change their accounting reference date and intimate this to OSCR in terms of Charities and Trustee Investment (Scotland) Act 2005 s.17; in addition, the new charity has to ensure that its accounts start from its commencement date—the date of incorporation for a guarantee company, or the date of registration for a SCIO—and will have to lodge an OSCR annual return too).

(e) a statement by the trustees of the original charity that the transfer has been completed;

(f) a statement by the new guarantee company that it has received all the assets, liabilities and undertaking of the original charity[135];

(14) to receive notification from OSCR, that the original charity has been removed from the Register of Charities, with the register entry for the removed charity still being cross-referenced to the new guarantee company;

(15) for the trustees of the original charity to confirm to HMRC that it no longer holds any assets, after the transfer to the new guarantee company, and that it no longer exists; and[136]

(16) if necessary, for the trustees of the guarantee company to apply to.

Change from a charitable trust or unincorporated association to a SCIO

For a change of legal form from a charitable trust or an unincorporated association to a SCIO, the procedure is as follows: **12–177**

Preliminaries

(1) to check that the original charity has power to transfer its assets to another charity (the new SCIO in this case) and to be dissolved—if not, it may as a vital preliminary step require to apply to OSCR to include these provisions by way of a reorganisation scheme[137]; **12–178**

(2) to check and list the identity, character and approximate current value of all of the assets and liabilities of the original charity, so as to clarify what steps will need to be taken within the process for the successful transfer of all of these to the new charity. See specific issues listed in para.12–180, step (11);

(3) to check that there are no restrictions on specific assets or restricted funds which would prevent their transfer to the new charity—if there are, consideration may be required to see if the nature of such restriction can be changed by agreement of the donor (who applied the restriction) or whether a restricted funds reorganisation scheme[138] may be appropriate and necessary;

(4) to check that the new SCIO should meet the charity test[139];

(5) to check that the proposed name of the SCIO is not likely to be "objectionable" in terms of s.10 of the 2005 Act[140];

(6) to prepare the draft constitution of the new SCIO;

(7) to hold a meeting of the members of the original charity and to obtain their formal approval:

---

[135] This may be included in the deed of transfer.

[136] Currently HMRC Charities Application Form ChA1 at *http://www.hmrc.gov.uk* [Accessed 4 June 2016].

[137] See para.12–45 onwards.

[138] See para.12–108 onwards.

[139] See para.1–10.

[140] See para.3–34.

(a) to incorporate a new SCIO in terms of the draft constitution, subject to OSCR's consent; and
(b) to transfer all the assets, liabilities and undertaking of the original charity to the new SCIO, so that the original charity can be dissolved after such transfer has been effected.

Application

12–179 (8) to send to OSCR:
(a) a completed and signed Application for Incorporation as a SCIO application (Stage 1) form,[141] which must have a different name to that of the original charitable trust or unincorporated association (it could, for example, simply add a year at the end of the existing name)—bearing in mind that, after the original charity has veen dissolved (see below), it would be possible for the new SCIO to apply to the OSCR for its consent to a change of name (but please note that if the new SCIO is to retain a different name to that of the original charity, careful consideration should be given to continuity—see paras 12–17—12–21);
(b) a copy of the proposed constitution of the new SCIO;
(c) trustee declaration forms[142] for the first trustees of the new SCIO; and
(9) to receive OSCR's response, after it has checked the points raised at (1)–(3) above and that the elements relating to the proposed new SCIO complies with the charity test, which if in approval leads to immediate registration of the SCIO as a new charity on the Charity Register.[143]

Post consent

12–180 (10) to send to OSCR an Application for Consent to Wind-Up or Dissolve a Charity[144] (which will also show all assets, liabilities and undertaking of the original charity to be transferred to the new SCIO);
(11) to arrange the transfer of all the assets, liabilities and undertaking of the original charity to the new SCIO on date of transfer—this will involve a deed of transfer between the trustees of the original charity and the new SCIO which lists all of the assets; this deed may be sufficient to transfer certain of the assets (such as intellectual property rights, future legacies, furniture and computer equipment) but others may require further documentation (such as specific notifications of change to suppliers, contractors and employees; assignations of leases, contracts, etc.; and/or a title deed of any heritable property), whilst bank accounts will in most

[141] Available at *http://www.oscr.org.uk* [Accessed 4 June 2016].
[142] Available at *http://www.oscr.org.uk* [Accessed 4 June 2016].
[143] See para.12–102.
[144] Available at *http://www.oscr.org.uk* [Accessed 4 June 2016].

cases involve the opening of new accounts for the new SCIO to which the closing balance in each of the original charity's bank accounts can be transferred;

(12) to provide evidence to OSCR of the transfer of all assets, liabilities and undertaking of the original charity to the new SCIO, by way of:
- (a) a copy of the deed of transfer;
- (b) the final accounts of the original charity drawn up to a date after the date of transfer;
- (c) a copy of the final bank statement of the original charity, showing the resultant nil balance after transfer to the new SCIO;
- (d) the bank statement of the new SCIO showing the credit of the original charity's closing bank balance;
- (e) a statement by the trustees of the original charity that the transfer has been completed; and
- (f) a statement by the new SCIO that it has received all the assets, liabilities and undertaking of the original charity.[145]

(13) to receive notification from OSCR that the original charity has been removed from the Register of Charities, with the register entry for the removed charity still being cross-referenced to the new SCIO; and

(14) for the trustees of the original charity to confirm to HMRC that it no longer holds any assets, after the transfer to the new SCIO, and that it no longer exists; and[146]

(15) if necessary, for the trustees of the SCIO to apply to HMRC for a charity tax code.[147]

Conversion from a guarantee company or registered society to a SCIO

For a change of legal form from either a guarantee company or a registered society[148] to a SCIO, the procedure is as follows: **12–181**

Preliminaries

(1) to check and list the identity, character and approximate current value of all of the assets and liabilities of the original charity, given that the transfer of these will (unlike in all other transfer processes) happen automatically in terms of s.58(5) of the 2005 Act which states: **12–182**

[145] This may be included in the deed of transfer.

[146] Currently HMRC Charities Application Form ChA1, at *http://www.hmrc.gov.uk* [Accessed 4 June 2016].

[147] This can done only online at *http://www.gov.uk/charity-recognition-hmrc* [Accessed 8 July 2016].

[148] Previously known as an Industrial and Provident Society (regulated by the Industrial and Provident Societies Act 1965 (c.12), now repealed) and now regulated by the Co-operative and Community Benefit Societies Act 2014 (c.14).

> "All property, rights and liabilities of the converting company or industrial & provident society[149] become by virtue of this subsection the property, rights and liabilities of the SCIO."

(2) to check that there are no restrictions on specific assets or restricted funds which would prevent their transfer to the new SCIO—if there are, consideration may be required to see if the nature of such restriction can be changed by agreement of the donor (who applied the restriction) or whether a restricted funds reorganisation scheme[150] may be appropriate and necessary;

(3) to consider the terms of all contracts and agreements so as to ensure that a transfer of these to a SCIO would have no adverse effect and, if appropriate, to consider with the other contracting party whether any variation of such contract or agreement would be preferred or required;

(4) as a SCIO cannot hold a floating charge or other complex loan instruments, to consider, where the original charity holds one, what alternative arrangements can be made to the satisfaction of the lender or other holder of such floating charge or loan instrument;

(5) to ensure that all filing requirements regarding annual accounts and annual returns are up-to-date with the Registrar of Companies (if the original charity is a guarantee company) or the Financial Conduct Authority (FCA) (if the original charity is a regulated society), because OSCR is required to check the position with the Registrar of Companies or the FCA as appropriate as to whether they have any objection to the proposed conversion to a SCIO—there are a number of reasons why the Registrar of Companies or the FCA might wish to object (such as being in default of filing requirements or failing to pay any penalties due);

(6) to check that the new SCIO should meet the charity test[151];

(7) to check that the proposed name of the SCIO is not likely to be "objectionable" in terms of s.10 of the 2005 Act[152];

(8) to prepare the draft constitution of the new SCIO;

(9) to hold a meeting of the members of the original charity and to obtain their formal approval to:

  (a) the conversion to a SCIO, subject to OSCR's consent, and to transfer all the assets, liabilities and undertaking of the original charity to the new SCIO (as the original charity will be dissolved automatically after such transfer has been effected); and

  (b) the terms of the draft constitution of the SCIO.

Application

12–183 (10) to send to OSCR:

---

[149] Now a registered society under the Co-operative and Community Benefit Societies Act 2014 (c.14).

[150] See para.12–108.

[151] See para.1–10.

[152] See para.3–34.

(a) a completed and signed Conversion into a SCIO Application Form[153];
(b) a copy of the original charity's current constitution;
(c) a copy of the proposed constitution of the new SCIO;
(d) trustee declaration forms (available on OSCR's website)[154] for the first trustees of the new SCIO; and
(e) a certified copy of the resolutions passed formally at the members' meeting (held in terms of step (9) above).

(11) to wait whilst OSCR writes to the Registrar of Companies (where the original charity is a guarantee company) or the FCA (where the original charity is a registered society) so that they can implement their part of the conversion process, notifying OSCR in response that the conversion has taken effect, as a result of which the following occur with immediate effect:
(a) the original charity converts into a SCIO with its new constitution and, if relevant, new name;
(b) the members of the original charity become the first members of the SCIO;
(c) those who signed trustee declaration forms (lodged with OSCR in terms of step (10)(d) above) become the first trustees of the SCIO;
(d) all assets, liabilities and undertaking of the original charity now belong to the SCIO; and
(e) the Scottish Charity Register shows the charity as now being a SCIO.

(12) to obtain confirmation from OSCR that the process has been completed; and

(13) for the trustees of the new SCIO to apply to HMRC for a charity tax code.[155]

Conversion from a community interest company to a guarantee company which is a charity

To close this chapter, and specifically this section about changing legal form, we look at one particular set of circumstances where a non-charity can use a specific conversion process in order to become a charity. **12–184**

A community interest company (CIC), which cannot be a charity, will have been constituted either as a guarantee company, or as a company limited by shares. There is a specific conversion process, which we will now follow, for a CIC which is constituted as a guarantee company to become a charity. **12–185**

As a company limited by shares cannot convert to a guarantee company, it cannot use this conversion process, which means that its directors would have to set up a new charity,[156] transfer its assets to the new charity and then arrange the dissolution of the limited company. **12–186**

153 Available at *http://www.oscr.org.uk* [Accessed 4 June 2016].
154 Available at *http://www.oscr.org.uk* [Accessed 4 June 2016].
155 This can done only online at *http://www.gov.uk/charity-recognition-hmrc* [Accessed 8 July 2016].
156 Which would not have to be a guarantee company.

12–187 A CIC will have been registered as a CIC by the CIC Regulator.[157] To have been eligible for registration as a CIC, it will have been required to include a number of specific features, including:

- a name which includes a CIC designation;
- a statement that it is a CIC; and
- a purpose which confirms that it provides community benefit.

These features will all have to be amended as part of the conversion process.

12–188 A careful check of its (memorandum and) articles of association should also be made to ensure that no other changes are required to enable charity registration, for example provisions with regard to remunerating directors.

12–189 In addition, as a CIC cannot be a charity, it is possible that, although primarily for community benefit, its existing purposes, as currently worded,[158] may not pass the charity test,[159] and thus a change to its purposes may also be required.

12–190 For these reasons, it may be preferable to prepare a brand new set of articles so that these can be adopted wholly to supersede the CIC set.

12–191 In addition to these technical aspects, the directors of the CIC should also give due prior consideration to other matters, including:

- the implications of its being a charity, including permanent compliance with the charity test;
- the appropriateness of its governance and management structures;
- the attitude of funding bodies and the terms of its existing funding contracts;
- whether any directors receive remuneration (and, if so, whether the terms of s.67 of the 2005 Act can be met)[160]; and
- relevant tax implications.

Procedure

12–192 The procedure for conversion of a CIC to a charity which is a guarantee company is as follows:

(1) for the board of the CIC:
  - (a) to decide in principle to change its status from a CIC to a charity;
  - (b) to agree a new name, at least to remove the CIC designation; and
  - (c) to instruct a thorough check of its articles of association with either draft amendments being made, or a new set of articles being prepared fully to supersede the existing articles.

---

157 *http://www.gov.uk/government/organisations/office-of-the-regulator-of-community-interest-companies* [Accessed 4 June 2016].

158 Apart from providing a community benefit, a CIC is not required to adopt any particular provisions in its purposes.

159 See para.1–10.

160 See para.4–120 onwards.

(d) to check that there is unlikely to be any dissenting members[161];

(2) to send to OSCR:

(a) a New Charity application[162];

(b) a copy of the amended (or new) articles of association; and

(c) trustee declarations forms[163] for the existing directors who are going to continue in office and will therefore become the first trustees of the guarantee company when it becomes a charity;

(3) to receive OSCR's response, after it has checked that the proposed articles would comply with the charity test,[164] which if in consent, provides a statement to the CIC that, in its opinion, if the proposed changes take effect, the company will be a Scottish charity and be entered onto the Scottish Charity Register, and this enables the CIC to proceed—however, please note that if OSCR does not give its consent, the charity cannot proceed further with the application, but can seek a review[165];

(4) for the CIC to convene an annual general meeting (AGM) or extraordinary general meeting (EGM) at which the following special resolutions require to be passed by the requisite special majority:

(a) that the company shall cease to be a community interest company and that the statement, "The company shall be a community interest company" be removed from its memorandum and/or articles of association;

(b) that the company name be changed to "[insert new name, without CIC designation]";

(c) either that the articles be amended, [specify amendments], or that the existing (memorandum and) articles of association be superseded by the new articles of association attached, approved by OSCR as passing the charity test under s.7 of the 2005 Act and to the exclusion of any previous (memorandum and) articles of association of the company previously registered with the Registrar of Companies.

(5) to obtain two copies either of a notification[166] of the passing of the special resolution or of the minutes of the relevant meeting, in either case signed by two trustees of the charity;

(6) to recognise that one or more dissenting members of the CIC have the right within a period of up to 28 days after the date on which the special resolutions are passed to apply to the court[167] for these resolutions to be cancelled, on the grounds that their interests as members would be unfairly

[161] See para.12–192 step (6).

[162] Available at *http://www.oscr.org.uk* [Accessed 4 June 2016].

[163] Available at *http://www.oscr.org.uk* [Accessed 4 June 2016].

[164] See para.1–10.

[165] See para.12–102.

[166] A notification is simply a written statement confirming that the wording of the special resolution(s), as laid out in full in the notification, have been passed either unanimously, or at least by the requisite special majority, at the particular meeting, which is signed by two trustees of the charity.

[167] In terms of Companies Act 2006 s.994.

prejudiced by the proposed conversion, in which event the resolutions would not take effect unless or until the court makes a ruling to that effect[168];

(7) to send the Registrar of Companies within 15 days either after the AGM or EGM (where no application has been made to the court), or after the date on which the court determines the application (where application has been made to the court):
   (a) the statement received from OSCR at step (3) above;
   (b) the articles of association (amended or new);
   (c) one of the signed notifications of the special resolution or of the signed minutes of the relevant meeting (step (5) above); and
   (d) the required fee payable to the Registrar of Companies for the change of name;[169]

(8) to wait whilst the Registrar of Companies contacts the CIC Regulator, who must decide whether the company is eligible to cease being a CIC; if the CIC Regulator decides that the company is eligible to cease being a CIC, they inform the Registrar of Companies who issues a new Certificate of Incorporation on Change of Name (but if the CIC Regulator decides that the company is not eligible to cease being a CIC, they will contact the company to try to resolve any issues and will advise the Registrar of Companies accordingly);

(9) to receive the Certificate of Incorporation on Change of Name from the Registrar of Companies, and to send a copy of it to OSCR along with a copy of the newly adopted articles of association, who will then enter the company on the Scottish Register of Charities, which completes the conversion process to a charitable guarantee company; and

(10) for the trustees of the new charity to apply to HMRC for a charity tax code.[170]

Conversion of guarantee company to a CIC

12–193 Just as a CIC can convert into a guarantee company which is a charity, so the reverse can occur, with a charitable guarantee company converting into a CIC. It may do so only with the consent of OSCR and, as a result of such conversion, would, of course, lose the tax benefits of being a charity. It would, however, remain subject to the protection of assets that were formerly charitable.[171] Whilst consideration of key matters[172] are recommended when converting a CIC to a charity, these are even more relevant when converting from a charity to a CIC.

[168] For this reason it may therefore be useful for the directors of the CIC informally to canvas member's views on the proposed conversion before proceeding far with the process or in holding the AGM or EGM.

[169] The current fee is £10.

[170] This can done only online at *http://www.gov.uk/charity-recognition-hmrc* [Accessed 8 July 2016].

[171] Charities and Trustee Investment (Scotland) Act 2005 s.19—see also para.2–62.

[172] See para.12–191.

DEREGISTRATION AS A CHARITY AND THE "SECTION 19 LOCK"

Any charity which seeks to deregister as a charity, whether by becoming a CIC or otherwise by remaining as an organisation (other than a SCIO) which no longer has charitable registration, has to bear carefully in mind the implications of the "section 19 lock". **12–194**

This statutory provision[173] means that any assets which previously were charitable, by virtue of their being held by a charity registered in Scotland, must continue to be held for or in furtherance of the original charitable purposes of the deregistered organisation, if necessary in a separate restricted fund (especially if the purposes of the former charity are changed upon or after deregistration). **12–195**

In addition, the organisation which has deregistered as a charity must continue to lodge annual accounts with OSCR, within nine months of its year end, for so long as any of those formerly-charitable assets remain. OSCR may, therefore, examine the activities and workings of the former charity so as to ensure that those formerly-charitable assets continue to be used for and in furtherance of the original charitable purposes.[174] **12–196**

IN CONCLUSION

In all aspects, it cannot be stressed too much how important forward planning and consideration of the possible consequences are whenever any charity wishes to effect a variation of whatever nature, be it changing any of its name, constitution or legal form, or its wishing to transfer its assets, amalgamate or be dissolved.[175] **12–197**

[173] Charities and Trustee Investment (Scotland) Act 2005 s.19.

[174] See also para.2–64.

[175] See Ch.13.

CHAPTER 13

DISSOLUTION AND WINDING-UP

Colin Liddell

INTRODUCTION

There comes a time when a charity wishes, or is forced to arrange, to dissolve or wind up (referred to as "dissolution" in this chapter). Reasons include a situation where a charity: **13–01**

- has run out of steam, or lost its main protagonist with no succession in place, or has achieved its objectives, and therefore simply wishes to close down;
- faces a large claim or liability, which it cannot meet from its existing resources and therefore cannot continue;
- wishes to amalgamate with another charity, new or existing, involving the transfer of its assets and liabilities to another charity, and then its dissolution; or
- is a guarantee company, where:
    - liabilities have come to exceed its assets;
    - the trustees have realised that this is (or is about to be) the case; and
    - there is no reasonably immediate prospect of this position being reversed,

  as a result of which the trustees accept that there is (or may be) "wrongful trading"[1] and that, in order to avoid any potential personal liability by them to creditors, they require the charity to stop trading and in due course thereafter to be dissolved.

DISSOLUTION PROCEDURES

In dealing with dissolution, there are different procedures for each of: **13–02**

(1) charitable trusts and unincorporated associations;
(2) guarantee companies and registered societies; and
(3) Scottish Charitable Incorporated Organisations (SCIO).

These are explained in turn below.

[1] Described in Insolvency Act 1986 (c.45) s.214.

13–03 There is also, in some cases, a distinction in procedure depending on whether the dissolution is:

(1) solvent; or
(2) insolvent.

Where relevant, these alternatives are explained below.

Preliminaries

13–04 Whenever trustees contemplate dissolution of their charity, professional assistance (legal and accounting) should be sought at the earliest opportunity. This is a critical time for any charity, involving research, planning, a number of preliminaries and an application for the Office of Scottish Charity Regulator's (OSCR) consent, before the actual steps required to achieve dissolution can be taken.

13–05 As soon as dissolution is contemplated, the following preliminary steps need to be taken:

(1) to ascertain whether the charity's constitution gives the trustees power to dissolve the charity[2];
(2) to research the nature and terms of all contracts and grant awards to ascertain the implications of dissolution upon them;
(3) to research the nature and terms of all restricted funds to ascertain the implications of dissolution upon them;
(4) to check and list the identity, character and approximate current value of all of the assets;
(5) to check and list the identity, character and approximate current value of all of the commitments and potential liabilities which will need to be addressed, to the extent possible, such as:
  (a) secured loans;
  (b) ordinary loans;
  (c) repayable grants; and
  (d) payments due to creditors;
(6) to check and list payments which would be due as a result of closure of the charitable business, including:
  (a) employee redundancy;
  (b) rent during a final notice period;
  (c) regular payments for services, and their termination;
  (d) charges for equipment (e.g. photocopier lease, etc.);
  (e) final payments due to self-employed consultants;
  (f) payments due under the termination of any contracts from others;
  (g) termination of contracts of supply by the charity to others; and
  (h) advance payments due to accountants, lawyers or other professionals up to the date of dissolution;

---

[2] See para.13–06 and 13–07.

(7) to establish whether dissolution is likely to be a solvent dissolution, or an insolvent one;
(8) if it is likely to be a solvent dissolution, to ascertain what sort of surplus may be available and to ascertain whether the constitution specifies how any remaining assets or surplus upon dissolution are to be dealt with[3]; and
(9) if it is likely to be an insolvent dissolution, to consider how best to proceed (see para.13–34 and following).

If the charity's constitution gives power for the charity to be dissolved[4] then, subject to obtaining OSCR's prior consent, the trustees can proceed in terms of its existing constitution. **13–06**

If the charity's constitution does not give power for the charity to be dissolved, one of the following options may apply: **13–07**

(1) the trustees may have to take formal steps, if permitted by the constitution to make changes to it, to insert a dissolution clause into the constitution and to intimate this change to OSCR;
(2) the trustees may have to consider a reorganisation scheme[5]; or
(3) the trustees may have to petition the court to dissolve the charity.

It is because of all these preliminary issues that forward planning is essential. It is obviously better, if possible, to dissolve a charity where the process still leaves an overall surplus (however small) to disperse than to leave matters unattended until it is too late to do so. **13–08**

A charitable trust is considered to have ceased to exist if it no longer holds any assets or property. However, in the case of dissolution, the charity is obliged in terms of s.16 of the Charities and Trustee Investment (Scotland) Act 2005 (the 2005 Act) to apply to OSCR for its consent to the proposed dissolution, and OSCR will not give that consent if the constitution contains no power to dissolve. **13–09**

A guarantee company does not need to have power to dissolve within its constitution in order to do so, provided that its constitution does not expressly prohibit its dissolution. **13–10**

In most cases, but not all, the dissolution clause will specify what is to happen to any assets upon dissolution of the charity. Such specification will usually state either that the recipient has to be a charity or that it has to be a charity with the same or similar purposes to those of the charity which intends to dissolve. This must be followed, as must any process for dissolution stated in the constitution (such as a formal meeting and/or a special resolution by a special majority of the members), unless that specification or process is changed formally as a change to the constitution (where permitted[6]). **13–11**

[3] See para.13–11 onwards.
[4] See para.12–22 onwards.
[5] See para.12–45 onwards.
[6] See para.13–15.

13–12 Where the dissolution clause makes reference to any recipient having to be a charity, this means that it has to be a charity entered on the Scottish Charity Register.[7] This does not mean that it has to be a Scottish charity, as charities from other jurisdictions may be, or may have to be, registered Scotland

> "if they occupy any land or premises in Scotland, or carry out activities in any office, shop or similar premises in Scotland".[8]

13–13 Where the dissolution clause makes reference to any recipient having to have the same or similar purposes to those of the charity which intends to dissolve, consideration must inevitably be given to what the dissolving charity's charitable purposes actually say, and these must then be compared to those of any proposed recipient charity. As long as the specification says "similar to", the charitable purposes of the dissolving charity and those of any proposed recipient charity do not need to match exactly, but they do need to be reasonably similar.

13–14 The constitution of the dissolving charity will usually specify how and by whom any decision in this respect should be reached, whether by the members whom failing the trustees, or whether by the trustees, and if by an ordinary resolution by a simple majority decision or if by a special resolution by a special majority decision. These provisions must again be followed.

13–15 Should the precise terms of the dissolution clause cause the members and/or trustees, as decision-makers, any difficulty (for example, if there is no other charity with similar charitable purposes in the locality), it then would be possible for the decision-makers to use the power within the constitution (if such power exists) formally to amend the terms of the dissolution clause (usually by special resolution). Examples would be to remove the requirement that any recipient charity must have the same or similar charitable purposes, or that the recipient charity must be located in or operate within a particular locality. Once intimated to OSCR,[9] this formal change could then widen the scope of potential recipient charities sufficiently to enable the decision-makers to reach an appropriate decision about the surplus.

13–16 It is possible that the dissolution clause may not specify that the recipient must be a charity (as in the case of many older constitutions or ones which may, for example, name a non-charity as recipient, such as the local authority or National Records of Scotland). This is not necessarily fatal to the application for dissolution. OSCR will look very carefully at the nature of the named recipient, any relationship which the dissolving charity has had in the past with the named recipient and the planned use of the dissolving charity's surplus by the named recipient to ensure that such use is likely to be commensurate with the charitable purposes of the dissolving charity.

13–17 In this respect, any restriction which can be placed by the dissolving charity upon the use of its surplus by the named recipient could be key to the success of the

[7] Charities and Trustee Investment (Scotland) Act 2005 s.106 defines a "charity" as a body entered in the Scottish Charity Register.

[8] Charities and Trustee Investment (Scotland) Act 2005 s.14(b).

[9] Charities and Trustee Investment (Scotland) Act 2005 s.17.

application, whether in line with the terms of its existing dissolution clause, or in accordance with any amendment it chooses formally to make to its dissolution clause, or as a result of a voluntary agreement with the named recipient.

APPLICATION FOR DISSOLUTION (EXCEPT BY SCIOS)[10]

Once it is known that dissolution is to proceed, the decision-makers of the charity must resolve formally (by special resolution where applicable): **13–18**

(1) to dissolve the charity, subject to obtaining OSCR's prior consent; and
(2) prior to dissolution, to transfer the charity's remaining assets (after satisfaction of all its liabilities) to the chosen recipient(s).[11]

The chosen recipient(s) must confirm in writing that it (or they) will agree to receive the dissolving charity's assets (or its proportion of them). **13–19**

An application can then be lodged by the charity (but not in the case of a SCIO, as previously indicated) with OSCR at least 42 days before the date of dissolution.[12] **13–20**

The date of dissolution depends on the type of charity which is seeking to dissolve, as follows: **13–21**

(1) for a charitable trust, it is the date on which the trust no longer holds any assets;
(2) for an unincorporated association, it is the date at which the members (or trustees) resolve to dissolve the charity (which at the earliest will be the date on which the formal decision to dissolve is taken);
(3) for a registered society, it is the date on which it is dissolved by the FCA, after due application to it; and
(4) for a guarantee company, it is the date on which it is dissolved and removed from the Register of Companies by Companies House, after due application to them.

The trustees must send to OSCR: **13–22**

(1) an Application for Consent to Wind-up or Dissolve a Charity form,[13] which includes a list and assessment of value of the charity's assets and liabilities;
(2) a copy of the charity's constitution (with all up-to-date amendments thereto);
(3) a copy of the appropriate resolutions to dissolve the charity and to transfer its remaining assets[14];
(4) confirmation that the recipient(s) will accept the remaining assets; and

---

10 See para.13–41 as follows.
11 See para.13–11 onwards.
12 See para.13–22.
13 Available from *http://www.oscr.org.uk* [Accessed 6 June 2016].
14 See para.13–18.

(5) if relevant, a copy of the constitution of any proposed recipient charity or named recipient.[15]

13–23 Within 28 days of receiving all the information it reasonably requires, OSCR will either:

(1) grant consent—enabling dissolution to proceed after expiry of the 42 day period, conditional upon the charity's distributing any remaining assets as stated in the application and therefore as agreed by OSCR;
(2) grant consent, with conditions attached—enabling dissolution to proceed after expiry of the 42 day period, conditional upon the charity's adhering to such specific conditions applied by OSCR, and its distributing any remaining assets as stated in the application and therefore as agreed by OSCR;
(3) refuse consent (usually if the charity does not have power in its constitution to dissolve or the proposals for dealing with any remaining assets are not approved by OSCR)—in which event the only remedy for the charity is to seek a review of OSCR's decision[16]; or
(4) issue a direction not to take any action for a period of not more than six months (this may be because of concern raised either by OSCR itself or by someone who has lodged a complaint with OSCR)—in which event, OSCR will provide the charity with an explanation and will follow this with a decision within the six month period.

13–24 If OSCR grants consent, the actual dissolution process can proceed (depending upon the type of dissolution available or chosen—see below) and, once completed, the charity has then to finalise its process with OSCR. This will include:

(1) settling all liabilities (including paying in advance the legal and accounting costs to closure);
(2) transferring the remaining assets to the chosen recipient(s), and obtaining a written receipt therefor;
(3) preparing final accounts to show a nil balance;
(4) sending to OSCR:
    (a) the final accounts; and
    (b) a copy of the receipt from the recipient(s); and
(5) advising HMRC that the charity has been dissolved and its remaining assets have been transferred to the chosen recipient(s).

---

15 See para.13–11.

16 See para.12–102.

Type of dissolution—charitable trusts and unincorporated associations

A charitable trust can be dissolved only with the consent of its trustees in accordance with the terms of its trust deed, whilst an unincorporated association can be dissolved only with the consent of its members in accordance with the terms of its constitution. 13–25

In the absence of a dissolution clause, a reorganisation scheme may be required. 13–26

Where there are insufficient assets to meet all the charity's liabilities, all the trustees of a charitable trust, and all the office-bearers (or committee of management) and (probably) all the members of an unincorporated association, are equally liable, on a joint or several basis, for the extent of the shortfall. However, in the case of an unincorporated association, liability may rest only with, or rest more greatly upon, the office-bearers (or committee of management) if they have failed in a particular duty of care to a specific creditor.[17] 13–27

This is, of course, the principal reason for the significant ongoing migration from unincorporated associations to guarantee companies and SCIOs. 13–28

Type of dissolution—registered societies and guarantee companies

Some registered societies (formerly industrial and provident societies) if set up as community benefit societies (sometimes known as "BenComs"), can be charities in certain circumstances. Although subject to their own Act,[18] they are treated[19] for the purposes of dissolution as though a company (but with the FCA as the relevant registrar rather than the Registrar of Companies). Reference to a guarantee company in this section therefore includes a registered society, unless stated otherwise. 13–29

In relation to a dissolution, a guarantee company has a number of options, whereby it can opt for one of: 13–30

(1) striking-off procedure;
(2) members' voluntary liquidation;
(3) compulsory liquidation; and
(4) company voluntary arrangement.

Each of these will be explained briefly in turn.

---

[17] For a useful summary of the law relating to unincorporated associations, see the Scottish Law Commission's Report, *Unincorporated Associations* (Scot. Law Comm. No.217) of November 2009 at *http://www.scotlawcom.gov.uk/law-reform-projects/completed-projects/unincorporated-associations/* [Accessed 6 June 2016].

[18] Co-operative and Community Benefit Societies Act 2014 (c.14).

[19] Insolvency Act 1986 (c.45) s.55.

Striking-off

13–31 Striking-off is the simplest and cheapest option. It is available only in relation to a solvent dissolution.

13–32 Here there is a difference in process between a guarantee company and a registered society. A registered society has to apply to the FCA with a completed instrument of dissolution[20] (in duplicate). If the registered society has issued withdrawable shares, its shareholders cannot be paid more than the nominal value of their shares.

13–33 In contrast, a guarantee company has to divest itself of all its funds and meet all its liabilities (including a pre-payment of any final professional fees for the period up to dissolution) and then, but only then, can it apply to the Registrar of Companies to strike off the guarantee company, with the appropriate fee.[21] The Registrar publishes that intention in the *Edinburgh Gazette* and approximately three months later will intimate that the guarantee company is to be dissolved on a specified date. The trustees as company directors remain personally liable if any debts due by the guarantee company were to arise after the striking-off procedure has been completed; the trustees therefore need to be sure that they know of all likely debts and liabilities, and have been able to settle these prior to their beginning the procedure.

Members' voluntary liquidation

13–34 The process of members' voluntary liquidation is usually chosen (even though it is more protracted and expensive as it involves the formal appointment of a liquidator) if and where the trustees:

- are not sure if the dissolution would be solvent or insolvent;
- are sure that it will be an insolvent one; or
- wish to ensure that they have no liability after dissolution (although the liquidator will require them to sign a declaration of solvency where they can).

13–35 Once the liquidator is formally appointed by the members (if two-tier) or trustees (if single-tier), they will arrange all matters, including ascertaining whether or not there is a surplus. If there is a surplus, after the liquidator's expenses and other liabilities have been met, the liquidator will ascertain the members' (if two-tier) or trustees' (if single-tier) decision in respect of the recipients of the surplus.[22] Whether it is a solvent or insolvent dissolution, the liquidator will then lodge the application for Consent to Wind-up or Dissolve a Charity[23] with OSCR and will finalise the necessary processes for dissolution thereafter (including paying out the surplus if there is one).

---

[20] Available from the Financial Conduct Authority at *http://www.fca.org.uk* [Accessed 6 June 2016].
[21] Currently £10.
[22] See para.13–11 onwards.
[23] Available at *http://www.oscr.org.uk* [Accessed 6 June 2016].

In the case of a registered society, if it has issued withdrawable shares, its shareholders cannot be paid more than the nominal value of their shares. 13–36

Compulsory liquidation

Where the charity is insolvent and is not in a position to negotiate or settle with any creditors, it is more likely that a compulsory liquidation would be initiated by one or more of its creditors. A liquidator would be formally appointed who would arrange all matters, including lodging the application for consent to wind-up or dissolve a charity with OSCR and finalising the necessary processes for dissolution thereafter (including paying out any dividend if there is one to the confirmed creditors). 13–37

Company voluntary arrangement

In terms of the Insolvency Act 1986,[24] there is the possibility of a company voluntary arrangement (CVA), whereby the trustees, or any appointed administrator, or any appointed liquidator, may make a proposal to the members of the guarantee company and to its creditors for either an agreement (known as "a composition") in satisfaction of its debts, or a voluntary arrangement of its affairs. The effect of the CVA is to put a stay on any dissolution process and to enable the guarantee company to continue in existence provided that it adheres to its financial and any other obligations thereunder. If it fails to do so, then a compulsory liquidation may be more than likely to follow. 13–38

Effect of dissolution for the members and trustees of a guarantee company

The extent of liability (or "guarantee") by each member of a guarantee company upon dissolution is as expressed in its constitution, namely for each to contribute a maximum of £1. In practice, it is highly unlikely that a creditor or liquidator would ask each member of a guarantee company for their £1 as it would cost far more in postage and administrative charges to collect this money. 13–39

The trustees (as directors) of a guarantee company may in certain cases find that they may have acquired an additional liability over and above the £1 guarantee if it can be shown that they have acted negligently or fraudulently or that they traded wrongfully.[25] 13–40

APPLICATION FOR DISSOLUTION BY SCIOS

The process for the dissolution of a SCIO will be one of three types depending upon the circumstances. These can be: 13–41

(1) dissolution of a solvent SCIO;

[24] Insolvency Act 1986 ss.1–7B.

[25] See para.13–01 and Insolvency Act 1986 s.214.

(2) dissolution of an insolvent SCIO; or
(3) dissolution of a SCIO by its creditors (known as "a creditor-led dissolution").

Each of these will be explained in turn.

13–42 For the avoidance of doubt, s.16 of the 2005 Act does not apply to SCIOs. This means that a SCIO which wishes to dissolve does not have to adhere to any specific timetable; this is because it is OSCR, not the SCIO, which determines when the SCIO will be removed from the Scottish Charity Register which automatically brings about its dissolution.

13–43 Section 18 of the 2005 Act does not apply either, which would otherwise enable a charity to apply to have its charitable registration removed but remain as a (non-charitable) body; this is because a SCIO can exist only if and as a charity.

SCIOs—solvent dissolution

13–44 If a SCIO is solvent at the time it wishes to apply for dissolution, it may apply to OSCR for its removal from the Scottish Charity Register. The process is as follows:

(1) for the SCIO to convene a meeting of its members in order to pass a special resolution (by at least a two-thirds majority of those voting) to confirm that, subject to OSCR's consent, the SCIO will:
   (a) wind up its affairs;
   (b) transfer any surplus to a named recipient body or bodies, the purposes of which are the same or resemble closely those of the dissolving SCIO; and
   (c) be removed from the Scottish Charity Register and thereby be dissolved;
(2) within 21 days of the members' meeting held in terms of step (1) above, to send to OSCR:
   (a) an application for Consent to Dissolve a Solvent SCIO,[26] which includes:
      (i) a statement of the SCIO's current assets and liabilities;
      (ii) details of any funds which require to be refunded by virtue of a funding agreement or other contracts;
      (iii) its proposals for settling any other outstanding liabilities; and
      (iv) the named recipient body or bodies to receive any surplus;
   (b) an undertaking signed by the SCIO to notify all known creditors that it has applied to be dissolved;
   (c) a copy of the resolutions passed at the members' meeting in terms of step (1), duly certified by either at least two-thirds of the SCIO's trustees (or, if so authorised, by one trustee on behalf of all of them, together with a copy of such authorisation);

---

[26] Available at *http://www.oscr.org.uk* [Accessed 6 June 2016].

(d) a copy of the dissolving SCIO's constitution;
(e) a copy of the SCIO's Register of Trustees;
(f) a declaration of solvency,[27] signed by at least two-thirds of the SCIO's trustees (or, if so authorised, by one trustee on behalf of all of them, together with a copy of such authorisation);
(g) notice of application for dissolution of the SCIO[28]; and
(h) a copy of the constitution of the named recipient body or bodies;

(3) OSCR will check the application and supporting papers and will acknowledge these; if it requires any more information or considers that any aspect of the application is incomplete, it will advise the SCIO of its requirements;
(4) once OSCR has the completed application and all required documentation, it will, within 14 days, publish the notice of application for dissolution on its website for not less than 28 days;
(5) during that 28 day period, anyone may contact OSCR to make a representation (which may be in support, or offer comment or further information, or be an objection)—those creditors to be notified by the SCIO (see step (2)(b) above) may of course object if they consider that the SCIO owes them outstanding debts which may not be paid as part of the solvent dissolution process; and
(6) within 21 days after expiry of the 28 day period, OSCR must make a decision on the application either to:
(a) consent to the application;
(b) consent to the application, subject to one or more conditions; or
(c) refuse the application.

If OSCR consents to the application, the process is as follows: **13–45**

(7) to agree a time limit with OSCR by which the SCIO must wind up its affairs;
(8) to wind up its affairs and pass its surplus to the named recipient body or bodies;
(9) to send to OSCR:
(a) evidence that the surplus has been passed to, and received by, the named recipient body or bodies; and
(b) confirmation by its trustees that the SCIO has settled all outstanding liabilities and now has no remaining assets; and
(10) if OSCR is satisfied, it removes the SCIO from the Scottish Charity Register and thereby the SCIO is dissolved and no longer exists.

If OSCR consents to the application, subject to one or more conditions, the process is the same as in para.13–45, except that the SCIO must also: **13–46**

(11) adhere to and fulfil any such condition or conditions; and
(12) provide evidence to OSCR that it has done so.

[27] Appendix 1 of the Application for Consent to Dissolve a Solvent SCIO.
[28] Appendix 2 of the Application for Consent to Dissolve a Solvent SCIO.

13–47 If OSCR refuses the application, the SCIO cannot proceed, but has a right to ask for a review of OSCR's decision.[29]

SCIOs—insolvent dissolution

13–48 If a SCIO is insolvent, and provided that it has outstanding debts of £1,500 or more,[30] it may apply to OSCR for its removal from the Scottish Charity Register. This involves not only OSCR but also the Accountant in Bankruptcy (AiB), which is a government agency charged with supervising insolvencies in Scotland.

The process is as follows:

(1) for the SCIO to convene a meeting of its members in order to pass a special resolution (by at least a two-thirds majority of those voting) to confirm, subject to OSCR being satisfied that the application meets the requirements of the dissolution regulations,[31] that:
   (a) the SCIO's "estate" (i.e. all of its assets and undertaking) will be sequestrated;
   (b) any surplus assets of the SCIO will be transferred to a named recipient body or bodies, the purposes of which are the same or resemble closely those of the dissolving SCIO; and
   (c) the SCIO will be removed from the Scottish Charity Register and thereby dissolved.

(2) within 21 days of the members' meeting held in terms of step (1), to send to OSCR:
   (a) an application to Dissolve an Insolvent SCIO,[32] which includes the named recipient body or bodies to receive any surplus;
   (b) a copy of the resolutions passed at the members' meeting in terms of step (1), duly certified by either at least two-thirds of the SCIO's trustees (or, if so authorised, by one trustee on behalf of all of them, together with a copy of such authorisation);
   (c) a copy of the dissolving SCIO's constitution;
   (d) a copy of the SCIO's Register of Trustees;
   (e) a declaration of insolvency,[33] signed by at least two-thirds of the SCIO's trustees (or, if so authorised, by one trustee on behalf of all of them, together with a copy of such authorisation);
   (f) an application of the SCIO to the AiB for sequestration of the estate of the SCIO,[34] signed by at least two-thirds of the SCIO's trustees (or, if so authorised, by one trustee on behalf of all of them, together with a copy of such authorisation), which includes a statement of the SCIO's current assets and liabilities;

---

29 See para.12–102.

30 See para.13–49 for options if the SCIO has debts which are less than £1,500.

31 Currently the Scottish Charitable Incorporated Organisations (Removal from Register and Dissolution) Regulations 2011 (SSI 2011/237).

32 Available at *http://www.oscr.org.uk* [Accessed 6 June 2016].

33 Appendix 1 of the Application to Dissolve an Insolvent SCIO.

34 Appendix 3 of the Application to Dissolve an Insolvent SCIO.

(g) notice of application for dissolution of the SCIO[35]; and
(h) a copy of the constitution of the named recipient body or bodies.

(3) OSCR will check the application and supporting papers and will acknowledge these; if it requires any more information or considers that any aspect of the application is incomplete, it will advise the SCIO of its requirements;

(4) once OSCR has the completed application and all required documentation, it will, within 14 days, publish the notice of application for dissolution on its website where it will remain until the AiB makes a decision as to whether the sequestration is accepted or refused—this is usually within four to six weeks (although the entire sequestration process will take a minimum of 15 months to complete);

(5) within 14 days of having published the notice of application for dissolution on its website, OSCR will:
(a) send the application to the AiB;
(b) notify the SCIO that it has done so; and
(c) advise the SCIO to pay the debtor application fee direct to the AiB.[36]

(6) within 21 days of the AiB receiving the application from OSCR, the SCIO, even though insolvent, must pay the debtor application fee—the various ways to pay are specified in the OSCR guidance on SCIOs[37]—the AiB cannot process the application until this fee is paid;

(7) if the AiB has not received the debtor application fee within 21 days of its receiving the application from OSCR, it must refuse the sequestration—in that event, the fee, even if received by the AiB after the time limit, is non-refundable;

(8) if the AiB has received the debtor application fee timeously, it will proceed to assess the application as follows:
(a) the AiB will establish the SCIO's assets and liabilities so as to determine that the SCIO is insolvent with outstanding debts of at least £1,500;
(b) if satisfied thus, the AiB will notify the SCIO of its decision to accept ("award") sequestration;
(c) the AiB will notify OSCR likewise;
(d) OSCR will remove the notice of application for dissolution from its website and replace it there with notification of the award of sequestration;
(e) the AiB will enter details of the sequestration into its Register of Insolvencies[38];
(f) the AiB will, if considered appropriate, convene a meeting of the SCIO's creditors;
(g) the AiB will realise the SCIO's estate and will make payments to the creditors if and to the extent that there are funds with which to do so;

[35] Appendix 2 of the Application to Dissolve an Insolvent SCIO.
[36] Set by the Bankruptcy Fees etc. (Scotland) Regulations, which are updated regularly. For the most current version, see *http://www.aib.gov.uk* [Accessed 6 June 2016].
[37] Available at *http://www.oscr.org.uk* [Accessed 6 June 2016].
[38] Available at *http://www.aib.gov.uk* [Accessed 6 June 2016].

(h) once sequestration of the SCIO's estate is complete, and if there is any surplus after all creditors' claims have been satisfied, the AiB will transfer such surplus to the named recipient body or bodies;
(i) the AiB will notify OSCR that the sequestration is complete (as stated above, this stage will take a minimum of 15 months to reach) and will provide copies of final accounts of the SCIO's estate;
(j) OSCR will remove the SCIO from the Scottish Charity Register and will thereby dissolve the SCIO; and
(k) OSCR will advise the applicants that the SCIO has been dissolved.

13–49 If a SCIO is insolvent, but has outstanding debts of less than £1,500, its options are either:

(1) to attract sufficient funds to enable it to apply for a solvent dissolution;
(2) to negotiate with creditors so that its outstanding debts are reduced sufficiently;
(3) to enable a solvent dissolution (perhaps by finding ways to settle, discharge or reduce debts);
(4) to wait until its outstanding debts amount to £1,500 or more (but having to be aware that any worsening of the situation through such a delay may give rise to a claim of negligence against the trustees);
(5) to negotiate with its creditors, so as to enter into some form of agreement or arrangement with them; or
(6) to encourage, or accept that there will be, a creditor-led dissolution (see below).

SCIOs—creditor-led dissolution

13–50 A SCIO's creditor or creditors may petition in the Sheriff Court for the sequestration of a SCIO, provided that they are owed at least £3,000 by the SCIO. A temporary administrator or a liquidator may also petition likewise. All are referred to as "the creditor" in this section. The process is as follows:

(1) the creditor notifies the SCIO of the intention to petition between seven and 14 days before the petition is lodged;
(2) the creditor notifies OSCR of the intention to petition between seven and 14 days before the petition is lodged;
(3) the creditor proceeds with the petition, providing proof to the sheriff that both the SCIO and OSCR have been so notified;
(4) as part of the petition the creditor may nominate a named trustee in bankruptcy, who may be the AiB or could be an insolvency practitioner—if the creditor does not do so the trustee in bankruptcy, if appointed, will be the AiB;
(5) the SCIO is given the opportunity to challenge the petition as part of the court procedure;

(6) if the petition is successful, the sheriff will award sequestration of the SCIO's estate and will appoint the trustee in bankruptcy (the named insolvency practitioner or the AiB);
(7) the trustee in bankruptcy will notify OSCR of the sheriff's award of sequestration and their appointment;
(8) OSCR will publish a notice of the award of sequestration on its website and this will state that the SCIO will be dissolved once the sequestration has been completed;
(9) if the AiB is the trustee in bankruptcy, it will enter details of the sequestration into its Register of Insolvencies[39];
(10) the trustee in bankruptcy will, if considered appropriate, convene a meeting of the SCIO's creditors;
(11) the trustee in bankruptcy will realise the SCIO's estate and will make payments to the creditors if and to the extent that there are funds with which to do so;
(12) once sequestration of the SCIO's estate is complete, and if there is any surplus after all creditors' claims have been satisfied, the trustee in bankruptcy will transfer such surplus to a body or bodies, the purposes of which are the same or resemble closely those of the dissolving SCIO—in doing so the trustee in bankruptcy may (and, if the AiB, will) ask OSCR to identify an appropriate recipient body or bodies, so as to ensure that the recipient is appropriate;
(13) the trustee in bankruptcy will notify OSCR that the sequestration is complete (as stated above, this stage will take a minimum of 15 months to reach) and will provide copies of final accounts of the SCIO's estate;
(14) OSCR will remove the SCIO from the Scottish Charity Register and will thereby dissolve the SCIO; and
(15) OSCR will advise the petitioners that the SCIO has been dissolved.

Effect of dissolution for the members and trustees of a SCIO

The members of a SCIO have no obligation to make any monetary contribution to the SCIO in respect of its dissolution. **13–51**

The trustees of a SCIO may in certain cases find that they may have acquired a liability if it can be shown that they have acted negligently or fraudulently. **13–52**

IN CONCLUSION

Whenever a charity faces financial difficulty or the possibility of its dissolution, proper planning (involving professionals, as appropriate) is essential. It may well enable the trustees, possibly with changes to the charity's business model and finances, to retain it as a viable entity for many years to come. However, if **13–53**

[39] Available at *http://www.aib.gov.uk* [Accessed 6 June 2016].

dissolution is inevitable, then at least the trustees may then enter this final phase of the charity's lifecycle with eyes open, alert and as prepared as they can be for what lies ahead.

INDEX

All references are to paragraph number